Blackstone's Guide to the

CHILDREN ACT 1989

Blackstone's Guide to the
CHILDREN ACT 1989

A. Jane Bridge, LLB, Barrister
of Gray's Inn and the North-Eastern Circuit

Stuart Bridge, MA, Barrister
Fellow of Queens' College, Cambridge

&

Susan Luke, LLB, Solicitor
Senior Lecturer, Nottingham Law School

BLACKSTONE
PRESS LIMITED

First published in Great Britain 1990 by Blackstone Press Limited,
9-15 Aldine Street, London W12 8AW. Telephone 01-740 1173

© A. J. Bridge, S. Bridge and S. Luke, 1990

ISBN: 1 85431 058 5

Brtish Library Cataloguing in Publication Data
A CIP catalogue record for this book is available from the British Library

Typeset by Style Photosetting Ltd, Mayfield, East Sussex
Printed by Livesey Ltd, Shrewsbury

Contents

Preface

This book is but one of many which will be published in the course of 1990 on the Children Act 1989. It attempts to explain, in a simple and straightforward way, the likely effect of this important statute on the existing law of children. It is directed primarily at the practitioner, whether he or she be legal or lay, but it is hoped that students of law and other related disciplines and even parents themselves will find the book helpful in casting some light on what has become a desperately complex structure of rules and regulations. There is little space in a book of this size for criticism of the new provisions, but where the authors have felt it is called for, they make the appropriate noises. By and large, however, the aim is exposition rather than exposure.

The task of any author in producing a guide of this nature is never easy, as the Bill in question charts the stormy seas of the Parliamentary process, jettisoning little en route but picking up an apparently never ending load of flotsam. Journey's end was initially predicted to be July, but the enthusiasms of the Parliamentary masters was such that it was November, and the very last week of their year, before her final port was reached. Only then was the epic scale of the venture to be seen in its full glory: what had set out twelve months earlier with less than eighty sections to its name returned fully laden with 108, and fifteen schedules in tow.

Jane and Stuart Bridge thank, unreservedly, Norma Martin Clement of Leeds University, for reading the proofs of chapters 1 to 5 and making many constructive comments and criticisms, and Albert and Nora Bridge, to whom parental responsibility for the Bridglets was delegated on occasions too numerous to mention, so enabling the first mentioned author to concentrate on writing (unquestionably a less demanding task than child care). Susan Luke wishes to thank Christine Forsey for typing some parts of the manuscript and her family for their patience and encouragement. All three authors thank the publishers for their customary, but nevertheless refreshing, patience, enthusiasm, and understanding. No thanks whatsoever are due to the Ministry of Transport whose genuine devotion to repairing the carriageway of the M1 between junctions 25 and 26 made the frequent trips between Yorkshire and Nottingham for authors' meetings considerably more unpleasant (not to say longer) than could reasonably be expected.

Jane Bridge
Stuart Bridge
Susan Luke

Chapter One
Introduction

'The Bill in my view represents the most comprehensive and far-reaching reform of child law which has come before Parliament in living memory. It brings together the public and private law concerning the care, protection and upbringing of children and the provision of services to them and their families.'

These words, spoken by Lord Mackay of Clashfern in opening the House of Lords debate on the second reading of the Bill which was subsequently enacted as the Children Act 1989 (HL Deb, col. 488, 6 December 1988), in no way exaggerate the significance of the Act. As the Lord Chancellor remarked later in the same speech, it repeals no less than eight post-war statutes (in chronological order the Nurseries and Child-Minders Regulation Act 1948, the Guardianship of Minors Act 1971, Guardianship Act 1973, the Children Act 1975, the Child Care Act 1980, the Foster Children Act 1980, the Children's Homes Act 1982, and the Children and Young Persons (Amendment) Act 1986) and limits others (most notably the Children and Young Persons Act 1969) to purely criminal provisions. The removal of so much of the existing law necessitates its replacement by something. The Children Act 1989 does this by setting out a comprehensive code of the law affecting children.

The practitioner in the fields of divorce and child care should not underestimate the importance of this legislation. In its tightly constructed provisions, it seeks to set up the basic structure and principles affecting children in both public and private law, thereby becoming the principal statute on child law. In the years to come, there can be no doubt that the Children Act 1989 will be viewed as a landmark in the history of child care legislation in this country.

The impetus for reform came from two concurrent reviews of the existing law. Following the publication of the report, *Children in Care*, by the House of Commons Social Services Committee in 1984, which advocated a thorough review of the body of statute law, regulations and case law relating to children, the Review of Child Care Law (a report of the Working Party on Child Care Law), discussing proposals for the codification of child care law, was produced in September 1985. The government then published its White Paper, *The Law on Child Care and Family Services* (Cm 62) in January 1987, and it is this document which promoted the reform of the public law affecting children and families now to be found in Parts III to VI of the Children Act 1989. At the same time as these proposals were emanating from central government, the Law Commission was at work on its own review of child law (see Working Papers Nos. 91, 96, 100 and 101, on guardianship, custody, care, supervision and interim orders in custody proceedings, and wards of court respectively). The Law Commission's proposals in its report on custody and guardianship (Law Com. 172) form the basis for Parts I and II of the Children Act 1989, dealing mainly (but not exclusively) with the private law affecting children.

However, reviews by eminent legislators or academics do not attract publicity in the way concrete manifestations of the inadequacies of the existing system do, and the media attention given to various inquiries focusing on particular cases has without question prompted the government to act with greater expedition than would have otherwise been likely. Thus, there have been well publicised investigations into the tragic deaths of Jasmine Beckford, Kimberly Carlile, and Tyra Henry, and reports which made criticisms of the present law and constructive suggestions for its improvement. Eclipsing even these, however, and in many ways the catalyst for the Children Bill, was the child abuse crisis which arose in Cleveland in the course of 1987. The lengthy report of Lord Justice Butler-Sloss (*Report of the Inquiry into Child Abuse in Cleveland 1987* (CM 412), the 'Cleveland Report') contains (amongst many other things) an examination of the practical workings of existing law and legal procedures, and a commentary on the likely efficacy of many of the reforms then proposed in the Government White Paper and now enacted in the Children Act 1989. The significance of Cleveland, the inquiry and the report, is arguably greater in relation to its identification of the need for reform of the law rather than the particular proposals made in the report. Indeed, in time, the Children Act 1989 may come to be criticised for paying insufficient attention to the lessons evidenced by the crisis and the arguments for change advanced in the report.

A summary of the provisions of the Children Act 1989 is not particularly easy to provide. However, if we divide it into provisions affecting private law and those affecting public law, it may be asserted that the changes to public law are more radical and therefore require more extended treatment. A book of this length cannot possibly refer to every single new provision, and the practitioner must of course be ready to 'dip into' the statute itself.

Parts III to V form the nub of the provisions governing the public law affecting children. Part III redefines the general powers and duties of local authorities in relation to children in the light of the basic principle that parents and local authorities should be free to work together in 'voluntary partnership' for the benefit of the children concerned. Although much of Part III consists of a restatement of old principles, albeit in places in a different form, there are certain significant reforms. In particular, the system of 'voluntary care' is dismantled, and parents whose children are 'accommodated' by the local authority will be able to reclaim them at any time 'on demand'. Part IV deals principally with care proceedings, which under the new regime assume a central role, and which will no longer be conducted exclusively in the magistrates' court. The grounds for making a care order are simplified, streamlined and extended — a child who is likely to suffer harm in the future being, by definition, a proper subject for the making of a care order. Most importantly, the need for accountability and open justice results in the removal of any alternative routes to the acquisition by a local authority of the care of a child: criminal courts and the High Court in wardship are no longer free to make care orders under the new regime. Part IV also states the principles applicable to supervision orders and creates a new form of disposition in 'education supervision orders' which is aimed at poor school attenders.

The emergency protection of children, on which so much media attention was focused during the Cleveland crisis, is radically reformed by Part V of the Children Act 1989. Place of safety orders are replaced by the more appropriately named and more skilfully tailored 'emergency protection orders', conferring on the courts powers to order the removal of children from their parents in cases of urgency for strictly limited periods (eight days, subject to one extension only of seven days). With the imposition of legal duties to ensure contact between the child and his parents, and the conferment on parents of an effective right to challenge the making of an order within the eight-day period, it is hoped that the new provisions avoid the difficulties endemic with place of safety orders. Where an emergency protection order appears too Draconian, but the court considers that enquiries into the welfare of a child are nevertheless necessary, the 'half-way house' of child assessment orders is now available.

The substantive principles of child law are not substantially changed by the new legislation. However, Part I, which is applicable across both public and private law, reasserts the most basic principle of all, that the child's welfare is paramount, introduces, to replace the existing rather notional 'parental rights and duties', the concept of parental responsibility, and delineates the circumstances in which parental responsibility is acquired and lost. It also restructures the law of guardianship, consequent upon the recommendations of the Law Commission.

Part II deals primarily with the private law of children, and creates an entirely new system of court orders which will be of particular (although not exclusive) application in the course of disputes between parents. Custody and access orders are replaced by orders for 'residence' and 'contact' respectively, and 'specific issue' and 'prohibited steps' orders are new orders created as an alternative to the use of wardship. The provisions governing financial relief for children, formerly found in several statutes, are consolidated, with minor amendments, in schedule 1.

Parts VI to X of the Children Act 1989 deal with the regimes for children in community homes, voluntary homes, and registered children's homes, with private fostering and with child-minding and day care for young children: to a large extent, these provisions are re-enactments of earlier legislation which is now repealed.

Finally, Parts XI and XII detail the supervisory functions of the Secretary of State, and enact various 'miscellaneous and general' provisions, some of which are of greater significance than this accolade infers: note particularly the restrictions on the use of the wardship jurisdiction by local authorities (s. 100: see 5.11 below).

The schedules to the Act must not be overlooked. Together with the usual range of transitional provisions (dealt with in this book with reference to each subject area), consequential amendments and repeals, there are extensive reforms of the law of adoption, a new legal regime for child minders and providers of 'day care' for children, and much more.

This book seeks to provide a practical guide to the Children Act 1989, and it does this by taking the statute part by part, and largely following the same order as the Act. However, the provisions of Part XII and the schedules are dealt with as and when they arise in relation to the other provisions. The book can therefore be fairly described as a commentary to the statute.

The Children Bill was introduced in the House of Lords on 23 November 1988, the Lord Chancellor assuming responsibility for its conduct through the higher chamber. Having received its third reading on 16 March 1989, it commenced its journey through the House of Commons four days later. The passage of the Bill was largely uncontentious, in the sense that the opposition in both Lords and Commons considered its objectives to be laudable and essential. However, reservations were expressed in certain respects.

The opposition was particularly concerned at the refusal of the government to introduce 'family courts' at this stage, and much criticism was voiced (some in Parliament, some in the professional literature) on the Bill's attack on the widely respected wardship jurisdiction of the High Court. These areas were hardly touched as the Bill proceeded, but others were, and the Bill returned to the Lords from the Commons with no less than 447 amendments. Despite earlier hopes that the Bill would be enacted before the summer recess, its passage occupied the entire Parliamentary year, receiving royal assent on 16 November 1989.

The new legal structure heralded by the Children Act 1989 is by no means complete at the time of writing. Much of the detail of the new law will be found in statutory instruments which have yet to be promulgated. Recognising the need for all those affected by this major piece of legislation to become fully apprised of its effects and consequences, the Lord Chancellor has indicated on several occasions that (with the exception of a handful of urgently required provisions: s. 108(2)) the Children Act will not be brought into force until at least 12 months (and possibly as long as two years) have elapsed from royal assent. Realising too, however, the public support for something to be done, the Lord Chancellor will not allow this statute to be 'limping legislation' (as was the case with, to cite but one example, the Children Act 1975), and two years is thought to be the maximum period which will elapse. At the time of writing, therefore, a commencement date no later than October 1991 would appear to be likely. It must be borne in mind, as this book is being read, that the authors are setting out provisions which are not as yet law and they are attempting on occasions to picture a legal edifice only the foundations of which are clearly visible. Enough is, however, evident from the Children Act 1989 to render the exercise of becoming acquainted with its substance both useful and, indeed, necessary, if the reader wishes to be able to act and advise in the field of child care law with an awareness of its imminent future developments.

Chapter Two
General Principles

2.1 Introduction

Ever since the enactment of the Guardianship of Infants Act 1925, the dominant principle in child care law has been the welfare of the child. The Children Act 1989 seeks to promote this principle still further, as the 'indications are that the paramountcy of the child's welfare needs to be strengthened and supported rather than replaced' (Law Commission Working Paper No. 96, 6.13). Section 1 reasserts, with some amendments, the basic tenet (contained previously in Guardianship of Minors Act 1971, s. 1, one of the several statutes repealed in their entirety by the Children Act 1989), and provides, for the first time, a 'statutory checklist' of factors to which a court must have regard in exercising its jurisdiction under the Children Act 1989, s. 8 and Part IV. It also emphasises that any delay in determining questions with regard to a child's upbringing is likely to prejudice the welfare of that child.

2.1.1 The paramountcy of welfare

The Children Act 1989, s. 1(1), although expressed in a slightly different way, will have the same effect in practice as the equivalent provision in the Guardianship of Minors Act 1971. The 'welfare principle' (i.e., that the child's welfare shall be the court's paramount consideration) is to be applied whenever a court (*any* court, High Court, county court, or magistrates' court: s. 92(7)) determines any question with respect to the upbringing of a child, the administration of a child's property or the application of any income arising from it. It wil not therefore apply to the determination of other questions, even though they will indirectly affect the child, for example, whether the court should make an order excluding a parent from the matrimonial home (*Richards* v *Richards* [1984] AC 174) or whether blood tests should be taken in an attempt to ascertain paternity (*S* v *McC* [1972] AC 24). Nor will the principle be applicable in adoption proceedings, where different statutory criteria apply (Adoption Act 1976, s. 6). It will primarily be of importance in determining the proper resolution of a custody or access (now 'residence' or 'contact') dispute, and the difficult decision as to whether a care order (or supervision order) should be made with respect to a child. As care and supervision orders are dealt with fully in chapter 5 below, it is with reference to residence and contact disputes that the practical application of the welfare principle will now be considered.

Under the existing law (Guardianship of Minors Act 1971, s. 1), the welfare of the infant is expressed to be '*the first and* paramount consideration', the italicised words now being omitted from the Children Act 1989, s. 1(1). Their omission, advocated as they 'had in the past led some courts to balance other considerations *against* the child's welfare rather than to consider what light they shed upon it' (Law Com. No. 172, 3.13), will clarify the position and assist in the practical application of the principle. In effect, the welfare of the child is treated as the sole consideration, and all other matters are only relevant to the extent that they impinge upon the child's welfare. The paramountcy of the child's welfare dictates that other considerations are to be given a distinctly subsidiary role. For example, the conduct of the parents towards one another will not displace the welfare principle, and will be of dubious significance save and insofar as that conduct has directly affected the child himself: *Re K (Minors) (Children: Care and Control)* [1977] Fam 179. Nor will the claims of natural parents to custody of the child necessarily outweigh those of foster parents. If the child's welfare demands that he reside with the foster parents rather than return to his natural parents, then that is the course the court must follow, *(J v C* [1970] AC 668). As Roskill LJ stated in *Re C (A Minor) (Wardship and Adoption)* (1979) 2 FLR 177, 184, the welfare principle must be applied 'without qualification, compromise or gloss'.

2.1.2 Delay in family proceedings
Section 1(2) requires the court, in any proceedings in which there arises any question with respect to the upbringing of a child, to have regard to the general principle that any delay in determining the question is likely to prejudice the welfare of the child concerned. This provision reflects the increasing anxiety amongst parents, practitioners, the judiciary and other interested persons, that 'prolonged litigation about their future is deeply damaging to children, not only because of the uncertainty it brings for them, but also because of the harm it does to the relationship between the parents and their capacity to cooperate with one another in the future' (Law Com. No. 172, 4.55). Regrettably, delays are often to the advantage of one of the parties since it adds strength to the argument that where the child has been with one party for a prolonged period of time, the child would be upset by being moved. In such cases of deliberate delay it is often found that the parent with whom the child is living pending the hearing is hindering the child's contact with the other parent in the mean time. A further cause of delay is the time taken for welfare reports to be produced (on which see 5.7).

This is by no means the only provision in the Children Act 1989 which addresses the problem of delay. Particularly significant also are ss. 11 and 32 which require the court to draw up a timetable with a view to eliminating undue delay in proceedings for a section 8 order and care proceedings respectively (see 3.8 and 5.7.4).

2.1.3 The statutory checklist
The Children Act 1989 breaks new ground by introducing, in s. 1(3), a statutory checklist of factors which the court must consider in deciding how the welfare of

the child is to be satisfied. The checklist is to be used *only* in the circumstances mentioned in s. 1(4), that is:

(a) When the court is exercising its jurisdiction under s. 8 (to make, vary or discharge a residence, contact, prohibited steps, or specific issue order: see chapter 3) and the order contemplated is being contested.

(b) When the court is considering whether to make, vary or discharge an order under Part IV (i.e., care or supervision orders: see chapter 5).

Use of the checklist is not mandatory where the court is making an emergency protection order (see chapter 6).

The checklist, first mooted in the Law Commission Working Paper on custody (Working Paper No. 96, 6.34), was promoted by the Law Commission on the basis that:

There are clear advantages in establishing a non-exhaustive set of relevant factors which in no way hampers the development of substantive case law or risks creating a bias in favour of certain parties. It simply aims to ensure that all the relevant considerations are taken fully into account and also, perhaps, to provide some consistency from court to court and case to case. (6.35.)

The list is therefore seen as providing greater consistency and clarity in the law, and assisting parents and children in endeavouring to understand how judicial decisions are made (Law Com. No. 172, 3.18). These expectations may be too high. The checklist contained in s. 1(3) is short, both in content and in specificity. It is thought unlikely that a county court judge being called upon to decide a custody dispute before s. 1(3) comes into force would decide it any differently (as a residence dispute) with the statutory checklist in force and in mind. Section 1(3) simply sets out factors which are in practice the most significant in the determination of disputes concerning the child's upbringing, and demands that the court pays particular attention with regard to them. It does not attempt to give the factors an order of importance, nor does it state that the circumstances are of equal importance. Judges need not be intimidated by s. 1(3): its substantive effect will be negligible, although it may lead to a greater readiness to appeal on the basis that a particular judge failed to have particular regard to one of the circumstances listed.

The statutory checklist does, however, act as a useful indication of the circumstances which the courts view as significant in resolving disputes over children, and the case law prior to the Children Act 1989 can cast some light through the apparent opacity of the factors set out in s. 1(3).

2.1.3.1 The ascertainable wishes and feelings of the child concerned (considered in the light of his age and understanding) (Section 1(3)(a)) The stated wish of a child to reside with a particular parent, or to see (or not to see) a parent, is a factor of some weight, which in certain circumstances may be decisive of the matter in question. However, the court will be aware that a child is likely to be influenced, consciously or not, by the views of the parent with whom the child resides, and may communicate that parent's prejudices rather than his own genuine feelings.

The age and maturity of the child is clearly of significance in considering the weight to be placed on the child's wishes. Thus, in *Re D W (A Minor) (Custody)* [1984] Fam Law 17, the court overrode the views of a 10-year-old, on the basis that the wishes he expressed did not correspond with his best interests. However, in *M v M (Minor: Custody Appeal)* [1987] 1 WLR 404, the Court of Appeal overturned the decision of a county court judge that a 12-year-old daughter should live with her mother despite her strongly stating that she wished to live with her father. The judge had failed to take into account the adamant attitude of the girl. A similar decision was reached by the court in *Williamson v Williamson* [1986] 2 FLR 146. Some six years after the divorce of their parents (and the making of a custody order in favour of their mother) two daughters, now aged 13 and 12, 'voted with their feet' and arrived at their father's home indicating they did not want to return to live with their mother. The Court of Appeal held that in these circumstances the proper order was one transferring custody to the father.

The wishes or feelings of the child are also to be placed in the balance where the court is considering whether to make a 'prohibited steps' or 'specific issue' order under s. 8. One example may be that a parent applies to the court to change the surname of the child. In *W v A (Minor: Surname)* [1981] Fam 14, two children stated that they wished to be known by their stepfather's surname: the Court of Appeal upheld the decision of the judge refusing leave to change their names. The judge was 'entirely right not to attach decisive importance to the views of two young children of 10 and 12 who were about to embark on the excitement of going to Australia with their mother and their new stepfather' (per Dunn LJ at p. 21).

2.1.3.2   His physical, emotional and educational needs (section 1(3)(b))   The

physical needs, in the sense of material needs, of the child will rarely be decisive when the court makes a decision concerning residence. If, for example, the mother is impecunious and is financially unable to provide for the child, appropriate financial relief can be ordered in the course of the matrimonial proceedings. However, physical needs may have wider connotations. In *Stephenson v Stephenson* [1985] FLR 1140, the father of a two-year-old girl lived in a three-bedroom house (owned by his parents) in Middlesbrough while the mother lived in a two-bedroom council flat in Lewisham. Both parties had found new partners since the marital split, at which time the mother had left her daughter in Middlesbrough. Wood J, giving the judgment of the Court of Appeal, held that the 'disadvantages of a material sort' current in the Lewisham home were 'of little weight'. Much more important, in allowing the father's appeal against a grant of custody to the mother, was the lack of consistency or commitment by the mother to the child in the past, and the likely permanence of the relationship between the mother and her present partner, both of which posed risks in the future which could be obviated by returning the child to Middlesbrough. In a sense, these were all 'physical needs'.

Another possibility is that the child is in need of regular medical treatment, the provision of which is significantly better in the area where one parent lives. The 'physical needs' of the child might therefore be a deciding factor in determining with which parent the child is to reside.

Foremost among the *emotional* needs which the courts will recognise are those based on the closeness of the child's ties with one or other of his parents, or with his brothers and sisters, and the trauma consequent upon a breaking of such ties. It has been acknowledged that a young child's emotional needs are in most, though not all, cases, based upon his attachment to his mother, and again, in most, though not all, cases, young brothers and sisters should be brought up together in the same household. *C v C (Minors: Custody)* [1988] 2 FLR 291, which concerned custody of a seven-year-old girl and a 4½-year-old boy is a particularly good example. In 1986, the mother left the matrimonial home, taking the girl, C, with her. An interim order granting custody of C to the mother and of the boy, A, to the father, was made. Following breakdowns in the access arrangements, the father intimated that he would be prepared to concede care and control of both children to the mother, an intimation he subsequently reneged upon. The Court of Appeal allowed an appeal by the mother from the county court judge's order that the boy remain with the father. Purchas LJ stated, at p. 302:

> It is really beyond argument that unless there are strong features indicating a contrary arrangement that brothers and sisters should, wherever possible, be brought up together, so that they are an emotional support to each other in the stormy waters of the destruction of their family.

Heilbron J, in the same case (at pp. 305-6), restated the principle that:

> ... all things being equal it is a good thing for a young child to be brought up by his mother, though that is not to say that fathers cannot also look after children of that age and even younger; they can and they do.

See also *Allington v Allington* [1985] FLR 586, noted below.

There are few cases where the educational needs of the child have proved decisive, although as with the other adjectives in s. 1(3)(b), the word 'educational' can be interpreted widely. In its wide sense, it can denote almost anything to do with the upbringing of the child. In *May v May* [1986] 1 FLR 325, the fact that the father had 'firmer' values and higher standards than the man with whom the mother was living was an important element in the decision to grant custody to him. However, education in its narrow sense of schooling may still be of significance, for example, if one parent is moving away from the area at a time which is particularly important (e.g., the child is in the middle of his GCSEs) then it may tilt the balance in favour of the parent who will continue to live in proximity to the child's current school. Disruption to schooling will perhaps be of less weight the younger the child is. Whatever the child's age, adequate provision of special schools where the child requires this will also be an important factor.

2.1.3.3 The likely effect on him on any change in his circumstances (section 1(3)(c)) Possibly the most significant single factor in deciding disputes about residence or contact will be the desire, however expressed, to preserve the status quo. Under the existing law, there is no doubt that the parent who has *de facto* control of a child has a considerably better chance of obtaining legal custody of that child than one who is arguing for a transfer of care from the other parent. The cases see the courts responding to the dangers of transferring custody, and this item in the statutory checklist recognises the cogency of this element in the matrimonial equation. Its appearance some way down the order is misleading, and no particular significance should be placed on its position.

The general attitude of the courts to changing the child's place of abode is articulated by Ormrod LJ in *D* v *M* (*Minor:Custody Appeal*) [1983] Fam 33 at p.41:

> . . . it is generally accepted by those who are professionally concerned with children that, particularly in the early years, continuity of care is a most important part of a child's sense of security and that disruption of established bonds is to be avoided whenever it is possible to do so.

Thus in *T* v *T* (*Minors: Custody Appeal*) [1987] 1 FLR 374 the decision of a judge in a 'knife-edge case' to leave a five-year-old girl with her father was justifiable, *inter-alia*, because it meant that she would have the desired continuity of care. However, the status quo argument does not always prevail:

> [It] depends for its strength wholly and entirely on whether the status quo is satisfactory or not. The more satisfactory the status quo, the stronger the argument for not interfering. The less satisfactory the status quo, the less one requires before deciding to change. (Per Ormrod LJ in *S* v *W* (1980) 11 Fam Law 81, at p. 82.)

In *Allington* v *Allington* [1985] FLR 586, the question of custody of a two-year-old girl fell to be determined within some 10 weeks of her mother leaving the matrimonial home. During that time, the mother had cared for the child for a considerable proportion of each week. The father, an evangelist, led an unorthodox lifestyle, and had devised a complicated regime to ensure that his daughter was provided for. The Court of Appeal held that the judge had been wrong to grant custody to the father by reference to the need to preserve the status quo. Cumming-Bruce LJ summarised the matter thus (at p. 593):

> There was not really any status quo at all. There was a history of 18 months or so in which the child had been at home with both its parents and then a brief interval of weeks in which the care of the child was with father more than mother, but with mother having care of the child a great deal; and nothing at all had happened, as far as the evidence goes, significantly to impair the relationship of mother and child.

There has been confusion in the past in establishing exactly what the status quo is. Where one parent has snatched a child from the other, he will not be entitled to argue that, the child now being with him, that status quo should be retained (see, for example, *Jenkins* v *Jenkins* (1980) 1 FLR 148). A rather less extreme case is that of *Edwards* v *Edwards* [1986] 1 FLR 187. The father failed to return the child to its mother (who had *de facto* custody) following an access visit. The justices then made repeated interim custody orders in favour of the father on adjournments of the mother's application for custody under the Guardianship of Minors Act 1971, on the basis, *inter alia,* that to do so was to preserve the status quo. Wood J overturned the justices' decision on judicial review, and the Court of Appeal agreed. The real status quo was not with the father, with whom the child had lived for a few weeks, but with the mother, who had had the day-to-day care of him for the previous 4½ years.

2.1.3.4 His age, sex, background, and any characteristics of his which the court considers relevant (section 1(3)(d))   The age of the child will often be a significant factor in deciding what is best for the child. To take extreme examples, a baby's needs will in most cases be satisfied by his living with his mother, whereas a 16-year-old will generally be considered sufficiently mature to make up his own mind as to what is best for him. The age or, more accurately, the maturity of the child will be important to the court in assessing the proper weight to be given to that child's own wishes, as we have seen above. Age may also assist the court in gauging the emotional ties between the child and his parents. In *A v A (Custody Appeal: Role of Appellate Court)* [1988] 1 FLR 193, at p.205, Bingham LJ considered that there was no legal presumption that mothers should have custody of young children. He went on:

> . . . in resolving agonising disputes such as this, a judge must bring to the task of judgment all his experience of life, both personal and professional, all his knowledge of human nature and all the wisdom he can command. . . . If, viewing the case in the round, he is moved to attach importance to the bond which ordinarily exists between mothers and very young children, particularly where the evidence shows that that bond does exist, he cannot, in my judgment, be faulted.

The sex of the child is a somewhat more nebulous factor. Some importance can be attached to the assistance a girl can derive from her mother, particularly during the years of puberty, but this can be negated by the availability of a substitute mature female whom the girl in question knows and confides in. As remarked above, in most cases brothers and sisters should be brought up together, and it would be in unusual circumstances, perhaps where there is no strong emotional attachment between brother and sister, that a court would contemplate making an order which would separate them. English courts do not follow the example of other legal regimes which see girls with their mothers and boys with their fathers as the general rule.

The 'background' of a particular child can mean almost anything. It might mean his religious upbringing, it might mean his family environment. 'Characteristics' is even broader. They might be physical (for example, disability or chronic illness) or religious (the child being brought up in a certain faith: see *J v C* [1970] AC 668) or even sporting or intellectual. The checklist at this point becomes virtually open-ended.

2.1.3.5 Any harm which he has suffered or is at risk of suffering (section 1(3)(e))   'Harm' is a deliberately wide-ranging term, and this subsection covers both physical injury and psychological trauma. If a parent has a history of assaulting the child and causing him injury, that is obviously a major factor in deciding disputes over the child's future upbringing. The same applies if the child is for one reason or another reluctant to have contact with the parent in question. Courts should not force children against their genuinely held wishes, although they must be on their guard against indoctrination by the parent with whom the child resides. In these circumstances, the appropriate question may well concern the likelihood of harm to the child. Thus in *Re E (A Minor: Access)* [1987] 1 FLR 368, the mother and stepfather of an eight-year-old girl (with whom she lived) made clear to her that if she saw her natural father she would be defying their wishes. In effect, an order for access exposed her to this conflict and, in turn, the possibility of harm. Nevertheless, on the facts, and having considered the question of harm, the Court of Appeal refused to overturn the access order. Transfers of custody against the expressed wishes of the child will require the court to consider carefully the potential harm which the order contemplated might cause (see *M v M (Minor: Custody Appeal)* [1987] 1 WLR 404).

Sexual abuse is a hugely complicated matter, which the Children Act 1989 addresses in provisions to be considered later in this book. Where there is proven sexual abuse, then the harm (both past and future) to the child will be a dominant factor in determining the relationship between that child and the abuser. The presence of a blood tie will be of little significance (*Re R (A Minor) (Child Abuse: Access)* [1988] 1 FLR 206).

2.1.3.6   How capable each of his parents, and any other person in relation to whom the court considers the question to be relevant, is of meeting his needs (section 1(3)(f))   It is obviously important, when deciding with whom a child should reside, to evaluate the capability for child care of the persons concerned. As between two parents who are equally committed and able to care, the deciding factor may be that one works full time whereas the other is available throughout the day. The latter parent is the one more 'capable' of meeting the child's needs. Then one parent may have a particular lifestyle which does not indicate that he is particularly capable. In *Re R (Minors) (Custody)* [1986] 1 FLR 6, the Court of Appeal pointed out the necessity for judges adjudicating upon custody disputes to have possession of the fullest information concerning the capabilities of the parties. The father to whom custody of two young children had been granted had a drink problem and a criminal record, neither of which had been fully explored. A rehearing was ordered, with custody in the interim to the mother.

Relevant to capability may be the medical condition of the parents or others. A parent may be seriously physically disabled, or may be mentally ill. Once more, the court will need to be apprised of the fullest information.

It is not only the parents whose capability the court must examine. A wider approach is necessary, and the capability 'of any other person in relation to whom the court considers the quesion to be relevant' must also be looked at. This will include, for example, any new partner of one of the spouses, the court evaluating whether the children will be well cared for in his or her company. It may also include grandparents or other members of the parents' families. Frequently the scheme which is proposed by a parent who hopes to be granted a residence order will rely to some extent on the cooperation of grandparents or others, and the court will need to be satisfied of their suitability. Child care arrangements outside the family — child minders, nannies, and nurseries — may also be contemplated.

2.1.3.7 The range of powers available to the court under this Act in the proceedings in question (section 1(3)(g))   This paragraph emphasises the importance of the court considering fully the entire range of remedies open to it. The court does not have to make an order of any kind, and indeed may only make one if it considers that to do so is better for the child than making no order at all (s. 1(5)).

The range of orders is extensive, and the Children Act 1989 aims to facilitate the making of an appropriate order for the child irrespective of the specific proceedings. For example application may be made by a parent for a residence order. If, during the course of those proceedings, the court considers that a care or supervision order may be appropriate, it has power to adjourn and direct the local authority to investigate the circumstances of the child with a view to the authority making application for such an order (s. 37(1): although see 5.8 for the limitations of such a course of action).

Conversely (and departing more radically from the existing law), in the course of care proceedings, the court may consider that the best means of disposal (that is, the order best suited to the interests of the child) is the making of a residence order, perhaps in favour of a grandparent. This it is now empowered to do (s. 10(1)(b): see 3.2.1). However, a local authority cannot apply for a residence order, nor can such an order be made in their favour (s. 9(1) and (2)).

The court must therefore always be aware of the wide range of powers which it has. For a summary of the orders which are made available to the court as a result of the Children Act 1989, see appendix 1.

2.2 Parental responsibility

2.2.1 Nature of parental responsibility

Parental responsibility is a new concept introduced by the Children Act 1989. In the words of the Lord Chancellor:

> ... like the welfare principle ... the idea of parental responsibility runs through the Bill like a golden thread, knotting together parental status and the effect of orders about a child's upbringing whether in private family proceedings or in care proceedings where the State intervenes to protect the child (Joseph Jackson Memorial Lecture (1989) 139 NLJ 505).

Several existing statutes in the field of child welfare law refer to 'parental rights and duties' (e.g., Children Act 1975, s. 85(1); Adoption Act 1976, s. 12(1) and (2); Child Care Act 1980, s. 3(1); Family Law Reform Act 1987, Part II) or, less frequently, the 'powers and duties' (Child Care Act 1980, s. 10(2)) or 'rights and authority' (Guardianship Act 1973, s. 1(1)) of a parent. These terms are nowhere defined, and the precise ambit of the parent's relationship in law with his child has been left to the courts to delineate more closely. In the epochal case of *Gillick v West Norfolk & Wisbech Area Health Authority* [1986] AC 112, the House of

Lords made the most significant examination of the nature of the parental status so far conducted, and the speeches of their lordships, together with the lively juristic debate which followed, were the prime motivation for the change in emphasis (for it is perhaps little more than that) now given statutory force by this part of the Children Act 1989.

In *Gillick*, the House of Lords viewed the so-called 'rights' of a parent as being no more than a necessary concomitant of his duties. In the words of Lord Fraser of Tullybelton:

> . . . parental rights to control a child do not exist for the benefit of the parent. They exist for the benefit of the child and they are justified only insofar as they enable the parent to perform his duties towards the child and towards other children in the family.

Lord Scarman made a similar point:

> The principle of the law . . . is that parental rights are derived from parental duty and exist only so long as they are needed for the person and property of the child.

In the light of the decision in *Gillick*, the Law Commission took the view that 'to refer to the concept of "right" in the relationship between parent and child is . . . likely to produce confusion' (Law Com. No. 172, 2.4). The Commission conceded that the proposed change to the concept of parental responsibility now adopted in the Children Act 1989 'would make little difference in substance' but contended that it would at least 'reflect the everyday reality of being a parent and emphasise the responsibilities of all who are in that position' (Law Com. No. 172, 2.4).

The concept of parental responsibility is defined in the Children Act 1989, s. 3(1). The definition is not, however, complete. Parental responsibility 'means all the rights, duties, powers, responsibilities and authority which by law a parent of a child has in relation to the child and his property'. What these 'rights, duties, powers, responsibilities and authority' are is not stated in the Act, and the Law Commission made little apology for omitting to identify them, on the basis that the list would be continually changing 'to meet differing needs and circumstances' (Law Com. No. 172, 2.6). A useful guide to what constitutes 'parental rights and duties' can be found in *Bromley's Family Law*, 7th ed., by P. M. Bromley and N. V. Lowe (1987), at p. 270 et seq. However, such a list must be used with care. The Children Act 1989 gives statutory recognition to the change in emphasis from 'rights' to 'responsibilities' initiated by *Gillick*, in particular, that a parent has only such rights as are necessary to fulfil his responsibility towards his child, and abolishes the rule of law that the father is the natural guardian of his legitimate child (s. 2(4)).

The exercise of parental responsibility will frequently be qualified in some way by agreement of the parents or by order of the court. This may take the form of the father agreeing that the child is to reside with the mother. It may be more extensive: a court may decide that a father (who has perhaps been guilty of sexual abuse) should have no contact with his children at all. In both cases, however, the parent in question will continue to have 'parental responsibility': the ability to exercise that responsibility will be subject to the agreement between the parents or the order of the court.

'Parental responsibility' as a concept is to be used not only in relation to parents as such but to guardians as well, who are to be equated with natural parents for these purposes (s. 3(2)). The guardian is expressly enabled, by s. 3(3), to receive or recover in his own name, for the child's benefit, property which the child is entitled to receive or recover. For the changes in the law of guardianship effected by the Children Act 1989, see ss. 5 and 6 and 2.3 below. Moreover, local authorities (and others) may acquire 'parental responsibility', for example, on the making of a care order (see chapter 5).

2.2.2 Who has parental responsibility?

Although it is nowhere expressly stated, references in the Children Act 1989 to 'mother' or 'father' are clearly intended to denote the natural parents of the child, and the same terminology is used here.

Parental responsibility is conferred on the mother of a child irrespective of her marital status, and so her parental responsibility is in a sense 'automatic'. Whether the father also has parental responsibility prima facie depends on whether he was married to the mother at the time of the child's birth (s. 2(1)). If he was so married, he too will have 'automatic' parental responsibility. Even if the father was not lawfully married to the mother at the time of the birth, he will be treated for these purposes as having been married if (s. 2(3), importing Family Law Reform Act 1987, s. 1):

(a)   The child is treated as legitimate, being a child of a void marriage, if at the time of the act of intercourse resulting in the birth (or at the time of the celebration of the marriage if later) both or either of the parties reasonably believed that the marriage was valid.

(b)   The child is a legitimated person (e.g., a person legitimated or recognised as legitimated by the marriage of his parents subsequent to the birth); see further Legitimacy Act 1976, s. 10.

(c)   The child is an adopted child within Part IV of the Adoption Act 1976.

(d)   The child is otherwise treated in law as legitimate.

The father will also be deemed to have been married to the mother at the time of the birth if he was married to her at any time during the period beginning with the insemination (or if no insemination the conception) resulting in the birth and ending with the birth (Family Law Reform Act 1987, s. 1(4)).

Thus the position can be summarised by saying that if the father and mother of the child have been married at any time later than the date of conception the effect will almost certainly be that the father will have parental responsibility as well as the mother. Possible difficulties may arise where the father was not domiciled in England and Wales at a relevant time, on which see Legitimacy Act 1976, ss. 1 to 3.

If the father was not married to the mother at the time of the child's birth, and does not come within the extensions to this concept, it will follow that prima facie he will not have parental responsibility for the child. However, he may acquire parental responsibility in one of two ways:

(a)   He may apply to the court for an order that he shall have parental responsibility (Children Act 1989, s.4(1)(a)). Such an order must be made if the court makes a residence order in favour of such a father (s. 12(1)).

(b)   He may enter into an agreement with the mother whereby he acquires parental responsibility (s. 4(1)(b)). '. . . this should provide a simple and straightforward means for unmarried parents to acknowledge their shared responsibility, not only for the support, but also for the upbringing of their child' (Law Com. No. 172, 2.19). This agreement must be made in the prescribed form and recorded in the prescribed manner (s. 4(2)). 'The object is to ensure that, as far as possible, both parents understand the importance and effects of their agreement' (Law Com. No. 172, 2.19).

These are important reforms which will materially improve the legal position of the father of a child who was not married to the mother at the time of the birth. The Family Reform Act 1987, s. 4(1), granted the unmarried father the right to apply for 'parental rights and duties'. The Children Act 1989 now allows him to apply for parental responsibility instead, and, more significantly, permits parents who are unmarried to make 'parental responsibility agreements', thereby obviating the need to make any application to the court in cases where the mother wishes the father to be accorded proper recognition in his status as parent.

The Children Act 1989 does not, however, facilitate the proof of paternity, which will remain problematical in many cases. It will of course be necessary to satisfy the court (on the balance of probabilities) that the applicant is the father of the child concerned before an order vesting parental responsibility in him can be made. DNA fingerprinting is now available, on which see Family Law Reform Act 1987, s. 23, and note also the amendments made (with effect from the passing of the Children Act 1989) to the power of the court to order paternity tests (Children Act 1989, ss. 89 and 108(2)).

The unmarried father who does not seek (or even deliberately avoids) the conferment of parental responsibility will remain obliged to maintain the child (Children Act 1989, s. 3(4)).

The acquisition of parental responsibility by a *stepfather* does not differ from the acquisition of parental responsibility by any other person who is not a natural parent of the child. He may acquire parental responsibility:

(a)   By the making of a residence order in his favour (or in favour of the mother and himself jointly), parental responsibility being retained for as long as the order remains in force (s. 12(2)). However, the rights enjoyed by natural parents in relation to adoption and guardianship will not apply to him (s. 12(3)).

(b)   By the making of an adoption order in his favour (or in favour of the mother and himself jointly) (see 2.2.3).

A stepfather will be responsible for the maintenance of a child insofar as he is a party to a marriage (whether or not subsisting) in relation to whom the child concerned is a child of the family (sch. 1, para. 16; for a definition of 'child of the family' see s. 105(1)). This will be the case irrespective of whether the stepfather has 'parental responsibility' or not (s. 3(4)(a)). A stepfather who has care of a child may do what is reasonable in all the circumstances of the case for the purpose of safeguarding or promoting the child's welfare (s. 3(5)).

2.2.3 *Assignment of parental responsibility*

As with 'parental rights and duties' (Children Act 1975, s. 85(2)) the general principle is that parental responsibility is not alienable, although, as we have seen, certain of its characteristics may be qualified or restricted. A person with parental responsibility may not surrender or transfer any part of that responsibility (Children Act 1989, s. 2(9)). However, the parent may arrange that some part, or all, of that responsibility, be met by one or more other persons (ibid). In effect the primary responsibility for the child remains at all times with the person or persons with parental responsibility. However, delegation of powers to schools, local authorities, churches, and other like bodies, may be convenient and workable, and it is facilitated by the Children Act 1989. Where there is no 'arrangement' as such, the position of a person who has *de facto* care of a child is clarified by the Children Act 1989, s. 3(5): such a person may do what is reasonable in all the circumstances of the case for the purpose of safeguarding or promoting the child's welfare.

Controversially, the apparent effect of s. 2(9) is that parental responsibility will be rarely lost by a parent, and although on the making of a care order the local authority obtains parental responsibility for the child (s. 33(3)), the parent(s) will not lose it: it will therefore be (somewhat notionally) 'shared' (see further 5.5). The making of an emergency protection order confers parental responsibility on the applicant (s. 44(4)(c)) but, again, the parent(s) will retain it too.

The one situation in which parental responsibility will be irrevocably surrendered will be on the making of an adoption order. The natural parents of the child will thereupon cease to be considered to be the child's father and mother, and so the Children Act 1989, s. 2(1), will no longer apply to them. From the making of the order, the adoptive parent or parents will have parental responsibility (s. 2(1) and (3); Family Law Reform Act 1987, s. 1(3)(c)).

This position was confirmed by the Lord Chancellor (HL Deb, 19 December 1988, col 1175):

> When an adoption order is made it has the effect of depriving the person who previously had the parental responsibility of that responsibility. But that is not solely because the adoptive parents acquire parental responsibility under the adoption order; rather it is because the adoption order, by virtue of s. 12(3) of the Adoption Act 1968, specifically extinguishes the previous parent's responsibility.

2.2.4 *Discharge of parental responsibility agreements or orders*

Where a parent has 'automatic' parental responsibility, there is apparently no specific power to remove parental responsibility from him or her. The only circumstances which would have such an effect would be the making of an adoption order (see 2.2.3). However, where a father has obtained an order under s. 4(1)(a), or is a party to a parental responsibility agreement under s. 4(1)(b), such order or agreement may be brought to an end by order of the court where application is made by any person with parental responsibility for the child or (with leave of the court where the court is satisfied that the child has sufficient understanding to make the application) the child himself (s. 4(3) and (4)). However, parental responsibility cannot be removed from a father in whose favour a residence order is extant (s. 12(4)). It also appears that where a residence order has been made in favour of a person who is not a parent or guardian of the child, that person must also continue to have parental responsibility whilst the residence order remains in force (s. 12(2)). If not brought to an end earlier, an order conferring parental responsibility on a father (or an agreement to the same effect) will terminate on the child reaching the age of 18 (s. 91(7)).

2.2.5   Parental responsibility: transitional provisions

Schedule 14 to the Children Act 1989 contains transitional provisions, and of particular relevance are the following, concerning the conferment of parental responsibility:

(a)   A father may have obtained an order under the Family Law Reform Act 1987, s. 4(1), giving him parental rights and duties in relation to a child. If such an order is in force at the time of the Children Act 1989 coming into force, the order will be converted into an order under s. 4 of the new Act, thereby conferring parental responsibility on the father (see sch. 14, para. 4).

(b)   Where a father was not married to the mother at the time of the child's birth, but has obtained custody or care and control of the child by virtue of a court order (i.e., an 'existing order', as defined in sch. 14, para. 5(1)), then, on the Children Act 1989 coming into force, the court will be deemed to have made an order under s. 4 conferring parental responsibility on the father (sch. 14, para. 6(2)). The court cannot discharge the order under s. 4 whilst the father continues to have care and control by virtue of the earlier court order (sch. 14, para. 6(4)(b)).

(c)   A person who is neither parent nor guardian of a child shall have parental responsibility for him so long as he has custody or care and control by virtue of a court order (i.e., an 'existing order', see (b)) (sch. 14, para. 7(1)).

For further detail, the provisions themselves (sch. 14, paras 5 to 7) should be consulted.

2.3   Guardianship

The existing law on guardianship, contained in case law and the Guardianship of Minors Act 1971, ss. 3 to 7, is complex and convoluted. The Law Commission discussed various possible reforms to the existing provisions, and eventually concluded that 'a number of modifications to the present law seem desirable in order to integrate the existing patchwork of common law and statute in a coherent modern structure' (Law Com. No. 172, 2.22). These modifications are contained in ss. 5 and 6 of the Children Act 1989, which replaces the provisions in the Guardianship of Minors Act 1971 (itself repealed in its entirety by Children Act 1989, sch. 15).

Central to the new role of guardians as it is envisaged by the Law Commission is the conferment on them of parental responsibility (as defined in s. 3(1): see 2.2) for the child in question (s. 5(6)).

The power to control a child's upbringing should go hand in hand with the responsibility to look after him or at least to see that he is properly looked after. Consultation confirmed our impression that it is now generally expected that guardians will take over complete responsibility for the care and upbringing of a child if the parents die. If so, it is right that full legal responsibility should also be placed upon them. (Law Com. No. 172, 2.23.)

Such responsibility includes the duty to see that the child is provided with adequate 'food, clothing, medical aid and lodging' (Children and Young Persons Act 1933, s. 1(2)(a)) and to educate the child properly (Law Com. No. 172, 2.25).

There will no longer be different 'levels' of guardianship. The effect of s. 5 is that if a person is appointed guardian, then that person incurs parental responsibility. There is no longer a distinction to be drawn between guardians of the child's estate and guardians of the child's person, with the exception of transitional circumstances (on which see sch. 14, paras 12 to 14).

2.3.1 Appointment
Appointment of guardians may be made:

(a) By the court.
(b) By a parent who has parental responsibility.
(c) By an existing guardian.

The court (meaning the High Court, a county court, or a magistrates' court: s. 92(7)) may appoint a guardian in two circumstances only. First, where 'the child has no parent with parental responsibility for him' (s. 5(1)(a)). His parents may be dead, or his father may be alive but not have parental responsibility (as he was not married to the mother at the time of the birth and has not since acquired it by order or agreement). If his mother is alive, it seems that she must have parental responsibility for him, and therefore the court cannot make a guardianship order under this provision. Secondly, if 'a residence order has been made with respect to the child in favour of a parent or guardian of his who has died while the order was in force' (s. 5(1)(b)). Thus, the court may, on divorce, have ordered residence to the father and contact to the mother. Even though the mother will continue to have parental responsibility in respect of the child, the court will have full power, on the father's death, to appoint a guardian to look after the child.

It is immaterial that the court made an order for custody (or care and control) to the father at a time when the Children Act 1989 was not in force. The power of the court to appoint a guardian on the father's death would still be available (see sch. 14, para 8(1) and (2)).

An application to be appointed a guardian must be made by the intending guardian himself (s. 5(1)), although the court does have power, in family proceedings, to make an appointment of its own motion if it considers that it should be made (s. 5(2)).

A parent who has parental responsibility, or a guardian, may appoint a guardian to assume parental responsibility on the death of the appointer. Two (or more) persons may join together in making an appointment (s. 5(10)). Appointment need not be by will, nor even by deed. It was thought by the Law Commission that there was a reluctance (particularly among young adults) to make wills, and that in view of the desirability of encouraging the appointment of guardians, a simpler method was warranted (see Law Com. 172, 2.29). This is now to be found in s. 5(5): if not made by will, the appointment must be in writing, dated, and signed at the direction of the person making the appointment, in his presence, and in the presence of two witnesses who each attest the signature.

Although s. 5 refers to the appointment of 'an individual' to be a guardian of the child, the singular will include the plural (Interpretation Act 1978, s. 6) and it will be possible to appoint more than one guardian at one time. It is clear from s. 6(1) that an additional guardian (or guardians) can be appointed at a later date.

Where an appointment is made out of court (under s. 5(3) or (4)), the appointment will not necessarily take effect on the death of the appointing parent. The intention of the provisions set out in s. 5(7) and (8) is to remedy the situation under the Guardianship of Minors Act 1971 whereby, on the death of an appointing parent, the guardian took up his duties, despite the fact that a surviving parent was ready, able and willing to act. If, immediately before the death of the appointing parent, the child has another parent who has parental responsibility for him, and there is no residence order (or order for care and control: see sch. 14, para. 8) in force in favour of the appointing parent, the appointment will not take effect until the death of the surviving parent (s. 5(8)). If, however, the child does not have a surviving parent with parental responsibility, or he does have, but there was a residence order in force in favour of the appointing parent, then the appointment will take effect on the death of the appointing parent (s. 5(7)).

Example 2.1 W and H are married at the date of H's death. By his will, H appoints X to be the guardian of their children A, B and C. As W has parental responsibility for the children, and there was no residence order in force, X will not become a guardian as long as W is still alive.

Example 2.2 At the time of M's death, she and F had been divorced for five years. There is a custody order in force by which their children, J, K and L live with her. Although she dies intestate, M made an appointment of Y to be the guardian of the children by written declaration. Y will become guardian on M's death. F has parental responsibility for J, K and L, but there was a custody order in force in favour of M. Section 5(7) therefore applies. (For the effect of an order for custody which, necessarily, pre-dates the Children Act 1989, see sch. 14, para. 8(2).)

There remains potential for discontent, particularly amongst surviving parents, at the operation of these provisions. The effect of circumstances such as are outlined in example 2.2 is that parental responsibility is shared between a survivor and an appooned guardian, a guardian appointed, what is more, by an estranged spouse, and with whom the surviving parent may not see eye to eye. The remedy for the surviving parent is to apply to the court to have the guardianship terminated (s. 6(7)).

Another possible area of difficulty concerns the rights of the surviving parent in circumstances such as example 2.1. She does not have to share parental responsibility with the guardian appointed by her deceased husband. But can she herself appoint a guardian of her own choosing to take office in the event of her death, or is she bound by her husband's choice? The answer appears to be that she can appoint a guardian herself. This will not have the effect of revoking her husband's appointment: the two guardians will, in the event of the mother's death, act together. Although s. 5(3) refers to the appointment of one guardian by one parent, it does not deny to each parent the right to make a choice. Revocation of appointment can only be made by the person who made the appointment in the first place (s. 6(1) and (4)).

2.3.2   Revocation
Where the initial appointment of a guardian was by will (or codicil), the appointer can revoke it:

(a)   By revoking the will or codicil (s. 6(4)).
(b)   By a written and dated instrument (signed by the appointer or at his direction, in his presence, and the presence of two attesting witnesses) revoking the appointment (s. 6(2)).
(c)   By a later appointment (whether by will, codicil or declaration in writing) within s. 5(3) or (4), unless it is clear that the later appointment is of an additional guardian (s. 6(1)).

Where the initial appointment of a guardian was by declaration in writing (under s. 5(5)), the appointer can revoke it:

(a)   By destroying (or having some other person, in his presence, destroy) the document in question with the intention of revoking the appointment (s. 6(3)).
(b)   By a written and dated instrument (signed by the appointer or at his direction, in his presence, and in the presence of two attesting witnesses) revoking the appointment (s. 6(2)).
(c)   By a later appointment (whether by will, codicil or declaration in writing) within s. 5(3) or (4), unless it is clear that the later appointment is of an additional guardian (s. 6(1)).

Where the initial appointment of a guardian was by court order, the court retains jurisdiction to terminate the appointment at any time (s. 6(7)). Once the appointer has died, it is no longer possible to revoke the appointment by using the methods in s. 6(1) to (4). The proper method of terminating an appointment in those circumstances (whether or not the guardianship has taken effect) would be by application to the court under s. 6(7), which lists the persons who can make such an application.

If the appointment is not terminated earlier, it will come to an end automatically on the child reaching the age of 18, as will any court order made under s. 5(1) (s. 91(7) and (8)).

2.3.3   Disclaimer
The court does not seek to compel persons to act as guardians who do not wish to assume the substantial responsibilities of the office. Accordingly, there remains

provision for a guardian appointed other than by court order to disclaim the appointment by making an instrument in writing to that effect (s. 6(5)). The unwilling guardian has an indefeasible right to do this, as long as it is exercised within a reasonable time of his first knowing that the appointment has taken effect. Should the Lord Chancellor make regulations prescribing the recording of disclaimers (a rather obscure provision), any disclaimer must satisfy the regulations to have its intended effect (s. 6(6)).

2.3.4   Transitional provisions

Under the present law, guardians may be appointed pursuant to the Guardianship of Minors Act 1971, ss. 3 to 5, the Sexual Offences Act 1956, s. 38(3), and the inherent jurisdiction of the High Court. When the Children Act 1989 comes into force, an existing guardian whose appointment has taken effect will be deemed to have been appointed under s. 5 of the Act (sch. 14, para. 12 et seq.). He will have parental responsibility for the child (s. 5(6)) and will be able to appoint someone to succeed him in the event of his death (s. 5(4)).

2.4   Evidence of children

The courts have recently highlighted the vicissitudes of the rule against hearsay and the competence of child witnesses in the context of child abuse. It has long been established that the High Court when exercising its wardship jurisdiction has a discretion to admit hearsay evidence, and it had generally been accepted that this applied in all civil proceedings where the welfare of a child was in issue. However, in *Re H (A Minor); Re K (Minors) (Child Abuse: Evidence)* [1989] 2 FLR 313, the Court of Appeal denied that this was the case, and held that in matrimonial and guardianship proceedings at least, the rule against hearsay applied in its full force save and insofar as the parties consented to it being waived (or in certain interim applications). A similar decision was reached in the context of care proceedings by Otton J in *Bradford City Metropolitan Council* v *K* [1989] 2 FLR 507. However, the Court of Appeal was aware of the problems that its decision in *Re H; Re K* would cause:

> Compliance with the hearsay rule may well lead to confusing, inconsistent and anomalous results. Judges, with the welfare of the child as the paramount consideration, may be able to admit the statements of children in some cases and not in others, although the facts and circumstances of the children are similar. Alternatively, they may be able to receive the evidence to show the state of mind of the child but not to accept facts which the child or those concerned with the child's welfare seek to present to the court and which might have a marked influence on the exercise of the court's discretion. (Per Butler-Sloss LJ in *Re H; Re K* [1989] 2 FLR 313 at p. 336.)

The difficulties in eliciting admissible evidence in child abuse cases were underlined by a restatement of the principles of competence of child witnesses in *Re H; Re K*. A child may only give evidence in civil proceedings if he takes the oath (*R* v *Brasier* (1779) 1 Leach 199), and he may only take the oath if he understands its nature (on which see *R* v *Hayes* [1977] 1 WLR 234). The Civil Evidence Act 1968 does not help either (see *Re H; Re K* at pp 331–2).

Section 96(3) is an apparently innocuous rule-making provision, allowing the Lord Chancellor to provide for 'the admissibility of evidence which would otherwise be inadmissible under any rule of law relating to hearsay'. This power will be used, however, to reverse the effects of *Re H; Re K* and *Bradford Metropolitan City Council* v *K* and rationalise the admission of evidence of out-of-court statements made by children (and indeed others). To do so is particularly important as the availability of the wardship jurisdiction, which does presently allow the admission of hearsay, will be seriously curtailed under the Children Act 1989 (see 5.11). The Lord Chancellor is entitled to make the relevant rules when the Children Act 1989 received royal assent, as s. 96(3) was one of a mere handful of provisions which were brought immediately into force (see s.108(2)).

The competence of child witnesses is also addressed in s. 96. For the first time, children may give evidence unsworn in civil proceedings, as long as the court is of the opinion that the child understands that it is his duty to tell the truth, and has sufficient understanding to justify his evidence being heard (s. 96(2)). These conditions are not greatly dissimilar from those presently applicable to the admission of unsworn evidence in criminal proceedings (see Children and Young Persons Act 1933, s. 38(1)), but it is not a requirement of admissibility in civil proceedings that the child's evidence is corroborated 'in a material particular' (see *Phipson on Evidence*, 13th ed., 31-11). Section 96(2) will come into force on a day to be appointed.

Chapter Three

Orders with Respect to Children in Family and Other Proceedings

3.1 Introduction

Part II of the Children Act 1989 introduces a new scheme of orders, known as 'section 8 orders', to replace those available under the existing law in the form of custody, care and control and access orders. The changes have been introduced because of the high level of dissatisfaction with the present orders. The main criticisms were that:

(a)   The orders available differ according to the type of proceedings brought (Law Com. No. 172, 4.2).

(b)   The effect of such orders is no longer clear or well-understood, for example, the legal consequences following the making of a sole custody order as opposed to a joint custody order (Law Com. No. 172, 4.3).

(c)   The views and practices of various courts differ very considerably, for example, in the frequency with which joint custody orders are made (Law Com. No. 172, 4.4).

A more theoretical stance (adopted by the Law Commission) was that the existing system, in concentrating upon the allocation of parental 'rights', seemed more concerned with whether one parent could control what the other parent did while the child was with the other, than with ensuring that each parent properly met his responsibilities while the child was with him. This view is advanced most clearly by the new concept (discussed in 2.2 above) of 'parental responsibility' to replace 'parental rights and duties', but is also influential in the promotion of the scheme of court orders in Part II. The hope is that by devising a unified scheme which is consistent and clear, as opposed to the fragmented orders and applications available under the various existing legislative provisions, the parties will be able to see the interests of their children in a more pragmatic, less emotive, manner.

The main intention behind the new legislation is to ensure that, wherever possible, orders should be made in the course of existing proceedings about the family. For example, where the occupation of the matrimonial home is in dispute, the needs of the children are frequently an important factor in determining the relief sought. The new provisions will allow the court, at the same time as making an order excluding the father from the matrimonial home (pursuant to, for example, the Domestic Violence and Matrimonial Proceedings Act 1976), to order that the children should reside with the mother (who remains there), and to regulate the contact which they should have with the father. The orders contained in Part II of the Children Act 1989 will be applicable to a court hearing care proceedings, although, once a child is in care, applications to the court for such orders will be seriously restricted (see 3.10). Moreover, the new 'specific issue' and 'prohibited steps' orders will undoubtedly reduce the need to resort to wardship proceedings (to fill in gaps where no power exists to make a particular order in the course of particular proceedings: see 5.11), and the present temptation to go 'forum shopping' will diminish.

The new scheme acts upon the 'clear evidence that the children who fare best after their parents separate or divorce are those who are able to maintain a good relationship with them both' (Law Com. No. 172, 4.5). This will be implemented by allowing parents after divorce or separation to retain their equal parental responsibility, and with it their power to act independently, unless the court orders otherwise (s. 2(7)). This does not mean that the parent who does not have the child with him can exercise a power of veto over the other parent. But it does mean that he can refer any dispute over any aspect of parental responsibility to the court if necessary. The parent who does have the child with him should be able to exercise his parental responsibilities to the full during that time.

The Children Act 1989 attempts to move away from the concept that parents have rights over their children, and towards a recognition of their obligations to them. It follows that 'it is a mistake to see custody, care and control and access as differently-sized bundles of powers and responsibilities in a descending hierarchy of importance' (Law Commission Working Paper No. 96, para. 4.51). Therefore the fundamental necessity is that the parent who has the child with him must be in a position to meet his responsibilities as the circumstances and needs of the child dictate. In reality, the main questions to be decided by the courts are where is the child to live and how much is he to see of the other parent. The new section 8 orders have been devised to give effect to decisions upon these and any other relevant matters which need to be resolved.

3.2   Section 8 Orders

It will come as no great surprise to learn that the range of orders known as 'section 8 orders' is to be found in s. 8 of the Children Act 1989. The orders are as follows:

(a)   A 'residence order' — this settles the arrangements to be made about where the child is to live.

(b)   A 'contact order' — this requires the person with whom a child lives, or is to live, to allow the child to visit or stay with the person named in the order, or for that person and the child otherwise to have contact with each other.

(c)   A 'specific issue order' — this gives directions for the purpose of determining a specific question which has arisen, or which may arise, in connection with any aspect of parental responsibility for a child.

(d)   A 'prohibited steps order' — this states that no step which could be taken by a parent in meeting his parental responsibility for a child, and which is of a kind specified in the order, shall be taken by any person without the consent of the court.

Section 8 does not specify the principles to be applied by the court in deciding whether to make these orders. These principles are to be found in s. 1 (see 2.1) and in the existing case law. The court is under no duty to make a section 8 order when one is requested. It must not make such an order unless 'it considers that doing so would be better for the child than making no order at all' (s. 1(5)).

Example 3.1   Mr and Mrs Noble part amicably, and they agree that the two children, Tim and Tom, should live with their mother, but see their father regularly at weekends. In the divorce proceedings, Mrs Noble seeks an order from the court, to which Mr Noble consents, that Tim and Tom reside with her, and have reasonable contact with their father. Although the court makes the decree of divorce, it may refuse to make the orders for residence and contact. The parties to the divorce having shown that they are able to cooperate perfectly adequately, the court could properly take the view that making the order requested would not be better for the children than making no order at all.

This important change of emphasis has been further elucidated by the Lord Chancellor as follows:

In private law cases there is concern that some lawyers and courts at present perceive a custody order as part of the 'package', particularly in divorce cases. The government is anxious to change that perception and to make it clear in the Bill that families should generally be left to sort matters out for themselves unless it is shown that without an order the child's welfare will suffer. (Joseph Jackson Memorial Lecture (1989) 139 NLJ 505.)

3.2.1   Who Can Apply For Section 8 Orders?
Standing to apply for section 8 orders is governed by s. 10 which is unfortunately not the most coherently expressed provision in the Children Act 1989. Essentially, there are two broad circumstances in which the matter can come before the court (which may be the High Court, county court or magistrates' court).

First, the court may already be hearing proceedings in which the welfare of a child arises, or proceedings may have been initiated, and in the course of those proceedings, someone, or perhaps even the court itself, may consider that a section 8 order should be made. This situation is dealt with by s. 10(1), which states that in any family proceedings (widely defined in s. 8(3) and (4): note care proceedings are covered, as being under Part IV of the Children Act 1989) in which a question arises with respect to the welfare of any child, application may be made for a section 8 order, or the court may make an order of its own volition if it considers that such an order should be made.

Secondly, and perhaps more obviously, someone (most frequently a parent) may make a specific, 'self-contained' application to the court for a residence order or contact order or so forth. Section 10(2) provides for these circumstances, where the application is not made in the course of any existing proceedings.

With the exception of the court making an order of its own volition in existing proceedings (s. 10(1)), subsections (1) and (2) of s. 10 make no distinction between the persons given standing to apply for section 8 orders. In each case, certain persons are entitled to apply without further ado, and anyone else may only apply with leave of the court.

3.2.1.1   Who is 'entitled to apply'?   There is a distinction between those 'entitled to apply' for a residence or contact order, and those entitled to apply for a specific issue or prohibited steps order. Put simply, the class of persons who can apply as of right for residence or contact orders is appreciably wider. The persons entitled to apply to the court for *any* section 8 order (including specific issue and prohibited steps orders) are as follows:

(a)   Any parent or guardian of the child (s. 10(4)).

(b)   Any person in whose favour a residence order is in force with respect to the child (s. 10(4)).

(c)   Any person who has custody or care and control of the child by virtue of an 'existing order' (sch. 14, paras 5 and 7(3)(b)).

The class of persons who are entitled to apply to the court for a residence or contact order is extended by s. 10(5) to include:

(a)   Any party to the marriage (whether or not subsisting) in relation to whom the child is a child of the family (as defined in s. 105(1)).

(b)   Any person with whom the child has lived for a period of at least three years (the period of three years need not have been continuous but must not have begun more than five years before, or ended more than three months before, the making of the application (s. 10(10)).

(c)   Any person who, in any case where a residence order is in force with respect to the child (or an 'existing order' (sch. 14, para. 5) is in force conferring care and control: sch. 14, para. 8(3)), has the consent of each of the persons in whose favour the order was made.

(d)   Any person who, in any case where the child is in the care of a local authority by virtue of a care order, has the consent of that authority.

(e)   Any person who, in any other case, has the consent of each of those (if any) who have parental responsibility for the child.

This list is in addition to those referred to in s. 10(4), and it may be further extended by rules of court (s. 10(7)). Any person who has access to a child by virtue of an 'existing order' (see sch. 14, para. 5) is entitled to apply for contact, but not, as of right, residence (sch. 14, para. 9(2)).

3.2.1.2   Obtaining leave of the court   If a person wishes to apply for a section 8 order in relation to a child but does not fall within s. 10(4) or (5) (for residence or contact orders) or s. 10(4) (for specific issue or prohibited steps orders), he must first apply for leave of the court to make his application. If the child himself is applying for leave then the court may only grant leave if it is satisfied that the child has sufficient understanding to make the proposed application (s. 10(8)). However, if the person applying for leave is someone other than the child himself, then the court must consider specific matters when deciding whether or not to grant leave. Those matters are set out in s. 10(9) and are as follows:

(a)   The nature of the proposed application for the section 8 order.
(b)   The applicant's connection with the child.
(c)   Any risk there might be that the proposed application might disrupt the child's life to such an extent that he would be harmed by it.
(d)   If the child is being looked after by a local authority (see s. 22(1)), the court must consider the local authority's plans for the child's future, and the wishes and feelings of the child's parents.

3.2.1.3   Foster-parents

The rights of foster-parents to apply for section 8 orders are poorly defined in the Children Act 1989. Section 9(3) purports to restrict local-authority foster-parents from applying for leave to apply for a section 8 order without the consent of the local authority if the child concerned has lived with them for less than three years. What is the effect of this rather obscure provision, the consequences of which would appear to be somewhat vague in view of the apparently inconsistent s. 10(5)(c)(iii) (entitling those with the consent of the local authority to apply where the child is in care)?

It is tentatively submitted that all depends on whether or not the child who has been living with the foster-parents for less than three years is in the care of the local authority by virtue of a care order. If he is, then the foster-parents can apply for a residence or contact order as of right if they have the consent of the authority (s. 10(5)(c)(ii). If he is not (he is being 'accommodated' by the authority pursuant to its duties under s. 20; see 4.5), then the foster-parents must obtain both the consent of the local authority and the leave of the court before making application for the order itself (s. 9(3)). This would seem to accord with common sense as well as the wording of the statute. Whilst the child is being accommodated under s. 20, the parents may remove him at any time from the accommodation in quesion (s. 20(8)). It would create a situation of some difficulty if the foster-parents who were looking after such a child could make application to the court without a full analysis of the likely consequences for the child of the making of the application. However, once the child is in care, the local authority has parental responsibility (s. 33(3)) and is free to make long-term decisions concerning the child: it would seem oppressive to require the authority to obtain leave of the court to make an application which seeks to advance their statutory duties towards the child in their care.

Foster-parents who seek a specific issue or prohibited steps order will require local-authority consent and leave of the court if the child has lived with them for less than three years: s. 10(5) only applies to applications for residence or contact orders. When the child has lived with them for at least three years (for method of calculation, see s. 10(10)), they will be entitled to apply for a residence or contact order irrespective of the local authority's consent (s. 10(5)(b)). If they wish to apply for a specific issue order or a prohibited steps order at that stage, they can do so only with leave, but they do not need the consent of the local authority.

The object of the new statutory scheme is to allow anyone with a genuine interest in the child's welfare to make applications with respect to his upbringing, as can at present be done by making the child a ward of court. This should have the effect of reducing the number of cases in which the wardship jurisdiction of the High Court is invoked in future.

3.2.2 Duration of section 8 orders

Section 8 orders will continue in force until discharged by the court or otherwise until the child concerned reaches the age of 16 (s. 91(10)). However, if the court is satisfied that the circumstances are exceptional, it may direct that the order have effect beyond that age (s. 9(6)).

Certain orders in adoption proceedings will have the effect of bringing section 8 orders to an end (Adoption Act 1976, s. 12(3), as amended by Children Act 1989, sch. 10, para. 3), and the making of a care order will also discharge all current section 8 orders (s. 91(2)).

3.3 Residence Orders

A residence order settles the arrangements to be made as to the person with whom a child is to live. Its aim is to be flexibile enough to accommodate a much wider range of situations than a custody order was able to do. Where the child is to live with two (or more) people who do not live together, the order may specify the periods during which the child is to live in each household (s. 11(4)).

Example 3.2   Mr and Mrs Jones are divorced but live within a few miles of one another. They have two children, John, aged 10, and Susan, aged 12. Mrs Jones works on Fridays, Saturdays and Sundays. Mr Jones works on Mondays, Tuesdays, Wednesdays and Thursdays. The court decides that there should be a residence order specifying that the two children should with their mother from Monday to Thursday of each week, and with their father from Friday to Sunday of each week.

The Children Act 1989 displaces the presumption under the present system whereby, generally speaking, one parent is granted custody whilst the other is awarded access. The new residence orders can be formulated to cover the reality of parental responsibilities where the child lives with both parents but spends more time with one of them. This reflects the aim of the law to 'reduce the stakes' between parents competing for their children upon divorce or separation. The object is that changes in the child's residence should interfere as little as possible with his relationship with both parents. It is important to stress that the making of a residence order has no effect on the parental responsibility of either parent: it is an order which is intended to settle the living arrangements and no more.

If a residence order has been made in respect of a child but his parents, both of whom have parental responsibility for him, thereafter live together for a continuous period of six months, then the order ceases to have effect (s. 11(5)).

If a care order is made in respect of the child, then any residence order (together with any other section 8 orders) will be discharged automatically (s. 91(2)). Conversely, if a child in care is made the subject of a residence order, the care order will be similarly discharged (s. 91(1)).

3.3.1 Restrictions on change of surname and removal from jurisdiction

Where a residence order is in force with respect to a child, no person may cause the child to be know by a new surname or remove the child from the United Kingdom without either the written consent of every person with parental responsibility for the child, or the leave of the court (s. 13(1)). However, consent or leave is not required where the child is to be removed from the United Kingdom, by the person in whose favour the residence order has been made, for a period of less than one month (s. 13(2)). This allows the child to be taken on holiday abroad without the relevant parent having to go to the trouble of obtaining written consent or expense of applying for leave in the event of the other parent being uncooperative or unavailable. When the court makes the residence order it can grant general leave to remove the child for longer periods, or grant leave to remove for specified purposes (s. 13(3)). Where going abroad is within the terms of the order it should be treated as happening with the leave of the court for the purposes of the Child Abduction Act 1984.

The principles governing the grant of leave in these two circumstances are unlikely to change as a result of the Children Act. See, on change of surname, *W* v *A (Minor: Surname)* [1981] Fam. 14, and, on removal from the jurisdiction, *Belton* v *Belton* [1987] 2 FLR 343.

3.3.2 Residence orders and parental responsibility

Where a father who does not have parental responsibility (no doubt because he was not married to the mother at the time of the birth: see 2.2.2) applies for the child to live with him and the court makes a residence order in his favour, then the court must also make an order under s. 4 giving the father parental responsibility (s. 12(1)). The s. 4 order must last for the duration of the residence order, and can only be ended by order of the court (see ss. 12(4) and 4(3)).

Where a court makes a residence order in favour of any person who is not the parent or guardian of the child, and who does not otherwise have parental responsibility for him, then the court must order that that person shall have parental responsibility whilst the residence order is in force (s. 12(2)). However, it should be noted that the parental responsibility granted to these persons under s. 12(2) does not include the right to consent or refuse to consent to the making of adoption orders in respect of the child (s. 12(3)(a) and (b)) or the right to appoint a guardian for the child (s. 12(3)(c)).

3.4 Contact Orders

A contact order requires the person with whom a child lives to allow the child to visit, stay or otherwise have contact with the person named in the order. It aims to cater for the situation where the child is to spend much more time with one parent than with the other, so that the most realistic arrangement is for the child to reside with one parent and visit the other. The old 'access' order provided for the 'non-custodial' parent to have access to the child. The new contact order differs in that it provides for the child to have contact with the parent. Whilst the child is with that parent, the parent may exercise all his parental responsibilities but must not do anything that is incompatible with the order about where the child is to live. Examples of the type of parental behaviour that would, or would not, infringe this principle are set out in Law Com. No. 172, para. 2.11:

> . . . If the child has to live with one parent and go to a school near home, it would be incompatible with that order for the other parent to arrange for him to have his hair done in a way which will exclude him from the school. It would not, however, be incompatible for that parent to take him to a particular sporting occasion over the weekend, no matter how much the parent with whom the child lived might disapprove.

The normal form of order (as envisaged by the Law Commission: Law Com. No. 172, 4.17) will be for 'reasonable contact'. 'Contact' as a term is not limited to merely visiting the parent. If, for some reason, it is not practicable or appropriate for the child to visit the parent, it is open to the court to order other forms of contact including letters, telephone calls or visits by the parent to the child.

A contact order requiring one parent to allow the child to visit the other will lapse automatically if the parents live together for a continuous period of more than six months (s. 11(6)).

3.5 Specific issue orders

A specific issue order gives directions to determine a specific issue which has arisen, or which may arise, in connection with any aspect of parental responsibility for a child. Examples of such issues include a dispute between the parents over whether or not the child should be known by a new surname; whether or not he should be educated at a particular school; whether or not he should be brought up within a particular religion; whether or not the child should undergo certain medical treatment.

The Lord Chancellor has emphasised the breadth of the power to make specific issue orders, 'covering everything from disagreements about which school the child should attend to major decisions such as whether a child should undergo major and irreversible treatment such as an abortion or sterilisation' (Joseph Jackson Memorial Lecture, (1989) 139 NLJ 505, 506). The availability of such orders will reduce the need for disputes of this kind to be decided in wardship proceedings (see further 5.11).

The order may be made together with the residence or contact orders, or on its own. The aim of the order is to enable either parent to seek the determination of an issue by the court according to what is best for the child. The object is not to give a parent the 'right' to determine a particular point in relation to the child's upbringing. However, it is clear from s. 9(5) that no court may exercise its powers to make a specific issue order with a view to achieving a result which could be achieved by making a residence or contact order. This prevents the parties from using the power of the court to make a specific issue order as a 'back-door' method of ensuring that the child lives with them or has contact with them, whilst at the same time avoiding the legal effects of such orders.

Example 3.3   M and F are divorced. There is a residence order in force under which their son, S, now aged 5, lives with M in Newcastle. F lives in Sheffield and now applies to the court for a specific issue order that S attend a private day-school in Sheffield. The court decides that to accede to F's application would amount to an order that S should leave M and reside instead with F. It should therefore refuse to make a specific issue order. It could make a residence order in F's favour instead if the child's interests so demanded.

3.6   Prohibited steps orders

A prohibited steps order directs that no step which could be taken by a parent in meeting his parental responsibility for a child, and which is of a kind specified in the order, shall be taken by any person without the consent of the court.

It is perhaps best to leave the Law Commission to explain the function of these rather nebulous orders, and no apologies are made for a relatively lengthy quotation:

> Prohibited steps orders are . . . modelled on the wardship jurisdiction. The automatic effect of making a child a ward of court is that no important step may be taken without the court's leave. An important aim of our recommendations is to incorporate the most valuable features of wardship into the statutory jurisdictions. It is on occasions necessary for the court to play a continuing parental role in relation to the child, although we would not expect those occasions to be common. If this is in the best interests of the child, it should be made clear exactly what the limitations on the exercise of parental responsibility are. Hence, instead of the vague requirement in wardship that no 'important step' may be taken, the court should spell out those matters which will have to be referred back to the court. We would expect such orders to be few and far between, as in practice the wardship jurisdiction is more often invoked to achieve a particular result at the time than to produce the continuing over-sight of the court. One example, however, might be to ensure that the child is not removed from the United Kingdom, especially in a case where there is no residence order and so the automatic prohibition (now s. 13(1)) cannot apply. (Law Com. No. 172, 4.20.)

Insofar as the Law Commission indicates that a prohibited steps order will provide an alternative to the use of wardship, the passage is misleading. If a local authority is the applicant, they will not have a choice. They will only obtain leave to apply for the High Court to exercise its wardship jurisdiction where the result they wish to achieve cannot be achieved by some other method (s. 100(4); see further 5.11).

As with specific issue orders, no court may exercise its powers to make a prohibited steps order with a view to achieving a result which could have been achieved by making a residence or contact order (s. 9(5)).

3.7   Supplementary provisions

The object of the supplementary provisions contained in s. 11(7) is to preserve the existing flexibility of the court's powers within the new scheme of orders, so as to allow the court to make interim orders, delay implementation of orders or to attach other special conditions. These matters are within the absolute discretion of the court.

3.7.1   Power to give directions (section 11(7)(a))

The power of the court to give directions as to how an order is to be carried into effect is aimed at cases where the court orders a change in the existing arrangements in relation to the child. For example, such power may provide for a delay before the child's residence is changed, in order to smooth the transition from one residence to another.

Example 3.4   Mr and Mrs Smith were divorced in 1987, and Mrs Smith was granted custody of their child, Robert, aged 12. Since that time Robert has become increasingly unhappy at having to live with his mother, and wishes to go to live with his father. Mrs Smith wishes him to remain with her. Mr Smith applies to the court for a residence order so that Robert can come to live with him. The court decides that it is in Robert's best interests to move to live at his father's house, but wishes the move to be achieved so as to allow Robert to finish the current term at his old school, since his change of residence will mean that he has to attend a school closer to his father's house. Therefore the court orders that the residence order will take effect as from the last day of Robert's current school term, so as to cause as little disruption to his education as possible.

The exercise of such a power may also allow the court to ensure a gradual build-up of contact between a child and another person where that is deemed necessary in the circumstances.

Example 3.5   Mr and Mrs Brown were divorced in 1986, at a time when their daughter, Samantha, was only one year old. Mrs Brown was granted custody of the child with reasonable access to Mr Brown. However, Mr Brown never bothered to exercise access to Samantha, until, shortly after the Children Act 1989 came into force, he decided that he wanted to see her. Mrs Brown refused his request because of the length of time since Mr Brown had last seen his daughter. Mr Brown applied to the court for a contact order. The court decided that it was in Samantha's best interests to renew her relationship with her father, but that in view of the length of time since she had last seen him it would be wise to institute a gradual build-up of contact over a period of time, rather than making an order for 'reasonable contact' immediately. Therefore, the court ordered that Mr Brown could visit Samantha at her mother's home for the first three consecutive Saturday mornings, and then take her out on his own for two hours for the next three Saturday mornings. Thereafter, if all had proceeded smoothly, he could have contact with her every Saturday from 10 a.m. until 4 p.m., and the court would review the case in six months' time to assess the progress made, and to see if a 'reasonable contact' order would be appropriate.

3.7.2   Power to attach conditions (section 11(7)(b))

The power of the court to impose conditions (upon any person listed in s. 11(7)(b)) aims to enable the court to resolve present disputes and anticipate future ones. Three examples are set out in Law. Com, No. 172, 4.23: first, if there is a dispute about which school the child should attend, then the court could attach a condition to the residence order that the child concerned should attend a particular school; secondly, if there is a real fear that while the child is visiting one parent he will be removed from the country, then the court could attach a condition to the contact order prohibiting all removal (see 3.3.1); thirdly, as happened in the case of *Jane* v *Jane* (1983) 4 FLR 712, there might be a real concern that the parent with whom the child was to live would not consent to a blood transfusion for the child. Under the new legislation the court could make it a condition of the residence order that, if the need for a transfusion arose, then that parent must inform the other parent of the situation so that he could consent to it instead. An alternative solution would be for the court to order that transfusions be given on specified medical advice without such agreement. Once again, the object of such powers is to resolve practical problems rather than allocating 'rights' to parents for the future.

3.7.3   *Power to specify period of order* (section 11(7)(c))

The power of the court to specify the period for which the order, or any provision in it, is to have effect aims to preserve the existing position under the Matrimonial Causes Act 1973, whereby no firm distinction is drawn between 'interim' and 'final' orders. This flexibility is based upon the general principle that no order made in relation to a child is ever truly final, since there is always the possibility of the child's situation changing in some respect. Thus, it must always be open to the court to review the position where necessary. By virtue of s. 11(3) it is clear that where a question relating to the child arises in the course of any proceedings in which the court has power to make a section 8 order, the court has the power to make a final decision upon the matter. In the absence of directions to the contrary, the normal duration of a section 8 order is set out in s. 91 (see 3.2.2).

3.8   Duty of court to impose a timetable

In an attempt to remedy problems caused by delay (see also 2.1.2), Children Act 1989, s. 11(1), places a clear obligation upon the court to oversee the progress of cases involving section 8 orders, and to draw up a timetable with a view to determining such questions without delay. The court must also give such directions as it considers appropriate for ensuring that the timetable is adhered to. The details of how s.11(1) is to be implemented are to be provided by rules of court (s. 11(2)) which have yet to be formulated. If the required steps are not taken in time it will be for the court to consider how best to proceed for the child's welfare in the light of the information available at the time. The Law Commission (Law Com. No. 172, 4.58) envisages that usually the best way of doing this will be by setting return dates, but that sometimes it will be by requiring progress reports rather than a hearing.

3.9   Enforcement of residence orders

By s. 14, a person in whose favour a residence order has been made may enforce it in the magistrates' court under Magistrates' Courts Act 1980, s. 63. The court may order the person in breach to pay a sum not exceeding £50 for each day during which he is in default (to a maximum total of £2,000) or commit him to custody until he remedies his default or for a period not exceeding two months. This procedure is without prejudice to other means of enforcement of orders, and it can be used to enforce 'existing orders' (i.e., custody orders made before the Children Act 1989 came into force) (sch. 14, paras 5 and 10).

3.10   Relationship between section 8 orders and care orders

The Children Act 1989 aims to clarify the relationship between orders which may be made in private law and public law. One of the fundamental principles behind this aim is that care proceedings, like any other family proceedings, are concerned with the meeting of parental responsibilities for a child (Law Com. No. 172, 4.51).

When a child is in care, the local authority have parental responsibility and are given wide discretionary powers in respect of his upbringing (see generally chapter 5). At the same time, the freedom of parents and others to intervene and challenge the decisions of the authority is closely circumscribed. Thus, s. 9(1) prevents a court from making a contact order, specific issue order or prohibited steps order with respect to a child who is in the care of the local authority by virtue of a care order, reflecting the situation under the existing law whereby neither the wardship jurisdiction, nor the statutory powers of the courts to award access in private law, can be used to interfere with a local authority's exercise of their parental responsibilities (*A* v *Liverpool City Council* [1982] AC 363; *Re W (A Minor) (Wardship: Jurisdiction)* [1985] AC 791).

However, application may be made for a residence order whilst a care order is in force in relation to a child. Such an application will in substance comprise an application for the discharge of the care order, because if the court decides to make a residence order in these circumstances then the residence order will supersede the care order (s. 91(1)). This course may be attractive as the class of person who can apply for a residence order is much wider than those who can apply to discharge a care order (ss. 9 and 10; cf. s.39(1)).

A local authority cannot apply for a residence order or contact order, and the court is prevented from making either of those orders in favour of a local authority (s. 9(2)). However, they can apply for specific issue or prohibited steps orders, and will now have to do so where they would previously have used wardship if the result sought by the authority can be achieved by way of the new orders (s. 100(3) and (4), and see 5.11).

3.11   Existing orders: transitional provisions

For many years to come, courts will need to consider the position of children concerning whom orders for custody, access and the like were made before the Children Act 1989 came into force. The general principle is that 'existing orders' (defined in sch. 14, para. 5(1): they do not include care orders) will continue despite the new legislation, save where successful application is made to the court (a) for a residence order or a care order, or (b) for discharge of the order in question. The fact that an existing order subsists does not appear to restrict the jurisdiction of the court when it hears an application under Part II of the Children Act 1989: indeed, it can make, for example, a contact order with respect to a child to whom a custody order remains in force (sch. 14, para. 11(2)). The court has jurisdiction to discharge existing orders where the welfare of the child so demands (sch. 14, para. 11(3) to (6)).

3.12   Family assistance orders

The Children Act 1989 introduces the new 'family assistance order' which is designed to formalise the involvement of a probation officer (or an officer of the local authority) for a short period in helping a family at a time of marital breakdown. It was thought desirable to introduce a new type of order to run alongside the supervision order (Law Com. No. 172, 5.10 to 5.20). In future a supervision order made in the course of family proceedings will have the same effect as a supervision order made in care proceedings (on which see 5.9). The grounds for making a supervision order will relate to the harm or likely harm to children (see 5.4), and the court will be able to impose requirements upon parents as well as upon children. A supervision order will, therefore, be appropriate where the main concern is child protection. On the other hand, a family assistance order will aim to provide short-term help, in cases where there are 'exceptional circumstances', to parents or spouses to cope with the immediate problems of divorce and separation; it will aim to encourage a smooth transition for them and the children, to promote arrangements for contact where that is in dispute, and to promote cooperation in future. A further aim of the new order is to discourage the making of unnecessary residence orders, and therefore it will be available in family proceedings irrespective of whether or not any other order in respect of the child's residence or upbringing is made. Neither a supervision order nor a family assistance order will be available if a care order is made.

Where, in any family proceedings (as defined in s.8(3) and (4)), the court has power to make an order under Part II of the Children Act 1989 with respect to any child, it may (whether or not it makes such an order) make a 'family assistance order' requiring a probation officer or a local authority officer to advise, assist and befriend any person named in the order (s. 16(1)). The persons who may be named in the order are any parent or guardian of the child, any person with whom the child is living or in whose favour a contact order has been made with respect to the child, and the child himself (s. 16(2)). No court may make a family assistance order unless it is satisfied that the circumstances of the case are 'exceptional' and it has obtained the consent of every person named in the order other than the child (s. 16(3)). A family assistance order may direct the person named in the order to take specified steps to enable the officer to be kept informed of the address of any person named in the order and to be allowed to visit any person named in the order (s. 16(4)). The order will have effect for a period of six months, unless a shorter period is specified (s. 16(5)). There is no restriction in the Children Act 1989 on a second family assistance order being made on the expiry of the initial period.

In cases where both a section 8 order and a family assistance order are in force with respect to the child the officer may refer to the court the question of whether the section 8 order should be varied or discharged (s. 16(6)). It should be noted that it is not possible to attach to a family assistance order the wide range of requirements that can be made of named persons under a supervision order. The family assistance order meets the need for a more limited form of order in cases where under the existing legislation the full effect of a supervision order had to be invoked even though it was not needed.

The duties of local authorities in relation to family assistance orders are clarified in s. 16(7). An order cannot be made so as to require the authority to make an officer of theirs available unless the authority agree or the child concerned lives or will live in their area. Where a probation officer is required, arrangements made by the probation committee in the relevant area must be complied with (s. 16(8)).

3.13 Financial provision and property adjustment for children

The Children Act 1989 incorporates the powers in relation to financial provision and property adjustment for children which were formerly to be found in the Guardianship of Minors Act 1971, the Guardianship Act 1973 and the Children Act 1975 (all of which are now repealed). Where other legislation gives the court powers to make orders for the benefit of adults as well as children, for example under the Matrimonial Causes Act 1973 and the Domestic Proceedings and Magistrates' Courts Act 1978, the Law Commission came to the conclusion that it would be more convenient for all of the relevant orders to be made under the existing provisions, rather than trying to hive off the orders relating to children to bring them within the Children Act 1989 (Law Com. No. 172, 4.59). The assimilation and merger of the Guardianship of Minors Act 1971, the Guardianship Act 1973 and the Children Act 1975 have produced little change in the substance of the existing law, but have simplified it considerably.

One effect of the Family Law Reform Act 1987 is that orders for the benefit of children can now be made irrespective of whether there is an order for actual custody, and it gives the High Court and the county court power to award periodical payments, secured periodical payments and unlimited lump sums, and the ability to adjust the property rights of either parent. The object of the 1987 Act was to enable all children (irrespective of their parents' marital status) to have the benefit of the same range of powers as were previously available to the children of married parents when the parents divorced.

The effect of the Children Act 1989 can be summarised as follows:

(a)   Under the existing law, a guardian appointed by an unmarried mother cannot apply for financial relief against the father unless the father has some parental or custodial rights. Under the Children Act 1989 guardians will have the same rights of application as parents.

(b)   The full range of financial orders will now be available to persons with the benefit of residence orders, since to restrict the range of orders available outside divorce proceedings would be to discriminate against children whose parents were never married to each other.

(c)   Spouses who have treated a child as a 'child of the family' are placed in the same position as parents (sch. 1, para. 16). This principle is already established in proceedings under the Matrimonial Causes Act 1973, the Domestic Proceedings and Magistrates' Court Act 1978 and the Children Act 1975.

(d)   Criteria are set out governing the court's decision, including special factors to be applied when considering orders against a person who is not a parent of the child. These criteria have largely been adopted from the existing law.

(e)   The time-limits operative under the existing legislation in relation to interim financial orders are removed, and provision made for orders to be renewed. This reflects the principle that all orders are really 'interim' because circumstances are constantly changing. Therefore, the court is given powers to make further orders for periodical payments and lump sums after the original application has been determined. However, property adjustment orders remain a 'once and for all' provision.

(f)   The duration, variation and enforcement provisions in relation to financial orders remain the same as under the Guardianship of Minors Act 1971, the Guardianship Act 1973 and the Children Act 1975.

(g)   An application for 'financial provision' comes within the definition of 'family proceedings' for the purposes of the Children Act 1989. Accordingly, a court hearing such an application may make residence or contact orders (or any other section 8 order) if it considers such orders should be made (s. 10(1)).

(h)   Under the existing legislation the powers available to the High Court in the exercise of its wardship jurisdiction are much more limited than those available to other courts. Although the Children Act fails to rectify this in its present form, an amendment contained in the Crown and Legal Services Bill (sch. 10, para. 6(2)) currently before Parliament will regularise this position.

The Children Act 1989, s. 15, empowers the court to make provision in relation to financial relief for children, and the details of those powers are set out in sch. 1. For appeals concerning periodical payment orders, reference should be made to s. 94. In relation to their use in sch. 1 the following terms are defined by para. 16:

(a)   'child' includes, in any case where an application is made under para. 2 or 6 in relation to a person who has reached the age of 18, that person; and

(b)   'parent' includes any party to a marriage (whether or not subsisting) in relation to whom the child concerned is a child of the family. ('Child of the family' is defined in s. 105(1).)

3.13.1   Orders against parents
A parent, guardian or person in whose favour a residence order is in force may apply to the High Court or the county court for the following orders:

(a)   That either or both parents of a child make periodical payments to the applicant for the benefit of the child, or to the child himself (para. 1(2)(a)).

(b)   That either or both parents of a child make secured periodical payments to the applicant for the benefit of the child, or to the child himself (para. 1(2)(b)).

(c)   That either or both parents of a child pay a lump sum to the applicant for the benefit of the child, or to the child himself (para. 1(2)(c)). It is open to the court to order that such a sum may be paid by instalments (para. 5(5)).

(d)   That there be a settlement of property, to which either parent is entitled, for the benefit of the child (para. 1(2)(d)).

(e)   That either or both parents be required to transfer property, to which they are entitled, to the applicant for the benefit of the child, or to the child himself (para. 1(2)(e)).

If the application is made to a magistrates' court, then there is only power to grant orders under (a) and (c) above (see para. 1(1)(b)).

Orders for periodical payments or secured periodical payments can be varied or discharged upon the application of the payer or the payee (para. 1(4)). However, it is open to the court upon such an application to order the payer to make a lump-sum payment instead (para. 5(3)). The court can allow such a lump sum to be paid by instalments (para. 5(5)) and, if so, it can subsequently vary the number and amount of such instalments and the date upon which they become payable (para. 5(6)). If an application is made in the magistrates' court to vary or discharge a periodical payments order, and the court decides to order a lump sum instead, then it may do so even if the payer has been required to pay a lump sum by a previous order under the Children Act 1989 (para. 5(4)). However, the maximum lump sum that may be ordered by a magistrates' court is £1000 (para. 5(2)).

In any event, the court may order a lump sum under para. 1 for the purpose of meeting any liabilities or expenses, reasonably incurred before the making of the order, in connection with the birth of the child or in maintaining the child (para. 5(1)).

It is open to the court to make further orders for periodical payments, secured periodical payments or lump sums, provided that the child concerned has not attained the age of 18 (para. 1(5)(a)). However, if an order is made under para. 1(2)(a) or (b) for a parent of the child to make periodical payments or secured periodical payments, then the order will cease to have effect if the parents of the child live together for a period of more than six months (para. 3(4)). In respect of orders in relation to the settlement or transfer of property, the court may only make one order against the same person in respect of the same child (para. 1(5)(b)).

The powers set out above can be exercised by the court at any time (para. 1(3)). Furthermore, if the court makes, varies or discharges a residence order, then it can exercise any of its powers contained in sch. 1, even if no application has been made thereunder (para. 1(6)).

3.13.2   *Orders for persons over 18*
A person over 18 may apply for either or both of his parents to make periodical payments or pay a lump sum (which the court may allow to be paid in instalments) to him (sch. 1, para. 2(2)), provided that it appears to the court that:

(a)   he is (or will be if the payments are ordered) receiving instruction at an educational establishment or undergoing training for a trade, profession or vocation, whether or not while in gainful employment (para. 2(1)(a)); or

(b)   there are special circumstances justifying the making of an order (para. 2(1)(b)).

However, he may only make such an application provided that:

(a)   immediately before he was 16 there was no periodical payments order in force in respect of him (i.e., an order under Children Act 1989, sch. 1; Family Law Reform Act 1969, s. 6(3); Matrimonial Causes Act 1973, s. 23 or s. 27; Domestic

Proceedings and Magistrates' Courts Act 1978, Part I): (para. 2(4) and (6)); and
   (b)   his parents are not living together in the same household at the time of the application (para. 2(4)).

The court has power to vary or discharge any order for periodical payments (para. 2(5)), and if it decides to do so then it may order the payer to make a lump-sum payment instead (para. 5(3)). Where this power is exercised by the magistrates' court, it may order a lump sum even if the payer has been required to make a lump–sum payment by a previous order made under the Children Act 1989 (para. 5(4)). However, the maximum lump sum that may be ordered by a magistrates' court is £1,000 (para. 5(2)). The court can order such a lump sum to be paid in instalments (para. 5(5)) and, if so, it has power to vary the number and amount of such payments and the date upon which they become payable (para. 5(6)).

The powers set out above may be exercised by the court at any time (para. 2(7)), and while any such order remains in force the court may make further orders from time to time (para. 2(8)).

3.13.3   Duration of orders for financial relief

Orders for periodical payments or secured periodical payments may not, in the first instance, extend past the child's 17th birthday unless the court sees fit to specify a later date (sch. 1, para. 3(1)(a)). In any event, such payments may not extend beyond the child's 18th birthday unless it appears to the court that:

   (a)   the child is (or will be if the payments are ordered) receiving instruction at an educational establishment or undergoing training for a trade, profession or vocation, whether or not while in gainful employment (para. 3(2)(a)); or
   (b)   there are other special circumstances which justify the making of the order (para. 3(2)(b)).

Where the court makes an order for periodical payments under para. 1(2)(a) or para. 2(2)(a), then that order will cease to have effect upon the death of the payer (para. 3(3)).

3.13.4   Matters to which the court is to have regard in making orders for financial relief

In deciding whether, and if so, how, to exercise its powers under paras. 1 and 2 of sch. 1, the court is required by para. 4(1) to have regard to all the circumstances, including the following factors:

   (a)   the income, earning capacity, property and other financial resources which the persons listed in para. 4(4) have or are likely to have in the foreseeable future;
   (b)   the financial needs, obligations and responsibilities which the same persons have or are likely to have in the foreseeable future;
   (c)   the financial needs of the child;
   (d)   the income, earning capacity (if any), property and other financial resources of the child;

(e)   any physical or mental disability of the child;
(f)   the manner in which the child was being, or was expected to be, educated or trained.

Where the court is deciding whether, and if so, how, to exercise its powers under para. 1 against a person who is *not* the mother or father of the child, then para. 4(2) requires it to have regard to certain additional factors:

(a)   whether that person has assumed responsibility for the maintenance of that child and, if so, the extent to which and the basis on which he assumed that responsibility and the length of the period during which he met that responsibility;
(b)   whether he did so knowing that the child was not his child;
(c)   the liability of any other person to maintain the child.

If an order is made against a person who is not the *father* of the child then that fact must be recorded in the order.

3.13.5   *Variation etc. of orders for periodical payments*
When the court is deciding whether or not to vary or discharge an order under para. 1 of sch. 1 for the making or securing of periodical payments, then it must have regard to all the circumstances of the case, including any change in the matters to which the court was required to have regard when making the order (para. 6(1)). It is open to the court to suspend temporarily, and later revive, any provision of such an order (para. 6(2)). If the court does in fact decide to vary the order, then it may provide that the payments as so varied shall be made from a date specified by the court, provided that it is no earlier than the date upon which the application for variation or discharge was made (para. 6(3)). There is also provision for the guardian of the child concerned to apply for an order for the making or securing of periodical payments to be varied or discharged after the death of either parent (para. 6(8)).
   If there is an order in force under para. 1 for the making or securing of periodical payments to or for the benefit of a child, then the child himself may apply for the variation or discharge of that order, provided that he has reached the age of 16 (para. 6(4)). Indeed, where such an order ceases to have effect on the child's 16th birthday, or at any time between then and his 18th birthday, the child can apply to the court which made the order for its revival (para. 6(5)). The court may order the revival of the order from a specific date (provided that it is no earlier than the date upon which the application was made) if it appears to the court that:

(a)   the child is (or will be if the order is made) receiving instruction at an educational establishment or undergoing training for a trade, profession or vocation, whether or not while in gainful employment; or
(b)   there are special circumstances which justify the making of an order.

Any order which is so revived may be varied or discharged upon the application of any person by whom or to whom payments are required to be made under the revived order (para. 6(7)).

3.13.6 Variation of orders for secured periodical payments after death of parent

Where the parent liable to make secured periodical payments under para. 1(2)(b) of sch. 1 has died, his personal representatives are included amongst the persons entitled to apply for the variation or discharge of the order (para. 7(1)). When considering such an application, the circumstances to which the court must have regard under para. 6(1) include the changed circumstances resulting from the parent's death (para. 7(5)). An application to vary the order must be made within six months of the date on which representation in regard to the parent's estate was first taken out (see para. 7(6) for details of what property is to be taken into account for this purpose), unless the court gives leave to apply later (para. 7(2)). In any event, the personal respresentatives will not be liable for distributing any part of the estate after the end of that six month period on the ground that they should have taken into account the possibility that the court might allow an application for variation to be made after that date by the person entitled to payments under the order (para. 7(3)). However, para. 7(3) does not prejudice any power to recover any part of the estate so distributed arising by virtue of such a variation (para. 7(4)).

3.13.7 Financial relief under other enactments

Where a residence order is made with respect to a child whilst there is a 'financial relief order' in force under some Act other than the Children Act 1989 requiring a person to contribute to the child's maintenance, then the following persons may apply to revoke the latter order, or to vary it by altering the amount payable or substituting the applicant for any other person to whom the order would otherwise be paid (sch. 1, para. 8):

(a)   any person required by the order to contribute to the child's maintenance; or

(b)   any person in whose favour a residence order with respect to the child is in force.

3.13.8 Interim orders

Where an application is made under sch. 1, para. 1 or 2, the court has power to make an interim order prior to the disposal of the application. The order may require either or both parents to make periodical payments at such times and for such term as the court thinks fit, and the court may give any direction which it considers to be necessary (para. 9(1)). The court can specify the date from which the payments are to be made, provided that it is no earlier than the date upon which the application was made (para. 9(2)). The interim order will cease to have effect when the application is disposed of, unless the court has specified an earlier date (para. 9(3)); if the court has specified such an earlier date then it has power to vary the order by specifying a later date for its cessation (para. 9(4)).

3.13.9 Alteration of maintenance agreements

In sch. 1, paras 10 and 11, 'maintenance agreement' means any agreement with respect to a child which:

(a)   is or was made between the father and mother of the child (para. 10(1)(a)); and

(b)   contains provision for the making or securing of payments, or the disposition or use of any property, for the maintenance or education of the child (para. 10(1)(b)).

Where a maintenance agreement is subsisting, then either party to it may apply to the High Court, a county court or a magistrates' court for variation or revocation of any 'financial arrangements' contained in it. However, before such an application can be made, each of the parties to the agreement must for the time being be domiciled or resident in England and Wales (para. 10(2)). A magistrates' court may not hear such an application unless at least one of the parties is also resident within its commission area (para. 10(6)), and, in any event, it has no power to make an order except:

(a)   In any case where the agreement contains no provision for periodical payments by either of the parties, the court may make an order inserting a provision for one of the parties to make periodical payments for the maintenance of the child (para. 10(6)(a));
(b)   In a case where the agreement includes provision for one of the parties to make periodical payments, the court may make an order increasing or reducing the rate of, or terminating, any of those payments (para. 10(6)(b)).

Subject to the above restrictions in the case of magistrates' courts, the court may order such alterations to the agreement as appear just in all the circumstances if it is satisfied that:

(a)   because of a change in the circumstances which prevailed at the time the agreement was made (even if such a change was foreseen by the parties at that time), the agreement should be altered so as to make different financial arrangements (para. 10(3)(a)); or
(b)   the agreement does not contain proper financial arrangements for the child (para. 10(3)(b)).

If the agreement is altered by an order under para. 10, then that alteration takes effect as if it had been made by agreement between the parties and for valuable consideration (para. 10(4)).
Where the court decides to alter the agreement:

(a)   by inserting provision for one of the parties to make or secure periodical payments for the maintenance of the child (para. 10(5)(a), or
(b)   by increasing the rate of periodical payments to be made or secured by one of the parties for the maintenance of the child (para. 10(5)(b)),

then, in deciding the term for which such payments are to be made or secured, the court must apply the provisions of para. 3(1) and (2) (see 3.13.3) as if the order was an order under para. 1(2)(a) or (b).
It should, however, be noted that para. 10 does not affect the power of the court, where proceedings between the parties to a maintenance agreement are brought under other legislation, to make an order for financial arrangements;

nor does it affect the right of either party to apply for such an order in such proceedings (para. 10(7)).

3.13.9.1   Alteration of maintenance agreements after the death of one of the parties Where a maintenance agreement provides for the continuance of maintenance payments for a child after the death of one of the parties, and that party dies domiciled in England and Wales, the surviving party or the personal representatives of the deceased may apply to the High Court or the county court for an order under sch. 1, para. 10 (para. 11(1)). However, a county court must not hear an application under para. 11, or an application for leave to make such an application, unless it would have jurisdiction to hear and determine proceedings for an order under Inheritance (Provision for Family and Dependants) Act 1975, s. 2, in relation to the deceased by virtue of County Courts Act 1984, s. 25 (jurisdiction under the Act of 1975) (para. 11(5)).

The application must be made within six months of the date when representation in regard to the deceased's estate (see para. 11(4) as to what property is to be taken into account for this purpose) was taken out, unless the High Court or a county court other gives leave (para. 11(3)). The personal representatives will not be liable for having distributed any part of the estate after the six-month period on the ground that they ought to have taken into account the possibility that a court might grant leave for an application to be made by the surviving party after that period (para. 11(6)). It should be noted, however, that this does not prejudice any power to recover any part of the estate so distributed by virtue of the making of an order under para. 11 (para. 11(7)). If the court does decide to alter the agreement, then the agreement will take effect as if the alteration had been made, immediately before the death, by agreement between the parties and for valuable consideration (para. 11(2)).

3.13.10   Financial provision for child resident outside England and Wales
Where one parent of a child lives outside England and Wales, and the child lives outside England and Wales with:

(a)   another parent of his,
(b)   a guardian of his, or
(c)   a person in whose favour a residence order is in force with respect to the child,

then any of the persons specified at (a) to (c) above may apply to the court for an order under sch. 1, para. 1(2)(a) or (b) (for the making or securing of periodical payments) against the parent living in England and Wales (para. 14(1)).

3.13.11   Local authority contribution to child's maintenance
Where a child lives, or is to live, with a person as a result of a residence order, a local authority may make contributions to that person towards the cost of the child's maintenance and accommodation, unless that person is a parent of the child or the spouse of a parent of the child (sch. 1, para. 15).

Chapter Four
Children and Local Authorities

4.1 Introduction

Parts III and IV of the Children Act 1989 deal primarily with the child and his relationship with the State, in other words the 'public law' aspects of child welfare. Part IV concentrates on the orders which can be made on application by local authorities and other public bodies, namely, care orders, supervision orders and education supervision orders, and will be dealt with in chapter 5.

The Child Care Act 1980, which contains the present description of local authority powers and duties, is repealed in its entirety by the Children Act 1989, and Part III of the 1989 Act lists the duties imposed on local authorities in relation to children. These include a *general* duty to safeguard and promote the welfare of children in need who are within their area, and sundry *specific* duties, set out at length in sch. 2. The system of 'voluntary care' is replaced by the imposition of a duty on local authorities to accommodate children in need in certain circumstances, and the former power to assume parental rights over such children by administrative resolution is repealed.

The treatment of children accommodated by a local authority, whether under the exercise of their duty to 'accommodate' or under the ambit of a care order, is also dealt with in Part III. The Act imposes a general duty on the authority to safeguard and promote the child's welfare, and then sets out the specific duties the authority must fulfil, concerning such matters as contact with parents and the extent to which the authority may make use of secure accommodation. Particularly important is the requirement imposed on local authorities to review the cases of children it is looking after, at the instance of the child himself, a parent or a foster-parent. In general, the duties imposed on authorities in Part III will be enforceable in appropriate (and rare) cases by judicial review.

4.2 Aims and objects

The Children Act 1989 aims to achieve greater clarity and consistency in the law under which the State, mainly through the social services departments of local authorities, performs the following functions (*The Law on Child Care and Family Services* (Cm 62, 1987), para. 3):

(a)   The provision of child care services to families with children.
(b)   Regulation of the standard of private care facilities for children in the interests of their protection.
(c)   The protection of children at risk.
(d)   Removal of children from their natural families.
(e)   Discharging its responsibilities to children in care.

Formerly, these matters were covered by a number of different Acts, and the law was 'confusing and inconsistent in an area where the opposite is required' (ibid., para. 4). The powers and duties of the local authority to support families with children derive from two main areas of the law, child care law and health and welfare legislation. Child care law provides for children to be supported in the family, or to be received voluntarily or compulsorily into the local authority's care in specified circumstances. Health and welfare legislation enables the provision of services to children as part of the local authority's responsibilities to particular groups of all ages, such as those who are mentally handicapped or physically disabled. The Children Act 1989 unifies these two areas in an effort to bring all of the relevant provisions within one statute.

The Law on Child Care and Family Services (Cm 62, 1987), para. 5, sets out the principles underlying the new approach as follows:

(a)   the prime responsibility for the upbringing of children rests with parents; the State should be ready to help parents to discharge that responsibility especially where doing so lessens the risk of family breakdown;
(b)   services to families in need of help should be arranged in a voluntary partnership with the parents. Where such services include looking after the child away from home, close contact should be maintained so that the children can continue their relationships with their families and where appropriate be reunited with them as soon as possible . . .
(f)   where local authorities are caring for a child away from home their legal responsibilities for the child should be clear, as should be the powers and responsibilities of parents in these circumstances.

4.3   Provision of services for children and their families

The Children Act 1989 places a *general* duty upon a local authority to safeguard and promote the welfare of children within their area who are in need, and to promote the upbringing of such children by their families by providing a range and level of services appropriate to those children's needs (s. 17(1)). The definition of 'child in need' is important, as many of the duties and powers contained in Part III of the Children Act 1989 relate to such a child.

A child is taken to be 'in need' if:

(a)   he is unlikely to achieve or maintain a reasonable standard of health or development without the provision for him of local authority services (s. 17(10)(a));
(b)   his health or development is likely to be significantly impaired without the provision for him of such services (s. 17(10)(b));
(c)   he is disabled (s. 17(10)(c)).

In this context 'family' includes any person with parental responsibility for the child, and any other person with whom he has been living (s. 17(10)). 'Disabled', 'development' and 'health' are all defined in s. 17(11).

The *specific* duties and powers relating to the discharge of the local authority's general duty are set out in Part I of sch. 2. These provisions, which state an outline code of practice for social workers, should be referred to in the Act itself, but they can be summarised as follows:

(a)   The local authority must take reasonable steps to identify the extent to which there are children who are in need within their area, and publish information about the services provided for such children (sch. 2, para. 1).

(b)   The local authority must maintain a register of disabled children within their area (para. 2). In addition, they must provide specific services for disabled children (para. 6).

(c)   The local authority must take reasonable steps, through their provision of services, to prevent children within their area suffering ill-treatment or neglect. If they believe that a child in their area is likely to suffer harm but lives, or proposes to live in a different area, then they must inform the relevant local authority of the nature of the likely harm, and where the child lives (para. 4).

(d)   The local authority must take steps to reduce the need to bring, in relation to children in their area, care proceedings; criminal proceedings; family or other proceedings which might lead to the child being placed in local authority care; wardship proceedings (para. 7). The local authority are no longer under a duty to diminish the need to receive children into their care on a voluntary basis (that is, to accommodate them pursuant to Children Act 1989, s. 20) as the emphasis of the new provisions is on a voluntary partnership between parents and local authority, a partnership which would be threatened if the authority were statutorily bound to reduce the number of children being accommodated.

(e)   The local authority must make appropriate provision for the following services for children in need who are living with their families: advice, guidance and counselling; occupational, social, cultural or recreational activities; home help; assistance with travelling to and from home to take advantage of local authority services; assistance to enable the child and his family to have a holiday (para. 8).

(f)   The local authority must make appropriate provision for family centres (as defined) for children, their parents, persons with parental responsibility for children and any other persons looking after children, to attend for local authority activities or advice, guidance and counselling (para. 9).

(g)   The local authority must take reasonable steps, where a child in need is living apart from his family, to enable him to live with his family or to promote contact between him and his family, provided that it is necessary to do so to safeguard or promote his welfare (para. 10). This is of course a particularly significant provision where the child is in the care of the local authority, as opposed to being accommodated by them (see also 4.6.3 and 5.6).

The local authority have power to provide such services not only for the child in need, but also for any member of his family, so long as it is done in order to safeguard or promote the child's welfare (s. 17(3)). Furthermore, they may facilitate the provision of such services by others, and arrange for other agencies to provide them on their behalf (s. 17(5)). The authority may give assistance in kind, and, in exceptional circumstances, in cash (s. 17(6)), but they can attach conditions as to repayment (s. 17(7)). However, before giving assistance or imposing conditions, the authority must consider the means of the child and his parents (s. 17(8)). The authority have power to recoup the cost, or part of the cost, of providing the services concerned from the child, his parent, or a member of his family, in appropriate circumstances (s. 29(1); see 4.11).

An important addition to the local authority's available powers in this area is made by sch. 12, para. 36, which adds a new s. 3A to Education Act 1981. This empowers local authorities to make such arrangements as they think fit to enable children with special needs to attend establishments outside England and Wales which cater for such children. The new provision has been drawn up with a view to giving assistance to severely handicapped children who would benefit from the system of 'conductive education' provided by the Peto Institute in Budapest (see HC Deb., vol 158, col. 511 et seq.). It is not, however, restricted to that establishment. This provision will come into force two months after the Children Act 1989 receives royal assent (s. 108(2)).

4.4 Day care for under-fives and supervision of school children

The local authority are under a *duty* to provide such day care as is appropriate for children in need in their area who are aged five years and under, and who are not yet attending schools (s. 18(1)). They are also empowered to provide day care for children who are not in need, the likelihood being in such cases that the authority would charge a reasonable fee to the parent (ss. 18(2) and 29(1)). They may also provide 'facilities' for the carers themselves (note in particular 'training'), and for those who accompany the children whilst they are in day care (s. 18(3)). These provisions envisage the authority giving practical advice and assistance to the parents of children who attend their nurseries, perhaps including (but not restricted to) their upbringing of the children concerned.

'Day care' is defined in s. 18(4) as any form of care or supervised activity provided for children during the day. Care in the home of the child is therefore within the definition. The authority are not restricted to assisting the under-fives and their families: they may provide such care or supervised activities outside school hours, or during school holidays, for children who are attending school as is appropriate, and are under a statutory duty to do so in respect of children in need (s. 18(5) and (6)). The provisions in s.18 are intended to help prevent the breakdown of family relationships which might eventually lead to the committal of children to the care of the local authority (*The Law on Child Care and Family Services* (Cm 62, 1987), para. 18).

Section 19 imposes on every local authority a duty to review, not only the day care they themselves provide pursuant to s. 18, but also the extent of child-minding services and other day care for the under-eights available in their area. Reviews must be conducted no less than every three years (the first such review to be within one year of s. 19 coming into force). They must be conducted together with the local education authority, and regard must be had to the representations of health authorities and any other representations considered relevant (s. 19(1), (2) and (7)). Regard must also be had to the child-care provision in 'relevant establishments' (as defined in s. 19(5)) in the local authority's area. Provision is made for publication of the results of reviews (s. 19(6)). For the new statutory regime for child minders and day carers, see Part X and sch. 9.

4.5 Provision of accommodation for children

The existing regime of 'vountary care' is controversial and unpopular. In brief, a local authority are under a duty to receive a child under 17 into care where he has neither parent nor guardian, he has been and remained abandoned or lost, or his parents or guardians are for the time being prevented from providing for him (Child Care Act 1980, s. 2(1)). The effect of an admission into voluntary care is that if there is a parent, then that parent retains custody of the child, the local authority having temporary 'care and control'. Should the parent wish to take over the day-to-day care of the child, he can do so, subject to the giving of 28 days' notice to the authority if the child has been in care for six months. However, if the authority are of the view that returning the child to his parent will not be in the child's best interests, they can, on proof of one of eight conditions, pass a resolution transferring parental rights and duties to themselves (Child Care Act 1980, s. 3). The parent then has the right to object to the resolution and, on his doing so, the authority would have to satisfy the juvenile court that a ground existed for the passing of the resolution and that the resolution should remain in force.

The procedure described above conflicted with at least two of the objects stated in the White Paper. First, the power of the local authority to refuse to hand over a child who had been in voluntary care for six months in default of 28 days' notice being given derogated from the principle that the parents and the authority were associated in a 'voluntary partnership' directed solely towards caring for the child. Secondly, the power of the local authority to acquire parental rights and duties as a consequence of an administrative resolution did not accord with the need for justice to be seen to be done, in 'a full court hearing following due legal processes'. The recommendation that the concept of voluntary care be abolished was accepted, and the Child Care Act 1980 is to be entirely repealed.

Although the system of voluntary care is dismantled by the Children Act 1989, there obviously remains a need for local authorities to look after children who are not otherwise being cared for. The general duty to safeguard and promote the welfare of children in need (Children Act 1989, s. 17(1)) must be fulfilled. The provision which fills the gap is s. 20, imposing on local authorities a duty to accommodate such children in the circumstances there set out. The provision attempts to emphasise the voluntary nature of the authority's actions, a parent being free to remove the child at any time, and the only way the authority can assume parental rights (now 'parental responsibility') over a child so accommodated is by the granting of a care order by the courts.

The local authority is under a duty to provide accommodation for a child in need who requires accommodation where:
(a) there is no person with parental responsibility for him (s. 20(1)(a));
(b) he is lost or abandoned (s. 20(1)(b));

(c)   the person who has been caring for him is prevented from providing him with suitable accommodation or care (s. 20(1)(c)).

'Parental responsibility' is defined by s. 3(1) (see 2.2). In the construction of earlier statutes, 'abandoned' has been held to connote 'leaving the child to his fate' (*Mitchell* v *Wright* (1905) 7 F 568 at p. 574). The classic instance of a person being *prevented* from providing for the child is where the parent concerned is ill, but the words of the statute would also cover his imprisonment, or, indeed, death. A parent who simply states that he no longer wants to care for the child will not satisfy s. 20(1)(c), although such a statement might lead to the authority applying for a care order, or seeking to exercise their power under s. 20(4) (below).

Accommodation may be provided by a local authority for a child in need if the child has reached the age of 16 and his welfare is otherwise likely to be severely prejudiced (s. 20(3)). The authority may also provide accommodation for a child (who is not necessarily 'in need') even though there is someone with parental responsibility for him who is willing to accommodate him, so long as it considers that to do so would safeguard or promote the child's welfare (s. 20(4)). If a person (again not necessarily a former child 'in need') has reached 16 but is under 21, accommodation in a community home may be provided, so long as the home is run for people over 16 and to do so would safeguard or promote that person's welfare (s. 20(5)).

A local authority is also under a duty to provide accommodation for children who are subject to an emergency protection order, in police protection or detention, or on remand (s.21). However, the provisions of s. 20 (including the right of parents to remove the child in question from local-authority accommodation) do not apply in such cases for obvious reasons. The following text therefore refers only to children who are accommodated under s. 20.

Before the local authority provide accommodation, they must find out and take into consideration the child's wishes upon the matter (having regard to his age and understanding (s. 20 (6)). Where accommodation is provided, the authority must comply with their statutory duties under the Children Act 1989, ss. 22 and 23, and these will include the duty to ascertain the wishes of the child and others before making any decision about him (see further 4.6.1)).

The new arrangements for accommodation contained in s. 20 are intended to emphasise the voluntary nature of the relationship between parents and local authorities. If a person with parental responsibility for a child objects to the child being accommodated *and* is willing and able to provide or arrange the child's accommodation himself, then the authority cannot provide accommodation under the section (s. 20(7)). Moreover, once a child is accommodated by a local authority, any person with parental responsibility for the child may *at any time* remove the child from the local authority accommodation (s. 20(8)). These parental powers are wide, and exceptions are made in only two instances:

(a)   Where a person in whose favour a residence order has been made in respect of the child, or who has care and control of the child by virtue of an order made in the exercise of the High Court's inherent jurisdiction (s. 20(9)) or by virtue of an 'existing order' (see sch. 14, para. 8(4)) agrees to the child being looked after by the local authority (s. 20(9)). If there are two such persons, both must agree (s. 20(10)).

(b) Where a child who has reached 16 himself agrees to being accommodated by the local authority (s. 20(11)).

Example 4.1 Mr and Mrs Jones are divorced. Their son, Tommy, lives with Mrs Jones. When Mrs Jones goes into hospital, she asks the local authority to provide Tommy with accommodation. They do so. When Mr Jones finds out that his son is with short-term foster-parents, he physically removes him and takes him to live at his own house. In doing this, Mr Jones is acting lawfully, unless (a) Tommy lives his with mother pursuant to a residence order of the court (or she has care of him pursuant to an order of the High Court), or (b) Tommy is 16 or over and has himself agreed to be accommodated by the local authority.

This freedom of parents to remove their children from foster-parents or others with whom they may have been living for some considerable time has been criticised. 'Where parents are separated, they may be using the child as a pawn in their own dispute. Only time will tell whether this will be a further reason for children being moved in and out of local-authority accommodation.' (Richard White, 'Progress of the Children Bill' (1989) 139 NLJ 515). The problem is that the parent who is looking after the child may not necessarily have a residence order in his favour. Application may not have been made, or the court may have decided that there was no need to make such an order (the principle being that an order should only be made where to do so would be better for the child than making no order at all: s. 1(5)). In those circumstances, the parent who has not been looking after the child would be in a strong position.

The power to remove 'at any time' is controversial. Whilst an 'agreement' between parent and local authority could include a term that the parent give so many days' or hours' notice before removing the child, such a term would not be legally binding on the parent. In consequence, there is nothing to prevent a child being removed in the middle of the night, or without any warning or preparation, and the very suddenness of such a move could well be detrimental to the child's welfare. Children seeking clarification of their position from social workers or foster-parents can no longer be reassured about how and when the parent may take them home, and they are bound to feel less secure than at present.

The local authority may consider that the return of the child to his parent or parents would not be for his welfare. The repeal of the Child Care Act 1980 prohibits the authority from assuming parental rights and duties by administrative resolution. What other steps could the authority take? In the past, the issue of wardship proceedings would be a serious possibility. This too is now denied to the local authority (s. 100(1): see 5.11). There appear to be two options available to the authority in these circumstances:

(a) The authority may apply to the court for a care order. They must be able to satisfy the court that the statutory grounds for such an order (set out in s. 31(2)) are made out: it is not enough that the making of such an order is for the welfare of the child.

(b) In cases of urgency, the local authority may apply to the court for an emergency protection order (s. 44(1)). For the duration and effect of such orders, see 6.5 and 6.6.

Each of these courses of action will be open to the authority whether or not the removal of the child has occurred or is merely anticipated, although obviously if there is a risk of significant harm to the child, it will be desirable to obtain the order before removal does occur. When a parent approaches a local authority and requests that his child be accommodated by them, the authority should consider whether it is appropriate to accommodate the child, or whether taking care proceedings would be in the child's best interests. Particularly relevant to this decision will be the power of the parent to remove the child at any time if the child is simply 'accommodated', and the resultant damage which might ensue if the child is frequently moved in and out of local authority accommodation at the parent's behest. The authority should therefore point out the legal position to the parents and that they may well apply for a care order to protect the child should there be a risk of this eventuality occurring.

4.5.1   Children in voluntary care: transitional provisions
On Part III of the Children Act 1989 coming into force, children who are in 'voluntary care' pursuant to Child Care Act 1980, s. 2(1), will be treated as being provided with accommodation by the local authority under Part III (sch. 14, para. 20). Where, however, a resolution under Child Care Act 1980, s. 3, is in force in respect of the child, he will be treated as being in care pursuant to a care order (sch. 14, para. 15(1)(c); and see further 5.12).

4.6   Duties of local authorities in relation to children looked after by them

A child is 'looked after' by a local authority for the purposes of the Children Act 1989 if he is in their care by virtue of a care order, or is provided with accommodation by them (for a continuous period of more than 24 hours) under a voluntary arrangement (s. 22(1); see also s. 105(4)).

4.6.1   General Duties
Where a local authority looks after any child, they have a duty to safeguard and promote his welfare, and to make use of services available for children cared for by their own parents (s. 22(3)). They must act as a good parent; this entails planning for the child's well-being, monitoring the outcome of the plan, and ensuring that any placement is satisfactory (*The Law on Child Care and Family Services* (Cm 62, 1987), para. 29). Before making a decision with respect to the child the authority are required to ascertain the wishes and feelings of the child, his parents, and any person who is not a parent of his but who has parental responsibility for him, regarding the matter to be decided (s. 22(4)). Furthermore, in actually making such a decision the authority must give due consideration to the wishes and feelings of those persons, and to the child's religious persuasion, racial origin and cultural and linguistic background (s. 22(5)). It is, however, possible for the authority to exercise their powers with respect to the child without fulfilling all of these duties if it is necessary to do so in order to protect members of the public from serious injury (s. 22(6)), and it must

be emphasised that the imposition of a duty to give due consideration to the wishes of someone else does not imply that the authority, having given due consideration, must act in accordance with those wishes.

4.6.2 Provision of accommodation and maintenance

Where a local authority looks after any child they must provide him with accommodation while he is in their care, and must also maintain him (s. 23(1)). The authority may do this in the following ways (s. 23(2)):

(a) By placing him with a family, a relative of his, or other suitable person ('a local-authority foster-parent'), who will be paid by the authority. Schedule 2, para. 12, allows for regulations to be made governing the placement of children with local-authority foster-parents; these will cover such matters as the health, education and religious upbringing of the child, together with arrangements for the inspection and supervision of such placements by the authority.

(b) By maintaining him in a community home (see chapter 7).

(c) By maintaining him in a voluntary home (see chapter 7).

(d) By maintaining him in a registered children's home (see chapter 7).

(e) By maintaining him in a home provided by the Secretary of State under s. 82(5) which caters for children in need of particular facilities and services.

(f) By making such other arrangements as are appropriate and which comply with regulations made by the Secretary of State. (Schedule 2, para. 13, allows for such regulations to be made.)

There is now a statutory presumption that a local authority looking after a child must make arrangements enabling him to live with (a) a parent of his, (b) a person who is not a parent but who has parental responsibility, (c) a person in whose favour a residence order was in force immediately before a care order was made (see also sch. 14, para. 8(5)) or (d) a relative, friend or other person connected with him, unless that would not be reasonably practicable or consistent with his welfare (s. 23(6)). However, if the child is in care (i.e., pursuant to a care order), this presumption is apparently reversed (s. 23(5)).

Schedule 2, para. 14, provides for regulations to be made as to how the authority make their decision to allow children in care to live with such persons, as to the supervision or medical examination of the child, and as to the removal of the child from the person with whom he has been allowed to live. The existing regulations are the Accommodation of Children (Charge and Control) Regulations 1988 (SI 1988/2183), which came into force on 1 June 1989.

Where the authority do provide accommodation for a child they must, so far as is practicable and consistent with his welfare, ensure that it is near the child's home, and where they are providing accommodation for brothers and/or sisters they must, again so far as is practicable, secure that they are accommodated together (s. 23(7)). Where the child concerned is disabled, the authority must, so far as is reasonably practicable, secure that the accommodation is not unsuitable to his particular needs (s. 23(8)).

4.6.3 Contact between child and family

Where a child is being looked after by a local authority, the authority must endeavour, so far as is practicable and consistent with his welfare, to promote contact between the child and his parents, any person who is not a parent of his but who has parental responsibility for him, and any other person connected with him (sch. 2, para. 15(1)). The authority must take reasonable steps to keep the child's parents, or any other person with parental responsibility for him, informed of where he is being accommodated (sch. 2, para. 15(2)). However, there is no duty to inform anyone of the child's whereabouts if the child is in the care of the local authority and the authority have reasonable cause to believe that informing the person would prejudice the child's welfare (sch. 2, para. 15(4)). This is a welcome clarification of a local authority's power to withhold details of a child's whereabouts from his parents.

In order to facilitate contact between the child and the persons set out above, the authority are empowered to pay travelling expenses incurred in visiting the child where certain conditions apply (sch. 2, para. 16). If a child is not being visited by those persons referred to, the authority may be under a duty to appoint an independent person to visit the child (para. 17).

For parental contact with children in care, see further 5.5.

4.6.4 Arrangements to assist children to live outside England and Wales
A local authority may, with the approval of the court, arrange for any child in their care to live outside England and Wales (sch. 2, para. 19). It may be, for example, that long-term foster-parents decide to emigrate. The local authority must first seek the approval of every person who has parental responsibility for the child. The court must not give its approval unless it is satisfied that living abroad would be in the child's best interests, that suitable arrangements have been made for the child in the country in which he is to live, and that the child and those persons set out above consent to him living in that country (para. 19(3)). The child's consent can be dispensed with if he does not have sufficient understanding, and a parent's consent can also be dispensed with if the person concerned cannot be found, is incapable of consenting (for example, due to mental illness), or is withholding his consent unreasonably (para. 19(5)). (See also the power to arrange for children with special needs to attend establishments outside England and Wales (sch. 12, para. 36; see 4.3).)

4.6.5 Death of children being looked after by local authorities
Schedule 2, para. 20 (re-enacting, with amendments, Child Care Act 1980, s. 25) sets out the procedures to be followed where a child being looked after by a local authority dies.

4.7 Advice and assistance for certain children

Section 24 imposes duties and confers powers on local authorities in respect of children who are being looked after by the authority and in respect of children and adults under 21 who were (but are no longer) accommodated by an authority or other specified body. It is a complex provision, the exact duties and powers being dependent upon whether the person in question is or has been looked after by a local authority, and reference should be made to the statute for the detailed position. Particular attention should be paid to the duty imposed on a local authority, where a child is being looked after by them, to advise, assist and befriend him with a view to promoting his welfare when he ceases to be looked after by them (s. 24(1)). This represents a welcome reform of local-authority responsibilities, since children and young people often face difficulties in adjusting to leaving the protective environment of, for example, a community home or foster-parents. Those who do not return to their families must learn to adapt to independent living, 'and the difficulties may be exacerbated for young people who are handicapped or whose history and circumstances make them especially vulnerable. The existing legislation which sets out the local authorities' responsibilities to young people in these circumstances is confused.' (*The Law on Child Care and Family Services* (Cm 62, 1987), para. 32.)

4.8 Secure accommodation

A child who is being looked after by a local authority may not be placed in 'secure accommodation' (that is to say, accommodation provided to restrict his liberty), unless:

    (a) he has a history of absconding, is likely to abscond from any other type of accommodation, and if he does so is likely to suffer significant harm (s. 25(1)(a)); or

    (b) if he is kept in any other type of accommodation he is likely to injure himself or other people (s. 25(1)(b)).

Provision is made for regulations to be formulated specifying the periods during which a child may be kept in secure accommodation, and will empower the court to authorise such periods or extensions thereto. The regulations may also provide that such applications to the court must only be made by local authorities (s. 25(2)). A duty is imposed upon a court hearing such an application to determine whether any relevant criteria for keeping a child in secure accommodation are satisfied in his case (s. 25(3)). The child in such proceedings is entitled to legal aid if he wishes to be legally represented (s. 99(2)). If the court finds that the criteria are satisfied, then it must make an order authorising that the child be kept in secure accommodation and specifying the maximum period for which he may be so kept (s. 25(4)). If the hearing is adjourned, then the court has power to make an interim order permitting the child to be kept in secure accommodation during the adjournment (s. 25(5)). No court may exercise its powers under section 25 in respect of a child who is not legally represented, unless, having been informed of his right to apply for legal aid and having had the opportunity to do so, he refused or failed to apply (s. 25(6)). There is provision for regulations to be made specifying the description of children to whom the section will apply (s. 25(7)). If a court authorises the keeping of a child in secure accommodation, this does not prevent any court in England, Wales or Scotland from giving directions in relation to that child (s. 25(8)).

Section 25 is expressed to be subject to s. 20(8) (see s. 25(9)), under which any person with parental responsibility may remove a child from local-authority accommodation. However, as the parental power to remove applies only where the authority have provided accommodation under their s. 20 duty, a child who is in care (pursuant to a care order) and in secure accommodation cannot be legitimately removed by his parent.

4.9   Review of cases

The Children Act 1989 introduces a new requirement that local authorities provide a procedure, with an independent element, to resolve disputes and complaints raised when a child, a parent of his, a person who is not a parent but who has parental responsibility for him, or a local-authority foster-parent is unhappy with the arrangements made for his care (s. 26(3)). The procedure must ensure that at least one person who is not a member or officer of the authority takes part in the consideration of the representations made, and in discussions held about any action to be taken in relation to the child in the light of the consideration of those representations (s. 26(4)). There is provision for regulations to be made setting out the procedures to be followed in, consider-ations to be applied during, and the frequency such reviews are to be held (s. 26(1) and (2)). The regulations may also require the authority, before conducting any review, to seek the views of those entitled to make representa-tions, and any other person whose views are relevant (s. 26(2)(d)). Further specific requirements which the regulations may make of the authority are as follows:

(a)   Where the child is the subject of a care order, to consider whether an application should be made to discharge the order (s. 26(2)(e)).

(b)   Where the child is accommodated by them, to consider whether the accommodation accords with the requirements of Part III of the Children Act 1989 (s. 26(2)(f)).

(c)   To inform the child, so far as is reasonably practicable, of any steps he may take under the Act (s. 26(2)(g)).

(d)   To make arrangements to implement any decision which they propose to make in the course of, or as a result of, the review (s. 26(2)(h)).

(e)   To notify details of the result of the review, and any decision taken as a result thereof, to the child, his parents, any person who is not a parent of his but who has parental responsibility for him, and any other person whom they consider ought to be notified (s. 26(2)(i)).

(f)   To monitor the arrangements which they have made with a view to ensuring compliance with the regulations (s. 26(2)(j)).

When the local authority consider representations at such a review, they must comply with any regulations that have been made (s. 26(5)). Once the review has been held, the authority must have regard to the findings made by those considering the representations, and must take reasonable steps to notify in writing the person making the representations, the child (if he has sufficient understanding), and such other persons as appear likely to be affected, of the authority's decisions and reasons therefor, and any action they have taken or propose to take (s. 26(7)). Finally, the authority must give appropriate publicity of their procedure for such reviews (s. 26(8)).

4.10   Cooperation between authorities

Power is given to a local authority to request help in the exercise of any of their functions under Part III of the Children Act 1989 from any other local authority, local education authority, local housing authority, health authority and any person authorised by the Secretary of State for this purpose (s. 27(1) and (3)). Those authorities and persons must comply with the request unless it is incompatible with their own statutory duties and functions (s. 27(2)). There is a particular duty laid upon every local authority to assist any local education authority with the provision of services for any child within the local authority's area who has special educational needs (s. 27(4)). Where a local authority propose to provide accommodation for a child (whom they are looking after) in an establishment at which education is provided, they must (so far as is reasonably practicable) consult the local education authority and inform that authority of the arrangements made for the child's education (s. 28).

4.11   Recoupment of cost of providing services

Where a local authority provide services for children and their families under s. 17, or day care for under-fives and supervision of schoolchildren under s. 18 (other than advice, guidance and counselling), they may recover such charge as they consider reasonable from the following persons (s. 29(1) and (4)):

(a)   where the service is provided for a child under 16, each of his parents;
(b)   where it is provided for a child who has reached the age of 16, the child himself; and
(c)   where it is provided for a member of the child's family, that member.

However, where the person's means are insufficient for him to pay the charge, the authority must only require him to pay that sum which it is reasonable to expect him to pay, and a person who is in receipt of income support or family credit will not be liable to pay a charge (s. 29(2) and (3)).

Provision is also made for local authorities to collect contributions towards the maintenance of children who are being looked after by them, if they consider it reasonable to do so (sch. 2, Part III). This consists of the re-enactment with modifications of provisions in Part V of the Child Care Act 1980. The persons liable to contribute are (sch. 2, para. 21(3)):

(a)   where the child is under 16, each of his parents;
(b)   where the child has reached the age of 16, the child himself.

The authority may only recover such contributions as are agreed or determined in accordance with Part III of sch. 2, and before doing so they must serve a 'contribution notice' on the contributor specifying the details set out in para. 22 of sch. 2. If a contributor is served with a contribution notice and has failed to reach an agreement with the local authority within one month, or has served written notice withdrawing his agreement to the contribution arrangements, then the authority may apply to a court for an order that contributions be made (para. 23). Paragraph 23 of sch. 2 states the terms that may be contained in such an order, together with provisions for its revocation or variation. Rules of court will provide for an appeal from any contribution order (para. 23(11)). The provisions for the enforcement of contribution orders will be found in para. 24 of sch. 2. Regulations will be made to define the considerations which a local authority must take into account in deciding whether it is reasonable to recover contributions and what the arrangements should be (para. 25(a)). Regulations will also set down the procedures to be followed by a local authority in reaching agreements with contributors and any other local authority (para. 25(b)).

In certain circumstances, one local authority may be able to recover expenses from another local authority. See generally s. 29(7) to (9).

Chapter Five
Care and Supervision Orders

5.1 Introduction

With the demise of voluntary care and the repeal of local authority powers to assume parental rights and duties by administrative resolution (on which see chapter 4), together with the new restrictions on the use of wardship by local authorities, the principles and procedure governing care orders become of even greater importance than before. The Children Act 1989 makes substantial changes to the existing law, the main hallmarks of the new law being as follows:

(a)   The court may only make a care order on being satisfied of the statutory grounds set out in s. 31(2) and that the child's welfare demands that a care order be made.

(b)   Care orders may be made on specific application, or in the course of family proceedings. Criminal courts no longer have jurisdiction to make care orders but can still make supervision orders.

(c)   Local authorities cannot use the wardship jurisdiction to achieve a transfer of care to them. It is no longer available as a 'longstop' in cases where the authority cannot prove the statutory grounds.

(d)   Jurisdiction to make care orders will be concurrent in that the magistrates' court, the county court and the High Court are all empowered to make them. However, rules will determine precisely how application is to be made.

(e)   On the making of a care order, the authority will assume parental responsibility for the child concerned, and existing residence and contact orders will terminate. However, the care order will not extinguish the parental responsibility held by others at the time.

(f)   A new regime for contact between the child and his parents (and certain others) is established, there being a statutory presumption that the authority will allow the child to have reasonable contact with such persons.

(g)   The courts retain the power to make supervision orders in the course of care proceedings.

The new law concerning care orders will now be considered in more detail. For purposes of exposition, supervision orders will be dealt with separately (see 5.9).

It should, however, be noted that the procedure and grounds for supervision and care orders are the same. As with so much of the Children Act 1989, the detailed position, particularly with regard to procedural matters, will not be entirely clear until the regulations contemplated by the Act are promulgated.

5.2   Who can apply for a care order?

Application for a care order may be made by 'any local authority' (s. 31(1)). It is not necessary for the child to be ordinarily resident within the area of the applicant authority. However, if the care order is made, it will have the effect of placing him in the care of the authority in whose area the child ordinarily resides ('the designated authority') (s. 31(8)(a)). The only exception to this will be where the child does not reside in the area of any local authority. In such a case, the designated authority will be the authority 'within whose area any circumstances arose in consequence of which the order is being made' (s. 31(8)(b)).

Example 5.1   Tony's parents live in Nottingham. He runs away from home and he is found three months later sleeping rough in London in the company of drug addicts. His parents refuse to have him back. In these circumstances, Tony not being resident in the area of any local authority, the authority to be designated on the making of a care order would be the one in whose area he was found sleeping rough (s. 31(8)(b)). If, however, he had run away to live permanently with a relative, he would become 'ordinarily resident' in that local authority area, and s. 31(8)(a) would therefore apply. (For the meaning of 'ordinary residence', see s. 105(6).)

Application for a care order may also be made by an 'authorised person', meaning the NSPCC (and any of its officers) or any other person authorised by the Secretary of State (s. 31(9)). Where an authorised person proposes to make an application for a care order, then before doing so he must (if it is reasonably practicable) consult the local authority in whose area the child concerned is ordinarily resident (s. 31(6)). Moreover, the court must not entertain an application by an authorised person if, at the time when it is made, the child is (s. 31(7)):

(a)   the subject of an existing application for a care or supervision order which has not been disposed of; or
(b)   subject to a care or supervision order, an order under Children and Young Persons Act 1969, s. 7(7)(b), or a supervision requirement within the meaning of the Social Work (Scotland) Act 1968.

There is nothing to stop an authorised person from applying for a care order in respect of a child who is accommodated by the local authority, and in a case where, perhaps, the NSPCC has been instrumental in rescuing a child from a particular crisis, it might seem appropriate, and convenient, for that organisation to make the application. However, as it is the local authority which will accommodate the child, in most instances it will be more appropriate for the proceedings to be taken by the local authority.

No one other than local authorities or authorised persons may initiate care proceedings. Thus, the police can no longer bring care proceedings, as they could under Children and Young Persons Act 1969, s. 1, one of the bases of the new reforms being to decriminalise the care process (for repeal, see s. 90). Moreover, the procedure whereby parents could pressure local authorities into commencing proceedings (Children and Young Persons Act 1963, s. 3) has been repealed. A parent who is unable to control his own child will only be able to compel action on the part of a reluctant local authority by resorting to the rather cumbersome procedure of judicial review. Moreover, challenging the decision of a local authority not to initiate care proceedings will be even more difficult than before as a result of the wider discretion now vested in local authorities.

A care order can only be made where the child concerned is under the age of 17, or, where the child is married, under the age of 16 (s. 31(3)). Furthermore, as the High Court loses its inherent jurisdiction to make a care order in respect of a child, children aged 17 and married 16-year-olds cannot in any circumstances be made the subject of a care order (cf. *Re S.W. (A Minor) (Wardship: Jurisdiction)* [1986] 1 FLR 24).

5.3 Before the application

It will of course be part of the practice under the new law as under the old that, before applying for a care order, a local authority or authorised person will take all reasonable steps to apprise itself fully of the material facts and satisfy itself that the course it is taking is the proper one. Whilst this is as much a matter of good social-work practice as of law, and to that extent outside the scope of this book, the Children Act 1989 does, by several rather disparate provisions, reinforce the duties of local authorities in the making of the decision in question. Central is the general duty to safeguard and promote the welfare of children in need within the local authority's area (s. 17(1)); but mention should also be made of the duty contained in s. 22(4). This requires the authority (so far as is reasonably practicable) to ascertain the wishes and feelings of the child, his parents, anyone else with parental responsibility (e.g., a guardian), and any other person whose wishes and feelings the authority consider to be relevant *before* making a decision with respect to the child. The duty applies to children whom the authority are looking after (e.g., already in care or accommodated by the authority), and also to children whom they are *proposing to look after*. This must include children who are still living at home with their parents but in relation to whom care proceedings are contemplated. In those circumstances, therefore, the authority are statutorily bound to ascertain the wishes of the persons listed, but in a case of urgency, where it is thought, for example, that communication with the parents might result in the swift disappearance of the child, application without full consultation would be permissible on the ground that it was not 'reasonably practicable' to conduct the usual exercise.

Where a local authority are informed, or have cause to suspect (*inter alia*) that a child who lives, or is found, in their area has suffered significant harm or is likely to do so, then the authority are under a duty to investigate, so that they can decide whether any action should be taken to safeguard and promote the child's welfare (s. 47(1)). The enquiries must be directed particularly towards establishing whether the authority should apply to the court for a care order, for example (s. 47(3)). A particularly important provision, which effects a significant change to the existing law is s. 47(8), governing the duty of local authorities to take care proceedings (and, indeed, proceedings for an emergency protection order or a supervision order). By this provision, a local authority which conclude that they should take action to safeguard or promote the child's welfare are obliged to take that action 'so far as it is both within their power and reasonably practicable for them to do so'. Although 'within their power' is a statement of the obvious, as a local authority may not act *ultra vires*, the reference to reasonable practicability widens the scope of their discretion. Under the existing law (contained in Children and Young Persons Act 1969, s. 2(2), and now repealed), the local authority have a specific duty to commence care proceedings in respect of a child 'unless they are satisfied that it is neither in his interest nor the public interest to do so or that some other person is about to do so or to charge him with an offence'. Under Children Act 1989, s. 47(8), the authority could decide that proceedings were necessary to safeguard the child, but not take them on the basis that it was not reasonably practicable to do so, what is practicable being influenced by considerations unrelated to the interests of the child. These could arguably include the availability of resources such as social workers, solicitors, foster-parents and so on. In a time of financial constraints, where local authorities are concerned about the allocation of funds, the argument of reasonable practicability is perhaps a dangerous one to allow. It should be emphasised that prior to the Cleveland crisis (which is still uppermost in people's minds) the major enquiries that have taken place have concerned relatively inactive and not over-active authorities. However, a challenge by judicial review of an authority's decision not to initiate proceedings will be even more difficult than before, as a result of the wider discretion now conferred by s. 47(8).

5.4   The statutory grounds

The existing grounds for committing children to the care of a local authority are to be found in Children and Young Persons Act 1969, s. 1. A child can also be committed to care in the course of matrimonial proceedings under Matrimonial Causes Act 1973, s. 43, guardianship proceedings under Guardianship Act 1973, s. 2, proceedings under the inherent jurisdiction of the High Court in wardship (or under Family Law Reform Act 1969, s. 7), or as a result of criminal proceedings against him. Child Care Act 1980, ss. 2 and 3, govern the reception of a child into voluntary care and the grounds for passing a resolution assuming parental rights and duties. All of the existing provisions are repealed and the only way of admitting a child into the care of a local authority in future will be on the court being satisfied of the existence of grounds pursuant to Children Act 1989, s. 31.

Children and Young Persons Act 1969, s. 23, under which, in the course of criminal proceedings, a child could be remanded to the care of a local authority, is redrafted by Children Act 1989, sch. 12, para. 26, and such a remand is now 'to local authority accommodation'. It is declared to be lawful for the local authority to 'detain' the remanded child. A 'young person' (over 14 and under 17) shall be committed to a remand centre or prison if the court certifies him to be 'of unruly character', and he may be so certified on the application of the local authority who are accommodating him. The effect of this amendment is that a child remanded under s. 23 of the 1969 Act is not in the care of the local authority.

The new provisions for the making of an order in care proceedings have jettisoned the specific grounds found under the existing legislation, such as the committing of an offence or non-attendance at school. The grounds which must be satisfied in order for a care order to be made are set out in s. 31(2). A court may *only* make a care order if it is satisfied that:

(a)   the child is suffering, or is likely to suffer, significant harm; *and*
(b)   the harm, or likelihood of harm, is attributable to:

(i)   the care given to the child, or likely to be given to him if the order is not made, not being what it would be reasonable to expect a parent to give to him; *or*
(ii)   the child's being beyond parental control.

Note that grounds (a) and (b) are cumulative: both must be satisfied, although (b) may be satisfied by either of its subparagraphs. When the grounds have been successfully made out, the court has a discretion as to making the order, and in the exercise of that discretion it must abide by the dictates of s. 1. In particular, it must be aware that in determining the application before it:

(a)   the child's welfare is the paramount consideration (s. 1(1)); and
(b)   the court must not make an order unless it considers that making it would be better than making no order at all (s. 1(5)).

In deciding how best to promote the child's welfare, the court must have regard to the 'statutory checklist' of factors in s. 1(3) (see s. 1(4)(b) and 2.1.3), and to the general principle that any delay is likely to prejudice the child (s. 1(2)).

Returning to s. 31(2), ground (a) refers to 'harm', defined as ill-treatment or the impairment of health and development. 'Development', means physical, intellectual, emotional, social or behavioural development, and 'health' means physical or mental health; 'ill-treatment' includes sexual abuse and forms of ill-treatment which are not physical (s. 31(9)). 'Significant' does not add a great deal: the lawyer would in any case construe the statute by reference to the '*de minimis*' principle. The layman should not equate 'significant' with 'substantial'. Where the question of whether the harm suffered by the child is 'significant' turns upon the child's health or development, then his health or development is to be compared with that which could reasonably be expected of a similar child (s. 31(10)).

Ground (a) refers both to present harm and to future harm.

The requirement that the child *is suffering* significant harm, in its use of the present tense, mirrors the existing ground contained in Children and Young Persons Act 1969, s. 1(2)(a), and it is no doubt intended that the new section should receive the same liberal interpretation as does the existing one. The court must not adopt blinkers and look solely at the position of the child at the very moment in time when it is deciding whether or not to make a care order.

The decision in *M* v *Westminster City Council* [1985] FLR 325 provides an example of the approach a court must adopt when considering whether a child 'is suffering' significant harm. Both mother and father had a drink problem. As a result their twin daughters had been left alone in the house and had witnessed violent scenes between their parents. The parents showed a 'lack of reaction' to the twins in times of stress. Following interim care orders, the twins were returned to the mother, and for the four weeks prior to the full hearing, she cared for the children satisfactorily. The Divisional Court held that despite the four-week lull there was ample evidence on which the magistrates could find that the children's proper development was being avoidably prevented or neglected. In a passage which is most illuminating, Bush J (at p. 340) considered the effect of the use of the present tense in the Children and Young Persons Act 1969:

> The development of a child is a continuing matter and encompasses the past, present and, to a certain extent, the future. The magistrates, in determining the primary condition, must have regard to the past treatment of the child as well as to the present. They must ask themselves on the day of the hearing: 'Are we satisfied that his proper development is being avoidably prevented or neglected, or his health is being avoidably impaired or neglected?' They are not bound to answer the question in the negative if, for example, there has been a temporary respite in the condition or treatment of the child. *In my view 'is being' is not temporal in the sense that it means 'now', 'this minute'; it is descriptive of the child, that is the child must fall into the category mentioned in the section.* If the words used had been different then different considerations would apply. 'Has been' would indicate some time in the past; 'will be' would indicate some time in the future; 'is being' would indicate a situation over a period, not now at this precise moment but over a period of time sufficiently proximate to the date of the inquiry to indicate that it is the present, not history and not the days to come. It is the description of a continuing set of circumstances which may not obtain on the particular day on which the matter is being considered but represents a category which the description of the child fits. (Emphasis added.)

These words were considered, with approval, by the House of Lords in *Re D (A Minor)* [1987] AC 317 which concerned the availability of a care order in the case of a child born to a drug addict and suffering at birth from withdrawal symptoms. Lord Goff of Chieveley states (at p. 351):

> ... when magistrates are considering whether there is a presently existing state of affairs, and there is evidence before them of events which indicate the existence of such a state of affairs in the past, the magistrates are entitled and, indeed, bound to consider whether at the time when they are considering making an order, there is an existing likelihood that the state of affairs revealed by those past events will continue into the future, in order to decide whether the necessary continuum exists at the relevant time.

Both of these passages must be read subject to the changes in wording consequent upon the Children Act 1989 (in particular, the removal of any reference to the 'avoidability' of the relevant harm). The question for courts to answer when faced with an application under Children Act 1989, s. 31, will be: in the light of the words emphasised above, and weighing as appropriate the relevance of the past, is the child who is the subject of the care application 'suffering significant harm'?

The inclusion of future harm in the new grounds is a considerable simplification from the existing law (see Children and Young Persons Act 1969, s. 1(2)(b) and (bb)), and is necessary as the authority will no longer be able to use wardship proceedings to obtain care of the child, as was the case previously where harm to the child was anticipated rather than actual. Two brief examples may assist in explaining how this element of s. 31(2)(a) is intended to function.

Example 5.2 The local authority are accommodating Darren pursuant to their duty under Children Act 1989, s. 20. It comes to their notice that Darren's grandfather, who lives with Darren's parents, has been convicted of sexual offences against young boys (but not Darren). His release from prison is imminent, and he is going back to live with Darren's parents. Darren's mother has indicated that she will soon be asking for Darren to be returned to her (see Children Act 1989, s. 20(7) and (8)). The local authority can apply for a care order, and will argue that Darren is likely to suffer significant harm (i.e. ill-treatment, which includes sexual abuse: s. 31(9)) if a care order is not made.

Example 5.3 Julie, who is mentally retarded (with a mental age of six), gives birth to a baby, Sean. She has no previous children, or, indeed, experience of caring for a child. Before the birth, the local authority take the view that the baby will be at risk if cared for by Julie. The authority may apply for an emergency protection order and take care proceedings on the grounds that Sean is likely to suffer significant harm, the evidence being the mother's inability to care for herself, her care of Sean in hospital, and any social work assessment made during contact between Julie and Sean. Whilst all these factors may or may not be present, it is open to a court on sufficient evidence of risk to the child to make a care order on birth.

These examples are intended to emphasise that the authority may be able to show 'likely harm' both where the child is still at home, and the purpose of taking care proceedings is to remove him from a potential source of danger, and where the child is away from home, and care proceedings are initiated to preserve the existing position. The difficulty which an authority will face frequently is to show, as it will need to, on the balance of probabilities, that the child is likely to suffer harm. There must be something more than mere surmise.

The Law on Child Care and Family Services (Cm 62, 1987), para. 60, is perhaps helpful here:

> It is intended that 'likely harm' should cover all cases of unacceptable risk in which it may be necessary to balance the chance of the harm occurring against the magnitude of that harm if it does occur. . . . the court will have to judge whether there is a risk and what the nature of the risk is.

Local authorities will have experience, based on their use of the wardship jurisdiction, of whether there is in a given case a sufficiently serious risk to initiate proceedings on the basis of future harm. High Court judges, and to a lesser extent county court judges, will also be well versed in the evaluation of evidence of this nature. However, magistrates must realise that the new care grounds require them to perform a wholly different task in these cases. Even magistrates familiar with care proceedings will not have had to make care orders where the only evidence before them relates to the harm which the child is likely to suffer in the future rather than the harm he has suffered in the past. Their readiness to accept evidence of future harm (and make care orders in appropriate cases where that is the only evidence available) will be essential if the new system of care proceedings is to function effectively.

Ground (b), in its alternative guises, requires the court to find the cause for the harm, or likely harm, which has satisfied ground (a). Ground (b)(i) looks to the standard of care which the child obtains, or is likely to obtain if the care order is *not* made. The court must evaluate that standard of care, and then ask itself the question: Is that standard below that which it would be reasonable to expect the parent of such a child to give to him? The court should therefore focus on the care being given to the child, and then ask itself whether it meets the required standard. In this way, the court will avoid being too subjective in its analysis of the parent who is caring for the child, and giving too much weight to the individual parent's ability. The words of the White Paper (at para. 60) are a helpful guide, stating that s. 31(2)(b)(i) 'is not intended to imply a judgment on the parent who may be doing his best but is still unable to provide a reasonable standard of care'.

Ground (b)(ii) is a simpler question: Is the child beyond parental control? This is reproduced, with cosmetic amendment only, from Children and Young Persons Act 1969, s. 1(2)(d). The parent may not be 'at fault' for this ground to be satisfied: for example, he may attempt to discipline the child, who then refuses to accept it. Note that a parent who considers that his child is beyond his control cannot himself apply for a care order to be made, nor can he request the local authority to bring proceedings with the sanction of complaining to the juvenile court and forcing the issue if they refuse to act: Children and Young Persons Act 1969, s. 3, is repealed by Children Act 1989. He may, informally, ask the authority to act and if they fail to do so there is an outside chance that he will have a remedy in judicial review. He will, however, have to show that the decision of the authority not to take any action was one which no reasonable local authority could have made: a very considerable burden.

As a general comment, although s. 31(2) undoubtedly simplifies the law, it is less 'new' than its proponents would allow. A close comparison between Children and Young Persons Act 1969, s. 1(2)(a) and the Children Act 1989, s. 31(2), such as is beyond the scope of this book, would reveal the derivation of the 'new' grounds. The substantial change is the power to make care orders in the case of anticipated rather than actual harm, a necessary reform in view of the restrictions now imposed on local authorities' use of the wardship jurisdiction.

To summarise the exercise s. 31(2) requires the court to carry out:

(a)   Is the child suffering significant harm, *or* is he likely to suffer significant harm?
(b)   What is the harm (or likelihood of harm) attributable to?
If it is attributable to (i) the standard of care being below that which it would be

reasonable to expect the parent of such a child to give, *or* (ii) the child's being beyond parental control, then

(c)   the court has a discretion whether to grant a care order.

In deciding whether to make such an order, the child's welfare is the paramount consideration.

5.5   Effect of care orders

Once a care order has been made, the local authority are under a duty to receive the child into their care and keep him there while the order remains in force (s. 33(1)). Where the order was made upon the application of an 'authorised person' rather than a local authority, and the authority were not informed about the application (a relatively rare occurrence, as the authority will normally be consulted prior to the 'authorised person' making application: see s. 31(6)), then the authorised person may keep the child in his care until the child is received into the care of the authority (s. 33(2)).

Whilst the care order is in force with respect to a child, the local authority have parental responsibility for him (s. 33(3)(a)). This does not mean that the person who had parental responsibility (let us call him a parent for the sake of simplicity) immediately prior to the care order being made loses it when the order is made. Thereafter, the position will be that both local authority and parent will have parental responsibility for the child.

An attempt is made to resolve this rather awkward situation in s. 33(3)(b), which confers on the designated local authority the power to determine the extent to which a parent of a child in care may meet his parental responsibility for the child. However, this power may not be exercised unless the authority are satisfied that it is necessary to do so in order to safeguard or promote the child's welfare (s. 33(4)). Furthermore, a parent who has *de facto* care of the child may do what is reasonable in all the circumstances of the case for the purpose of safeguarding or promoting his welfare (s. 33(5); see also s. 3(5)). Only time will tell whether these cumbersome provisions meet the criticisms of the parents' retention of parental responsibility made by Eekelaar and Dingwall (1989) 139 NLJ 217, 760.

Despite having parental responsibility, there are certain things which the local authority have no right to do in respect of the child. The authority may not:

(a)   Bring the child up in any religious persuasion other than that in which he would have been brought up if the order had not been made (s. 33(6)(a)). This does not necessarily preclude the child, if of sufficient understanding, from choosing to practise a different religion from his parents: he is entitled to be consulted by the authority about such matters (s. 22(4) and (5)).

(b)   Consent to or refuse the making of an application freeing the child for adoption (s. 33(6)(b)(i)).

(c)   Agree or refuse to agree to the making of an adoption order in respect of the child or an order authorising removal of a child from the jurisdiction for the purpose of adoption abroad (s. 33(6)(b)(ii)).

(d)   Appoint a guardian for the child (s. 33(6)(b)(iii)).

All these matters will presumably remain the prerogative of the parents. Thus, if the authority decide that the child's welfare demands that he be adopted, the parent's rights in the adoption proceedings are unaffected by the existence of the care order. It is clearly right that the parents' ability to oppose an adoption order (which would terminate their parental responsibility) should be retained, but it must of course be recognised that a parent is likely to be held to be withholding consent unreasonably in the case of a child of his who is the subject of a care order.

Furthermore, while a care order is in force no person may cause the child to be known by a new surname, or remove him from the United Kingdom without either the written consent of every person who has parental responsibility for the child or the leave of the court (s. 33(7)). However, such consent is not necessary where the authority wish to remove the child from the jurisdiction for a period of less than one month (s. 33(8)(a)). Foster-parents who wish to take the child on holiday with them (and who have the consent of the local authority) are therefore free to do so without the need of the natural parents' consent, unless the holiday is over a month in duration. If the authority wish to apply for the child to live abroad, then that application is governed by sch. 2, para. 19, to which reference should be made (s. 33(8)(b)).

The power of a local authority to place a child in its care with one or both of its parents is governed by Children Act 1989, s. 23(4) and (5) (see 4.6.2, above), although the detail is left to regulations which have yet to be made. It is, however, envisaged that such regulations will follow, in general terms, the Accommodation of Children (Charge and Control) Regulations 1988 (SI 1988/2183), which came into force on 1 June 1989.

A care order has the effect of discharging all existing residence or contact orders, or, for that matter, prohibited steps or specific issue orders (s. 91(2)). Obviously, the central concept of a care order (i.e., the transfer of immediate care over the child from the parent to the local authority) demands that a residence order which is in force at the time of the care order is automatically discharged. Less obvious is the position concerning contact orders: it may be clearer once we have examined the important reforms the Children Act 1989 makes in relation to children in care retaining contact with their parents.

5.6   Parental contact with children in care

In *A* v *Liverpool City Council* [1982] AC 363, the House of Lords rejected a claim by a mother to make her child, who was in the care of the local authority, a ward of court and grant her access, on the grounds that the wardship jurisdiction could not be used to challenge decisions lawfully made by local authorities. In 1983, Parliament responded to proceedings pending before the European Court of Human Rights (*R* v *The United Kingdom* (Case No. 6/1986/104/152) [1988] 2 FLR 445) by enacting ss. 12A to 12G of the Child Care Act 1980 (in Health and Social Services and Social Security Adjudications Act 1983, s. 6 and sch. 1) which gave parents the right to apply for an access order when access was terminated. Further guidance with regard to access was then contained in the Code of Practice, 'Access to Children in Care' (the so-called 'Access Code'), promulgated under the powers in s. 12G of the 1980 Act.

The provisions in the Child Care Act 1980 are now repealed. The difficult area of parental contact with children in care is now dealt with in two provisions of the Children Act 1989: s. 34 and sch. 2, para. 15. A parent who is seeking contact cannot apply for a section 8 contact order if his child is in care (s. 9(1)).

By sch. 2, para 15, a local authority are placed under a duty to 'endeavour to promote' contact between any child they are looking after and his parents, those who have parental responsibility (e.g., guardians), and any relatives, friends or other persons connected with him. This duty is applicable unless contact is not reasonably practicable or consistent with his welfare.

Where the child being looked after is actually in care, the Children Act 1989 now imposes a statutory presumption that the authority must allow the child to have reasonable contact with his parents, any guardian of his, and any person in whose favour a residence order was in force with respect to the child immediately before the care order was made (s. 34(1)). This is a welcome innovation in the area of child-care law. The duty imposed by s. 34(1) is enforceable in the courts, and the remainder of s. 34 works out the manner of enforcement.

The local authority designated in the care order, and the child himself, may apply to the court for an order directing the contact which is to be allowed between the child and a particular named person (s. 34(2)). As the authority have, by definition, parental responsibility, they would only use this power in rare cases, perhaps where there is substantial doubt about the advisability of contact with, for example, an abusing relative, and the sanction of the court is sought. The child may wish to apply to maintain contact with a relative (including brothers and sisters), a close friend, or, indeed, anyone with whom he wishes to keep in touch. If the purpose of the application is to prohibit contact between the child and a named person, the proper provision under which to apply will be s. 34(4).

Any of the persons set out in s. 34(1), or any person who has leave of the court to do so, may apply to the court for an order with respect to the contact which is to be allowed between the child and the applicant (s. 34(3); see also, for transitional cases, sch. 14, para. 7(3)(c)).

It may be, of course, that the very object of care proceedings has been to eliminate contact between the child and a particular person (perhaps a parent who is suspected of abuse) who would otherwise be presumed to have contact with the child. In such circumstances, the court may order that the local authority are authorised to refuse contact between the child and the person in question (s. 34(4)). The only persons who can apply for an order under s. 34(4) are the local authority designated in the care order and the child himself. It would not be open to, for example, a parent of the child in care to apply for an order terminating contact between the child and the other parent, and he would have to rely on the authority sharing his concern for the child and acting upon that concern.

It is open to the court to impose such conditions as it considers appropriate upon making an s. 34 order (s. 34(7)). The court would normally specify in the order the timing, nature and duration of the contact, but it is not obliged to do so. In deciding what order to make, indeed whether to make an order at all (see s. 1(5)), the court's paramount consideration must be the welfare of the child (s. 1(1)) and it must have regard to the general principle that any delay is likely to prejudice the welfare of the child (s. 1(2)). It must be stressed that s. 34 is a child-centred provision, giving rights to the child and not to the parents. Where, for instance, a child in care did not wish to see his parents, the local authority would satisfy their duty under s. 34(1) by being prepared to make contact arrangements. However, the parent can make application, under s. 34(3), and it would then be up to the court to decide whether to make an order in the light of the child's refusal.

It may be a cause of some concern that s. 34 does not extend to allow contact where appropriate with the wider family. Grandparents, for example, would not normally fall within any of the categories listed in s. 34(1). Do they have any right to see their grandchild who is in the care of the local authority? Strictly speaking, the answer is no: they have no *right* to see him. However, in an appropriate case, perhaps where links between grandchild and grandparent are strong, the grandparent could ask the court for leave to apply for a contact order under s. 34(3). In considering the application for leave, and indeed the substantive application itself, the court should be apprised of the duty owed by the authority under sch. 2, para. 15. It is a duty to endeavour to promote contact between the child and (*inter alios*) 'any relative'. In brief, while contact between grandparents and grandchildren is not 'presumed' in the way contact between child and parents is, there would normally be a reasonable prospect of a grandparent obtaining an order for contact under s. 34(3).

A possibly more worrying omission from the list of those with whom the local authority are obliged to allow the child reasonable contact are the child's brothers and sisters. As with grandparents, they have a notional right to make application, with the leave of the court, but in view of their likely ages, such application is unlikely to be initiated by them. They would also fall within the ambit of the local authority's duty under sch. 2, para. 15.

The authority do have some discretion in relation to the contact they allow with a child in their care even where the court has made an s. 34 order. They may refuse contact with the persons listed in s. 34(1), or those in relation to whom an s. 34 order has been made, as a matter of urgency without an application to the court, provided that the refusal does not last for more than seven days and is necessary in order to safeguard or promote the child's welfare (s. 34(6)). The extent to which an authority may allow contact between the child and a person who has been refused contact by the court pursuant to s. 34(4) is unclear, and this difficulty will, it is hoped, be resolved by regulation (see particularly s. 34(8)(b)).

The court may vary or discharge any s. 34 order on the application of the person named in the order, the authority or the child concerned (s. 34(9)). Where a person other than a local authority has made an application for any s. 34 order, and that application has been refused, then that person may not make a similar application in respect of the same child until at least six months have elapsed since the refusal, unless he has obtained leave of the court (s. 91(17)). This provision may seriously inhibit a local authority's ability to plan for the long-term care of a child in a case where a parent makes repeated application (perhaps every six months) for contact with the child.

An s. 34 order may be made at the same time as the care order itself or later (s. 34(10)). Before making a care order the court must consider the arrangements which the authority have made, or propose to make, for affording contact between the child and the persons to whom s. 34 applies (s. 34(11)). This is an important provision. In essence, when a care order is made, the court will frequently make whatever order it considers appropriate regarding access at the same time, and (subject to any court rules or directions in the proceedings themselves) all parties may have to be prepared to present evidence and make submissions on the question of contact.

The provisions contained in s. 34 are likely to lead to an increase in the amount of court work in this area, but they represent an important step in making the legal framework fairer to parents who disagree with the local authority's restrictions on contact with children who are subject to a care order. However, the freedom of parents to challenge the decisions of local authorities concerning their children who are in their care receives little support elsewhere in the Children Act 1989.

5.7 Care order procedure

5.7.1 Parties

The applicant for a care order must be either a local authority or an authorised person (see 5.2). The Children Act 1989 does not specify which other persons will be entitled to party status, leaving the issue to be determined by rules of court (s. 93(2)(b)). In the White Paper (*The Law on Child Care and Family Services,* para. 55), it is stated that anyone whose legal position could be affected by the proceedings, and anyone who is permitted to seek and is seeking legal responsibility for the child, will be able to be a party. In the House of Lords, the Lord Chancellor initimated that the child would be a party in every case, and that those with parental responsibility would normally be parties (HL Deb., 23 January 1989, col. 550). The position is as yet far from clear, and we must await the rules themselves for clarification. There is a substantial school of thought that relatives should have rights to be heard in the course of care proceedings, one member being Neill LJ:

> Speaking for myself, I see great force in the contention that where the parents of a child are themselves unwilling or unable to care for him, members of the extended or wider family, if willing to help, are often in a unique position to help with his care and upbringing. Indeed, it could be argued that it would be desirable that members of the wider family should be given a statutory right to be heard in proceedings involving infant children to whom they are closely related. (*Re W (A Minor) (Care Proceedings: Wardship)* [1985] FLR 408, at p. 433.)

It is hoped that when the rules are promulgated relatives are given such rights, perhaps subject to the leave of the court.

5.7.2 Representation

This particularly difficult subject is dealt with largely in s. 41 of the Children Act 1989. The government has decided not to implement the proposal in the Cleveland Report (para. 16.91) that there should be an Office of Child Protection. Instead, the role of advancing the child's interests (as opposed to his wishes) in the course of care proceedings will continue to be that of the guardians *ad litem.* The common criticism that guardians *ad litem* are often social workers appointed by the same authority which is seeking to obtain the care order and that the panel of guardians is administered by the same authority is countered by an attempt to distance the guardian appointed for a particular case from the applicant local authority and by making new regulations concerning the administration of panels. Legal representation is also dealt with by s. 41.

The court is under a duty to appoint a guardian *ad litem* for a child for the purpose of 'specified proceedings' unless it is satisfied that it is not necessary to do so in order to safegurd his interests (s. 41(1)). The Lord Chancellor has said:

> We accept that the courts are unlikely to find many cases in which it would not be appropriate to appoint a guardian to represent the child's interests. However, there may be some — perhaps a straightforward case involving an older child who has already instructed his own solicitor. (HL Deb., 19 January 1989, col. 407.)

'Specified proceedings' are defined in s. 41(6), to which reference should be made. They include applications for a care order and an interim care order (see 5.7.5), as well as applications to discharge a care order and appeals against a care order. The definition may be extended by rules of court (ss. 41(6)(i) and 43(12)). The court is under the same duty to appoint a guardian *ad litem* for the purpose of proceedings for an emergency protection order (see s. 41(6)(g)).

Rules of court (yet to be made) will govern the method of appointment of a guardian *ad litem,* who will be placed under a duty to safeguard the interests of the child in the manner prescribed by those rules (s. 41(2)). The guardian *ad litem* will be selected from a panel of persons, the Secretary of State continuing to have power to provide for the establishment of such panels (s. 41(7)). Whilst the further details relating to the establishment and administration of such panels will be laid down by regulations and rules of court which have yet to be formulated, it is fairly clear that the government favours joint management of a panel by neighbouring local authorities. The existence of such a panel would enable the guardian *ad litem* for a particular case to be selected from the number provided by a local authority which is not involved in the case concerned. The selection process is likely to be rendered fairer in appearance by directing the authorities associated in a joint panel to appoint as 'panel manager' a person who does not also have duties of case management. See generally HL Deb., 19 January 1989, col. 418.

An important reform is contained in s. 42. This confers on a guardian *ad litem* the right to examine (and take copies of) local-authority records compiled in connection with the making of the application, and goes on to render such records admissible in the ensuing proceedings. In the words of the Solicitor-General:

> If a guardian *ad litem* is to protect a child's interests when that child is subject to an application by a local authority, and if the guardian is to advise the court fully on that application, he must have access to the information held by the local authority when making decisions about that child's future (HC Deb., vol. 158, col. 626).

The court may appoint a solicitor to represent the child provided that he is not already represented by one, *and* one of the conditions in s. 41(4) is satisfied (s. 41(3)). These are that no guardian *ad litem* has been appointed for him, that the child has sufficient understanding to instruct a solicitor and wishes to do so, or that it appears to be in the child's best interests for him to be represented by a solicitor. Any solicitor so appointed must represent the child in accordance with the relevant rules of court (s. 41(5)). By s. 99(4), the provisions of the Legal Aid Act 1988 governing availability of legal aid in care proceedings cease to have effect. Presumably, the Lord Chancellor will promulgate rules under s. 99(5) determining eligibility for legal aid in care proceedings under the Children Act 1989.

5.7.3 Jurisdiction

Rules of court, to be made by the Lord Chancellor, will state to which courts application for a care order should be made, and which courts will have jurisdiction (for the Lord Chancellor's powers, see sch. 11). However, the Lord Chancellor has already made fairly clear the outline of what is intended.

(a) Application will be made initially to the 'family proceedings court' (as the domestic court is renamed: s. 92(1)). The juvenile court loses its jurisdiction in care cases.

(b) A decision will then be made (by the clerk or the justices themselves) on the level of court at which the matter is to be tried. The criteria for transfer up from family proceedings court to county court or High Court will include the forensic or legal complexity of the case.

(c) An appeal against the decision on the level of court may be made to the county court.

(d) In summary, family proceedings courts, county courts and the High Court will have a concurrent jurisdiction. It is anticipated, however, that the majority of care cases will be heard in the family proceedings court.

This outline scheme (and it must be stressed that discussions are still continuing) has been subjected to criticism. One commentator has argued that:

> the power to transfer, though a useful one, is not sufficient since in other areas it is evident that lower courts are loath to divest themselves of a case. In any event, a transfer will inevitably cause delay. Moreover, it does not seem appropriate for such key decisions to be taken by officials of the lower courts. (Nigel Lowe, (1989) 139 NLJ 87.)

The Lord Chancellor, giving the Joseph Jackson Memorial Lecture on 12 April 1989, recognised the scepticism on this jurisdiction question, and conceded that:

> the decision to require care cases to start in magistrates' courts will be kept under review once the Bill is in force and if our surmise is proved wrong there will be power under the Bill to allow care-related proceedings to start in a higher court or, perhaps, to allow the parties some choice in the matter ((1989) 139 NLJ 505 at p. 507).

The likelihood is that the magistrates' courts will see an increase in their workload, which may have resource implications. Indeed, if they are inundated, as is a distinct possibility, the fears expressed by Lowe may be unfounded: the justices will be only too ready to shed some of the cases by transferring them up the judicial hierarchy. It must be hoped that the system functions credibly and consistently throughout England and Wales, and to that end the Lord Chancellor has sought the advice of an experienced circuit judge, Her Honour Judge Joyanne Bracewell, QC, on the judicial administration necessary to facilitate the transition to the new procedures.

An appeal against a decision by a family proceedings court to make or not to make a care order will lie to the High Court (s. 94), as recommended by the Law Commission (*The Law on Child Care and Family Services,* paras 66 to 68). Presumably, care orders made in the High Court itself will be appealed (as of right?) to the Court of Appeal. The reference to 'any refusal . . . to make . . . an order' in s. 94(1) appears to give local authorities rights of appeal from a court decision in care proceedings, which is necessary as they will not be able to use the wardship jurisdiction as a *de facto* appeal mechanism as previously (s. 100(1) and (2); cf. *Re C (A Minor) (Justices' Decision: Review)* (1981) 2 FLR 62). For the continuation of interim care orders where application for a full care order has been refused, and where an appeal is pending, see s. 40.

5.7.4   Delay

The court is under a duty, when hearing an application for a care order, to have regard to the general principle that any delay in disposing of the application is likely to prejudice the welfare of the child concerned (s. 1(2)). The court is obliged to draw up a timetable for the speedy disposal of the application, and to give such directions as it thinks appropriate to ensure that the timetable is adhered to (s. 32(1)). Rules of court may be made in an attempt to assist the object of these provisions (s. 32(2)).

5.7.5   Interim care orders

Despite the presumption that delay in the court procedures is prejudicial to the welfare of the child concerned, it may frequently be unavoidable to adjourn the care proceedings. In these circumstances, the question of the child's welfare in the interim will of course arise. By s. 38(1), the court has power to make an interim care order (or interim supervision order: see 5.9) where proceedings on an application for a care order are adjourned. However, by s. 38(2), the court may *only* make such an interim order if it is satisfied that 'there are reasonable grounds for believing that the circumstances with respect to the child are as mentioned in section 31(2)'. The court does not have to be satisfied that s. 31(2) grounds exist: to do so would defeat the purpose of an adjournment, and require the authority to prove their case on the first hearing before the court if the child was to be fully protected. It will be extremely rare for the authority to be in such a position, as they will not have completed their own investigations, and there will need to be time for the guardian *ad litem* to undertake his enquiries and report on them. In effect, to obtain an interim care order, the authority are being asked to show a 'prima facie case', as is (by and large) the case under the existing law.

An interim order will last for an initial period of no more than eight weeks, with provision for the court to extend it for a further period of four weeks (s. 38(4) and (5)). There appears to be nothing preventing further extensions at four-week intervals, although rules of court may impose a more rigid timetable than is at present evident from the Act itself. In determining the period for which the interim order should remain in force, the court must consider whether any party who was, or might have been, opposed to the making of the order was in a position to argue his case fully (s. 38(10)).

Whilst it might be hoped that in most cases an application for a care order will not be adjourned for as long as eight weeks (and in those circumstances, the interim order will last only until the application is disposed of: s. 38(4)(c)), the reality is likely to be that the guardian *ad litem* will require eight weeks to complete his enquiries, and so eight-week adjournments following the first hearing will probably become the norm. In view of the present shortage of guardians *ad litem*, and the increased demand for them which will arise under the Children Act 1989, this prognosis may be unduly optimistic. The hope amongst the proponents of the legislation, that the new care proceedings will be dealt with more quickly than before, may not be realised. Whether speed is always desirable is a moot point (see 5.11).

When the court makes an interim care or supervision order (or later, whilst the order is still in force (s. 38(8)) it may give directions with regard to the medical or psychiatric examination of the child (s. 38(6)); such a direction can be to the effect that no such examination is to take place (s. 38(7)).

5.7.6 *Discharge of care orders*
A care order may be discharged by the court on the application of any person with parental responsibility for the child, the child himself, or the local authority (s. 39(1)). Where a care order is in force, a person who is entitled to apply for it to be discharged may apply for a supervision order to be substituted for the care order (s. 39(4)). By s. 39(5), when considering whether to substitute a supervision order for a care order, the court need not repeat the exercise of going through the statutory grounds in s. 31(2). During the period of six months following disposal of an application to discharge a care order, or to substitute a supervision order for a care order, no further such application can be made (s. 91(15)).

A care order will be 'automatically' discharged if a residence order is made in respect of the child concerned (s. 91(1); such an order is permitted by s. 9(1)).

Otherwise a care order will continue in force until the child reaches the age of 18 (s. 91(12)).

5.8 Care orders at the instigation of the court

The above text has concentrated on the situation where there are no proceedings current when the local authority make application for a care order. It may be, however, that the possible need for a care order becomes apparent in the course of some other proceedings. A father may apply for a residence order in respect of his child, and the evidence which is given leads the court to believe that the child's welfare does not demand that he reside with father, far from it, or the mother, for that matter. The court may decide that a care order is on the cards. In this situation, what does it do? It directs the 'appropriate local authority' (defined in

s. 37(5)) to undertake an investigation of the child's circumstances, normally giving the authority eight weeks in which to provide their report (s. 37(1) and (4)). In the mean time, it would be open to the court to make an interim care or supervision order (see 5.7.5). If the authority decide to apply for a care order (and they must of course be able to satisfy s. 31(2) in order to succeed), then they need not take out a separate application, but can intervene in the existing proceedings (s. 31(4)).

If the local authority decide not to apply for a care order, then they must inform the court of the reasons for their decision, the service and assistance they have provided or intend to provide, for the child and his family, and any other action taken or to be taken (s. 37(3)). They must also consider whether it would be appropriate to review the case at a later date (s. 37(6)). The local authority's decision not to apply for a care order in these circumstances does not appear to be open to question. The court has no power (as it had previously under its inherent jurisdiction, now removed by s. 100; see 5.11) to commit the child into care unless the local authority concerned make express application.

5.9   Supervision orders

The court may make an order placing a child under the supervision of a local authority or a probation officer (s. 31(1)). The local authority may only be designated as supervisor if the authority agree, or the child concerned lives or will be living within their area (sch. 3, para. 9(1)). A probation officer may only be designated as supervisor if the appropriate authority so request, and an officer is already carrying out, or has carried out, his duties in respect of another member of the child's household (sch. 3, para. 9(2)).

Supervision orders may only be made if the court is satisfied that the grounds in s. 31(2) (the same grounds as for a care order) are made out, and the making of a supervision order is for the welfare of the child concerned. Many of the rules concerning care orders apply equally to supervision orders:

(a)   The child must be under 17, or 16 if married (s. 31(3)).

(b)   Any delay in the application will be presumed to prejudice the welfare of the child, and a timetable should accordingly be drawn up (s. 32).

(c)   The court may take the initiative and direct the local authority to investigate under s. 37.

(d)   Interim supervision orders may be made, on the same principles as interim care orders (s. 38(1)).

(e)   The guardian *ad litem* provisions apply equally (s. 41(1)).

The supervisor (whether local authority or probation officer) does not acquire parental responsibility for the child. The supervisor's main duty is to advise, assist and befriend the child concerned and to take such steps as are reasonably necessary to give effect to the order (s. 35(1)(a) and (b)). The supervisor is also under a duty to consider whether or not to apply to the court for the variation or discharge of the order where the order is not wholly complied with or may no longer be necessary (s. 35(1)(c)). A supervision order will last for an initial period of one year, but the supervisor may apply to the court to have it extended for a period of up to three years beginning with the date on which the order was first made (sch. 3, para. 6). Three years is therefore the maximum period for which a child may be the subject of a single supervision order. If, towards the end of the three–year period, the authority decide that a supervision order is still necessary, it will have to apply to the court again, and prove that s. 31(2) grounds are still in existence.

The making of a supervision order brings to an end any earlier care or supervision order made in respect of that child which would otherwise continue in force (sch. 3, para. 10).

Parts I and II of sch. 3 make further provision as to the requirements that may be contained in supervision orders, and are here dealt with in outline. (Schedule 12 contains considerable amendments and additions to the existing powers of courts in criminal proceedings to make supervision orders with conditions: this should be referred to.)

5.9.1 *Power to give directions to supervised child*
A supervision order may require the supervised child to comply with directions given by the supervisor as to where he lives; presenting himself to specified persons at specified times and places; and/or participating in specified activities (sch. 3, para. 2). Such matters will be within the discretion of the supervisor (sch. 3, para. 2(2)), but the child may only be required to comply with such directions for a maximum total of 90 days (sch. 3, para. 7). These provisions would therefore enable the supervisor to require the child to participate in a so-called 'intermediate treatment' programme, which would involve residence away from home for up to 90 days. The total of 90 days is what it says — a total. There is no necessity that the 90 days on which the child may be required to comply with his supervisor's directions be a single period, and that will indeed be rarely the case.

Local authorities have on occasion required as a condition of a supervision order that the child reside with a particular person, for example, a grandparent. It is strongly arguable that the imposition of such a requirement, if having effect for a total of over 90 days, will break the 90-day rule as stated above. The authority may be better served by asking the grandparent to seek a residence order from the court under s. 8. Such an application would require leave in most cases (see s. 10), and must be made by the grandparent himself (not by the local authority: s. 9).

The supervisor has no power to give directions in respect of any medical or psychiatric examination or treatment (sch. 3, para. 2(3)). Such directions can only be given by the court (see 5.9.3 and 5.9.4).

5.9.2 *Imposition of obligations on responsible person*
The White Paper (*The Law on Child Care and Family Services*, para. 62) accepted the recommendation of the Child Care Review that the court should be able to impose obligations on the parent of the child as well as the child himself, and this recommendation is implemented in sch. 3 to the Children Act 1989.

Obligations can be imposed on a 'responsible person'. A 'responsible person' in relation to a supervised child means any person with parental responsibility for the child, and any other person with whom the child is living (sch. 3, para. 1). This definition therefore includes step-parents, who will not normally have parental responsibility (see 2.2.2).

With the consent of any responsible person, a supervision order may include a requirement that he take all reasonable steps to ensure that the child complies with his supervisor's directions (sch. 3, para. 3). He may also be required, again if he consents, to take all reasonable steps to ensure that the child complies with any requirements contained in the supervision order concerning psychiatric and medical examinations or treatment (ibid.). However, the total number of days in respect of which the responsible person can be required to comply with directions must not exceed 90 (sch. 3, para. 7).

Note that the consent of the parent is the *sine qua non* of the imposition of obligations upon him. In so providing, the Children Act 1989 stresses again the voluntariness of the partnership between the parent and the local authority. Moreover, if, subsequent to consenting to these obligations being imposed on him, the parent wishes to withdraw his cooperation, he may apply to the court to have any requirement affecting him varied (s. 39(2) and (3)). The court is not apparently obliged to remove an obligation earlier agreed to by the parent, but it may see little point in engaging in compulsion.

5.9.3   Psychiatric and medical examination

A supervision order may require the child to submit to a medical or psychiatric examination, or to do so from time to time as directed by his supervisor (sch. 3, para. 4(1)). Before a court includes such a requirement it must be satisfied that the child consents to it (where he has sufficient understanding to do so), and that satisfactory arrangements have been made for the examination (para. 4(4)). The order must require that the examination be conducted by a specified medical practitioner at a specific place (para. 4(2)). The examination itself may be delegated by the named practitioner, as long as it continues to be under his direction. If the child is to be made a resident patient in order for the examination to take place, the court must first be satisfied (on the evidence of a registered medical practitioner) that the child may be suffering from a physical or mental condition that requires, or may be susceptible to, treatment, and that a period as a resident patient is necessary if the examination is to be carried out properly (para. 4(3)).

There is no express provision allowing the court to require a person subject to a supervision order to undergo an examination by a psychologist, as opposed to a psychiatrist. However, as such an examination would not be a 'medical or psychiatric examination', sch. 3, para. 2(3) (see 5.9.1), does not appear to preclude a supervisor from giving directions in this regard.

5.9.4   Psychiatric and medical treatment

A court making or varying a supervision order may include in it a requirement that the child shall submit to psychiatric or medical treatment by a registered medical practitioner at a specific place (sch. 3, para. 5). Before the court includes such a requirement it must be satisfied (on the evidence of a registered medical practitioner approved under the Mental Health Act 1983) that the child's mental condition requires, and may be susceptible to, treatment, that it is not such as to warrant his detention in pursuance of a hospital order (para. 5(1)), that the child consents to it (where he has sufficient understanding to do so), and that satisfactory arrangements have been made for the treatment (para. 5(5)).

When treatment has commenced, the medical practitioner may become unwilling to continue to treat the child, or become of the opinion that the treatment should continue beyond the specified period or should take a different form, or that the child is not susceptible to treatment or does not require further treatment. In such circumstances, he must make a written report to that effect to the supervisor (para. 5(6)). On receiving such a report the supervisor must refer it to the court, and the court may then make an order cancelling or varying the requirement (para. 5(7)).

5.10 Education supervision orders

Section 36 responds to the problems caused in the case of a child who is not being properly educated. Under the existing law (Children and Young Persons Act 1969, s. 1(2)(e)), a local education authority can apply for a care order on the ground that the child 'is of compulsory school age and is not receiving efficient full-time education'. This could prove to be a rather harsh remedy, as exemplified by cases where well-behaved and disciplined children have been made the subject of care orders because their parents were implacably opposed to the form of schooling which the local education authority offered (see, for example, *Re S (A Minor) (Care Order: Education)* [1978] QB 120). The Children Act 1989, s. 36, attempts to proffer the local education authority a remedy which is effective, but less Draconian in consequence than the care order previously available. Where similar (though not identical) grounds exist as would before the coming into force of the Children Act 1989 have justified the making of a care order, the local education authority will now seek an education supervision order instead. They may not obtain such an order where the child is already in care (s. 36(6)).

A court may, on the application of a local education authority, make an order placing a child under the supervision of that authority where the court is satisfied that the child is of compulsory school age and is not being properly educated (s. 36(1) to (3)). A child is to be regarded as being properly educated only if he is receiving efficient full-time education suitable to his age, ability and aptitude and any special educational needs he may have (s. 36(4)). (The reference to 'special educational needs' is new.) It will be assumed that the child is not being properly educated if he is the subject of a school attendance order which has not been complied with or if he is a registered pupil at a school which he is not attending regularly (s. 36(5), corresponding to Children and Young Persons Act 1969, s. 2(8)(b), though note omission of the child who is taken with a person who habitually wanders from place to place). It should be stressed that s. 36(5) does not have to be satisfied: an education supervision order can be made as long as s. 36(3) and (4) are met. However, the court must be satisfied that the making of an education supervision order is for the welfare of the child concerned, having regard to the statutory checklist of factors (s. 1(1) to (4)), and the court must only make the order if it is better for the child than making no order at all (s. 1(5)).

Before making application for an education supervision order, the local education authority must consult the social services committee of the appropriate local authority (s. 36(8) and (9)). Where an education supervision order is in

force, the supervisor is under a duty to advise, assist, befriend and give directions
to the child, his parents and any person with parental responsibility for him in
order to ensure that the child is properly educated (sch. 3, para. 12(1)). Before
giving any such directions the supervisor should do his best to ascertain, and give
due consideration to, the wishes and feelings of the child, his parents and every
person who is not a parent of his but who has parental responsibility for him
(para. 12(2) and (3)). Unlike supervision orders, the parent can be compelled to
comply with the supervisor's directions under an education supervision order
even though he does not consent to them. Persistent failure so to comply is a
criminal offence punishable with a fine (sch. 3, para. 18).

An education supervision order is intended to transfer the primary obligation
to ensure that the child is educated from the parent to the local education
authority. Thus, once an education supervision order is made, existing school
attendance orders cease to have effect, and other provisions in the Education
Acts are no longer applicable (see generally sch. 3, para. 13).

An education supervision order will have effect for an initial period of one
year, but the court may extend it on more than one occasion provided that no one
extension is for a period of more than three years (sch. 3, para. 15). The order will
cease to have effect when the child ceases to be of compulsory school age, or upon
the making of a care order with respect to the child (para. 15(6)). The court may
discharge an education supervision order on the application of the child, his
parents, any person who is not a parent of his but who has parental responsibility
for him, or the local education authority concerned (para. 17). For full details of
the further provisions that may be made with respect to education supervision
orders see Part III of sch. 3.

An education supervision order is not the only possibility open to the State
where the child appears to be failing to obtain a proper education:

(a)   It remains open to the local education authority to prosecute parents
under the Education Act 1944 for failing to ensure that their child receives an
efficient full–time education (the offence ceases to be imprisonable: sch. 12,
para. 4). However, it is hoped that the local education authority will in future
take the more conciliatory course of applying for an education supervision order.
Before commencing a prosecution, the local education authority must consider
the appropriateness of applying for an education supervision order instead of (or
as well as) prosecuting (Education Act 1944, s. 40(2A) added by Children Act
1989, sch. 13, para. 8(2)).

Where an education supervision order is in force, the duties of parents under
the Education Act 1944, ss. 36 and 39, will be superseded by their duty to comply
with any directions under the education supervision order (Children Act 1989,
sch. 3, para. 13(1)). In other words, a parent could not be prosecuted for failing to
ensure that his child received a full-time education with respect to a time when the
education supervision order was in force.

(b)   A court could still make a care order where the provisions of s. 31(2) are
satisfied. If a child has, for example, suffered, or is likely to suffer, a significant
impairment of his intellectual development, which is attributable to the standard
of care given to him being below that which it would be reasonable to expect the
parent of such a child to give to him, or alternatively attributable to his being

beyond parental control, then the court has jurisdiction to grant a care order
(s. 31(2) and (9)), and must do so if the welfare of the child so demands (s. 1(1)).

(c) School attendance orders are still available, and will be probably used as a
warning shot before the making of an education supervision order (see also
sch. 3, para. 13(2)).

(d) A supervision order in criminal proceedings (as opposed to a supervision
order under the Children Act 1989, s. 35) may include an education requirement
(Children and Young Persons Act 1969, s. 12A; see also Children Act 1989, sch. 3,
para. 13(2)(c) and (d)).

For amendments to the Education Act 1944, see Children Act 1989, sch. 13,
paras 8 to 10.

5.11 Wardship and local authorities

Prior to the Children Act 1989 coming into force, the High Court can make a
child a ward of court, and vest care and control in a local authority (a) under the
statutory power contained in the Family Law Reform Act 1969, s. 7(2), or (b)
pursuant to its inherent jurisdiction. The power under the 1969 Act arises where
'there are exceptional circumstances making it impracticable or undesirable for a
ward to be, or continue to be, under the care of either of his parents', and is
limited in its exercise to minors under the age of 17 (Family Law Reform Act
1969, s. 7(2) and (3)). The inherent power is not so restricted, and can be utilised
where the interests of the child so demand (see, for example, *Re S.W. (A Minor)
(Wardship: Jurisdiction)* [1986] 1 FLR 24, 27).

The use of the wardship jurisdiction outlined above in order to commit a child
to care has been an increasingly dominant feature of local-authority practice in
recent years. The grounds upon which a juvenile court can make a care order
(contained in Children and Young Persons Act 1969, s. 1) are generally limited to
proof of recent actual harm to the child, and so in cases of anticipated future
harm, the High Court jurisdiction has had to be invoked. However, local
authorities have not restricted their use of the High Court to such cases, that
court having certain other advantages over the juvenile court in terms of
efficiency, flexibility, quality of justice, and the ability to respond swiftly when
required. The disadvantage of the High Court as a tribunal is that it is generally
more expensive than the juvenile court.

Section 100 of the Children Act 1989 is a most important provision, and one
which will have major implications for the law of child care. Put at its simplest, it
prohibits local authorities from resorting to wardship in order to achieve the
admission of a child into their care, and imposes substantial restrictions on the
freedom of local authorities to use wardship for other puposes. These reforms
must be considered in the light of the fact that it will become easier for local
authorities to obtain care orders where harm to the child is anticipated rather
than actual (s. 31(2); see 5.4), and that care proceedings will on occasion (where
the matter is sufficiently complex; see 5.7.3) be heard in the High Court. The
simplification and rationalisation of the grounds for making a care order herald a
new policy of diverting local authorities away from the use of wardship and
towards the use of care proceedings instead. Even without section 100, the effect

of the reforms to care proceedings would have led to an inevitable decrease in the number of wardship applications by local authorities, and the courts could have disapproved of such applications where care proceedings were a viable alternative (such disapproval has been rare: but see *Re D (A Minor)* [1987] AC 317). Section 100 does not leave the courts with any such discretion. It repeals s. 7 of the Family Law Reform Act 1969, and prevents the High Court from exercising its inherent jurisdiction so as to require a child to be placed in the care of, under the supervision of, or to be accommodated by or on behalf of, a local authority. The effect of these provisions is quite clear: the only way a child can be admitted into care once the Children Act 1989 comes into force is by the court making a care order on being satisfied of grounds contained in s. 31(2). There is no 'longstop', 'stopgap', 'safety net' or 'fall-back' of the wardship jurisdiction.

The use of wardship as a means whereby the court's assistance can be invoked to answer particularly difficult or sensitive questions has been frequently sanctioned by the courts themselves:

> ... it has become customary, or perhaps not customary but quite frequent, for the local authorities nowadays to resort to the ward of court procedure to help them over their difficulties. This court has never said, and I hope never will say, anything to discourage that practice. It has always seemed to me that when a serious dispute arises about the welfare of a child, it is asking too much for the social workers to be made to be judges as well as social workers in the case, and that it is to the advantage of all parties, including the local authority, to resort to the court in order that a judge may take the responsibility for the decision. (Per Ormrod LJ in *Re C.B. (A Minor) (Wardship: Local Authority)* [1981] 1 WLR 379, 382.)

However, it is submitted that one effect of s. 100 is to limit this particular use by local authorities of wardship and, arguably, to curtail it altogether. Authorities may only apply to the High Court in wardship with leave (s. 100(3)). Leave for the local authority to make application for the court to exercise its inherent jurisdiction is governed by s. 100(4). The court may only grant leave if the two conditions in that subsection are satisfied. First, the result which the authority wish to achieve must not be capable of being achieved through the making of some other court order (see s. 100(5) for definition of 'order'). Secondly, the court must be satisfied that there is reasonable cause to believe that if the jurisdiction is not exercised the child will suffer significant harm.

In the circumstances outlined by Ormrod LJ in *Re C.B.,* the authority may have an alternative course of action to wardship. They can arguably apply to the court for a specific issue order, defined in s. 8(1) as 'an order giving directions for the purpose of determining a specific question which has arisen, or which may arise, *in connection with any aspect of parental responsibility* for a child'. The words italicised are wide, and would appear to cover such matters as consent to medical treatment (including sterilisation, life-saving operations for Down's syndrome babies, blood transfusions for children of Jehovah's Witnesses) which have recently been determined by exercise of the wardship jurisdiction. The authority having that alternative, the court would seem to be precluded from granting them leave to invoke the wardship jurisdiction, as a result of s. 100(4).

The proponents of s. 100 have asserted that it does not entirely prohibit local authorities' use of wardship. If it does not, it goes very close to doing so. One possible residual use might be where the authority wishes to exclude from the family home a man with whom the mother is living and who has been violent towards the child. The mother is too frightened to apply for an ouster injunction herself, and so the authority wish to exercise the court's inherent jurisdiction to protect the child by obtaining an injunction excluding the man from the home. There does not appear to be an alternative course available to the local authority in these circumstances. Although application can be made for a prohibited steps order, its definition would seem to prevent its use other than against parents (see s. 8(1) and 3.6). If it was the child's father whom the authority sought to exclude, however, then a prohibited steps order would be viable, and accordingly leave to apply in wardship could not be obtained (s. 100(4)).

The court may not delegate to a local authority power to determine an issue which has arisen in connection with parental responsibility for the child (s. 100(2)(d)). As far as children who are not in the care of the local authority are concerned, the effect of s. 100(2)(d) is to prevent the High Court giving the authority powers over those children. It is part of the legislative policy that intervention by the State in the life of a child must be justified by reference to the matters set out in the Children Act 1989, s. 31(2), and not otherwise. It is, however, difficult to see what relevance this rather obscure provision might have in relation to children who are already in care under a care order.

Section 100 has proved to be one of the most controversial provisions in the Children Act 1989. It is ironic that the Children Act 1989 has been promoted as being the government's answer to the Cleveland crisis, and yet in its rejection of wardship as an instrument for the protection of children fails to heed the clear conclusion of the Cleveland Report that wardship was invaluable, Lord Justice Butler-Sloss stating (at 16.37):

It has proved in Cleveland to be an invaluable procedure to enable extremely difficult, complex and emotive issues to be fully considered and adjudicated upon. Wardship has an ethos which is recognised by those who use and are engaged in the jurisdiction. We see wardship having a role to play in care proceedings in the future.

The argument against s. 100 is that if the new regime for care proceedings is as effective and comprehensive as its proponents claim, then local-authority use of wardship can be retained, to die a natural death: it will be little used if it is an inferior system, and the courts can discourage wardship in cases where care proceedings could have been brought. To remove the safety net of wardship is premature, as only time (and judicial interpretation) will tell whether the new care grounds are all-embracing, and dangerous, as it may leave certain children unprotected. Ultimately, s. 100 smacks of complacency.

Particularly galling to the critics of s. 100 is their suspicion that its prime, if not only, purpose is to save public expenditure. As was noted in the Cleveland Report (at 16.55), 'Wardship proceedings are likely almost always to be substantially more expensive than juvenile court proceedings', and the same can be said if the comparison is made with the domestic court. The Explanatory

Memorandum to the Children Bill as initially laid before Parliament was forthright, stating, 'There will be savings from the transfer of most local authority wardship applications to care proceedings in lower courts'. This succinct summary of the rationale for s. 100 disappeared from later prints of the Bill. However, it is difficult to disagree with the opposition peer, Lord Irvine of Lairg, that 'the thumb-prints of the Treasury are all too visible'.

Final judgment on s. 100 should perhaps be reserved until the full details of the revamped care proceedings are forthcoming. Many a local authority will look with concern on the section in the mean time. Wardship had become an effective and expeditious way of securing the interests of the child, and its removal from the local authority's armoury will be generally bemoaned.

5.12   Care and supervision orders: transitional provisions

The provisions concerning care and supervision orders made before the coming into force of the Children Act 1989 are contained in sch. 14. These transitional provisions are, of necessity, complex, and they must be referred to for their full effect. What follows is a summary of the most important of them. References to paragraphs are to the relevant paragraph in sch. 14.

(a)   With the exception of criminal care orders (see (f) below) existing care orders are converted into ('deemed to be') care orders made under the Children Act 1989, the authority in whose care the child is becoming the 'designated authority' (para. 15). The law applicable to such orders thereafter will be that contained in Part IV of the new Act. For those in care beyond the age of 18, see para. 16.

(b)   Where the child in care is allowed to be under the charge and control of his parent or guardian, then the provisions of Children Act 1989 (see 4.6.2) will apply as if the child had been placed with that person pursuant to s. 23(5) (para. 17).

(c)   Where an access order (under Child Care Act 1980, s. 12C) is in force, then it will continue to have effect as a contact order under Children Act 1989, s. 34 (para. 18; see 5.6).

(d)   Where the child is in voluntary care, he will be treated as being provided with accommodation by the local authority under Part III of the Children Act 1989 (para. 20; see 4.5 and 4.5.1).

(e)   Existing supervision orders (if made under Children and Young Persons Act 1969, s. 1(3)(b) or s. 21(2)) are converted into ('deemed to be') supervision orders made under the Children Act 1989 and their duration is governed by para. 25. Supervision orders made under other legislation will not, however, be so treated, but will nevertheless continue in force for a maximum period of one year after the Children Act 1989 comes into force (paras 25 and 26).

(f)   Criminal care orders (i.e., those made under Children and Young Persons Act 1969, s. 7(7)(a) or s. 15(1)) will continue to have effect for a maximum period of six months after the Children Act 1989 comes into force (para. 36).

Chapter Six
Emergency Protection of Children

6.1 Introduction

The need to provide an effective and flexible means of protecting children who are in a situation of risk has been highlighted in many child abuse enquiries and was again emphasised in the course of the investigations into the child abuse 'crisis' in Cleveland in 1987. Part V of the Children Act 1989 was described during debates in the House of Commons as the heart of the legislation because it gives social workers the means of investigating and protecting children at risk. Protection of a child at risk may require the immediate removal of the child from a dangerous home environment, or alternatively may necessitate the retention of the child in a hospital, or local authority accommodation, from which there is an imminent danger of removal by the parent. The Cleveland Report highlighted the inadequacies of the existing law governing the emergency protection of children, with particular reference to justice to parents, and supported the earlier recommendations for reform contained in the White Paper, *The Law on Child Care and Family Services* (Cm 62, 1987), which outlined the new remedy called the emergency protection order, the relevant provisions for which are now contained in Part V of the Children Act 1989.

Under the law effective immediately prior to the Children Act 1989 coming into force, the statutory provision most frequently employed to provide immediate protection for children who had, or were likely to be, abused was Children and Young Persons Act 1969, s. 28. Under the 1969 Act any person might be granted a place of safety order by a magistrate giving authority to detain the child in a place of safety. Such an order could also be used to retain a child or young person, for example, in hospital when a parent was likely to discharge the child in circumstances where such a discharge would place the child at risk. The police were also given powers under Children and Young Person Act 1969, s. 28, whereby any constable might on his own authority detain a child for up to eight days in a place of safety without obtaining a court order.

In addition the wardship jurisdiction was available to give immediate protection in certain circumstances. In particular wardship could be employed to prevent a child being removed from a 'safe' place to one where he might be at risk; by issuing an originating summons in the Family Division of the High Court the child's position could be frozen so that no steps which materially affected the child's welfare could be taken without an order of the court. Under the provisions of the Children Act 1989, the wardship jurisdiction will no longer be available to be used in these circumstances.

Children and Young Persons Act 1969, s. 28, is repealed by the Children Act 1989. The principal objections to the place of safety order put forward in the Review of Child Care Law and in *The Law on Child Care and Family Services* (Cm 62), paras 45 and 46, were that the period of 28 days was too long to detain a child without provision for challenge by the parent or child, and that the grounds for such an order did not address the emergency nature of the need to remove the child. The impossibility of challenging a place of safety order within the 28-day period was confirmed in *Nottinghamshire County Council* v *Q* [1982] Fam 94.

The introduction of emergency protection orders seeks to answer the criticisms of the existing law by substantially reducing the maximum duration of an order to eight days and allowing only one extension of a maximum of seven days; conferring on parents and others the right to challenge such orders once 72 hours have elapsed; and imposing on the person who obtains the emergency protection order a duty to allow the child contact with certain individuals. In addition the new regime gives the lower courts important powers, which they did not formerly enjoy, to direct whether the child be medically examined and to determine with whom the child has contact. These are fundamental changes to the present legal position and their practical implications must be appreciated by all those concerned with children in need of emergency protection.

6.2   Child assessment orders

Those experienced in child care law, either as social workers or as lawyers, were aware that the inadequacy of the legislation was not just the place of safety order but also that it did not deal with a situation in which there was reason to believe that a child was being abused or neglected but, because of an inability to see the child, evidence could not be adduced. Organisations such as the NSPCC, the Association of Directors of Social Services, the British Association of Social Workers and the British Agencies for Adoption and Fostering, and many other groups, put forward suggestions on how to deal with this situation and expressed their concern that the emergency protection order did not allow for action to be taken in these circumstances.

The result is the child assessment order which enables a social worker, or authorised person, to make an assessment with or without removing the child from home. Mr Mellor, Minister of Health, explained the inclusion of the child assessment order as follows;

> There are other circumstances in which there might be serious cause for concern about the welfare of a child. There may be a repeated failure to produce a child and perhaps it cannot be asserted that the matter is quite so urgent that there is an immediate need to intervene to take the child away — it is at the heart of our concerns that the emergency protection order is used only in those very serious circumstances, so the issue is whether there should be a lesser order requiring the production of a child and one which allows for the assessment of the child to take place. (HC Deb., vol. 158, col. 593.)

The decision as to whether a child should be removed from home under a child assessment order will be made at the time of the application and if the court is of the view that removal is necessary to facilitate an assessment then a direction will need to be included in the child assessment order authorising removal of the child. The maximum duration of such an order and of such period of removal is seven days. It is not intended that this order should be used as an easier means of removing a child from home than applying for an emergency protection order but that an application for a child assessment order should only be made where there is a genuine inability to assess whether a child is at risk without an order of the court.

6.2.1 Who can apply for a child assessment order

An application for a child assessment order can only be made by a local authority or an authorised person as defined in Children Act 1989, s. 31(9), in other words the same persons who can apply for a care or supervision order. The class of persons who can apply for a child assessment order is, therefore, more restricted than for an emergency protection order but it is clearly correct to limit the right to apply for this type of order to those who will carry out any assessment.

6.2.2 Jurisdiction

Section 43(1) states that the application will be made to the court and it is left to rules of court to give further details. It is likely that in most instances the application will be to magistrates but it is clearly not intended that the application should be heard *ex parte* as there is a specific requirement in the section for reasonable steps to be taken to serve notice of the application on a class of persons (see 6.2.3).

6.2.3 Service of notice of application

By s. 43(11), the applicant must take such steps as are reasonably practicable to ensure that notice of the application for a child assessment order is given, before the hearing of the application, to the following persons:

(a) The child's parents.

(b) Any person who is not a parent of the child but who has parental responsibility for him.

(c) Any person caring for the child.

(d) Any person in whose favour a contact order is in force with respect to the child.

(e) Any person who is allowed to have contact with the child by virtue of an order under s. 34.

(f) The child.

6.2.4 The statutory grounds

The court may only make a child assessment order if it is satisfied that the applicant has reasonable cause to suspect that the child is suffering, or is likely to suffer, significant harm (s. 43(1)(a)). Before making the order the court must also be satisfied that an assessment of the state of the child's health or development, or way in which he has been treated, is required to enable the applicant to determine whether or not the child is suffering, or is likely to suffer, significant harm and in addition that it is unlikely that such an assessment will be made, or be satisfactory, in the absence of such an order (s. 43(1)(b) and (c)).

The court must not make a child assessment order if it is satisfied that there are grounds for making an emergency protection order and that is the more appropriate order (s. 43(4)). The court is empowered to treat an application for a child assessment order as an application for an emergency protection order (s. 43(3)).

6.2.5 Commencement, duration and directions

The court must specify in a child assessment order the date by which the assessment is to begin and how long the order is to last up to a maximum period of seven days (s. 43(5)).

A child can only be kept away from home if the order contains a direction to that effect and can then only be kept away from home in accordance with that direction and for such period or periods as may be specified in the order (s. 43(9)). In addition a child may only be kept away from home if it is necessary for the purposes of the assessment (s. 43(9)(b)). Therefore, if when granting a child assessment order the court envisages that it will be necessary for the child to be kept away from home, and makes a direction to that effect, the child should in fact only be kept away from home for as long as is necessary for the assessment. If during the period which the direction allows the child to be kept away from home it is no longer necessary for assessment but it is thought necessary for the protection of the child then an immediate application either for an emergency protection order or an interim care order will be necessary. This is in keeping with the philosophy of the Act to put those who remove children under an obligation to return them home as soon as possible.

If a child is kept away from home then the child assessment order must contain such directions as the court thinks fit with regard to the contact which the child must be allowed to have with other persons while away from home (s. 43(10)).

6.2.6 Effect of a child assessment order

When a child assessment order is made then any person who is in a position to produce the child must produce him to any person named in the order (s. 43(6)(a)). As it appears that the order will limit those to whom the child must be produced then care must be taken that the order includes the correct persons and that the order does not fail to be of effect because the person named becomes ill or goes on holiday. In addition it will be the duty of any person who is in a position to produce the child to comply with such directions relating to the assessment of the child as the court thinks fit to specify in the order (s. 43(6)(b)). By confining those who must comply with directions to persons who are in a position to produce the child will mean that in many cases the court will be unable to direct the involvement of others who are as important, or more important, to the successful outcome of an assessment.

A child assessment order authorises any person carrying out the assessment, or part of the assessment, to do so in accordance with the terms of the order (s. 43(7)). This gives those carrying out the assessment the flexibility to involve any person that they deem appropriate.

Reflecting the emphasis of this Act on the child's rights, a child may refuse to submit to a medical, psychiatric or other assessment if he is of sufficient understanding to make an informed decision (s. 43(8)). The inclusion of this provision is to be welcomed as it recognises the child as an individual who has a right to be consulted and not just as the property of the parent. However, the dangers of adult pressure on the child needs to be recognised. It may cause social workers and other professionals difficulty when dealing with young children in deciding whether the child is of sufficient understanding to make an informed decision but the social worker will need to be making some assessment of the child with regard to the child's maturity and abilities in any event. It does mean that the person carrying out the assessment must discuss matters with the child before commencing the assessment.

The criticisms of this order are primarily twofold. First that assessment is not possible in such a short time and secondly that the order will simply cause confusion as to which is the appropriate application and what kind of assessment can be achieved within seven days. Mr David Hinchliffe MP expressed this concern when he said, 'I fear that the child assessment order will cause immense confusion among social workers, because it will not facilitate the use of many existing models of assessment; it will not be possible to make a proper assessment of the kind envisaged . . . with a seven-day time-scale' (HC Deb., vol. 158, col. 604).

Clearly neither under a child assessment order, with a maximum duration of seven days, nor under an emergency protection order, with a maximum duration of eight days plus an extension of seven days, can a full assessment be carried out. It will not usually be possible in such a short space of time to assess whether there is a problem, the nature of the problem, consider what can be done to improve matters, discuss the help that can be given with the parents and child and then for the social worker to consider the right course of action to be taken. The best that can be achieved in such a short period is to carry out an initial assessment of whether there are signs of abuse or neglect. The results of this initial assessment might then give the social worker enough information to decide whether to seek an emergency protection order or care order or to deal with the matter in some other way.

6.2.7 *Variation and discharge of a child assessment order*
The Children Act 1989 allows for rules of court to be made to provide for the circumstances in which those on whom a notice of the application should be served, and such other persons as may be specified in the rules, may apply to the court for a child assessment order to be varied or discharged (s. 43(12)).

6.3 **Emergency protection orders**

6.3.1 *Who can apply for an emergency protection order*
Under the Children Act 1989 'any person' can apply for an emergency protection order (s. 44(1)). Whereas there is nothing in the Children and Young Persons Act 1969 to suggest that 'any person' means other than an individual, and orders are always granted to individuals, in the Children Act 1989 'any person' is not just used to refer to individuals. This is an improvement on the existing law. The

consequence of a particular social worker being the applicant for a place of safety order was that personal responsibility could be conferred on someone who was not involved in management of the case concerned. The Children Act 1989 clearly contemplates both individuals and local authorities (acting in their social services capacity) applying for emergency protection orders: there are references to emergency protection orders obtained by a local authority (e.g., s. 47(2)) and to a local authority making a decision as to whether to apply for an emergency protection order (e.g., s. 47(6)). In future, it would seem desirable, and consistent with the scheme of the legislation, that courts granting emergency protection orders view the local authority rather than the individual social worker as the applicant.

6.3.2   Jurisdiction
The Children Act 1989 merely states that application is made to 'the court' (s. 44(1)). There is provision for rules of court to be made with respect to the procedure to be followed in connection with emergency protection orders (s. 52). It is likely that most applications will be made *ex parte* to a single justice of the peace, but will also be able to be made to a magistrates' court, a county court, or even, in appropriate circumstances yet to be defined, the High Court.

6.3.3   The statutory grounds
There is a general ground for application which can be relied on by a local authority, authorised person or any other person. In addition, where the applicant is a local authority, there is a second separate ground, and if the applicant is an authorised person then a similar additional ground is available.

The court, on the application of any person, may make an emergency protection order if it is satisfied that there is reasonable cause to believe that the child is likely to suffer significant harm if he is not removed to accommodation provided by the applicant, or does not remain where he is presently accommodated (s. 44(1)). As under the existing law, the emergency provision depends upon grounds which are not totally separate from those relevant to care proceedings (and reference should be made to 5.4 accordingly). However, it does differ in three respects. First, the evidential burden is on the applicant: the court must be satisfied *that there is reasonable cause to believe* (and does not need to be satisfied) that the child is likely to suffer harm. Secondly, there is no need to attribute a reason for the harm which is anticipated (cf. s. 31(2)(b)). Thirdly, it is not enough for the court to be satisfied of harm having occurred in the past: emergency protection orders can only be granted where there remains a likelihood of future harm.

Where the applicant is a local authority, the separate and additional ground that can be relied on is that the court may make an emergency protection order if the local authority are making enquiries under s. 47(1)(b), which imposes a duty to investigate (see 6.5.1), and those enquiries are being frustrated by access to the child being unreasonably refused to a person authorised to seek access and the applicant has reasonable cause to believe that access to the child is required as a matter of urgency (s. 44(1)(b)).

Where the application is made by a local authority as above, or by an authorised person as described in the following paragraph, then the test with regard to the need for urgency is whether the applicant has reasonable cause to believe that access to the child is required as a matter of urgency and not whether the court is satisfied on the evidence.

If the applicant is an authorised person, the additional and separate ground is that the court may make an emergency protection order if the applicant has reasonable cause to suspect that a child is suffering, or is likely to suffer, significant harm, and the applicant is making enquiries with respect to the child's welfare, and those enquiries are being frustrated by access to the child being unreasonably refused to a person authorised to seek access and the applicant has reasonable cause to believe that access to the child is required as a matter of urgency (s. 44(1)(c)).

'A person authorised to seek access' is defined as being an officer of a local authority or a person authorised by the local authority to act on their behalf in connection with the enquiries, where the local authority are the applicant, and where the application is made by an authorised person then it means that person (s. 44(2)(b)). Any person who purports to be an authorised person seeking access must if asked to do so produce a duly authenticated document as evidence that he is such a person (s. 44(3)).

In deciding whether or not to grant an emergency protection order, the child's welfare must be the paramount consideration of the court (s. 1(1)). Furthermore, the court shall not make an emergency protection order unless it considers that to do so is better for the child than making no order at all (s. 1(5)). In determining where the child's welfare lies, the court is not under a duty to have regard to the matters set out in the 'statutory checklist' in s. 1(3) (see s. 1(4)). However, it will still be open to the court to look to the list for guidance as to the principles applicable.

Evidential rules are understandably relaxed when an application for an emergency protection order is being considered. This is because the person who presents the application before the court will frequently, by virtue of the emergency nature of the application, be relying upon information which has been gathered from a variety of sources. Accordingly, s. 45(7) provides that where a court is considering such an application it may disregard any enactment or rule of law which would prevent it from taking into account the following:

(a)   any statement contained in any report made to the court in the course of, or in connection with, the hearing; or

(b)   any evidence given during the hearing, which, in the opinion of the court, is relevant to the application.

6.3.4   Effect of an emergency protection order

An emergency protection order may be sought in two distinct circumstances. The first is where the child is living in a potentially dangerous situation. For example, the child has severe bruising to the abdomen, and complains to his teacher that his father beats him regularly. In these circumstances, the local authority may apply for an emergency protection order, which will operate as a direction to any person, in a position to do so, to comply with any request to produce the child to the authority, and the authority are then authorised to remove the child to their accommodation (s. 44(4)(a) and (b)(i)). The second circumstance is where the child is not living in such a situation, but the applicant considers that an attempt may be made to remove him into a situation where he may be at risk. For example, the child has been living with his aunt for some time. His mother, whose cohabitee has convictions for sexual offences, intends to resume caring for him. The local authority (or for that matter the aunt) may apply for an emergency protection order. There will be no need to invoke s. 44(4)(a) to produce the child: however, the applicant will now be authorised to prevent his removal from the aunt's home (s. 44(4)(b)(ii)). This provision will be frequently used to retain children who are being accommodated on a voluntary basis by the local authority (see 4.5) and whose return home is viewed with justifiable concern.

An emergency protection order authorises the removal of the child at any time while it is in force so that the child can be placed in accommodation provided by the applicant or on behalf of the applicant. It also acts as authority for the applicant to keep the child in that accommodation throughout the duration of the order (s. 44(4)).

During the period of an emergency protection order the applicant acquires parental responsibility for the child (s. 44(4)(c)). Any person who has parental responsibility for the child while an emergency protection order is in force, that is to say, either the applicant or a local authority to whom the order has been transferred, must exercise the power conferred by the order to remove the child, or prevent removal from a safe place, only in order to safeguard the welfare of the child (s. 44(5)(a)). In addition the person with parental responsibility under the order is only allowed to take such action as is reasonably required to safeguard and promote the welfare of the child. In meeting their responsibilities under the order and deciding on the action they should take, particular regard must be given to the duration of the order (s. 44(5)(b)). It would appear to follow from this limitation that, other than removing the child from his home, major changes should not be made in the child's life and upbringing. One of the implications of this may be difficulties in deciding where or with whom the child should be accommodated during the period of the order. Regulations to be made by the Secretary of State may further control actions which may be taken in exercising parental responsibility under an emergency protection order (s. 44(5)(c)).

Anyone who intentionally obstructs any person exercising the authority given to him by an emergency protection order to remove or prevent removal will be guilty of an offence and liable to a fine (s. 44(15) and (16)).

The position with regard to the cost of accommodating and maintaining the child when the applicant is not the local authority is unclear. However, in such circumstances a local authority are obliged to consider whether it would be in the child's best interests to be in accommodation provided by the authority, and local authorities are obliged to make provision for the reception and mainten-ance of children who have been removed (s. 47(3)(b)). There does not appear to be a *duty* upon the local authority to take on the responsibility for accommodat-ing and maintaining a child even if they consider that it is in the child's best interests to be in such accommodation. If, however, they consider that action should be taken to safeguard or promote the child's welfare they are under a duty to take that action, so far as it is within their power and reasonably practicable for them to do so (s. 47(8); see 5.3). This may involve the authority in accommodating the child concerned. In the absence of the local authority assuming responsibility it appears that the cost of accommodating and maintaining will remain with the applicant.

The applicant for the emergency protection order is under a duty to return the child, or allow him to be removed from where he is, as soon as the applicant considers it safe to do so (s. 44(10)). He must return the child to the care of the person from whom he was removed; if it is not reasonably practicable to do so the applicant should 'return' him to one of the following people: a parent, any person with parental responsibility or such other person as the applicant, with the agreement of the court, considers appropriate (s. 44(11)). This provision imposes a duty to 'return': if the local authority consider it is in the interests of the child to return him, it is presumably within their powers to do so, and the court cannot effectively intervene.

Use of the word 'return' in s. 44(10) is misleading as it is clearly possible to place a child with persons other than those from whom he was removed. It should be noted by local authorities and other applicants that once they have formed the view that it is safe for the child to be returned, the duty to return contained in s. 44(10), which is mandatory, is immediately imposed upon them, and must therefore be complied with. If the applicant considered it safe to return or allow the child to be removed during the emergency protection order, but while that order is in force there is a change of circumstances, then the applicant may again exercise his powers with respect to the child if it is necessary for him to do so (s. 44(12)).

Example 6.1 The local authority obtain an emergency protection order in respect of Tracey, on the basis that her father has been sexually abusing her, and she is removed to local authority accommodation. Two days later, her father is charged with indecent assault and remanded in custody. The authority consider that it is safe for Tracey to return home, and therefore return her, as they are bound to do (s. 44(10)). Three days later, the father is granted bail. The local authority may take the view that this change in circumstances makes it necessary to exercise their powers with respect to Tracey, and so they remove her once again from home under the authority of the earlier emergency protection order (s. 44(12)). If, however, the emergency protection order had expired, the authority would have to make fresh application to the court under s. 44(1).

6.3.5 Duration and extension of emergency protection orders

The maximum period for the duration of an emergency protection order is eight days, with one exception; the exception being that where the court takes the view that the appropriate period for the order is eight days but the eighth day would be a Sunday, Christmas Day, Good Friday or a Bank Holiday the court may make an order that lasts until noon on the first day which is not such a holiday (s. 45(1) and (2)). The day on which the order is made counts as the first day of the order. If it were otherwise there would be no authority given by the order on the day it was made. Where a child has been taken into police protection (see 6.4) the period of eight days begins with the first day on which the child was taken into police protection (s. 45(3)).

The only person able to apply for the period of the emergency protection order to be extended is a person who is entitled to apply for a care order and who also has parental responsibility as a result of the emergency protection order (s. 45(4)). Those entitled to apply for a care order are local authorities or an 'authorised person' (see 5.2). A person with parental responsibility as a result of an emergency protection order will either be the applicant for the original order or a local authority which have had the order transferred to them. Thus, an applicant who is neither a local authority nor an 'authorised person' cannot apply for an extension to the order. Where such an applicant (an 'individual') has obtained an emergency protection order, the local authority will only be able to continue with his application (and seek an extension) where the order is in the mean time transferred to them (pursuant to regulations made under s. 52(3)). Otherwise the local authority will not have parental responsibility as a result of the emergency protection order, and will lack the necessary standing to make an application to extend. This apparent difficulty may be resolved by the regulations governing transfer of emergency protection orders.

Where an application to extend the period of an emergency protection order has been made the court may only grant such an extension if there is reasonable cause to believe the child is likely to suffer significant harm if the order is not extended (s. 45(5)). The maximum period for which an order may be extended is seven days (s. 45(5)). The order may only be extended once (s. 45(6)).

6.3.6   Who must be informed
The Children Act 1989 is silent about who must be informed that an emergency protection order has been made. There is provision for rules of court to be made that would include, amongst other matters, the persons who must be notified of the making of an emergency protection order (s. 52(2)).

6.3.7   Challenging an emergency protection order
In answer to the criticisms levelled at the inability of parents to challenge the making of place of safety orders in respect of their children, the Children Act 1989 provides that an application for an emergency protection order to be discharged can be made by a parent, the child himself, any person with whom the child was living immediately before the order was made or any person who is not a parent but has parental responsibility (s. 45(8)). An application to discharge the order cannot be heard until 72 hours have elapsed since the order was made (s. 45(9)). The time limitation only states that the hearing cannot occur until after 72 hours. This would imply that an application could be filed with the court during the 72 hours.

The right to apply for discharge is limited by the fact that a person who has been given notice, in accordance with rules of court, of the hearing and was present at that hearing has no entitlement to apply for discharge of the order (s. 45(11)(a)). It should also be noted that there is no right to apply for discharge of an emergency protection order which has been extended (s. 45(11)(b)).

Although a right to apply for discharge of an emergency protection order is given to certain persons, it is clearly stated that there is no right of appeal against the making of, or the refusal to make, an emergency protection order (s. 45(10)).

The Review of Child Care Law (at p.89, 13.22) considered whether an emergency protection order should last for only 72 hours, but the proposal was rejected for several reasons, one of which was that it was thought that this would lead to social work staff spending the duration of the order preparing for the court hearing rather than investigating the case. Instead, the period of eight days was adopted. The power to apply for the discharge of the order to be considered immediately after 72 hours have elapsed is likely to ensure that the result the Review of Child Care Law wished to avoid will in fact occur.

6.3.8 Contact

Where a place of safety order is obtained, any access allowed is at the discretion of the person who was ganted that order. No application can be made under the Children and Young Persons Act 1969 by a parent, or any other person, for access to the child while a place of safety order is in force save by challenging the local authority's decision in that respect by way of judicial review which, due primarily to time-scales, is unlikely to be of much assistance. The Children Act 1989 provides a new regime for contact (the meaning of which is discussed in 3.4) during the period of an emergency protection order.

By s. 44(6) of the Children Act 1989, a court which has made an emergency protection order may give such directions as it considers appropriate with respect to contact between the child and any named person. Subject to any direction that may have been made by the court in this regard, the applicant for the emergency protection order must allow the child reasonable contact with parents, any person with parental responsibility, any person with whom the child was living immediately before the order, any person in respect of whom a contact order is in force, any person allowed contact by an order under s. 34 and any person acting on behalf of any of these people (s. 44(13)). Including 'any person acting on behalf . . .' could cause difficulties. When is a person 'acting on behalf'?

The applicant for the emergency protection order is under no obligation to allow contact with grandparents, aunts or uncles unless the child was living with any of these relatives immediately prior to the making of the order. This does not, of course, mean that such contact should not be allowed, and these relatives remain in exactly the same position as they are under the present legislation where contact will be at the discretion of the person who has obtained the emergency protection order. The Review of Child Care Law did not consider it was within its brief to create new rights of contact with regard to children and so did not recommend including contact rights for the wider family. However, a new right does appear to have been created by providing that reasonable contact should be allowed with any person with whom the child was living immediately before the order (s. 44(13)(c)) and, moreover, enabling such persons to apply to vary a direction with regard to their contact with the child (s. 44(9)(b)), subject to rules of court.

There is no duty to provide reasonable contact with brothers and sisters of the child. It may be that brothers and sisters with whom the child was living immediately prior to the order could come within the category 'any person with whom he was living immediately before' the order but this would still leave out those with whom the child was not living prior to the order. It is clear to anyone who works in this area that contact with brothers and sisters is as important, and sometimes more important, to a child than contact with parents.

Where a direction in respect of contact has been made, an application to vary that direction can be made by a category of persons yet to be prescribed by rules of court but which will presumably include parents, those with parental responsibility, those with whom the child has been living, the applicant and the local authority (s. 44(9)(b)). It is clear that the court can make a direction in respect of contact at any time while the order is in force, and the procedure whereby the matter would come back before the court will presumably be dealt with in the rules of court themselves.

What will amount to 'reasonable contact' is likely to be an area of dispute between those seeking contact and those with responsibility for the child while the emergency protection order is in force. Is reasonable contact a telephone call or letter? There seems to be an assumption that, in the absence of a direction, there will be some contact with all those listed. Where a child is in police protection there is a requirement under s. 46(10) to allow 'contact (if any)', but the power to deny contact, other than by a direction of the court, is not provided for in any other circumstances. It must be stressed that contact is a right of the child, and not a right of the adults (or others) concerned. This may provide a limitation on contact with all those listed in s. 46(10) where the child indicates that he does not wish to have contact with a particular person or persons.

Clearly the person with responsibility under the emergency protection order would have to show clearly the reasons for allowing the degree of contact that has been allowed. Local authorities will need to keep full records of what was taken into account and the reasoning behind any decision in respect of contact. Where the applicant wishes to deny contact between the child and persons with whom he is prima facie entitled to have contact, the applicant should apply for the appropriate direction at the time of making application for the emergency protection order. Although it is open to the court to make such a direction later, it would obviously be advantageous that the matters are all dealt with at the initial hearing.

6.3.9   Other orders and directions that may be made by the court

The Children Act 1989 gives the court power to make directions either at the time of the making of the emergency protection order or on any subsequent application, in respect of contact and medical or psychiatric examination or other assessment (s. 44(6) and (9)(a)).

The court's power to issue a search warrant (presently contained in Children and Young Persons Act 1933, s. 40) has been developed. In addition, other orders can be made to assist in the identification and discovery of children who may be in need of emergency protection.

6.3.9.1   Contact   The power of the court to give directions with regard to contact is dealt with in 6.3.8.

6.3.9.2   Medical or psychiatric examination or other assessment   The court will now have power to make directions with respect to the medical or psychiatric examination or other assessment of the child (s. 44(6)(b)). Psychological examination is not specifically mentioned but would presumably come within 'other assessment'. Assessments by social workers, paediatricians or the NSPCC could also come within 'other assessment'.

A direction in this respect may be to the effect that there is to be no examination or assessment at all or no examination or assessment unless the court directs otherwise (s. 44(8)). The High Court has always had the power under its inherent jurisdiction to direct or prohibit medical and psychiatric examination of wards of court and in general this has not caused any difficulties. Magistrates' courts (which have had no experience of giving directions of this nature) will need to appreciate the complexity of such questions. For example, a decision on whether or not to medically examine a child in respect of whom sexual abuse is suspected can be extremely difficult. If medical examination is prevented or delayed then evidence may be lost, but clearly not all children who have been sexually abused should be examined since if this was done inappropriately it might in itself amount to an abuse of the child.

A direction in respect of medical or psychiatric examination can be made at the time the emergency protection order is made or at any time while the order is in force (s. 44(9)(a)). It may be varied at any time on the application of any person falling within a category to be prescribed by rules of court (s. 44(9)(b)).

Where a direction has been given allowing examination or assessment a child may refuse to submit to it if of sufficient understanding to make an informed decision (s. 44(7)). Given the court's power to involve guardians *ad litem* at this early stage, any difficulties that may arise in this respect could be brought to the court's attention.

6.3.9.3 Powers to assist in identification and discovery of children

A major weakness in the law relating to powers under a place of safety order is to some extent met by the Children Act 1989, s. 48(1) which allows the court on the making of an emergency protection order to include a provision requiring a person with knowledge of the whereabouts of the child to disclose that information to the person making the application for the order (s. 48(1)). If such a provision is included then that person is not excused from complying with the requirement on the grounds that it might incriminate himself or his spouse. Any statement or admission made in complying with such a provision will not be admissible in evidence in proceedings for any offence other than perjury (s. 48(2)). However, as the restriction only applies to *offences* (i.e., criminal proceedings), any statement or admission would be admissible in care proceedings and any other civil proceedings.

The power of the magistrates' court under Children and Young Persons Act 1933, s. 40, to issue a warrant authorising a constable to search premises and remove a child is replaced in the Children Act 1989 by the power of the court when issuing an emergency protection order to authorise the applicant to enter premises specified in the order to search for the child concerned (s. 48(3)). Furthermore, if the court is satisfied that there is reasonable cause to believe there may be another child on the premises who ought to be made the subject of an emergency protection order it may also authorise a search for that child (s. 48(4)). When making an order authorising the search to include another child, that child should be named unless it is not reasonably practicable to do so, and if he cannot be named then he must be described as clearly as possible (s. 48(13)). Where the court has authorised the applicant to search for such another child and that child is found on the premises and the applicant is satisfied there are grounds for an emergency protection order, then the order made by the court will have effect as if it were an emergency protection order (s. 48(5)). Where an order has been made authorising the applicant to search for another child the applicant must notify the court of the outcome (s. 48(6)).

Insofar as these provisions appear to provide protection for children found upon the premises whose presence was not anticipated at the time the emergency protection order was made, such protection is illusory. By referring to another child who 'ought' to be made the subject of an order (s. 48(4)) the scope of the provision is limited. The court cannot form a view as to whether there may be another child in respect of whom an order ought to be made without some knowledge that such a child is likely to be there. Where a child is found who is not contemplated by the emergency protection order but who is at risk there is no power to remove him unless the applicant is accompanied by a constable who could act under the powers of s. 46 and take the child into police protection. The only way to protect the 'unexpected' child is to apply for an emergency protection order in respect of him, in the hope that he will still be there when the order is executed.

Where authority has been granted to search for the child to whom the emergency protection order relates, or any other child whom it is believed may be on the premises, anyone who intentionally obstructs the person exercising the authority shall be guilty of an offence and liable to a fine (s. 48(7) and (8)).

Where it appears to the court that a person acting under an emergency protection order has been refused entry to the premises concerned, or prevented from having access to the child, or it is likely that this will occur, the court may issue a warrant authorising any constable to assist the person attempting to exercise powers under the order and the constable may use reasonable force if necessary (s. 48(9)). The warrant must be addressed to and executed by a constable (s. 48(10)).

The constable searching for the child must be accompanied by the person applying for the warrant (who may not be the same person as the applicant for the emergency protection order) if the applicant wishes to do so and the court has not directed that the applicant must not accompany the constable (s. 48(10)). When issuing a search warrant the court may direct that the constable executing the warrant may be accompanied by a registered medical practitioner, registered nurse or registered health visitor (s. 48(11)). The inclusion in the Children Act 1989 of registered nurses and health visitors brings the provision (which is otherwise substantially a re-enactment of part of the Children and Young Persons Act 1933) up to date and recognises the role of nursing staff and health visitors in the investigation of child abuse. The procedure for making application for a warrant will be prescribed by rules of court (s. 48(12)). A direction can also be made when the emergency protection order is issued to allow the applicant to be accompanied in exercising powers under the order by a registered medical practitioner, registered nurse or registered health visitor if the applicant so chooses (s. 45(12)).

6.3.10   Position of child and guardian ad litem

A guardian *ad litem* must be appointed by the court where an emergency protection order is made unless the court is of the view that such an appointment is not necessary to safeguard the interests of the child (s. 41). The duties and responsibilities of the guardian *ad litem* where there is an emergency protection order will be the same as in other proceedings under the Children Act 1989 (see 5.7.2). In most areas of the country there are already insufficient suitably qualified guardians *ad litem,* and in many areas there are cases waiting for a guardian to be allocated. It is therefore doubtful that this provision will be of any practical benefit.

Where the child is not represented by a solicitor, the court may appoint a solicitor to represent the child provided that it has not appointed a guardian *ad litem,* that the child has sufficient understanding to instruct a solicitor and wishes to do so, and it appears to the court that it would be in the interests of the child (s. 41(3) and (4)).

The child has a right to apply for an emergency protection order to be discharged (s. 45(8)).

Contained in rules of court will be a list of persons who can apply for variation of a direction in respect of contact and medical or psychiatric examination, and it may be that the child could come within that category (s. 44(9)(b)).

6.4 Police removal and accommodation of children

Under the law existing immediately prior to the Children Act 1989 coming into force, the police can detain a child for up to eight days in a place of safety without the authority of an order of court (Children and Young Persons Act 1969, s. 28). The Children Act 1989 provides for a child being taken into police protection for a maximum of 72 hours without an order (s. 46).

Where the police have reasonable cause to believe that the child is likely to suffer significant harm they may remove the child and keep the child in suitable accommodation, or take reasonable steps to ensure the child is not removed from hospital or any other place in which he is accommodated (s. 46(1)). Where the police exercise this power the child is referred to as having been taken into 'police protection' (s. 46(2)). When a child is taken into police protection the case must be enquired into by an officer designated by the chief officer for that area to enquire into these matters (s. 46(3)(e)). It will obviously be necessary, in the light of these provisions, for appropriately experienced officers to be designated by the police to carry out child protection functions.

The designated officer may apply, while the child is in police protection, for an emergency protection order. The officer applies on behalf of the local authority in whose area the child is ordinarily resident whether or not the authority know or agree (s. 46(7)).

When the officer enquiring into the case has completed any enquiries, the officer must release the child from police protection unless the officer considers that there is still reasonable cause to believe that the child would suffer significant harm if released (s. 46(5)). However, the child cannot be kept in police protection for more than 72 hours and if the designated officer forms the opinion that the child would be at risk after the 72 hours an emergency protection order will have to be applied for (s. 46(6) and (7)).

Where a child is taken into police protection by being removed to accommodation that is not provided by or on behalf of a local authority and is not a refuge under s. 51 (see 6.8 below), the constable concerned shall, as soon as reasonably practicable, arrange for the child to be removed to such accommodation (s. 46(3)(f)).

The constable who has taken the child into police protection must as soon as is reasonably practicable inform the local authority within whose area the child was found of the steps that have been taken in respect of the child and the reasons for doing so and also inform this authority of any proposed actions and the reasons for the proposed actions (s. 46(3)(a)). The constable also has a duty, as soon as reasonably practicable, to give details of where the child is accommodated to the authority within whose area the child is ordinarily resident (s. 46(3)(b)). If the police apply for an emergency protection order they do so on behalf of the authority within whose area the child is ordinarily resident (for definition, see s. 105(6)) (s. 46(7)). It therefore seems inappropriate that the duty of the police in respect of this authority is simply to give details of where the child is accommodated and not also to give that authority the same information as the police are obliged to give to the authority within whose area the child was found. An emergency protection order can be made on behalf of this authority even though the authority do not agree with the application or do not even know of the application. The difficulties that could arise where a child is taken into police protection in an area where the child is not ordinarily resident are discussed later in this chapter.

If the constable who has taken the child into police protection is of the view that this child is capable of understanding, then the constable must as soon as reasonably practicable inform the child of the steps that have been taken and the reasons for doing so and of the further steps that may be taken (s. 46(3)(c)). The constable must take such steps as are reasonably practicable to ascertain the child's wishes and feelings (s. 46(3)(d)).

The constable taking the child into police protection must take steps as are reasonably practicable inform the child's parents, any other person who has parental responsibility and any person with whom the child was living before the child was taken into police protection of the steps that the constable has taken and the reasons for this action and also inform them of any further steps that may be taken with respect to the child (s. 46(4)).

While a child is in police protection neither the constable who has taken the child into police protection nor the designated officer enquiring into the case has parental responsibility for the child (s. 46(9)(a)). However, the designated officer must do what is reasonable in all the circumstances of the case to safeguard and promote the welfare of the child and in carrying out this duty the officer must have regard to the length of time that the child will be in police protection (s. 46(9)(b)).

While a child is in police protection the designated officer must allow contact, if any, with the child to the child's parents, any person with parental responsibility, any person with whom the child was living immediately before being taken into police protection, any person in whose favour a contact order is in force, any person allowed contact by virtue of an order under s. 34 and any person acting on behalf of any of these persons (s. 46(10)). The designated officer is only required to allow such contact as in his opinion is both reasonable and in the best interests of the child. This contrasts with the position of the person who has obtained an emergency protection order who is under a duty to allow reasonable contact with those persons unless the court directs otherwise. Where a child in police protection is accommodated by the local authority, in whose area the child is ordinarily resident, that authority's duty with regard to allowing contact will be the same as the designated officer's (s. 46(11)).

Where the child is found by the police in an area where he is not ordinarily resident, and is taken into police protection, two local authorities will be involved. The respective powers and duties of these authorities in these circumstances are not clearly defined by the Children Act 1989 and as a result disputes may arise between the authorities. Here an indication is given of the difficulties that could arise.

The police must inform the local authority in whose area the child is found (authority A) of the steps that have been taken and the reasons for such action (s. 46(3)(a)). Authority A is under a duty to investigate and decide whether action should be taken to safeguard and promote the child's welfare (s. 47(1)). In carrying out their enquiries authority A must consult the local authority in whose area the child is ordinarily resident (authority B) (s. 47(12)). Authority B may undertake the necessary enquiries on behalf of authority A (ibid.).

The police are required to give details to authority B of the place at which the child is being accommodated (s. 46(3)(c)). If an emergency protection order is applied for by the police they do so on behalf of authority B and under that order authority B will have parental responsibility (ss. 47(7) and 44(4)(c)).

It is likely that authority A will accommodate the child but if the police have obtained an emergency protection order authority A will not have parental responsibility and authority B, who will have parental responsibility, may not be prepared to allow authority A to act in their place. Conflict may also occur because authority A will be under a duty to investigate and make decisions about the child's welfare when authority B have parental responsibility.

A further potential difficulty is that the right to apply for an extension of an emergency protection order is only available to the authority which has parental responsibility under the order (s. 45(4)). Therefore, the local authority with the duty to investigate will not have the power to apply for an extension of the order where the child is ordinarily resident in the area of another authority.

6.5 Local authority duties and responsibilities

6.5.1 Investigations

The local authority within whose area a child lives or is found are under a duty to investigate if one of three circumstances exist in relation to that child. First, if they are informed that a child who lives or is found in their area is subject to an emergency protection order, secondly, if they are informed that a child is in police protection and thirdly, where the local authority have reasonable cause to suspect a child is suffering significant harm or is likely to suffer such harm (s. 47(1)). The authority are under a duty to make, or have made on their behalf, such enquiries as they consider necessary to enable them to decide whether they should take any action to safeguard or promote the child's welfare (s. 47(1)). The same duty to investigate applies where the local authority have themselves obtained an emergency protection order (s. 47(2)). In addition, a local authority must investigate where, in the course of family proceedings, the court so directs (s. 37(1) and sch. 3, para. 17) and where they are notified by a local education authority of persistent failure by a child to comply with directions under an education supervision order (sch. 3, para. 19).

Where a local authority are making enquiries as a result of their duty to investigate under s. 47 then the local authority concerned must obtain access to the child, or ensure that this is done for them, unless they are satisfied that they have sufficient information to enable them to determine what action to take (s. 47(4)).

The Children Act 1989 specifies particular matters that the authority must consider. The authority must consider whether they should make any application to the court and whether they should exercise any of the powers available to them under the Children Act 1989. The authority must consider, where the child is not in accommodation provided by the authority or on their behalf, whether it would be in the best interests of the child during the remaining period of the emergency protection order to be moved to such accommodation. In addition, the authority must consider, where they are informed that a child is in police protection, whether it would be in the best interests of the child to request the police to make an application for an emergency protection order (s. 47(3)).

Where, as a result of the authority's enquiries, it appears to them that there are matters connected with the child's education that require investigation they are under a duty to consult 'the relevant local education authority' (s. 47(5)).

Where a local authority are making enquiries and an officer of that authority, or a person authorised by the local authority to act on their behalf, is refused access to the child or denied information as to the whereabouts of the child then the local authority must apply for an emergency protection order, a child assessment order, a care order or a supervision order unless satisfied that the child's welfare can be satisfactorily safeguarded without their doing so (s. 47(6)). Children Act 1989 provides a list of 'persons' who must assist the local authority investigating by providing relevant information and advice if that authority ask them to do so (s. 47(9)). The persons under a duty to assist are any local authority, any local education authority, any local housing authority, any health authority and any person authorised by the Secretary of State for the purposes of this section (s. 47(11)). It is perhaps surprising that the police and probation service are not included among those with a duty to assist, considering the contents of the DHSS Circular, 'Child Abuse — Working Together', published in 1988 (not to mention the findings of almost every major inquiry into the death of a child and, indeed, the Cleveland Report), which emphasised the importance of cooperation between all relevant agencies including the police in the protection of children. Nor is there an obligation on family members closest to the child or members of the public who may have relevant information. Those under an obligation to assist the local authority can avoid their obligation where it would be unreasonable in all the circumstances of the case for them to assist (s. 47(10)). It is difficult to envisage any circumstance in which it would be unreasonable to assist enquiries into alleged child abuse.

Where a local authority conclude that in order to safeguard or promote the child's welfare they should take action then the duty that follows is to take action so far as it is within their power and reasonably practicable for them to do so

(s. 47(8)). For commentary on the possible effect of this provision, in particular the inclusion of the words 'reasonably practicable', see 5.3.

Section 21(1) requires every local authority to make provision for the reception and accommodation of any child removed under Part V of the Children Act 1989 any child who is in police protection, any child detained under Police and Criminal Evidence Act 1984, s. 38(6), and children on remand or under a supervision order with a residence requirement pursuant to the Children and Young Persons Act 1969. Where a local authority making such provision does so other than by placing the child in a community home, controlled community home or a hospital vested in the Secretary of State, they are able to recover the expenses of maintaining the child from the local authority in whose area the child is ordinarily resident (s. 29(8)). If there is any doubt about whether a child is ordinarily resident in an area and the local authorities cannot agree, the matter can be decided by the Secretary of State (s. 30(2)).

6.5.2   Reviews

Where a local authority have completed their investigations in compliance with their duty under Children Act 1989, s. 47(1) and (2), and have decided that they should not apply for an emergency protection order, care order, of supervision order, they must consider whether it would be appropriate to review the case at a later date. If the authority decide that it would be appropriate to review, they must determine the date on which that review is to begin. Whenever the authority carry out such a review, one of the matters they must consider, if they decide not to seek an order in respect of the child, is whether a further review is required, and, if so, set a date on which it is to begin (s. 47(7)).

It is not particularly clear what is meant by a 'review', but it is suggested that the intention of this provision (supported by the use of the word 'begin', which suggests a process taking place over a period of time) is that further enquiries will be made, and simply to reconvene the earlier meeting would not fulfil the authority's duty.

6.6   Practical consequences

In deciding on the duration of an emergency protection order, the court can make an order for more than eight days to take account of Sundays and bank holidays (see 6.3.5). However, the same does not apply to Saturdays. Therefore, applications for the extension of such orders, or for the making of an interim care order, may have to be heard on Saturdays. There are various other applications which by their nature will require an immediate court hearing, for example, for directions regarding contact or medical examination, or for discharge of an emergency protection order. With regard to the latter, there would appear to be little value in giving parents the right to apply once 72 hours have elapsed from the making of the emergency protection order if in the case of that period ending on a Friday evening they are then expected to wait until Monday morning to make the application.

There will therefore be a need to make provision for court hearings at weekends. Local authorities, the NSPCC, solicitors and courts must revise their staffing arrangements at these times, in particular, by ensuring that employees who at present are not required to work at weekends are able to do so. For example, a social worker investigating a case during the week would need to attend court at the weekend on the authority's application for an interim care order, as the authority could not be adequately represented by an emergency duty social worker who would not be able to give direct evidence pertinent to the case.

As the maximum duration of an emergency protection order is eight days (barring extensions which are unlikely to be granted automatically), the local authority have in reality a maximum of five working days in which to investigate or less if a bank holiday or Christmas falls during the period. During that period, the social worker investigating will have to do some or all of the following:

(a)   arrange for accommodation for the child;

(b)   place the child with foster-parents or in an institution, and explain to the child what is happening and give sufficient information to those who will be caring for the child to do so appropriately;

(c)   explain to the parents why their child has been removed from them, and discuss concerns and allegations with them;

(d)   spend further time with the child, to satisfy himself that the child's welfare is being met, and also ask the child about any concerns or allegations;

(e)   take the child for medical examination and/or treatment, and obtain the doctor's diagnosis;

(f)   make decisions about who the child should be allowed to have contact with (from those listed in s. 47(11));

(g)   arrange for such contact to take place;

(h)   instruct the authority's solicitor to make application for directions governing contact or medical examination, and respond to any such applications made by others;

(i)   prepare to respond to applications for discharge of the emergency protection order;

(j)   discuss the case with a guardian *ad litem,* if one has been appointed;

(k)   convene a case conference, trying to get a sufficient number of those involved with the family to attend;

(l)   keep under review whether it is safe to return the child home;

(m)   decide, with senior social work staff, whether action needs to be taken to promote or safeguard the child's welfare;

(n)   instruct the local authority solicitor to commence appropriate proceedings, and provide sufficient information for him to do so;

(o)   attend court in respect of an application for an interim care order, or for an extension of the emergency protection order (as the social worker requires more time to complete his investigations!).

6.7   Abduction of children in care and recovery orders

It will be an offence to abduct a child who is in care from the 'responsible person': the 'responsible person' is defined as any person who for the time being has care of the child by virtue of a care order, emergency protection order or where the child is in police protection (s. 49(1) and (2)). The children to whom this offence relates are those who are the subject of a care order, the subject of an emergency protection order or who are in police protection (s. 49(2)).

The offence can be committed in three ways: (a) where a person knowingly and without lawful authority or reasonable excuse takes a child away from the responsible person; or (b) where a person knowingly and without lawful authority or reasonable excuse keeps a child, to whom the section relates, away from the responsible person; or (c) where a person knowingly and without lawful authority or reasonable excuse induces, assists or incites a child, to whom the section relates, to run away or stay away from the responsible person (s. 49(1)). A person guilty of this offence is liable to imprisonment for up to six months and/or to a fine (s. 49(3)).

A court may make a recovery order if it appears to the court that there is reason to believe that one of the following circumstances applies to a child in care:

(a)   that a child has been unlawfully taken away or is being unlawfully kept away from the responsible person;
(b)   that a child has run away or is staying away from the responsible person; or
(c)   that a child is missing (s. 50(1)).

A recovery order acts as a direction to any person who is in a position to do so to produce the child to any authorised person (s. 50(3)(a)). In this context an authorised person includes any person specified by the court, any constable and any person who is authorised after a recovery order is made by the person with parental responsibility under a care order or emergency protection order (s. 50(7)). Where a person is authorised by the person with parental responsibility under a care or emergency protection order then the authorisation must identify the recovery order and any person claiming to be authorised in this manner must, if asked to do so, produce duly authenticated documentation (s. 50(8)).

A recovery order also authorises the removal of the child by an authorised person and authorises any constable to enter premises specified in the order and search for the child using reasonable force if necessary (s. 50(3)(b) and (d)). Premises can only be specified in an order if it appears to the court that there are reasonable grounds for believing that the child is on those premises (s. 50(6)). Limiting this to a specified address means that if the child is moved next door when the police constable is seen approaching the house then the order is ineffective. A further effect of a recovery order is that it requires any person who has information about the child's whereabouts to disclose that information, if asked to do so, to a constable or to an officer of the court (s. 50(3)(c)). No person can be excused from complying with such a request on the ground that to do so might incriminate him or his spouse. However, a statement or admission made in complying is not admissible in evidence against them other than for an offence of perjury (s. 50(11)). But such a statement or admission could possibly be adduced in family proceedings.

A recovery order can only be made on the application of a person with parental responsibility by virtue of a care order or emergency protection order or, if the child is in police protection, the designated officer (s. 50(4)). The order must name the child and any person with parental responsibility under a care or emergency protection order or, if the child is in police protection, the designated officer (s. 50(5)).

It is an offence to intentionally obstruct an authorised person exercising power under a recovery order to remove the child (s. 50(9)). A person guilty of this offence is liable to a fine (s. 50(10)).

Where a recovery order is made while a child is being looked after by a local authority then any reasonable expenses incurred by an authorised person are recoverable from the local authority (s. 50(12)).

A recovery order is effective in Scotland and is to be treated as if it had been made by the Court of Session (s. 50(13)).

Part (a)

6.8   Refuges for children at risk

Introduced in the Children Act 1989 is an immunity from certain offences in favour of those who provide refuges for children at risk. As a result of concern expressed, in particular by the Children's Society, about the position of organisations which assist runaway youngsters who would otherwise be at great risk and by doing so may themselves be at risk of prosecution for such offences as harbouring, there has been introduced a system by which the Secretary of State may issue a certificate in respect of a refuge the effect of which would be that the persons involved with that refuge would not be in danger of prosecution in respect of certain specified offences (s. 51).

The Secretary of State may issue a certificate where it is proposed to use a voluntary home or registered children's home to provide a refuge for children who apepar to be at risk of harm and the certificate would be in respect of one home (s. 51(1)). There is nothing included in the provision which indicates who needs to have formed the view that a child is at risk of harm. Where a local authority or a voluntary organisation arrange for a foster-parent to provide such a refuge then the Secretary of State may issue a certificate with respect to the foster-parent (s. 51(2)). A foster-parent is defined to be a person 'who is, or who from time to time is, a local-authority foster-parent (itself defined in s. 23(2)) or a foster-parent with whom children are placed by a voluntary organisation, (s. 51(3)).

The Secretary of State is empowered to make regulations which may provide for the manner in which certificates may be issued, impose requirements which must be complied with while a certificate is in force and provide for the circumstances of withdrawal of certificates (s. 51(4)).

Where a certificate is in force then the following provisions will not apply to the person providing the refuge to which it relates or the foster-parent who provides a refuge for a child in accordance with arrangements made by the local authority or voluntary organisation:

(a)   Children Act 1989, s. 49 (abduction of a child in care):
(b)   Social Work (Scotland) Act 1968, s. 71 (harbouring abscondees from residential homes);
(c)   Children and Young Persons Act 1969, s. 32(3) (compelling, persuading, inciting or assisting any person to be absent from detention);
(d)   Child Abduction Act 1984, s. 2.

6.9 Transitional provisions

A court cannot make a place of safety order after the repeal of Children and Young Persons Act 1969, s. 28(1) by the Children Act 1989. However, such orders which have been made prior to that date will continue to have effect, allowing the child in question to be detained pursuant to the order. See generally sch. 14, para. 27, which deals with other analogous powers of the court. Reference should also be made to sch. 14, paras 28 to 30 which similarly preserves the position following the arrest or recovery of children in care (Child Care Act 1980, ss. 15 and 16, and Children and Young Persons Act 1969, s. 32).

Chapter Seven
Residential Care for Children

7.1   Introduction

The law governing residential care for children is an important but often overlooked aspect of child care law. The need to assist parents who do not care adequately for their children so as to prevent children coming into the care of local authorities and the legal processes by which they come into care receive greatest attention. However, what happens to a child once in the care of the local authority is of equal and vital importance.

If a child lives in a home provided by a local authority or voluntary organisation (whether voluntarily or as a result of a statutory order) there are two particularly important issues. First the authority or voluntary organisation must ensure, so far as possible, that the child is accommodated in an appropriate institution or foster home (fostering is discussed in chapter 8) and in order to provide the child with good care the individual needs of each child must be taken into account: the child's age, personality, life experiences, ethnic and cultural background and religion are examples of some of the matters that should be considered. To provide appropriate accommodation, local authorities, in conjunction with voluntary agencies, need to have available a diversity of establishments. The mentally handicapped toddler, the sexually abused child and the rebellious teenager unable to cope with the demands of family life will require differing types of establishments to meet their needs.

Secondly, when a child is placed in residential care it is essential that there is sufficient regulation to protect the child and ensure that his best interests are being served. At the same time the regulations must not inhibit assistance being given to the child and plans being made for his future welfare. There is no greater tragedy than a child removed from neglectful or abusing parents only to be abused again by those to whom he is entrusted.

In December 1985 an independent review of residential care was commissioned by the Secretary of State for Health and Social Services. This resulted in 1988 in the publication of *A Positive Choice,* more widely referred to as the Wagner Report after Gillian Wagner who chaired the review. The scope of the Wagner Report encompassed all forms of residential care. The major recommendations so far as they relate to children in care are as follows:

(a)   Information about the agencies' complaints procedure should be made available to children and parents. Children in all forms of residential care should have access to an independent advocate. Consideration should be given to extending the system of guardians *ad litem* to enable families and children to request a guardian *ad litem* to safeguard children's interests (p. 116).

(b)   Residential services for children should be among the options available to children and their parents and should be developed to offer: respite care; a staged transition from hospital to family care; integrated education and care; a means of keeping siblings together (p. 117).

(c)   Greater importance should be attached to the educational and health needs of children in care.

(d)   The needs of children and young people from ethnic minority groups should receive particular attention.

(e)   Adequate accommodation should be made available to young people on leaving care.

(f)   The Department of Health and Social Security should draw up national guidelines for the registration and inspection of residential establishments, and should give equal attention to standards of accommodation, quality of life and the qualifications of mangement and staff (p. 118).

The Wagner Report also includes several recommendations with regard to staffing of residential establishments and emphasises the need for appropriate grading of staff, training and reflection of ethnic composition of the residents.

Some developments have been made by the Children Act 1989 but the majority of the provisions which relate to residential care of children are not new but reflect previous legislation. There is provision in the Act for regulations to be made that could lead to greater improvements. However, it should be recognised that under the Child Care Act 1980, and prior to this in the Children Act 1948, there was provision for regulations covering important issues such as health and communication between parents and child and although some regulations were made they were not very far-reaching.

Without more dynamic regulations the Children Act 1989 will become a missed opportunity to make important developments in the provision for children of residential care. In a time of financial constraint on local authorities and others it needs more than reliance on good social work practice to ensure that children in residential establishments receive a high standard of care and achieve their potential.

7.2   Community homes

The primary provisions relating to community homes are presently contained in Child Care Act 1980, ss. 31 and 35 to 44. These provisions will be repealed and replaced by Children Act 1989, ss. 53 to 58 and sch. 4. There is very little that is new in the provisions in the Children Act 1989 which are in effect a rewording of the previous provisions. The rewording, so far as it has taken place, has led to greater clarity and is therefore welcome.

7.3   Definition of community home

The term 'community home' has two preliminary definitions. First, a community home may be a home provided, managed, equipped and maintained by a local authority. Secondly a community home may be a home provided by a voluntary organisation but in respect of which a local authority and the voluntary organisation jointly propose that one of them will have responsibility for its management, equipment and maintenance (Children Act 1989, s. 53(3)). Where a community home is provided by a voluntary organisation and a local authority are to be responsible for the management, the authority have to designate the home as a 'controlled community home' (s. 53(4)). The voluntary organisation are able to appoint one third of those who will be on the board of managers (sch. 4, para. 1(5)(a)). Where the home is provided by a voluntary organisation and that organisation is to be responsible for the management then the local authority must designate the home as an 'assisted community home' (s. 53(5)) and the local authority are able to appoint one third of the board of managers (sch. 4, para. 1(5)(b)). However, in such cases the duties imposed upon voluntary organisations and local authorities by ss. 61 and 62 do apply (see 7.12).

7.4   Provision and management of community homes

By s. 53 of the Children Act 1989 every local authority must make such arrangements as they consider appropriate to ensure that community homes are available not only for the care and accommodation of children but also for purposes connected with the welfare of children (whether or not the local authority are looking after the child). To fulfil the duty imposed upon them to make appropriate provision of community homes, two or more local authorities may act jointly (s. 53(1)). Local authorities are given wide discretion but, in deciding what arrangements are appropriate, a local authority must have regard to the need for ensuring the availability of different descriptions of accommodation and accommodation which is suitable for different purposes and the requirements of different descriptions of children (s. 53(2)).

Instruments of management for controlled and assisted community homes, providing for the constitution of a body of managers, may be made by order of the Secretary of State (sch. 4, para. 1(1)). Where a voluntary organisation have provided two or more homes which are either controlled or assisted community homes, and the same local authority are to be represented on the body of managers for each of these homes then a single instrument of management may be made by the Secretary of State constituting one body of managers for these homes (sch. 4, para. 1(2) and (3)).

There is provision governing the number of managers and the proportion of managers that are to be appointed by the local authority. The number of managers can be specified in the instrument of management but must be in multiples of three (sch. 4, para. 1(4)). With a controlled community home there must be provision in the instrument of management for the local authority to appoint two thirds of the managers (sch. 4, para. 1(5)(a)). Where it is an assisted community home the instrument of management must provide that the local authority can appoint one third of the managers (sch. 4, para. 1(5)(b)).

The managers that are not appointed by the local authority are referred to as 'foundation managers'. The instrument must include provision for the manner by which the foundation managers will be appointed and who will make the appointment (sch. 4, para. 1(6)). When deciding who is to make appointments and the method of appointment the following must be taken into account. First, the choice must be made so as to represent the interests of the voluntary organisation by which the home is provided and secondly for the purpose of ensuring that, so far as is practicable, the character of the home as voluntary will be preserved and that the terms of any trust deed relating to the home are observed (sch. 4, para. 1(6)). Before a voluntary home can be known as either a controlled or assisted community home, according to its designation, it must have an instrument of management in force (sch. 4, para. 1(8)).

An instrument of management can contain such provisions as the Secretary of State considers appropriate but nothing in the instrument must affect the purposes for which the premises are held (sch. 4, para. 2(1) and (2)). The instrument of management may contain provision with regard to the nature and purpose of the home, the availability of places for use by local authorities and other specified bodies and the management and charging of fees (sch. 4, para. 2(3)). There is provision for variation and revocation of any of the provisions in the instrument of management. The Secretary of State may, by order, vary or revoke any provision after consultation with the voluntary organisation concerned and with the local authority specified in the instrument of management (sch. 4, para. 2(5)).

Where a community home is designated as a controlled community home, the local authority specified in the instrument of management are responsible for the management, equipment and maintenance of the home (sch. 4, para. 3(1)). If the home is designated as an assisted community home, the voluntary organisation which provided the home are responsible for management, equipment and maintenance (sch. 4, para. 3(2)). The Children Act 1989 allows for these functions to be carried out by the appointed managers and makes it clear that the managers act as agents for the 'responsible body' (sch. 4, para. 3(4) and (5)): either the local authority or voluntary organisation depending on the home's designation. Employment of community home staff is a matter that must be reserved for the decision of the responsible body and is not a function that can be delegated to the managers (sch. 4, para. 3(8)). In addition, the responsible body can reserve any other matter for their decision either specifically in the instrument of management or by serving on the managers a notice (sch. 4, para. 3(6)). In deciding upon matters of employment, and any other matter that has been reserved, the responsible body must take into account any representations made to them by the managers (sch. 4, para. 3(7)).

The local authority responsible for management of a controlled community home are empowered to enter into arrangements with the voluntary organisation whereby persons not employed by the local authority undertake duties at the home (sch. 4, para. 3(9)). Where a vountary organisation responsible for the management of an assisted community home propose to engage a member of staff or terminate any person's employment at the home, the voluntary organisation must consult with the local authority specified in the instrument of management (sch. 4, para. 3(10)(a)). If, after such consultation, the local authority so direct, the voluntary organisation must not carry out their proposal without the local authority's consent (sch. 4, para. 3(10)(a)). Additionally, the local authority specified in the instrument of management may, after consulation with the voluntary organisation, require them to terminate the employment of any person at the assisted community home (sch. 4, para. 3(10)(b)). There is provision under which the restrictions on appointing and terminating employment can be reduced. First, the local authority concerned can serve a notice in writing on the voluntary organisation specifying the cases and circumstances in which these provisions will not apply (sch. 4, para. 3(11)(a)). Secondly, in the home's instrument of management it can be specified, in relation to the employment of any persons or class of persons, that these provisions will not apply (sch. 4, para. 3(11)(b)).

The responsible body specifies the accounting year for the community home and the managers must submit each year estimates of expenditure and receipt for the forthcoming year (sch. 4, para 3(12) and (13)). Any expenses approved by the responsible body must be paid for by the responsible body (sch. 4, para. 3(14)).

As might be expected there is provision that the managers must keep proper accounts with respect to the home and proper records in relation to those accounts (sch. 4, para. 3(15)). Where there is one instrument of management for two or more homes then the accounts that have to be kept may be kept maintained in respect of all homes rather than each individual home (sch. 4, para. 3(16)).

7.5 Regulations in respect of community homes

The Children Act 1989 extends the matters in respect of which regulations can be made by the Secretary of State (sch. 4, para. 4). New in the Act is provision for the Secretary of State to make regulations in respect of:

(a) the placing of children in community homes;
(b) the conduct of community homes;
(c) securing the welfare of children in community homes;
(d) imposing requirements as to the staff in community homes;
(e) providing for the control and discipline of children in community homes;
(f) imposing requirements as to the keeping of records and giving of notices in respect of children in community homes;
(g) providing for the Secretary of State to be consulted in respect of applicants for the appointment of officer-in-charge of the home and to prohibit appointment of particular applicants.

The Wagner Report (see 7.1) recommended that there should be guidelines with regard to management and staffing of children's residential establishments and the new provisions will enable the Secretary of State to make regulations in this respect.

Another recommendation of the Wagner Report was that there should be greater emphasis placed on health and education. The existing enabling provision (Children and Young Persons Act 1969, s. 39) refers to 'medical arrangements to be made for protecting the health of children in the homes'.

Under the Children Act 1989 provision, the scope of regulations may be wider as the reference to 'medical' has been omitted and therefore regulations could be made in respect of any arrangements for protecting the child's health. The needs of children from ethnic minority groups, which the Wagner Report recommended should receive particular attention, are dealt with under s. 61(3)(c) (see 7.12). Education is not specifically mentioned but could be dealt with by regulations under the general ambit of conduct and securing the welfare of children.

The Wagner Report emphasised the need for children in care to have independent advocates, not only in the course of court proceedings but generally to safeguard a child's interests while in care. Under Child Care Act 1980, s. 11, local authorities are under a duty to appoint an 'independent visitor' to visit any child over the age of five accommodated in a community home or other establishment, when he has not been allowed to leave the premises for the preceding three months for the purpose of education, and communication between the child and parent had been infrequent or the child had not lived with or visited his parent in the preceding 12 months. This duty is widened under the Children Act 1989 and now applies to any child being looked after by a local authority and is not restricted to children who have not been receiving education outside the community home. The local authority's duty to appoint an independent visitor now arises where communication between the child and his parent, or any person with parental responsibility, has been infrequent or where the child has not visited or lived with or been visited by his parent, or any person with parental responsibility, during the preceding 12 months and it would be in the child's best interests (sch. 2, para. 17). It is to be hoped that local authorities will take greater account of this wider duty placed upon them than they do of the existing duty.

The provision for regulations to be made in respect of various matters under Child Care Act 1980, s. 39, is re-enacted in the Children Act 1989 with the omission of a provision that regulations could be made requiring the approval of the Secretary of State to the use of buildings for the purpose of community homes and doing anything which materially affected the buildings or grounds or other facilities or amenities available for the children's homes. The reader is referred to sch. 4, para. 4(2) and (3), for the details of the other regulations that may be made by the Secretary of State.

7.6 Disputes between local authority and voluntary organisation

Where there is a dispute in respect of a controlled or assisted community home between the local authority specified in the home's instrument of management and the voluntary organisation providing the home (or another local authority), the matter may be referred, by either party, to the Secretary of State for his determination (s. 55(1) and (2)). If there is a dispute between the responsible body for an assisted or community home and a local authority who have placed, or wish to place, a child in the community home, the dispute may be referred, by either party, to the Secretary of State. The Secretary of State may make such directions as he thinks fit to the local authority or voluntary organisation, whichever is the responsible body (s. 55(3)). If a dispute arises in respect of religious instruction given in a controlled or assisted community home and there is a trust deed which contains provision whereby a bishop or any other ecclesiastical or denominational authority has power to decide questions relating to religious instruction then the matter can only be referred to the Secretary of State if it is not capable of being dealt with in accordance with the provision in the trust deed (s. 55(5)).

7.7 Home ceasing to be used as an assisted or controlled community home

In the Children Act 1989 there is provision for the Secretary of State to direct, by notice in writing served on the responsible body, that from a specified date premises must not be used for the purposes of a community home (s. 54(1)). The circumstance in which the Secretary of State can make such a direction is where it appears that any premises used as a community home are unsuitable for that purpose, or the conduct of a community home is not in accordance with regulations made by the Secretary of State or is otherwise unsatisfactory. This provision applies to community homes provided and managed by local authorities as well as to assisted and controlled community homes (s. 54(3)). Where the Secretary of State has given such a direction he may at any time, by order, revoke the instrument of management for the home concerned (s. 54(2)).

Where a voluntary organisation which provide a controlled or assisted community home wish to discontinue its use as a community home they must give to the Secretary of State and the local authority concerned at least two years' notice in writing of their intention (s. 56(1)). The notice must specify the date from which the voluntary organisation intend to cease to provide the home as a community home and, if a notice is not withdrawn on that date, the home's designation as controlled or assisted and the home's instrument of management will automatically cease to have effect (s. 56(2) and (3)). If, in the intervening period between notice having been given and the home actually closing, the managers are unable or unwilling to continue, they may give notice in writing to the Secretary of State to this effect (s. 56(4)). The Secretary of State may then, by order, revoke the home's instrument of management and require the local authority specified in the instrument of management to manage the home until the date on which the home is to cease to be a community home and further may order that cessation to be brought forward to an earlier date (s. 56(4)).

There is provision in the Children Act 1989 for a local authority to withdraw their designation of a home as a controlled or assisted community home. The local authority would have to give the Secretary of State and the voluntary organisation which provide the home at least two years' notice in writing of their intention to withdraw the designation (s. 57(1)). If in the intervening period between notice of intention to withdraw designation and cessation of use as a community home the managers give notice in writing to the Secretary of State that they are unable or unwilling to continue as managers then the Secretary of State may, by order, revoke the home's instrument of management at an earlier date (s. 57(3)).

Children Act 1989, s. 58, covers the financial consequences of a controlled or assisted community home ceasing to be used as such. This section is primarily concerned with identifying to whom any increase in the value of the premises, which is attributable to the expenditure of public money, should be paid to.

7.8 Registration and regulation of voluntary homes

A 'voluntary home' is defined as any home or other institution providing care and accommodation for children which is carried on by a voluntary organisation (s. 60(3)). The following are specifically excluded by s. 60(3) from the definition of 'voluntary home':

(a) a nursing home, mental nursing home or residential care home;

(b) a school;

(c) any community home;

(d) any health service hospital;

(e) any home or other institution provided, equipped and maintained by the Secretary of State;

(f) any home which is exempted by regulations made by the Secretary of State.

By Children Act 1989, s. 60(1), a voluntary home cannot be used as such unless it is registered by the Secretary of State. Failure to comply with this provision is an offence and any person guilty of this offence is liable to be fined (sch. 5, para. 1(5) and (6)). An application for registration must be made by the persons intending to carry on the home to which the application relates and in such manner, and accompanied by such particulars, as the Secretary of State may prescribe (sch. 5, para. 1(1)).

The Secretary of State may refuse to register and if he grants the application he may do so subject to conditions (sch. 5, para. 1(2)). Once registered the Secretary of State may from time to time, with or without an application from the person carrying on the home, vary any condition or impose an additional condition (sch. 5, para. 1(3)). Before he can vary a condition or impose an additional one, the Secretary of State must give notice to any person carrying on a voluntary home of his proposal to do so (sch. 5, para. 2(4)). Any person who fails to comply with a condition of registration, without reasonable excuse, is guilty of an offence and liable to a fine (sch. 5, para. 1(5) and (6)).

The Secretary of State may at any time, where it appears to him that the conduct of any voluntary home is not in accordance with regulations or is otherwise unsatisfactory, cancel the registration of the home and remove it from the register (sch. 5, para. 1(4)). Before doing so the Secretary of State must serve a notice on the person carrying on the voluntary home of his proposal to cancel registration (sch. 5, para. 2(4)).

The Secretary of State is under an obligation to notify the local authority within whose area a voluntary home is situated of registration of that home or cancellation of registration (sch. 5, para. 1(7)). Bringing the provision up to date, the Secretary of State is enabled to maintain a register of voluntary homes by means of a computer (s. 60(2)).

7.9 Procedure for application and decisions of Secretary of State

The provisions with regard to procedure, right to make representations, decision of the Secretary of State and appeals appear in Children Act 1989, sch. 5, paras 2 to 5.

Under para. 2, where the Secretary of State proposes to grant an application and impose conditions, he must give written notice of his proposal to the applicant unless the conditions are ones which the applicant specified in his application or the Secretary of State and the applicant have already agreed the conditions. If the Secretary of State proposes to refuse an application he must always give notice of his proposal to the applicant.

The Secretary of State is required to give written notice of five categories of proposals: where he proposes to impose conditions on a new registration that were not specified in the application, to refuse an application, to cancel the registration of a home, to vary any conditions already imposed or to impose any additional conditions (sch. 5, para. 2(2), (3) and (4)). For ease of reference these will all be referred to as 'notices of proposal'.

Where the Secretary of State is required to serve a notice of proposal the notice must include a statement that the person served may, within 14 days, require the Secretary of State, in writing, to give him an opportunity to make representations (sch. 5, para. 3(1)).

Where a notice of proposal has been served, the Secretary of State shall not determine the matter until representations have been made, the period during which a person could have required the Secretary of State to give him an opportunity to make representations has elapsed or the Secretary of State has been required to give such an opportunity and has allowed a reasonable period for such representations to be made and none have been made (sch. 5, para. 3(2) and (3)).

A person who wishes to make representations, and has written to the Secretary of State requiring that he be given such an opportunity, may choose to do so either in writing or orally (sch. 5, para. 3(4)). If he chooses to make his representations orally the Secretary of State must give him an opportunity to appear before a person appointed by the Secretary of State (sch. 5, para. 3(5)).

If the Secretary of State decides to go ahead with the proposal then he must serve notice to that effect on any person on whom he served the original notice of proposal. By sch. 5, para. 4(2), this subsequent notice must be accompanied by a further notice which explains the right of appeal conferred by para. 5.

A decision by the Secretary of State to grant registration subject only to conditions that were contained in the application or to refuse an application for registration takes effect immediately. All other decisions take effect after 28 days, unless an appeal is brought, when the decision will take effect when the appeal is either determined or abandoned (sch. 5, para. 4(3)).

An appeal may be made by any person on whom a notice of decision has been served. An appeal must be brought by way of notice in writing given to the Secretary of State within 28 days after service of the notice of decision (sch. 5, para. 5(2) and (3)). No appeal may be brought after the 28 days has elapsed. Any appeal will be considered by the Registered Homes Tribunal. The tribunal may confirm the Secretary of State's decision or direct that the decision shall not be effective (sch. 5, para. 5(4)). In addition, the tribunal may vary a condition in respect of which the appeal relates or direct whether or not any such condition shall have effect (sch. 5, para. (5)).

7.10   Regulations as to conduct of voluntary homes

Under the Children Act 1989, sch. 5, para. 7, there is provision for the Secretary of State to make regulations regarding the conduct of voluntary homes. The matters in respect of which the Secretary of State may make regulations are as follows:

(a)   as to the placing of children in voluntary homes;
(b)   as to the conduct of such homes;
(c)   for securing the welfare of children in such homes;
(d)   to prescribe standards to which the premises used for such homes are to conform;
(e)   to impose requirements as to the accommodation, staff and equipment to be provided in such homes and as to the arrangements to be made for protecting the health of children in such homes;
(f)   to provide for the control and discipline of children in such homes;
(g)   to authorise the Secretary of State to limit the number of children who may be accommodated in any particular voluntary home;
(h)   to prohibit the use of accommodation for the purpose of restricting the liberty of children in such homes;
(i)   to impose requirements as to the keeping of records and giving of notices with respect to children in such homes;
(j)   to impose requirements as to the facilities which are to be provided for giving religious instruction to children in such homes;
(k)   to require notice to be given to the Secretary of State of any change of the person carrying on a voluntary home or of the premises used by such a home;
(l)   to require that information be given to the Secretary of State as to the facilities available at such homes for parents, those with parental responsibility and other persons connected with children in the home to visit and communicate with such children.

The regulations may also provide that a contravention of, or failure to comply with, any specified provision of the regulations without reasonable excuse shall be an offence and any person guilty of such an offence will be liable to a fine (sch. 5, para. 7(3) and (4)).

7.11   Provision of accommodation by voluntary organisations

Children Act 1989, s. 59, sets out where a voluntary organisation may place a child whom they are accommodating and enables the Secretary of State to make regulations of a similar kind in respect of children accommodated by a local authority. The duty imposed upon a voluntary organisation is that where they provide accommodation for a child then they must do so by:

(a)   placing the child with a family, relative of the child or any other suitable person;
(b)   maintaining the child in a voluntary home;
(c)   maintaining the child in a community home;

(d)   maintaining the child in a registered children's home;
(e)   maintaining the child in a home provided by the Secretary of State;
(f)   making such other arrangements as seem appropriate.

The Secretary of State may make regulations in respect of a voluntary organisation placing a child with foster-parents and a voluntary organisation's power to place a child in a home that comes within (a) above is subject to any such regulations. The voluntary organisation, should they accommodate a child in a place that comes within (a), may make such payments as they decide (s. 59(1)(a)). The Secretary of State is also enabled to make regulations in respect of the arrangements that may be made under (f) above (s. 59(3)).

The Secretary of State may make regulations that would require a voluntary organisation to review the case of any child that they are accommodating and consider any representations, including any complaints, made to them by a person who comes within a class of persons to be prescribed (s. 59(4)).

It may be an offence to contravene or fail to comply with any regulations made under s. 59; if so, the penalty will be a fine (s. 59(6)).

7.12   Duties of voluntary organisations in relation to the welfare of children

Where a child is accommodated by a voluntary organisation or on behalf of such an organisation, three fundamental duties are imposed on the organisation by Children Act 1989, s. 61(1). First, a duty to safeguard and promote the child's welfare. Secondly, to make use of services and facilities that are generally available to children in the community. Thirdly, to advise, assist and befriend the child with a view to promoting his welfare when he ceases to be accommodated by the voluntary organisation.

Before a voluntary organisation make any decision with respect to a child accommodated by them, or on behalf of them, the organisation must, so far as is reasonably practicable, ascertain the wishes and feelings of the child (s. 61(2)(a)). In making any decision the organisation must give due consideration, having regard to the child's age and understanding, to his wishes and feelings so far as they have been able to ascertain them (s. 61(3)(a)). The voluntary organisation must also asertain the wishes and feelings of the child's parents, any person with parental responsibility and any other person whose wishes and feelings the organisation consider to be relevant (s. 61(2)(b) to (d)). The organisation must give due consideration to the wishes and feelings of these individuals so far as they have been able to ascertain them (s. 61(3)(b)). Additionally the organisation must give due consideration to the child's religious persuasion, racial origin and cultural and linguistic background (s. 60(2) and (3); compare s. 22(4) and (5)).

7.13   Duties of local authorities in respect of children accommodated by voluntary organisations

Every local authority must satisfy themselves that any voluntary organisation providing accommodation for any child within the authority's area and any voluntary organisation providing accommodation outside that area for any child on behalf of the authority are satisfactorily safeguarding and promoting the welfare of those children (s. 62(1)). In order to carry out this duty a further duty is imposed so that every local authority must arrange for children who are accommodated within their area by, or on behalf of, a voluntary organisation to be visited from time to time (s. 62(2)). This second duty of visiting children does not apply where the accommodation provided by the voluntary organisation is a community home (s. 62(4)).

The Secretary of State may make regulations requiring a local authority, by one of their officers, to visit every child provided with accommodation by a voluntary organisation in their area (s. 62(3)(a)). The regulations may prescribe when visits must be made. In addition the regulations may impose requirements which must be met by any local authority, or officer of a local authority, carrying out functions under s. 62 (s. 62(3)(b)).

To enable a local authority to carry out these duties, any person authorised by a local authority may enter, at any reasonable time, and inspect any premises in which children are being accommodated by or on behalf of a voluntary organisation (s. 62(6)(a)). In addition the authorised person may inspect any child in the accommodation (s. 62(6)(b)). Further, the authorised person may require any person to provide him with such records as regulations may require or allow the authorised person to inspect such records (s. 62(6)(c)). Where an authorised person is exercising the power to inspect records he is entitled, at any reasonable time, to have access to any computer and any associated apparatus or material which is or has been used in connection with such records (s. 62(8)(a)). The authorised person is also entitled to inspect and check the operation of any such computer, associated apparatus or material. Additionally the authorised person is empowered to require the person by whom, or on whose behalf, the computer is or has been used to keep records to give him such assistance as he may reasonably require (s. 62(8)(b)). The authorised person may alternatively require any person having charge of, or otherwise concerned with the operation of, the computer, apparatus or material to give him such assistance (s. 62(8)(b)).

When an authorised person is exercising the power to enter and inspect premises, inspect any child or be provided with or inspect any records he must produce some duly authenticated document showing his authorisation if he is asked to do so (s. 62(7)). Any person who intentionally obstructs another in the exercise of any power with regard to inspecting premises, children or records or having access, inspecting or checking any computer or associated apparatus or material is guilty of an offence and liable on summary conviction to a fine (s. 62(9)).

7.14   Persons disqualified from running or being employed in a voluntary home

The Secretary of State is empowered by Children Act 1989, sch. 5, para. 8, to make regulations with regard to the disqualification of certain persons from being involved with voluntary homes. The provisions made by such regulations are to be similar to the provisions of s. 65 — see 7.21.

7.15   Registered children's homes

The term 'children's home' is given a basic definition in Children Act 1989, s. 63, and that definition is clarified by means of listing what is not a children's home.

The basic definition is that a 'children's home' means a home which provides, or usually provides or is intended to provide, care and accommodation wholly or mainly for more than three children at any one time (s. 63(3)(a)). Excluded is a home which is exempted under regulations that may be made by the Secretary of State and all of the following (s. 63(3)(b) and (5)):

(a) a community home;
(b) a voluntary home;
(c) a residential care home, nursing home or mental nursing home;
(d) a health service hospital;
(e) a home provided, equipped and maintained by the Secretary of State;
(f) a school, except that, by s. 63(6), an independent school is a children's home if it provides accommodation for not more than 50 children and the school is not approved by the Secretary of State under the Education Act 1981.

For clarification it is provided that a child is not cared for and accommodated in a children's home when he is cared for and accommodated by a parent of his, a person with parental responsibility for him or any relative (s. 63(4)). Further, a child who lives in a children's home will not be treated as cared for and accommodated in a children's home if one of his parents or any person with parental responsibility for him also lives at the home (s. 63(7)(a)). In addition, a child being cared for by a person in a personal capacity and not as part of that person's duties in relation to the home will not be treated as being cared for and accommodated in a children's home (s. 63(7)(b)). The circumstances in which a person may foster more than three children and not be treated as running a children's home are dealt with in sch. 7 (see chapter 8).

A 'home' is simply defined to include any institution (s. 63(9)). Children must not be cared for and provided with accommodation in a children's home unless it is registered and that register may be maintained by means of a computer (s. 63(1) and (2)). If a child is at any time cared for and accommodated in a children's home which is not registered then the person carrying on the home, unless he has a reasonable excuse, is guilty of an offence and liable to a fine (s. 63(10)).

7.16 Application for registration of children's homes

An application for registration of a children's home must be made by the person carrying on, or intending to carry on, the home to the local authority for that area (sch. 6, para. 1). The Secretary of State may in regulations prescribe the manner of an application and the particulars that must accompany that application. The application must be accompanied by a fee, the amount of which can be determined by the local authority but which must be 'reasonable' (para. 1(2)).

Before a local authority decide whether or not to grant an application they must comply with any requirements imposed by regulations made by the Secretary of State (sch. 6, para. 1(5) and (6)). Those regulations may make provision for the inspection of the home (para. 1(6)).

If a local authority are not satisfied that a children's home complies, or will comply, with requirements prescribed by the Secretary of State or with other requirements that appear to the local authority to be appropriate they must refuse the application (sch. 6, para. 1(4) and (8)). Where an application has neither been granted nor refused with a period of 12 months, beginning from the date when it was served on the local authority, it shall be deemed to have been refused by them and the applicant is deemed to have been notified of their refusal at the end of the period of 12 months (para. 1(9)). There is a restriction on further applications being made. If an application for registration is refused a further application cannot be made until six months have elapsed beginning with the date when the applicant was notified of the refusal (para. 9).

If a local authority are satisfied that a children's home complies, or will comply, with requirements prescribed by the Secretary of State and any requirements as appear to the local authority to be appropriate they must grant the application and in so doing may impose conditions, relating to the conduct of the home, as they think fit (paras 1(4) and 2). Where an application is granted the local authority must notify the applicant that the home has been registered as from such date as may be specified in the notice (para. 1(7)). From time to time a local authority may, with or without application from the person carrying on the home, vary any condition or impose an additional condition (para. 2(2)). If the person carrying on the home fails to comply with any condition, without reasonable excuse, he is guilty of an offence and liable on summary conviction to a fine (para. 2(3)).

The local authority which register the children's home become known as the 'responsible authority' and as such must review its registration every 12 months commencing with the anniversary of the date of the original registration (para. 3(1) and (2)). If when reviewing the registration the responsible authority are satisfied that the home is being carried on in accordance with relevant requirements then they must conclude that the registration should continue (para. 3(3)). 'Relevant requirements' include not only requirements prescribed by the Secretary of State and the local authority but also those imposed by the Secretary of State or local authority on the registration or regulations made under ss. 63 to 65 or under sch. 6, para. 10 (para. 3(6)). The responsible authority are required to serve a notice on the person carrying on the home of their decision as to whether registration should continue (sch. 6, para. 3(4)). The notice will require the person carrying on the home to pay a reasonable fee in respect of the review, the amount of which will be determined by the authority. Under para. 3(5) it is a condition of continued registration of the children's home that this fee is paid within 28 days of the notice being received by the person carrying on the home.

7.17 Cancellation of registration as a children's home

The person carrying on a registered children's home may at any time make application, in such manner and providing such particulars as may be prescribed by the Secretary of State, for the registration to be cancelled by the responsible body (sch. 6, para. 4(1)). In the case of a school registered as a children's home, if the authority are satisfied that the school is no longer one to which s. 63(6) (see 7.15) applies, the authority must give the person carrying on the home notice that registration is to be cancelled as from the date of the notice (para. 4(2)).

If, on any annual review of registration, or at any other time, it appears to the responsible authority that the home is being carried on otherwise than in accordance with relevant requirements then they may cancel the home's registration (para. 4(3)). In addition the responsible authority may at any time decide that a home's registration should be cancelled on the grounds that the person carrying on the home has been convicted of an offence or that any other person has been convicted of an offence in relation to the home (para. 4(4)).

7.18   Procedure

The procedure for registration of a children's home is the same as for registration of a voluntary home with some modifications (see sch. 6, para. 5).

As with voluntary homes, appeals lie to the Registered Homes Tribunal. By sch. 6, para. 8(6), a local authority must comply with any direction that is given by the Tribunal.

Restrictions are imposed as to when further applications can be made if registration is either refused or cancelled (sch. 6, para. 9). If an application is refused there cannot be a further application within six months beginning from the date on which the applicant received the notice of refusal (para. 9(1)). If the applicant appeals against refusal to register, the date on which the six-month period will start to run will be the date on which the appeal was either decided or abandoned (para. 9(2)). If the registration of a home is cancelled then again application for registration cannot be made for a period of six months beginning with the date of cancellation (para. 9(3)). If the person carrying on the home appeals against cancellation the date on which the six-month period will start to be calculated will be the date on which the appeal was decided or abandoned (para. 9(4)).

7.19   Regulations

The Secretary of State is enabled to make many regulations with regard to children's homes. Regulations made under sch. 6, para. 10, may:

    (a)   deal with the placing of children in a children's home;

    (b)   deal with the conduct of a children's home and make provision for securing the welfare of children in such homes;

    (c)   prescribe standards to which the premises are to conform;

    (d)   impose requirements as to the accommodation, staff and equipment to be provided in such homes;

    (e)   provide for the control and discipline of children in such homes;

    (f)   require information to be furnished to the local authority in respect of the facilities provided for visits and communication between the children in the home and their parents, anybody with parental responsibility and other persons connected with the child;

    (g)   impose requirements as to the keeping of records and giving of notices with respect to children in such homes;

    (h)   impose requirements as to the facilities which are provided for giving religious instruction to the children in the home;

    (i)   make provision for annual reviews;

    (j)   authorise the responsible authority to limit the number of children who may be accommodated in a children's home;

(k)   prohibit the use of accommodation for the purpose of restricting the liberty of children in such homes;

(l)   require notice to be given to the responsible authority of any change of person carrying on or in charge of a children's home or the premises used for such a home;

(m)   make provision similar to that made under Children Act 1989, s. 26, in respect of reviews of cases and procedures for considering representations and complaints.

The regulations may provide that to contravene or fail to comply with the regulations will be an offence (para. 10(3)) and the penalty for being guilty of such an offence will be a fine (para. 10(4)).

7.20   Duty of the person carrying on a children's home in respect of children's welfare

The duties that are imposed on the person carrying on a children's home in respect of children's welfare are the same as those imposed on a voluntary organisation running a voluntary home (s. 64: see 7.12). The local authority within whose area the children's home is situated have the same duties in respect of child welfare as they do where a home is run by a voluntary organisation. Section 64(4) states that s. 62 will apply to children's homes, which puts local authorities under a duty to satisfy themselves as to the welfare of children accommodated in such homes and gives them powers of entry, inspection of premises and children and of records (see 7.12 and 7.13).

7.21   Persons disqualified from running or being employed in a children's home

A person who is disqualified from privately fostering children (see chapter 8) is prohibited from running a children's home, being concerned in the management of a children's home or even having any financial interest in such a home unless he has disclosed to the responsible authority the fact that he has been disqualified and has obtained their written consent to his involvement in the children's home (s. 65(1)). A further prohibition is that anyone disqualified from privately fostering children may not be employed in a children's home without the local authority having been informed and giving their written consent (s. 65(2)). If a local authority refuse to give such written consent they must inform the applicant by way of a written notice which must include the reason for the refusal, the applicant's right to appeal to a Registered Homes Tribunal and the time within which his appeal must be made (s. 65(3)). If written consent has not been obtained or has been refused, any disqualified person who runs a children's home or is in any way involved with a children's home, or any disqualified person who is employed in such a home, will be guilty of an offence and liable to imprisonment for a term of up to six months and/or to a fine (s. 65(1) and (4)). Where a person has employed someone who has been disqualified from being a private foster-parent they also shall be guilty of an offence with the same penalty unless they prove that they did not know, and had no reasonable grounds for believing, that the person they were employing was so disqualified (s. 65(2), (4) and (5)).

Chapter Eight
Arrangements for Fostering Children

8.1 Introduction

Private fostering arrangements can be used in various situations where parents find themselves unable to care for their children. Sometimes parents feel unable to cope or there may be practical reasons, for instance, they may be in hospital, studying in other parts of the country or be abroad. Private foster-parents do not always keep adequate details, resulting in great difficulties, where local authorities have to intervene, in tracing the parents.

There are many excellent caring private foster-parents but it is those who cannot be so described who attract the greatest attention. In many areas of the country there have been cases of private fostering at its worst where clearly the prime motivation is money and the care of the foster-child is below any acceptable standard. The parents themselves may not always be fully aware of the standard of care that is being provided for their child. There have been cases where children have been presented clean, well dressed and with their own toys and bedroom when the parent visits, whereas in reality the child is frequently grubby, poorly dressed and sharing a bedroom with several other children but has not disclosed this to his or her parents because of threats from the private foster-parent.

As private fostering can tempt ruthless people interested only in earning money and not in the welfare of the children that they care for, it is important to impose upon local authorities duties to protect privately fostered children and give local authorities sufficient powers to enable them to do so. The provisions in the Children Act 1989 which relate to private fostering vary very little from the provisions in the Foster Children Act 1980 which was merely a re-enactment of the Children Act 1958. There are some minor additions and some rather worrying omissions.

Children Act 1989 places limits on the number of children that a person can foster. These limits apply to all fostering arrangements, whether arranged privately, by a local authority or by a voluntary organisation.

This chapter deals first of all with limits placed on the number of children who can be fostered by a person and then with the provisions which relate only to private fostering arrangements.

8.2 Limitation on the number of children that a person can foster

A person who fosters a child cannot foster more than three children at any one time. A person who exceeds this limit, and who does not come within an exception or is not exempted by a local authority, will be treated as running a children's home and will be subject to all the requirements and procedures that relate to such homes (s. 63(12) and sch. 7). The limitation on the number of children that a person can foster applies to all foster-parents and a person who fosters a child is interpreted to include a local-authority foster–parent, a foster–parent with whom a child has been placed by a voluntary organisation and a person who fosters a child privately (sch. 7, para. 1).

The description that is adopted for the rule that a person may not foster more than three children is 'the usual fostering limit' (sch. 7, para. 2). The usual fostering limit does not apply where a foster-parent is caring for more than three children when those children are siblings to each other (sch. 7, para. 3).

Another exception to the usual fostering limit is where a person is exempted from the usual fostering limit by the local authority within whose area the foster-parent lives (sch. 7, para. 4(1)). In deciding whether to exempt a person from the usual fostering limit the local authority must, by sch. 7, para. 4(2), have particular regard to the following matters:

(a) the number of children to be fostered;
(b) the arrangements for care and accommodation of the children;
(c) the intended and likely relationship between the children and foster-parent;
(d) the proposed duration of the fostering arrangement;
(e) whether the welfare of the fostered children, and any other children living in the same accommodation, will be safeguarded and promoted.

Where a local authority decide that it would be appropriate to exempt a person from the usual fostering limit they must inform that person of the exemption by written notice (sch. 7, para. 4(3)). The notice must include in addition to the fact of exemption the children described by name whom he may foster and any conditions that are a requirement of the exemption (para. 4(3)).

Where a local authority grant exemption from the usual fostering limit they may at any time, by notice in writing, vary or cancel the exemption itself or impose, vary or cancel a condition of that exemption (para. 4(4)).

The Secretary of State is enabled to make regulations which would amplify or modify these provisions insofar as is necessary to provide cases where children need to be placed as a matter of urgency (para. 4(5)).

If a person exceeds the usual fostering limit and is not fostering a sibling group and is not exempted by a local authority, then the person will be treated as if he were carrying on a children's home (para. 5(1)). A person who is exempted but fosters a child who is not named in the exemption and is then fostering more than three children will also be treated as if he were carrying on a children's home (para. 5(1)).

The fact that the children must be described by name in a notice of exemption clearly indicates that a person cannot be given a general exemption to foster a particular number of children in excess of the usual fostering limit. It is clear that if a foster-parent ceases to care for a foster-child then he cannot simply take on the care of another child but would need to ask the local authority to consider afresh whether they will grant exemption. Voluntary organisations must confirm that a person is exempted for each child that they propose to place with him or her as a foster-parent when they know that the usual fostering limit is being exceeded. A local authority would also need to be able to show that every exemption granted to a foster-parent, including their own foster-parents, had been considered anew on each occasion, taking into account the individual needs of each child and any change in circumstances in the household.

Every local authority is required to establish a procedure by which they will consider any representations or complaints made in respect of exemptions granted or denied or conditions imposed (para. 6(1)). The Secretary of State may make regulations as to how local authorities should consider representations and complaints (para. 6(2)).

8.3   Definition of a privately fostered child

Children Act 1989 contains an initial definition of a privately fostered child and then a list of instances that are deemed not to be private fostering. 'A privately fostered child' is stated by s. 66(1) to mean a child who is under the age of 16 years and who has been cared for, and provided with accommodation by, someone other than a parent, someone with parental responsibility or a relative. A child is not a privately fostered child if the person caring for and accommodating him has done so for a period of less than 28 days and does not intend to do so for any longer period (s. 66(2)). A child is not to be considered a privately fostered child in any of the following situations:

(a)   while the child is being looked after by a local authority (sch. 8, para. 1);

(b)   when he is being cared for in premises in which any parent, relative who has assumed responsibility for his care or person with parental responsibility is for the time being living (para. 2(1)(a));

(c)   in any children's home (para. 2(1)(b));

(d)   in accommodation provided by or on behalf of any voluntary organisation (para. 2(1)(c));

(e)   in any school in which he is receiving full-time education (subject to certain exceptions where children are cared for during school holidays at school (para. 2(1)(d) and see para. 9);

(f)   in any health service hospital (para. 2(1)(e));

(g)   in any residential care home, nursing home or mental nursing home (para. 2(1)(f));

(h)   in any home or institution not specified in para. 2 but provided, equipped and maintained by the Secretary of State (para. 2(1)(g));

(i)   if the child is being cared for by any person in compliance with either an order under Children and Young Persons Act 1969, (s. 7(7)(b) (supervision order in criminal proceedings) or a supervision requirement within the meaning of the Social Work (Scotland) Act 1968 (para. 3);

(j)   where the child is liable to be detained, or subject to guardianship, under the Mental Health Act 1983 (para. 4);

(k)   if the child is placed in the care of a person who proposes to adopt him under arrangements made by an adoption agency or the child is a protected child (para. 5).

Exemptions (c) to (h) do not apply if the person caring for the child is doing so in a personal capacity and not as part of their duties in relation to one of the establishments mentioned (sch. 8, para. 2(2)).

Under the Foster Children Act 1980 there were two situations when the definition of a fostered child was extended. First where a child lived at a school not maintained by a local education authority during school holidays and secondly where a child was over 16 but under 18 years of age and continued to live in a situation which but for his age would have been considered to be a fostering arrangement. The Children Act 1989 does not include the second extension to children who continue to be cared for by the same foster parents until they are 18 years of age. However, it does maintain and clarify the provision with regard to schools. Where a child is under 16 and a pupil at a school which is not maintained by a local education authority, if the child lives at the school for a period of more than two weeks during school holidays then the provisions in respect of private fostering will apply as if he were a privately fostered child. There are further detailed provisions with regard to notices and local authority exemptions in sch. 8, para. 9.

The welfare of children who board at independent schools has been of great concern since the exposé in the BBC television programme 'That's Life'. The reader is referred to chapter 10 which deals with the provisions of the Children Act 1989 concerning such children.

There is an important new addition to the extension of the meaning of a privately fostered child in the Children Act 1989. Where a child is disabled, the definition of 'a privately fostered child' being one who is under the age of 16 is extended to relate to a child under the age of 18 (s. 66(4)).

8.4   Notification of private fostering arrangements to local authorities

There has been concern that the procedure for notifying local authorities of children who are, have been or it is proposed will be, privately fostered is to be dealt with by regulations made by the Secretary of State and is not defined in the Children Act 1989. One of those to voice this concern was Tom Clarke, MP for Monklands West:

> . . . regulations to be made by the Secretary of State at some future date may define the notification procedure for private fostering arrangements. What is worrying about that is that a similar regulation-making power in the Foster Children Act 1980 was inserted and regulations were not made. We support the view of the Save the Children Fund, which argues convincingly that there is an absolute need for regulations on private fostering to be inserted into primary legislation and not left in limbo, perhaps never to be introduced. (HC Deb., 27 April 1989, col. 119.)

The regulations that the Secretary of State can make may (sch. 8, para. 7):

(a)   require any person who is, or proposes to be, involved (whether or not directly) in arranging for a child to be fostered privately to notify the appropriate local authority;

(b)   require any person who is a parent or has parental responsibility and who knows that it is proposed to arrange for his child to be fostered privately to notify the appropriate local authority;

(c)   require any parent of a privately fostered child, or person who has parental responsibility, to notify the appropriate local authority of any change of his address (the context of 'his address' indicates that this is the parents' address);

(d)   require any person who proposes to foster a child privately to notify the appropriate local authority of his proposal;

(e)   require any person who is fostering a child privately, or proposes to do so, to notify the appropriate local authority of any convictions, disqualification imposed on him from being a private foster-parent or any prohibition imposed on him to privately foster;

(f)   require any person who is fostering a child privately to notify the appropriate local authority of any change of his address;

(g)   require any person who is fostering privately to notify the appropriate local authority in writing of any person who begins, or ceases, to be part of the household;

(h)   require any person who has been fostering a child privately to notify the appropriate local authority that he has ceased to privately foster and, if the reason for ceasing to foster is that the child has died, require him to 'indicate' this in notifying the local authority.

'The appropriate local authority' is defined as the local authority within whose area the child is being fostered or within whose area it is proposed that he will be fostered (sch. 8, para. 6(6)(a)).

It is noteworthy that the regulation-making power in the Foster Children Act 1980 enabled parents to be subjected to more extensive requirements.

8.5   Persons disqualified from being private foster-parents

Under Children Act 1989, s. 68, the Secretary of State is empowered to make yet more regulations, this time in respect of persons who will be disqualified from being private foster-parents. Even though disqualified under such regulations a person can act as a private foster-parent if he or she discloses the facts to the appropriate local authority and obtains their written consent (s. 68(1)). The list of matters that may be covered by regulations (s. 68(2)) is rather vague, for example, that a person will be disqualified where 'a requirement of a kind [specified in the regulations] has been imposed at any time with respect to [any child who has been in his care], under or by virtue of any enactment'. More specifically, the list includes reference to persons who have been convicted, placed on probation or discharged absolutely or conditionally for an offence and persons who have had imposed upon them a prohibition against privately fostering. The other matters that the list refers to are, for example, where a child has been removed from the person's care as a result of a place of safety order, emergency protection order or care order; where that person's parental rights and duties have been assumed by a local authority under the Child Care Act 1980 or where that person has been refused registration under legislation in respect of nurseries and child-minders.

Requiring clarification is a matter raised by Michael Shersby, MP for Uxbridge:

> One of the points that the police have raised with me is whether [s. 68(2)(d), which refers to convictions, probation and discharge for an offence] applies to spent convictions under the Rehabilitation of Offenders Act. . . . the police and honourable members would find it helpful to know what procedures operate in respect of people who apply. . . . is there adequate protection to ensure that undesirable persons are not used as foster-parents? (HC Deb., 27 April, col. 1139.)

Whether this applies to spent convictions is not made clear in the provision. Regulations made under the provision or case law will have to supply the answer.

8.6   Local authority duties and powers

A duty is imposed on every local authority to satisfy themselves that the welfare of children who are privately fostered within their area is being satisfactorily safeguarded and promoted. Further, the local authority must ensure that those caring for privately fostered children are given such advice as appears to the local authority to be needed (s. 67(1)).

The Secretary of State is empowered to make regulations requiring that every child who is privately fostered within a local authority's area is visited by an officer of that authority in prescribed circumstances, on specified occasions or within specified periods (s. 67(2)). Regulations may also impose requirements which are to be met by any local authority, or officer of a local authority, in carrying out any of their functions under s. 67. Foster Children Act 1980 provided a similar regulation-making power but no regulations were ever made. However, under Foster Children Act 1980, s. 3(3)(a), local authorities were placed under a statutory duty to visit privately fostered children until such time as regulations were made. Therefore, unless the Secretary of State on this occasion does make regulations, privately fostered children will not be specifically protected and visited by an officer of a local authority who would be under a duty to be satisfied that the child's welfare was being met. The only protection left, without regulations, is that afforded to all children under s. 47 (see 5.3 above).

When regulations are made, if any person who is authorised by a local authority to visit a privately fostered child has reasonable cause to believe that such a child is being accommodated in premises within the authority's area, or it is proposed that he should be so accommodated, the local authority officer may, at any reasonable time, inspect those premises and any children who are there. In carrying out this duty the local authority officer must produce some duly authenticated document showing his authority if he is asked to do so (s. 67(3) and (4)).

If a local authority are not satisfied that the welfare of any privately fostered child within their area is being satisfactorily safeguarded or promoted they must take such steps as are reasonably practicable to secure that the care and accommodation of the child are undertaken by a parent, a person with parental responsibility or a relative (s. 67(5)(a)). The local authority are not required to take such steps if they consider that it would not be in the best interests of the child to do so. In addition, the local authority must consider whether they should exercise any of their other functions under the Children Act 1989 (s. 67(5)(b)). Foster Children Act 1980, ss. 12 and 13, specifically provided for local authorities to make applications to the juvenile court for authority to remove privately fostered children from unsuitable surroundings or from persons who were unfit to care for them and, furthermore a justice of the peace was able to issue a search warrant. The relevant provision is now s. 102, to which reference should be made.

Local authorities are given the power to prohibit a person from undertaking private fostering. Under s. 69, the local authority for the area within which a child is being privately fostered, or it is proposed that he should be fostered, may impose a prohibition if they are of the opinion that the private foster-parent is not a suitable person to foster a child, the premises are not suitable or it would be prejudicial to the welfare of the child for him to be, or continue to be, accommodated by that person in those premises. Section 69 applies where a person proposes to foster a child privately or is already fostering a child privately (s. 69(11)).

A prohibition imposed may prohibit the person from privately fostering any child in any premises within the local authority's area or any child in specified premises (s. 69(3)(a) and (b)). In addition, a local authority may prohibit a person from fostering privately an identified child in specified premises (s. 69(3)(c)). Where a local authority have imposed such a prohibition they may, if they think fit, cancel the prohibition either of their own volition or on application of the person concerned if they are satisfied that the prohibition is no longer justified (s. 69(4)). Previously, under the Foster Children Act 1980, a person prohibited from privately fostering could only make an application for cancellation on the ground that his or her circumstances had changed. Although this is not included it is likely that in reality such an application would not be successful unless the applicant's circumstances had altered.

Where such a prohibition is imposed the person on whom it is imposed must be informed by notice in writing informing him of the reason for the prohibition, his right of appeal and the time within which such an appeal may be made (s. 69(7)).

Local authorities are given a power to impose requirements on those who are privately fostering children (sch. 8, para. 6). Where a person is privately fostering any child, or proposes to do so, the local authority for the area concerned may impose requirements in respect of:

(a)   the number, age and sex of the children who may be fostered,
(b)   the standard of the accommodation and equipment to be provided for the children,
(c)   the arrangements to be made with respect to their health and safety,
(d)   particular arrangements which must be made with respect to the provision of care for the children.

Where such a requirement is imposed it is the duty of the private foster-parent to comply with any requirement before the end of such period as the local authority may specify (sch. 8, para. 6(1)). The duty to comply with a requirement does not arise where the person was only proposing to foster privately and does not in fact carry out that proposal.

When imposing a requirement, a local authority may also impose a prohibition which will come into effect when the time specified for compliance with the requirement has expired and the person has not in fact complied with the requirement (s. 69(6)).

Under Foster Children Act 1980, s. 9(1)(d) to (h), there were further matters in respect of which requirements could be imposed. These included such matters as particulars of the person in charge of the children, the number and qualifications of persons employed in looking after children and fire precautions. Presumably, such matters could still be subject to requirements under sch. 8, para. 6(1)(d): 'particular arrangements which must be made with respect to the provision of care'. However, it is surprising that such important matters should have been omitted.

A local authority may limit a requirement to a particular child or a class of child (sch. 8, para. 6(2)). Further, the local authority may limit the requirement so that it will only apply when the number of children fostered exceeds a specified number, except that such a limitation cannot be made to a requirement if it refers to the number, age and sex of the children who are to be fostered (para. 6(1) and (3)).

Any requirement must be imposed by way of notice in writing addressed to the person on whom it is to be imposed and informing him of the reason for the requirement, his right of appeal and the time within which he may appeal (para. 6(4)).

8.7 Offences

Under Children Act 1989, s. 70, a person is guilty of an offence in the following situations;

(a)   Being required to give any notice or information, he fails, without reasonable excuse, to give the notice within a specified time or, without reasonable excuse, to give the information within a reasonable time (s. 70(1)(a)(i) and (ii)). What is new to this offence is the inclusion of 'without reasonable excuse'.

(b)   Being required to give any notice or information, he makes, or causes or procures another person to make, any statement in the notice or information which he knows to be false or misleading in a material particular (s. 70(1)(a)(iii)).

(c)   He refuses to allow a privately fostered child to be visited by a duly authorised officer of a local authority.

(d)   He intentionally obstructs an authorised officer exercising the power to inspect the premises and children.

(e)   He contravenes s. 68 (see 8.5). If a person contravenes s. 68(3), which relates to persons disqualified from fostering being in the same household or employed in the household of a person who is privately fostering, he is not guilty of an offence if he proves that he did not know, and had no reasonable ground for believing, that any person was so disqualified.

(f)   He fails without reasonable excuse to comply with any requirement imposed by a local authority.

(g)   He accommodates a privately fostered child in any premises in contravention of a prohibition imposed by a local authority.

(h)   He knowingly causes to be published, or publishes, an advertisement which he knows contravenes sch. 8, para. 10 (see 8.8).

In addition, any person who is required to give a notice (which is likely to include parents and others in addition to private foster-parents) and fails to give the notice within the time specified, proceedings for the offence may be brought at any time within six months from the date when evidence of the offence came to the knowledge of the local authority despite the provisions of Magistrates' Courts Act 1980, s. 127(1), in respect of time-limits for proceedings.

A person guilty of an offence in respect of failure to give notice or provide information (as set out in (a) and (b) above) is liable to a fine not exceeding level 5 (s. 70(3)). A person guilty of an offence in respect of refusing to allow an officer of a local authority to visit or intentionally obstructing an officer wishing to inspect premises or with regard to prohibited advertising (as set out in (c), (d) and (h) above) is liable to a fine not exceeding level 3 (s. 70(4)). A person guilty of an offence as set out in (f) above is liable to a fine not exceeding level 4 (s. 70(6)).

A person guilty of an offence in respect of disqualification or prohibition (as set out in (e) and (g) above) is liable on summary conviction to imprisonment for a term not exceeding six months and/or to a fine not exceeding level 5 (s. 70(5)). Under the Foster Children Act 1980 there was specific provision enabling local authorities to prosecute for these offences but no such provision is included in the Children Act 1989.

8.8   Prohibition of advertisements

Under sch. 8, para. 10, there is a prohibition on publishing advertisements which indicate that a person will undertake, or will arrange for, a child to be privately fostered, unless the advertisement states that person's name and address. Omitted from the Children Act 1989 is the Secretary of State's ability to make regulations prohibiting parents and many others from placing advertisements in respect of private fostering which was contained in Foster Children Act 1980, s. 15.

8.9   Avoidance of insurances on lives of privately fostered children

Under Children Act 1989, sch. 8, para. 11, a person who fosters a child privately, and for reward, shall be deemed for the purposes of the Life Assurance Act 1774 to have no interest in the life of the child.

8.10   Appeals

A person notified of a requirement, refusal, prohibition, condition, variation or cancellation has a right to appeal to the court but must do so within 14 days from the date on which he was so notified, presumably the date on which he received the notification (sch. 8, para. 8(1) and (2)). A private foster-parent may appeal against any of the following but a local-authority foster-parent or a foster-parent for a voluntary organisation may only appeal against (a) to (d) of the following (sch. 8, para. 8(8)):

(a)   a requirement as to:

    (i)   the number, age and sex of the children to be fostered,
    (ii)   the standard of accommodation and equipment,
    (iii)   the arrangements with respect to health and safety,
    (iv)   particular arrangements with regard to provision of care;

(b)   a refusal of consent to foster a child when disqualified;
(c)   a prohibition on fostering privately;
(d)   a refusal to cancel a prohibition;
(e)   a refusal to make an exemption to the usual fostering limit;
(f)   a condition imposed on an exemption to the usual fostering limit;
(g)   a variation or cancellation of such an exemption.

Where an appeal is made against (a), (f) or (g) then these shall not have effect while the appeal is pending (para. 8(3)). Where the court allows an appeal against (a) or (c) then the court may, instead of cancelling a requirement, vary it or allow more time for compliance, and if an absolute prohibition has been imposed, the court may substitute a prohibition on using the premises after a specified time if certain requirements are not complied with (para. 8(4)). Any requirement or prohibition imposed by a court will be deemed to have been made by a local authority (para. 8(5)).

Where the court allows an appeal against (e), (f) or (g), the court may make an exemption, impose a condition on an exemption or vary an exemption (para. 8(6)).

8.11   Transitional provisions

Where a foster child, as defined in the Foster Children Act 1980, is being cared for in circumstances which would lead to his being treated as being provided with accommodation in a children's home and not as privately fostered then if he continued in such accommodation once Part VIII of the Act is in force an offence would be committed. However, if an application for registration is made within three months of this part coming into force and the application has not been refused or, if it has been refused, either the time for appeal has not expired or an appeal is pending then no offence is committed (sch. 14, para. 32). During this period of grace the child will be treated as if privately fostered.

Chapter Nine
Adoption

9.1 Introduction

Children Act 1989, s. 88(1), states that 'The Adoption Act 1976 shall have effect subject to amendments made by Part I of Schedule 10', and subsection (2) makes a similar statement in relation to the Adoption (Scotland) Act 1978. Part I of sch. 10 contains many amendments which merely bring the adoption legislation into line with the Children Act 1989, for example, by substituting 'parental responsibility' for 'parental rights and duties'. There are, more importantly, clarifications of existing provisions and some innovative provisions. Before dealing with sch. 10, however, it is necessary to consider other changes to adoption law made by the Children Act 1989.

Adoption Act 1976, s. 26, which gives the judge hearing an adoption application the power to commit a child to care or place him under supervision if the application is dismissed is now repealed. As a result of this, where a judge hearing an adoption application considers that a child should be committed to care or placed under supervision he will have to invite the local authority to make an application for such an order (see Children Act 1989, s. 37). Adoption proceedings will be 'family proceedings' under s. 8(4) of the Children Act 1989 and as a result the court considering the adoption application, although no longer able of its own volition to make care or supervision orders, will be in a position to make orders with regard to matters not presently within the court's remit, for example, residence orders and contact orders. In recent years judges have been more prepared to attach conditions of access to adoption orders especially in respect of grandparents. Conditions have only been made where all concerned are in agreement. A judge will now be able, it appears, to make a contact order in the course of adoption proceedings but, as with conditions of access, it is unlikely that such an order would be made if the adopters and all concerned were not in full accord. This could have a significant effect on the adoption of children in the care of local authorities.

Where an adoption application is made in respect of a child in care, the application to dispense with parental agreement in the majority of cases is on the basis that the child is subject to a care order and access has been terminated so, as the parent has neither the child nor access to the child, the parent is unreasonable in withholding agreement to adoption. Under existing adoption law the judge, unless the adoption is in the High Court, is unable to discharge a care order or order that access be reinstated. However, as adoption proceedings will be family proceedings then it appears that the adoption judge will have the power to order contact, make a residence order or discharge the care order. This should not adversely affect applications where the parents were given every opportunity to achieve rehabilitation or the parents abused or neglected a child to such a degree that rehabilitation was never possible. However, there are many cases where it is not clear that the parents were given an adequate opportunity. The parent who wants to resist adoption of his or her child who is in care now has the opportunity of making applications in the adoption proceedings that could lead to a review of the child's position in care.

9.2 Who can adopt

The Children Act 1989 retains the existing legal position that if two people want to adopt a child then they must be married to each other. It also retains the position that where a couple apply to adopt, if neither the husband nor the wife is a parent of the child, then they must both have attained the age of 21 years (sch. 10, para. 4; Adoption Act 1976, s. 14(1) and (1A)). A change that is brought about by the Children Act 1989 is that where one of the couple seeking to adopt is the father or mother of the child, then he or she need only have attained the age of 18 years so long as his or her spouse has attained 21 years (sch. 10, para. 4; Adoption Act 1976, s. 14(1B)). Most frequently this will apply to young mothers who have had a child while unmarried and have subsequently married a man other than the father. If she is under 21 years of age then it is likely that their marriage will be of fairly short duration. Clearly a judge would take into account the length of the marriage but as the application would be by agreement, the role of the reporting officer in explaining the legal consequences of adoption to such a mother, who has sole parental responsibility, will be even more important than with older mothers. Given the young age of the mother the reporting officer would also need to be careful to ascertain that before she signed her agreement to adoption that she did so with full understanding and without undue influence from her husband or other relatives.

9.3 Step-parent adoptions

Adoption Act 1976, s. 14(3) (which obliges the court considering the adoption of a stepchild to dismiss the application if it considers that the matter would be better dealt with by a custody order) is to be repealed. It remains to be seen whether this will affect the outcome of such applications.

9.4 Freeing for adoption

As wardship will no longer be available to local authorities to assist them in their plans for adoption of children in their care (see 5.11), there is likely to be an increase in applications to free children for adoption. The making of an order freeing a child for adoption will give the adoption agency the power to deny contact with the child to a person with parental responsibility and that person will be unable to apply to the court for an order for contact.

9.4.1   Pre-conditions for the application

Where an application to free a child for adoption is made, then, as with an adoption application, each parent or guardian must agree or an application to dispense with their agreement must be made.

By Adoption Act 1976, s. 18, an application to free a child for adoption can only be made if one of the parents, or guardians, consents or the child is in the care of the adoption agency making the application and that agency is also applying for an order dispensing with parental agreement. There have been two interpretations of what is meant by 'care' in this context. First, that the child must be in care under a court order or subject to a local authority resolution assuming parental rights and duties, as otherwise there is no authority for the child to be retained by the adoption agency should a parent request the child's return before the commencement of proceedings to free for adoption. The second view is that 'care' includes *de facto* care: the fact that the adoption agency has the child and places him with foster-parents or elsewhere amount to the child being in the 'care' of the adoption agency. This interpretation has been particularly attractive to voluntary adoption agencies who do not have any powers to seek a court order committing a child to their care.

The opportunity has been taken in the Children Act 1989 to clarify what is meant by being in 'care' in Adoption Act 1976, s. 18. A new subsection (2A) is added to s. 18 which states that 'a child is in the care of an adoption agency, if the adoption agency is a local authority and he is in their care' (Children Act 1989, sch. 10, para. 6). Under the Children Act 1989, if a child is 'in the care of' a local authority, rather than 'accommodated' by them, then this means he is subject to a care order (see s. 105(1); sch. 10, para. 30(9)). It is now clear that if neither parent consents to adoption and the child is not the subject of a care order then an application to free the child for adoption cannot be made. This is in keeping with the spirit of the Children Act 1989 of partnership between the parent and the local authority.

The same clarification of the meaning of 'care' is made with regard to removal of children while an application is pending (Children Act 1989, sch. 10, para 13; Adoption Act 1976, s. 27(2A)).

9.4.2   Fathers who do not have parental responsibility

Where an application is made for an order freeing a child for adoption then there is a specific requirement to ascertain whether the putative father intends to seek an order for custody and if so whether he would be likely to succeed (Adoption Act 1976, s. 18(7)). The Children Act 1989 rephrases this obligation to bring the provision up to date. Before making an order freeing a child for adoption the court must satisfy itself, with regard to any man claiming to be the father but who does not have parental responsibility, that he does not intend to apply for parental responsibility nor for a residence order (under ss. 4 and 9 respectively) or that if he did then it is likely that the application would be refused (sch. 10, para. 6(3); Adoption Act 1976, s. 18(7)).

9.4.3   Effect of revoking an order freeing a child for adoption

The position with regard to the class of persons who can apply to revoke an order freeing a child for adoption is unchanged. The opportunity to widen the scope of those who can make such an application has not been taken. The adoption agency remains unable to apply for revocation where it has become clear that the child will not be adopted. If the parents of the child made a declaration that they wished to have no further involvement then they can not apply to revoke the order. As a freeing order acts as an adoption order in favour of the adoption agency the child would remain a 'freed' child without an individual whom he could call his parent but with an organisation who would be his legal parent for ever.

Example 9.1   An order is made freeing Tony, who is mentally handicapped, for adoption. His parents have made a declaration that they wish to have no further involvement once the freeing order has been made and they understand that this means they will not come within the definition of 'former parent' and therefore will have no right to seek revocation of the order should Tony not have his home with adopters on the anniversary of the freeing order. Tony is placed with prospective adopters but they reject him. It becomes apparent that another adoptive home will not be found for Tony. As Tony has been freed for adoption the agency who were granted the order have in effect adopted him and have sole parental responsibility for him. If at any time during Tony's life there should be a need to know who his legal parents are, for example, for the purposes of the mental health legislation, then this would be the adoption agency for as long as it existed.

Where an order freeing a child for adoption is revoked this acts to extinguish the parental responsibility given to the adoption agency under that order (sch. 10, para. 8(2); Adoption Act 1976, s. 20(3)). Revocation of the freeing order operates so as to give parental responsibility to the child's mother and to the father where he was married to the mother at the time of the birth (sch. 10, para. 8(2); Adoption Act 1976, s. 20(3)). In addition it operates to revive a parental responsibility order made under Children Act 1989, s. 4, any parental responsibility agreement or any appointment of a guardian, whether appointed by a court or by any other means (sch. 10, para. 8(2); Adoption Act 1976, s. 20(3)).

Other than the orders specifically stated to be revived by the revocation of a freeing order, such revocation does not act to revive other orders made under the Children Act 1989 nor does it revive duties with regard to maintenance or parental responsibility for the period of the freeing order (sch. 10, para. 8(2); Adoption Act 1976, s. 20(3A)).

9.5   Protected child

Where a child who has not been placed by an adoption agency but is to be the subject of an adoption application and, in accordance with the requirements of Adoption Act 1976, s. 22, the local authority have been notified of the applicant's intention to adopt then the child becomes a 'protected child'. For as long as the child is a protected child then the local authority are under a duty to ensure that the child is visited from time to time and satisfy themselves as to the child's well-being. The Children Act 1989 takes the opportunity of clarifying when a child ceases to be a protected child. In addition to the existing circumstances set out in Adoption Act 1976, s. 32(4), the Children Act 1989 provides that a child will cease to be a protected child in the following circumstances: (a) on the refusal of an adoption application; (b) on the child's marriage; (c) where no application for adoption has been commenced after the expiry of two years from the giving of the notice of intention to adopt (sch. 10, para. 18(4); Adoption Act 1976, s. 32(4)). This last circumstance is perhaps the most important as it means that a local authority having been given notification of intention to adopt will no longer be in doubt about when their obligation to visit a protected child will cease.

9.6   Notification to local authority of intention to adopt

Where a child has not been placed with an adoption applicant by an adoption agency then the applicant is required by Adoption Act 1976, s. 22, to notify the local authority of his intention to adopt at least three months before the hearing of his application to adopt. The Children Act 1989 amends this requirement to the extent that the notification to the local authority must have been at least three months but not more than two years before the hearing of the adoption application (sch. 10, para. 10; Adoption Act 1976, s. 22(1A)). This amendment is required to bring the provision into accord with s. 32 concerning the circumstances when a child ceases to be a protected child (see 9.4).

The requirement refers to notification of the local authority in whose area the applicants have their home but as the applicants may have moved between giving notice and the adoption hearing, clarification was thought desirable. It has been made clear that this reference is to the area in which the applicants were living at the time when they gave notice of their intention to adopt (sch. 10, para 10; Adoption Act 1976, s. 22(1B)).

9.7   Disclosure of birth records of adopted children

An adopted person who is at least 18 years old and whose birth records are kept by the Registrar General may apply for information that will enable him to obtain his original birth certificate (Adoption Act 1976, s. 51(1)). The Registrar General must supply this information and must inform the applicant that counselling services are available to him (Adoption Act 1976, s. 51(1) and (3)). These provisions have been reworded by the Children Act 1989 without making substantial changes (sch. 10, para. 20).

9.7.1   Person adopted before 12 November 1975

The right to receive information that would enable the adopted person to obtain his original birth certificate at present only applies to people who had been adopted after 12 November 1975. Those adopted before this date are only able to receive such information if they attend for an interview with a counsellor: either at the General Register Office or one employed by a local authority or an adoption agency where an arrangement existed with that agency. This means that the person adopted before 12 November 1975 has no choice but to receive counselling whereas the person adopted after that date only has to be offered this facility. This is justified on the basis that the parents of those adopted prior to this date had gone through the adoption process believing that in the future there would be no way in which their child would be able to trace them. However, it had the important consequence that adopted persons not living in England or Wales were unable to obtain any information unless they were in a position to travel and for people living outside the United Kingdom this was often not possible. This has been a very real problem for hundreds of people adopted in this country but who now live abroad. The opportunity has been taken in the Children Act 1989 to facilitate information being given to adopted persons who live outside the United Kingdom.

Where an application is received from a person adopted before 12 November 1975 the Registrar General can still only supply the information if the person has attended an interview with a counsellor (sch. 10, para. 20; Adoption Act 1976, s. 51(7)). However, where the Registrar General is prevented from providing information by this provision to a person who was adopted before 12 November 1975 and who is not living in the United Kingdom then the Registrar General may supply the information to any body of persons which the Registrar General is satisfied is suitable to provide counselling to the applicant and which has notified the Registrar General that it is prepared to provide such counselling (sch. 10, para. 20; Adoption Act 1976, s. 51(7) and (18)). Those adopted before 12 November 1975 whether they live in the United Kingdom or abroad will now be able to receive information via a counsellor.

9.7.2 Adoption contact register

The system of providing information sufficient to enable the adopted person to obtain his or her birth certificate and counselling usually only provides the adopted person with information about his or her parents which is out of date. It does not allow for brothers, sisters, grandparents or any other relative to make it known in any way that they would be interested in being contacted by the adopted person. An innovative step is taken in the Children Act 1989 by making provision for an Adoption Contact Register (sch. 10, para. 21; Adoption Act 1976, s. 51A).

Under this provision the Registrar General must maintain an Adoption Contact Register in two parts with Part I to be in respect of the adopted persons and Part II in respect of relatives of adopted persons (sch. 10, para. 21; Adoption Act 1976, s. 51A(2)).

In Part I of the register must be entered, on payment of any fee that may be required, the name and address of any adopted person who gives notice that he wishes to contact any relative provided certain conditions are fulfilled (sch. 10, para. 21; Adoption Act 1976, s. 51A(3)). These conditions are that (a) the Registrar General keeps a record of that adopted person's birth, (b) the adopted person has attained 18 years of age and (c) he has been provided with information under Adoption Act 1976, s. 51, or the Registrar General is satisfied that the adopted person already has sufficient information for him to obtain his birth certificate (sch. 10, para. 21; Adoption Act 1976, s. 51A(4)).

The address to be entered in either Part I or Part II need not be the individual's address but can be a contact address. 'Address' is defined to include any address at or through which the person can be contacted (sch. 10, para. 21; Adoption Act 1976, s. 51A(13)(b).

In Part II of the register must be entered, on payment of any fee that may be required, the name and address of any person who gives notice that he wishes to contact an adopted person provided he fulfils certain conditions (sch. 10, para. 21; Adoption Act 1976, s. 51A(5)). The person wishing to contact an adopted person must be at least 18 years old, a relative and have such information as would enable him to obtain the adopted person's birth certificate. 'Relative' is widely defined as any person, other than an adopted person, who is related to the adopted person by blood, including half-blood, or by marriage (sch. 10, para. 21; Adoption Act 1976, s. 51A(13)(a)).

The Adoption Contact Register may be kept by means of a computer and will not be open to public inspection. Any person whose name is entered in either Part may notify the Registrar General that he wishes the entry in respect of him to be cancelled (sch. 10, para. 21; Adoption Act 1976, s. 51A(10) to (12)). Any adopted person whose name appears on Part I of the register must be informed by the Registrar General of any name and address of a relative of his that is entered in Part II of the register (sch. 10, para. 21; Adoption Act 1976, s. 51A(9)). The expression used in the provision is that the Registrar General must 'transmit' the information and it appears that the expectation is that the Registrar General will send the information by post.

Although this development has been welcomed it has also been criticised for being inflexible, not providing an adequate support system and for the manner in which information will be provided. Mr Ronald Fearn MP commented that the 'consortium of adoption support groups . . . were naturally pleased when this measure was introduced . . . however, they felt that the proposed operation of the service as outlined . . . will benefit few and have the potential to result in great distress for many individuals and their families' (HC Deb., vol. 158, cols 497 and 498). As a result of this concern some amendments were made. The fact that an adopted person or a relative must be at least 18 years of age before they could be entered on the register was included as a result of this concern. This also led to the inclusion of a definition of 'address' as meaning any address at or through which the person concerned may be contacted. Mr David Mellor, Minister for Health, accurately stated that 'many relatives will no doubt be happy to give their own address, but care and sensitivity are needed where people are seeking knowledge of each other in these often delicate circumstances. Some people prefer to make a first approach through an intermediary with skill and experience in smoothing the path for both parties . . . some voluntary agencies . . . have already expressed a willingness to provide their addresses and services and no doubt others will be equally willing' (HC Deb., vol. 158, col. 499).

However, the main concern has perhaps been about the method by which the information will be passed on to the adopted person. Mr David Mellor, Minister for Health, gave the following explanation: 'the register will be held by the Registrar General in circumstances where he will have no facilities for offering assistance to those who wish to make contact. However, the changes that we have introduced will enable people to make use of professional and other specialist services. As part of the administration of the scheme, the Registrar General will inform all users of the services, such as the social services departments and other agencies, from whom advice and assistance may be obtained.' (HC Deb., vol. 158, col. 498.) Mr Mellor did not dismiss the genuine doubts felt and recognised these issues but stated that 'Obviously, all these issues will, in due course, be part of a wider review of adoption law, but I cannot advocate any further changes until that point' (HC Deb., vol. 158, col. 499).

9.8 Adoption allowances

Children Act 1989, sch. 10, para. 25, inserts s. 57A into the Adoption Act 1976 to deal with adoption allowances. Adoption allowance schemes approved under Adoption Act 1976, s. 57(4), are to be revoked when s. 57A comes into force and future adoption allowance provision will be made in accordance with s. 57A and any regulations made under that section by the Secretary of State. The regulations that the Secretary of State may make will be for the purpose of enabling adoption agencies to pay allowances to persons who have adopted or who intend to adopt a child placed by an adoption agency (sch. 10, para. 25; Adoption Act 1976, s. 57A(1)).

The regulations may in particular make provision with regard to the following:

(a) the procedure to be followed by a adoption agency when deciding whether a particular person should be paid an allowance;
(b) the circumstances in which adoption allowances may be paid;
(c) the factors to be taken into account when deciding the amount of an adoption allowance;
(d) the procedure for review, variation and termination of adoption allowances;
(e) the information about adoption allowances to be given to prospective adopters by an adoption agency (sch. 10, para. 25; Adoption Act 1976, s. 57A(3)).

Adoption Act 1976, s. 57(1), which prohibits payments in consideration of adoption, will not apply to adoption allowance payments made under this provision (sch. 10, para. 25; Adoption Act 1976, s. 57A(2)). Similarly s. 57(1) will not apply to any payment made in accordance with a scheme which has been revoked and will not apply to any person to whom payment was made under such a scheme before its revocation (sch. 10, para. 25; Adoption Act 1976, s. 57A(5)). A person who may lawfully receive payments under a scheme prior to its revocation may choose instead to receive payments under these new regulations.

9.9 Panels of guardians *ad litem* and reporting officers

Local authority administration of panels of guardians *ad litem* and reporting officers who are appointed in adoption proceedings has, like the panels for care proceedings, been criticised. Under the Children Act 1989 the Secretary of State is empowered to mitigate this problem by providing by regulation that panels be administered jointly by two or more local authorities. Although not an ideal solution, if such regulations are made they will in part answer some of the criticisms of the existing system.

Under Adoption Act 1976, s. 65A (sch. 10, para. 29), the Secretary of State may make regulations providing for the establishment of panels of persons from whom guardians *ad litem* and reporting officers must be selected. The regulations may deal with the following matters; (a) constitution, administration and procedures of panels; (b) requiring two or more local authorities to manage such a panel jointly; (c) defrayment of local authority expenses incurred by members of the panels; (d) payment by local authorities of fees and allowances for members of panels; (e) qualifications for membership of a panel; (f) training to be given to panel members; (g) as to the cooperation required of specified local authorities in the provision of panels in specified areas; (h) for monitoring the work of guardians *ad litem* and reporting officers.

Rules of court may make provision as to the assistance which a court may require of any guardian *ad litem* or reporting officer (sch. 10, para. 29; Adoption Act 1976, s. 65A(3)).

Chapter Ten

Welfare of Children Accommodated in Independent Schools, Child-Minders and Day Care of Young Children

10.1 Introduction

During the passage of the Children Act 1989 through Parliament, concern was expressed about gaps in the legislation which as a result of which children in independent boarding-schools and children with child-minders and in day care were less protected than other children who are accommodated or cared for away from their parents.

The concern with regard to day care and child-minders arose largely from a recognition of the number of mothers who are employed, the increasing importance of private provision of day-care facilities and the resultant danger that without regulation such facilities might not provide adequate care for the children looked after. The result is the inclusion in Children Act 1989 of provisions which bring the degree of protection of children looked after by child-minders and in day care into line with other forms of non-parental care.

The inclusion of s. 87, which relates to the welfare of children accommodated at independent schools, acknowledges that there was no statutory provision requiring any agency to be satisfied about the welfare of children who were boarded at independent schools unless there was evidence of abuse and that even in that situation it would only be the welfare of those in respect of whom specific allegations of abuse were made. Public concern about such children started as a result of the broadcast on BBC television of the 'That's Life' investigation into sexual abuse of children at a particular boarding-school.

10.2 Duties imposed to protect children accommodated at independent schools

Mr David Mellor, Minister for Health, set out during the House of Commons debate on 23 October 1989 the three main elements contained in what is now s. 87 of the Children Act 1989:

First, a new duty is placed on the proprietor or any person conducting an independent school that provides accommodation for any child to safeguard and promote the child's welfare. This provision applies to independent schools

that are not categorised as children's homes or residential care homes. . . .
Secondly, any local authority, within the area of which the accommodation is
provided, must do what is reasonably practical to determine whether the
child's welfare is adequately safeguarded and promoted while he is accommodated by the school. . . . The third element is that where the local authority
consider that the person or proprietor conducting the school is failing to
discharge his welfare duty . . . the authority must notify the Secretary of State.
(HC Deb., vol. 158, col. 615.)

10.3   Independent schools that come within the provision

'Independent school' is defined in Education Act 1944, s. 114(1), as amended. It is
'any school at which full-time education is provided for five or more pupils of
compulsory school age (whether or not such education is also provided for pupils
under or over that age), not being a school maintained by a local education
authority or a special school not maintained by a local education authority'.

All independent schools fall within Children Act 1989, s. 87, unless the school
is deemed to be a children's home or is a residential care home (s. 87(2)).

An independent school is a children's home if it provides accommodation for
up to 50 children and it is not approved by the Secretary of State for Education
under the Education Act 1981 (s. 63(6)). As such a school would be a children's
home, there will be duties on those running the school and on the local authority
in respect of the welfare of the children who are accommodated there (see
chapter 7).

A 'residential care home', as defined by the Registered Homes Act 1984, is a
home that provides board and personal care for persons in need of personal care,
for example, by reason of disablement, dependence on alcohol or drugs or past or
present mental disorder. There are detailed provisions concerning registration
and inspection, and regulations have been made under this legislation.

10.4   Local authority powers

Any person authorised by a local authority for the purpose of enabling the local
authority to discharge their duty of determining whether a child's welfare is
adequately safeguarded and promoted may at any reasonable time enter any
independent school within their area which provides accommodation for any
child (Children Act 1989, s. 87(3) and (5)).

Any person entering an independent school in this capacity may carry out such
inspection of premises, children and records as is prescribed by regulations made
by the Secretary of State (s. 87(6)). As with so many of the provisions of the
Children Act 1989, this provision will only be really effective if the Secretary of
State provides adequate regulations. Any person authorised to inspect records is
entitled at any reasonable time to have access to, and inspect and check the
operation of, any computer and any associated apparatus or material which is or
has been in use in connection with the records in question (s. 87(8)(a)). The
person authorised to inspect records may not be conversant with computers or
the program in use and, perhaps with this in mind, the authorised person may
require the person by whom or on whose behalf the computer is or has been used,

or any person having charge of, or otherwise concerned with the operation of, the computer, apparatus or material, to afford him such assistance as he may reasonably require (s. 87(8)(b)).

Any person who intentionally obstructs another in exercising any power conferred under these provisions or regulations is guilty of an offence and liable to a fine (s. 87(9)).

10.5 Registration of child-minders and persons providing day care

Every local authority must keep a register of persons acting as child-minders within their area and those who provide day care for children under eight in their area (s. 71(1)). Any such register must be open to public inspection and may be kept by means of a computer (s. 71(15)).

A 'child-minder' is defined as a person who looks after on domestic premises one or more children under the age of eight, for reward and for a period or total period which exceeds two hours a day (s. 71(1) and (2)). 'Domestic premises' are defined as premises which are wholly or mainly used as a private dwelling and 'premises' includes any vehicle (s. 71(12)).

A person who provides day care is one who looks after children under eight years of age, other than on domestic premises, for a period or total period which exceeds two hours a day (s. 71(1) and (2)). If a person provides day care of this type at different premises then each must be separately registered with the local authority for the area within which the premises are situated (s. 71(3)).

Limiting these definitions to persons who look after children for more than two hours a day will take out of the scope of these provisions many, if not all, of those who care for children after school until their mothers arrive to collect them. However, many such persons would be exempt from registration because they do not look after the children 'for reward'.

Excluded from the need to be registered are the parent of the child, a relative of the child, any person with parental responsibility for the child or a foster-parent of the child (s. 71(4)). The term 'foster-parent' is given its expected meaning under this section of including local authority foster-parents, foster-parents for voluntary organisations and private foster-parents (s. 71(14)).

Also excluded from registration are nannies who are employed to look after children wholly or mainly in the home of their employer or nannies with two employers who care for the children wholly or mainly in the home of either of their employers (s. 71(5) and (6)). A nanny is defined as a person employed to look after children by either a parent of the child, or a person with parental responsibility or by a relative (for the scope of relative see s. 105) of the child who has assumed responsibility for the child's care (s. 71(13)).

Schedule 9 sets out the matters that must be contained in an application for registration and provides for payment of a fee (sch. 9, para. 1). It also includes provision for regulations to be made by the Secretary of State in respect of disqualification of certain persons from registering (para. 2). Further there are lists of certain schools and other establishments that are exempted from registration (paras 3 and 4). The schedule also allows for fees to be charged for inspection of premises and for cooperation between authorities in that an authority can request the help of another authority and that other authority must comply if the request is compatible with their own statutory duties (paras 7 and 8).

10.6   Refusal by local authority to register

A local authority may refuse to register a person as a child-minder on any of the following grounds:

(a)   they are satisfied that the applicant or any person looking after, or likely to be looking after, any children on any premises on which the applicant is, or is likely to be, child-minding is not fit to look after children under the age of eight (s. 71(7));

(b)   they are satisfied that any person living, or likely to be living, or any person employed, or likely to be employed, at any premises on which the applicant is, or is likely, to be child-minding is not fit to be in the proximity of children under eight years of age (s. 71(8));

(c)   they are satisfied that any premises on which the applicant is, or is likely to be, child-minding are not fit to be used for looking after children under the age of eight, whether because of any equipment used on the premises or for any reason connected with their situation, construction or size (s. 71(11)).

A local authority may refuse to register an applicant who proposes to provide day care on any of the following grounds:

(a)   they are satisfied that any person looking after, or likely to be looking after, any children on any premises to which the application relates is not fit to look after children under the age of eight (s. 71(9));

(b)   they are satisfied that any person living, or likely to be living, or any person employed, or likely to be employed at the premises to which the application relates is not fit to be in the proximity of children under the age of eight (s. 71(10));

(c)   they are satisfied that the premises to which the application relates are not fit to be used for looking after children under the age of eight, whether because of any equipment to be used or for any reason connected with their situation, construction or size (s. 71(11)).

10.7   Requirements to be complied with by child-minders

When a local authority register somebody as a child-minder then they must impose such reasonable requirements as they consider appropriate (s. 71(2)). When imposing requirements the local authority must include requirements in respect of the following:

(a)   The maximum number of children that the child-minder may look after or the maximum number of children within a specified age range that the child-minder may care for (s. 72(2)(a)). When deciding on the maximum number of children the local authority are required to take account of any other children who may be on the premises that the child-minder will, or may be, using to look after children (s. 72(4)).

(b) That any premises or equipment used in connection with looking after children be adequately maintained and kept safe by the child-minder (s. 72(2)(b)).

(c) That the child-minder keep a record of the name and address of any child, any person who assists in looking after the children and any person living, or likely to be living, at the premises where the children will be looked after and notify the local authority if there is any change of persons who assist or who live at the premises (s. 72(2)(c) and (d)).

The Secretary of State is empowered to make regulations that may add to the list of requirements that a local authority would have to impose (s. 72(3)). Any additional requirements imposed by a local authority must be compatible with those that the authority is required to impose (s. 72(5)).

A local authority may vary or remove a requirement or they may impose additional requirements at any time (s. 72(6)).

The requirements that must be imposed do not include any surprises but it is surprising that child-minders should not as a matter of course be required to keep a record of the child's general practitioner, any particular health details or a record of where a parent can be contacted in an emergency. It is to be hoped that local authorities will include such requirements.

10.8 Requirements to be complied with by persons providing day care

As with child-minders, local authorities are required to impose requirements when registering a person who is to provide day care for children and the requirements that a local authority must impose are the same as for child-minders with the addition of the following:

(a) That the person notify the local authority of any change in the facilities which he provides (s. 73(3)(c)).

(b) Specification of the number of persons required to assist in looking after the children (s. 73(3)(d)).

The remaining provisions as to variation, removal and additional requirements and determining the maximum number of children are the same as for child-minders (s. 73(6) to (8)).

10.9 Cancellation of registration

A local authority may at any time cancel the registration of a child-minder or a person who provides day care if any of the following matters apply:

(a) If it appears to the local authority that the circumstances then prevailing are such as would have justified registration being refused (s. 74(1)(a) and (2)(a)).

(b) The care provided by the child-minder when looking after any child or the day care provided on those premises to a child is seriously inadequate having regard to the needs of that child (s. 74(1)(b) and (2)(b)). As in other parts of the

Children Act 1989 when any person is required to consider the needs of a child and here where a local authority are required to consider the needs of a child they must have particular regard to the child's religious persuasion, racial origin and cultural and linguistic background (s. 74(6)).

(c) That the child-minder or person providing day care has contravened or failed to comply with a requirement or failed to pay any annual fee within the prescribed time (s. 74(1)(c) and (2)(c); sch. 9, para. 7).

Any cancellation of registration must be given by the local authority in writing (s. 74(5)).

When a local authority cancel the registration of a person who provides day care at more than one place they are limited to cancelling just one registration but may if the circumstances would have justified refusal of registration cancel all registrations of that person (s. 74(3)).

For clarity, a limit is imposed where a local authority have at any time imposed a requirement on a child-minder, or on a person who provides day care, that they carry out repairs or alterations or additions to the premises used for the purpose of looking after children. The registration cannot be cancelled if the time within which those matters were required to be carried out has not expired and the inadequate state of the premises is as a result of the work not being done (s. 74(4)).

10.10   Appeals

If a local authority intend to refuse or cancel registration, refuse consent to a disqualified person being involved in providing day care, refuse to grant an application for variation or removal of a requirement, or impose, vary or remove a requirement then they must send to the applicant or registered person written notice of their intention not less than 14 days before taking such action (s. 77(1)). The notice must include the local authority's reasons for their proposal and inform the person of their rights of objection and appeal (s. 77(2)).

Where the person receiving such a notice informs the local authority in writing of his desire to object to the proposed action then the local authority must give him an opportunity to object in person or by means of a representative (s. 77(3) and (4)). If, after considering the person's objections, the local authority decide that they should proceed with the proposal then they must give written notice and the person, if still aggrieved, may appeal against the action to the court (s. 77(5) and (6)).

Where the local authority proposal is to refuse registration or impose, remove or vary a requirement then the decision to go ahead with such action shall not take effect until the expiry of the time within which an appeal may be brought and, if an appeal is brought, not until its determination (s. 77(11)). In Scotland an appeal will be by summary application to the sheriff and must be made within 21 days (s. 77(10)). The court to which appeal will be made and the time within which such an appeal must be brought is not specified in the provision and we must await rules of court.

Where the court allows an appeal against a requirement it may cancel or vary the requirement and, if allowing an appeal against refusal or cancellation of registration, the court may impose requirements (s. 77(8) and (9)). If the court makes or varies requirements then these will be deemed to have been imposed by the local authority (s. 77(7)).

10.11 Protection of children in an emergency

If a local authority form the view that cancellation of registration or varying, imposing or removing a requirement is urgent and cannot be left until after the above procedure for consideration of objections and appeals has been completed then they can make an application to the court. The local authority can apply to the court for an order that registration be cancelled or a requirement be varied, removed or imposed (s. 75(1)(a)). The court may make the order if it appears to the court that a child who is, or may be, looked after by a child-minder or in day care is suffering, or is likely to suffer, significant harm (s. 75(1)(b)).

If such an order is made by the court then it has immediate effect from the date of the order (s. 75(2)). Where the court imposes or varies a requirement then it will be deemed to have been imposed by the local authority (s. 75(5)).

The application by the local authority may be made *ex parte* and the local authority must provide the court with a written statement of the authority's reasons for making the application (s. 75(3)). If the court grants the order then it is the local authority's responsibility to serve on the registered person, as soon as is reasonably practicable, notice of the order and its terms and a copy of the authority's statement that was provided to the court (s. 75(4)). As the local authority has to serve notice of the order and its terms, there is no need for the authority to delay service until they receive a copy of the court order.

10.12 Local-authority inspection

Every local authority is under a duty to inspect premises used in their area by child-minders or for day care of children under eight at least once a year (s. 76(4)). Any person authorised by a local authority may at any reasonable time enter any domestic premises used by a child-minder or any premises used for day care of children under eight (s. 76(1)). Any person so authorised who enters premises may inspect the premises, any children being looked after on the premises, the arrangements for the children's welfare and any records which are required to be kept (s. 76(3)). Any person inspecting records must be allowed at any reasonable time access to any computer or any associated apparatus or material and be given assistance to do so from any person by whom, or for whom, the computer is, or has been, so used or any person in charge of the computer or related apparatus or material (s. 76(5)).

The local authority have, in addition to their power to enter premises of a registered child-minder or person providing day care, a power to enter premises where the local authority have reasonable cause to believe a child is being looked after in contravention of Part X of the Children Act 1989 (s. 76(2)). If the local authority are to exercise this power they may enter premises at any reasonable time (s. 76(2)). Once the authority exercise their power of entry they have the same power of inspection of children, premises and records (s. 76(3)).

Any person exercising this power must, if asked to do so, provide duly authenticated documentation of his authorisation (s. 76(6)). Any person who obstructs a person attempting to exercise this power is guilty of an offence and liable to a fine (s. 76(7)).

10.13 Offences

In addition to the offence mentioned at the end of 10.12, s. 78 details several other offences.

If a person provides day care for children under the age of eight without being registered and does not have a reasonable excuse for so doing then he is guilty of an offence and liable to a fine not exceeding level 5 (s. 78(1), (2) and (12)(c)).

If a person acts as a child-minder without being registered then in effect he may be given a second chance as the local authority may serve that person with an 'enforcement notice' which will have effect for one year commencing on the day it is served (s. 78(4) and (5)). If a person who has been served with an enforcement notice continues to act as a child-minder without being registered then, unless he has a reasonable excuse, he will be guilty of an offence (s. 78(6)). If a person who has been served with an enforcement notice moves to the area of another authority and acts as a child minder without being registered within a year of the notice then he is guilty of an offence even though the local authority for that area has not served an enforcement notice (s. 78(7)).

Any person who, without reasonable excuse, contravenes a requirement is guilty of an offence and liable to a fine not exceeding level 4 (s. 78(8) and (12)(a)).

A person is guilty of an offence if he acts as a child-minder or provides day care when disqualified from doing so, or is involved in the management of day care or employs a person who is so disqualified or allows a person so disqualified to live on the premises that are used for looking after the children (s. 78(9)). A person guilty of this offence is liable to a fine not exceeding level 5 and/or to six months' imprisonment (s. 78(12)(b)). Where a person who lives in the same household as somebody who is disqualified or in a household where somebody who is disqualified is employed contravenes sch. 9, para. 2(3), he shall not be guilty of an offence if he proves that he did not know and had no reasonable grounds for believing that such a person lived or was employed there (s. 78(10)). Where a person employs a disqualified person he shall not be guilty of an offence if he proves that he did not know and had no reasonable grounds for believing that the person was so disqualified (s. 78(11)).

10.14   Transitional provisions

The Nurseries and Child-Minders Regulation Act 1948 is repealed by sch. 15. However, it will have some residual effect for a 'transitional period' of no more than twelve months commencing with the coming into force of Part X of the Children Act 1989. For further details, see sch. 14, paras 33 and 34.

Appendix

This appendix is intended to give a brief description of the more important orders which a court can make as a result of the Children Act 1989. Some will be familiar (e.g., care orders); others are entirely new (e.g., emergency protection orders). The list below is not comprehensive, concentrating on the orders in Parts I to V of the Act which the practitioner will encounter most frequently. In each case, the Part of the Act in which the order appears, the principal sections of the Act dealing with the order, and the paragraphs in this Guide commenting on it, are detailed in brackets. Reference should then be made to the relevant sections in the Act, and paragraphs in the text.

Care order   (Part IV; ss. 31 to 34; 5.2 to 5.5)
Imposes a duty on the local authority to receive the child and keep him in their care, the local authority being given parental responsibility with respect to the child. (Although the name for the order is not changed, the relevant law is radically affected by the Children Act 1989.)

Child assessment order   (Part V; s. 43; 6.2)
Directs the production of the child so that an assessment of his health or development or any other form of assessment can be made and a decision taken as to whether to proceed for an emergency protection order or a care order. The order may include a direction that a child may be kept away from home.

Contact order   (Part II; s. 8; 3.4)
Orders a person with whom the child lives to allow the child to have contact with another named person (and thereby replaces orders for 'access'). Where a child is in care, then no section 8 contact order can be made: however, there is the analogous contact order under s. 34(2) (Part III; s. 34(2); 5.6).

Education supervision order   (Part IV; s. 36; 5.10)
Places the child under the supervision of the local education authority, in an attempt to ensure that he receives proper education (the principal object being to secure attendance at school).

Emergency protection order   (Part V; s. 44; 6.3)
An emergency remedy where immediate action is required, it directs the production of the child and authorises his removal to local authority accommo-

dation (usually). Alternatively, it can prevent the child's removal from a particular place (e.g., a hospital, or local authority accommodation), where he is no longer in the situation of danger.

Family assistance order   (Part II; s. 16; 3.12)
Requires a probation officer or an officer of the local authority to 'advise, assist and befriend' a particular family.

Parental responsibility order   (Part I; s. 4(1)(a); 2.2.2.)
Confers parental responsibility on a father who was not married to the mother at the time of the child's birth.

Prohibited steps order   (Part II; s. 8; 3.6)
Prevents any specified 'step' being taken in relation to a child (e.g., removal from the United Kingdom) without the consent of the court (thereby replacing an aspect of the existing wardship jurisdiction).

Recovery order (Part V; s. 50; 6.7)
Enables the court to discover the whereabouts, and secure the production, of a child who is missing or away from home.

Residence order   (Part II; s. 8; 3.3)
Establishes with whom (and where) the child is to live (thereby replacing orders for custody).

Specific issue order   (Part II; s. 8; 3.5)
Enables the court to determine a specific question which has arisen in relation to a child (e.g., whether a mentally handicapped child should be sterilised), thereby replacing an important part of the existing wardship jurisdiction.

Supervision order   (Part III; ss. 31-32, 35, sch. 3; 5.9)
Puts the child under the supervision of the local authority or a probation officer, possibly subject to certain requirements or conditions.

Children Act 1989

CHAPTER 41

ARRANGEMENT OF SECTIONS

PART I INTRODUCTORY

PART II ORDERS WITH RESPECT TO CHILDREN IN FAMILY PROCEEDINGS

General

Financial relief

Family assistance orders

PART III   LOCAL AUTHORITY SUPPORT FOR CHILDREN AND FAMILIES

PART IV   CARE AND SUPERVISION

General

103. Offences by bodies corporate.
104. Regulations and orders.
105. Interpretation.
106. Financial provisions.
107. Application to Channel Islands.
108. Short title, commencement, extent, etc.

SCHEDULES

Children Act 1989

1989, c. 41 An Act to reform the law relating to children; to provide for local authority services for children in need and others; to amend the law with respect to children's homes and voluntary organisations; to make provision with respect to fostering and adoption; and for connected purposes.

[Royal Assent 16 November 1989]

BE IT ENACTED by the Queen's most Excellent Majesty, by and with the advice and consent of the Lords Spiritual and Temporal, and Commons, in this present Parliament assembled, and by the authority of the same, as follows:—

PART I   INTRODUCTORY

Welfare of the child.

1.—(1)   When a court determines any question with respect to—

    (a)   the upbringing of a child; or

    (b)   the administration of a child's property or the application of any income arising from it,

the child's welfare shall be the court's paramount consideration.

    (2)   In any proceedings in which any question with respect to the upbringing of a child arises, the court shall have regard to the general principle that any delay in determining the question is likely to prejudice the welfare of the child.

    (3)   In the circumstances mentioned in subsection (4), a court shall have regard in particular to—

    (a)   the ascertainable wishes and feelings of the child concerned (considered in the light of his age and understanding);

    (b)   his physical, emotional and educational needs;

    (c)   the likely effect on him of any change in his circumstances;

    (d)   his age, sex, background and any characteristics of his which the court considers relevant;

    (e)   any harm which he has suffered or is at risk of suffering;

    (f)   how capable each of his parents, and any other person in relation to whom the court considers the question to be relevant, is of meeting his needs;

    (g)   the range of powers available to the court under this Act in the proceedings in question.

    (4)   The circumstances are that—

    (a)   the court is considering whether to make, vary or discharge a section 8 order, and the making, variation or discharge of the order is opposed by any party to the proceedings; or

(b) the court is considering whether to make, vary or discharge an order under Part IV.

(5) Where a court is considering whether or not to make one or more orders under this Act with respect to a child, it shall not make the order or any of the orders unless it considers that doing so would be better for the child than making no order at all.

Parental responsibility for children.

2.—(1) Where a child's father and mother were married to each other at the time of his birth, they shall each have parental responsibility for the child.

(2) Where a child's father and mother were not married to each other at the time of his birth—

(a) the mother shall have parental responsibility for the child;

(b) the father shall not have parental responsibility for the child, unless he acquires it in accordance with the provisions of this Act.

(3) References in this Act to a child whose father and mother were, or (as the case may be) were not, married to each other at the time of his birth must be read with section 1 of the Family Law Reform Act 1987 (which extends their meaning).

(4) The rule of law that a father is the natural guardian of his legitimate child is abolished.

(5) More than one person may have parental responsibility for the same child at the same time.

(6) A person who has parental responsibility for a child at any time shall not cease to have that responsibility solely because some other person subsequently acquires parental responsibility for the child.

(7) Where more than one person has parental responsibility for a child, each of them may act alone and without the other (or others) in meeting that responsibility; but nothing in this Part shall be taken to affect the operation of any enactment which requires the consent of more than one person in a matter affecting the child.

(8) The fact that a person has parental responsibility for a child shall not entitle him to act in any way which would be incompatible with any order made with respect to the child under this Act.

(9) A person who has parental responsibility for a child may not surrender or transfer any part of that responsibility to another but may arrange for some or all of it to be met by one or more persons acting on his behalf.

(10) The person with whom any such arrangement is made may himself be a person who already has parental responsibility for the child concerned.

(11) The making of any such arrangement shall not affect any liability of the person making it which may arise from any failure to meet any part of his parental responsibility for the child concerned.

Meaning of "parental responsibility".

3.—(1) In this Act "parental responsibility" means all the rights, duties, powers, responsibilities and authority which by law a parent of a child has in relation to the child and his property.

(2)   It also includes the rights, powers and duties which a guardian of the child's estate (appointed, before the commencement of section 5, to act generally) would have had in relation to the child and his property.

(3)   The rights referred to in subsection (2) include, in particular, the right of the guardian to receive or recover in his own name, for the benefit of the child, property of whatever description and wherever situated which the child is entitled to receive or recover.

(4)   The fact that a person has, or does not have, parental responsibility for a child shall not affect—

(a)   any obligation which he may have in relation to the child (such as a statutory duty to maintain the child); or

(b)   any rights which, in the event of the child's death, he (or any other person) may have in relation to the child's property.

(5)   A person who—

(a)   does not have parental responsibility for a particulr child; but

(b)   has care of the child,

may (subject to the provisions of this Act) do what is reasonable in all the circumstances of the case for the purpose of safeguarding or promoting the child's welfare.

Acquisition of parental responsibility by father.

4.—(1)   Where a child's father and mother were not married to each other at the time of his birth—

(a)   the court may, on the application of the father, order that he shall have parental responsibility for the child; or

(b)   the father and mother may by agreement ("a parental responsibility agreement") provide for the father to have parental responsibility for the child.

(2)   No parental responsibility agreement shall have effect for the purposes of this Act unless—

(a)   it is made in the form prescribed by regulations made by the Lord Chancellor; and

(b)   where regulations are made by the Lord Chancellor prescribing the manner in which such agreements must be recorded, it is recorded in the prescribed manner.

(3)   Subject to section 12(4), an order under subsection (1)(a), or a parental responsibility agreement, may only be brought to an end by an order of the court made on the application—

(a)   of any person who has parental responsibility for the child; or

(b)   with leave of the court, of the child himself.

(4)   The court may only grant leave under subsection (3)(b) if it is satisfied that the child has sufficient understanding to make the proposed application.

Appointment of guardians.

5.   (1)   Where an application with respect to a child is made to the court by any individual, the court may by order appoint that individual to be the child's guardian if—

(a)   the child has no parent with parental responsibility for him; or

(b)   a residence order has been made with respect to the child in favour of a parent or guardian of his who has died while the order was in force.

(2)   The power conferred by subsection (1) may also be exercised in any family proceedings if the court considers that the order should be made even though no application has been made for it.

(3)   A parent who has parental responsibility for his child may appoint another individual to be the child's guardian in the event of his death.

(4)   A guardian of a child may appoint another individual to take his place as the child's guardian in the event of his death.

(5)   An appointment under subsection (3) or (4) shall not have effect unless it is made in writing, is dated and is signed by the person making the appointment or—

(a)   in the case of an appointment made by a will which is not signed by the testator, is signed at the direction of the testator in accordance with the requirements of section 9 of the Wills Act 1837; or

(b)   in any other case, is signed at the direction of the person making the appointment, in his presence and in the presence of two witnesses who each attest the signature.

(6)   A person appointed as a child's guardian under this section shall have parental responsibility for the child concerned.

(7)   Where—

(a)   on the death of any person making an appointment under subsection (3) or (4), the child concerned has no parent with parental responsibility for him; or

(b)   immediately before the death of any person making such an appointment, a residence order in his favour was in force with respect to the child, the appointment shall take effect on the death of that person.

(8)   Where, on the death of any person making an appointment under subsection (3) or (4)—

(a)   the child concerned has a parent with parental responsibility for him; and

(b)   subsection (7)(b) does not apply,

the appointment shall take effect when the child no longer has a parent who has parental responsibility for him.

(9)   Subsections (1) and (7) do not apply if the residence order referred to in paragraph (b) of those subsections was also made in favour of a surviving parent of the child.

(10)   Nothing in this section shall be taken to prevent an appointment under subsection (3) or (4) being made by two or more persons acting jointly.

(11)   Subject to any provision made by rules of court, no court shall exercise the High Court's inherent jurisdiction to appoint a guardian of the estate of any child.

(12)   Where rules of court are made under subsection (11) they may prescribe the circumstances in which, and conditions subject to which, an appointment of such a guardian may be made.

(13)   A guardian of a child may only be appointed in accordance with the provisions of this section.

Guardians: revocation and disclaimer.

6.—(1)   An appointment under section 5(3) or (4) revokes an earlier such appointment (including one made in an unrevoked will or codicil) made by the same person in respect of the same child, unless it is clear (whether as the result of an express provision in the later appointment or by any necessary implication) that the purpose of the later appointment is to appoint an additional guardian.

(2)   An appointment under section 5(3) or (4) (including one made in an unrevoked will or codicil) is revoked if the person who made the appointment revokes it by a written and dated instrument which is signed—

(a)   by him; or

(b)   at his direction, in his presence and in the presence of two witnesses who each attest the signature.

(3)   An appointment under section 5(3) or (4) (other than one made in a will or codicil) is revoked if, with the intention of revoking the appointment, the person who made it—

(a)   destroys the instrument by which it was made; or

(b)   has some other person destroy that instrument in his presence.

(4)   For the avoidance of doubt, an appointment under section 5(3) or (4) made in a will or codicil is revoked if the will or codicil is revoked.

(5)   A person who is appointed as a guardian under section 5(3) or (4) may disclaim his appointment by an instrument in writing signed by him and made within a reasonable time of his first knowing that the appointment has taken effect.

(6)   Where regulations are made by the Lord Chancellor prescribing the manner in which such disclaimers must be recorded, no such disclaimer shall have effect unless it is recorded in the prescribed manner.

(7)   Any appointment of a guardian under section 5 may be brought to an end at any time by order of the court—

(a)   on the application of any person who has parental responsibility for the child;

(b)   on the application of the child concerned, with leave of the court; or

(c)   in any family proceedings, if the court considers that it should be brought to an end even though no application has been made.

Welfare reports.

7.—(1)   A court considering any question with respect to a child under this Act may—

(a)   ask a probation officer; or

(b)   ask a local authority to arrange for—

(i)   an officer of the authority; or

(ii)   such other person (other than a probation officer) as the authority considers appropriate,

to report to the court on such matters relating to the welfare of that child as are required to be dealt with in the report.

(2)   The Lord Chancellor may make regulations specifying matters which, unless the court orders otherwise, must be dealt with in any report under this section.

(3)   The report may be made in writing, or orally, as the court requires.

(4)   Regardless of any enactment or rule of law which would otherwise prevent it from doing so, the court may take account of—

(a)   any statement contained in the report; and

(b)   any evidence given in respect of the matters referred to in the report,
in so far as the statement or evidence is, in the opinion of the court, relevant to the
question which it is considering.

(5)   It shall be the duty of the authority or probation officer to comply with
any request for a report under this section.

PART II   ORDERS WITH RESPECT TO CHILDREN IN FAMILY PROCEEDINGS

General

Residence, contact and other orders with respect to children.
8.—(1)   In this Act—
   "a contact order" means an order requiring the person with whom a child
   lives, or is to live, to allow the child to visit or stay with the person named in
   the order, or for that person and the child otherwise to have contact with
   each other;
   "a prohibited steps order" means an order that no step which could be taken
   by a parent in meeting his parental responsibility for a child, and which is of
   a kind specified in the order, shall be taken by any person without the
   consent of the court;
   "a residence order" means an order settling the arrangements to be made as
   to the person with whom a child is to live; and
   "a specific issue order" means an order giving directions for the purpose of
   determining a specific question which has arisen, or which may arise, in
   connection with any aspect of parental responsibility for a child.

(2)   In this Act "a section 8 order" means any of the orders mentioned in
subsection (1) and any order varying or discharging such an order.

(3)   For the purposes of this Act "family proceedings" means any proceedings—
   (a)   under the inherent jurisdiction of the High Court in relation to
children; and
   (b)   under the enactments mentioned in subsection (4),
but does not include proceedings on an application for leave under section
100(3).

(4)   The enactments are—
   (a)   Parts I, II and IV of this Act;
   (b)   the Matrimonial Causes Act 1973;
   (c)   the Domestic Violence and Matrimonial Proceedings Act 1976;
   (d)   the Adoption Act 1976;
   (e)   the Domestic Proceedings and Magistrates' Courts Act 1978;
   (f)   sections 1 and 9 of the Matrimonial Homes Act 1983;
   (g)   Part III of the Matrimonial and Family Proceedings Act 1984.

Restrictions on making section 8 orders.
9.—(1)   No court shall make any section 8 order, other than a residence order,
with respect to a child who is in the care of a local authority.

(2)   No application may be made by a local authority for a residence order or
contact order and no court shall make such an order in favour of a local
authority.

(3)   A person who is, or was at any time within the last six months, a local authority foster parent of a child may not apply for leave to apply for a section 8 order with respect to the child unless—

(a)   he has the consent of the authority;

(b)   he is a relative of the child; or

(c)   the child has lived with him for at least three years preceding the application.

(4)   The period of three years mentioned in subsection (3)(c) need not be continuous but must have begun not more than five years before the making of the application.

(5)   No court shall exercise its powers to make a specific issue order or prohibited steps order—

(a)   with a view to achieving a result which could be achieved by making a residence or contact order; or

(b)   in any way which is denied to the High Court (by section 100(2)) in the exercise of its inherent jurisdiction with respect to children.

(6)   No court shall make any section 8 order which is to have effect for a period which will end after the child has reached the age of sixteen unless it is satisfied that the circumstances of the case are exceptional.

(7)   No court shall make any section 8 order, other than one varying or discharging such an order, with respect to a child who has reached the age of sixteen unless it is satisfied that the circumstances of the case are exceptional.

Power of court to make section 8 orders.

10.—(1)   In any family proceedings in which a question arises with respect to the welfare of any child, the court may make a section 8 order with respect to the child if—

(a)   an application for the order has been made by a person who—

(i)   is entitled to apply for a section 8 order with respect to the child; or

(ii)   has obtained the leave of the court to make the application; or

(b)   the court considers that the order should be made even though no such application has been made.

(2)   The court may also make a section 8 order with respect to any child on the application of a person who—

(a)   is entitled to apply for a section 8 order with respect to the child; or

(b)   has obtained the leave of the court to make the application.

(3)   This section is subject to the restrictions imposed by section 9.

(4)   The following persons are entitled to apply to the court for any section 8 order with respect to a child—

(a)   any parent or guardian of the child;

(b)   any person in whose favour a residence order is in force with respect to the child.

(5)   The following persons are entitled to apply for a residence or contact order with respect to a child—

(a)   any party to a marriage (whether or not subsisting) in relation to whom the child is a child of the family;

(b)   any person with whom the child has lived for a period of at least three years;

    (c)   any person who—

        (i)   in any case where a residence order is in force with respect to the child, has the consent of each of the persons in whose favour the order was made;

        (ii)   in any case where the child is in the care of a local authority, has the consent of that authority; or

        (iii)   in any other case, has the consent of each of those (if any) who have parental responsibility for the child.

    (6)   A person who would not otherwise be entitled (under the previous provisions of this section) to apply for the variation or discharge of a section 8 order shall be entitled to do so if—

    (a)   the order was made on his application; or

    (b)   in the case of a contact order, he is named in the order.

    (7)   Any person who falls within a category of person prescribed by rules of court is entitled to apply for any such section 8 order as may be prescribed in relation to that category of person.

    (8)   Where the person applying for leave to make an application for a section 8 order is the child concerned, the court may only grant leave if it is satisfied that he has sufficient understanding to make the proposed application for the section 8 order.

    (9)   Where the person applying for leave to make an application for a section 8 order is not the child concerned, the court shall, in deciding whether or not to grant leave, have particular regard to—

    (a)   the nature of the proposed application for the section 8 order;

    (b)   the applicant's connection with the child;

    (c)   any risk there might be of that proposed application disrupting the child's life to such an extent that he would be harmed by it; and

    (d)   where the child is being looked after by a local authority—

        (i)   the authority's plans for the child's future; and

        (ii)   the wishes and feelings of the child's parents.

    (10)   The period of three years mentioned in subsection (5)(b) need not be continuous but must not have begun more than five years before, or ended more than three months before, the making of the application.

General principles and supplementary provisions.

11.—(1)   In proceedings in which any question of making a section 8 order, or any other question with respect to such an order arises, the court shall (in the light of any rules made by virtue of subsection (2))—

    (a)   draw up a timetable with a view to determining the question without delay; and

    (b)   give such directions as it considers appropriate for the purpose of ensuring, so far as is reasonably practicable, that that timetable is adhered to.

    (2)   Rules of court may—

    (a)   specify periods within which specified steps must be taken in relation to proceedings in which such questions arise; and

    (b)   make other provision with respect to such proceedings for the purpose of ensuring, so far as is reasonably practicable, that such questions are determined without delay.

(3)   Where a court has power to make a section 8 order, it may do so at any time during the course of the proceedings in question even though it is not in a position to dispose finally of those proceedings.

(4)   Where a residence order is made in favour of two or more persons who do not themselves all live together, the order may specify the periods during which the child is to live in the different households concerned.

(5)   Where—

(a)   a residence order has been made with respect to a child; and

(b)   as a result of the order the child lives, or is to live, with one of two parents who each have parental responsibility for him,

the residence order shall cease to have effect if the parents live together for a continuous period of more than six months.

(6)   A contact order which requires the parent with whom a child lives to allow the child to visit, or otherwise have contact with, his other parent shall cease to have effect if the parents live together for a continuous period of more than six months.

(7)   A section 8 order may—

(a)   contain directions about how it is to be carried into effect;

(b)   impose conditions which must be complied with by any person—

(i)   in whose favour the order is made;

(ii)   who is a parent of the child concerned;

(iii)   who is not a parent of his but who has parental responsibility for him; or

(iv)   with whom the child is living,

and to whom the conditions are expressed to apply;

(c)   be made to have effect for a specified period, or contain provisions which are to have effect for a specified period;

(d)   make such incidental, supplemental or consequential provision as the court thinks fit.

Residence orders and parental responsibility.

12.—(1)   Where the court makes a residence order in favour of the father of a child it shall, if the father would not otherwise have parental responsibility for the child, also make an order under section 4 giving him that responsibility.

(2)   Where the court makes a residence order in favour of any person who is not the parent or guardian of the child concerned that person shall have parental responsibility for the child, while the residence order remains in force.

(3)   Where a person has parental responsibility for a child as a result of subsection (2), he shall not have the right—

(a)   to consent, or refuse to consent, to the making of an application with respect to the child under section 18 of the Adoption Act 1976;

(b)   to agree, or refuse to agree, to the making of an adoption order, or an order under section 55 of the Act of 1976 with respect to the child; or

(c)   to appoint a guardian for the child.

(4)   Where subsection (1) requires the court to make an order under section 4 in respect of the father of a child, the court shall not bring that order to an end at any time while the residence order concerned remains in force.

Change of child's name or removal from jurisdiction.
13.—(1)   Where a residence order is in force with respect to a child, no person may—
    (a)   cause the child to be known by a new surname; or
    (b)   remove him from the United Kingdom;
without either the written consent of every person who has parental responsibility for the child or the leave of the court.
    (2)   Subsection (1)(b) does not prevent the removal of a child, for a period of less than one month, by the person in whose favour the residence order is made.
    (3)   In making a residence order with respect to a child the court may grant the leave required by subsection (1)(b), either generally or for specified purposes.

Enforcement of residence orders.
14.—(1)   Where—
    (a)   a residence order is in force with respect to a child in favour of any person; and
    (b)   any other person (including one in whose favour the order is also in force) is in breach of the arrangements settled by that order,
the person mentioned in paragraph (a) may, as soon as the requirement in subsection (2) is complied with, enforce the order under section 63(3) of the Magistrates' Court Act 1980 as if it were an order requiring the other person to produce the child to him.
    (2)   The requirement is that a copy of the residence order has been served on the other person.
    (3)   Subsection (1) is without prejudice to any other remedy open to the person in whose favour the residence order is in force.

Financial relief

Orders for financial relief with respect to children.
15.—(1)   Schedule 1 (which consists primarily of the re-enactment, with consequential amendments and minor modifications, of provisions of the Guardianship of Minors Acts 1971 and 1973, the Children Act 1975 and of sections 15 and 16 of the Family Law Reform Act 1987) makes provision in relation to financial relief for children.
    (2)   The powers of a magistrates' court under section 60 of the Magistrates' Courts Act 1980 to revoke, revive or vary an order for the periodical payment of money shall not apply in relation to an order made under Schedule 1.

Family assistance orders

Family assistance orders.
16.—(1)   Where, in any family proceedings, the court has power to make an order under this Part with respect to any child, it may (whether or not it makes such an order) make an order requiring—
    (a)   a probation officer to be made available; or
    (b)   a local authority to make an officer of the authority available,
to advise, assist and (where appropriate) befriend any person named in the order.
    (2)   The persons who may be named in an order under this section ("a family assistance order") are—

(a)   any parent or guardian of the child;

(b)   any person with whom the child is living or in whose favour a contact order is in force with respect to the child;

(c)   the child himself.

(3) No court may make a family assistance order unless—

(a)   it is satisfied that the circumstances of the case are exceptional; and

(b)   it has obtained the consent of every person to be named in the order other than the child.

(4) A family assistance order may direct—

(a)   the person named in the order; or

(b)   such of the persons named in the order as may be specified in the order, to take such steps as may be so specified with a view to enabling the officer concerned to be kept informed of the address of any person named in the order and to be allowed to visit any such person.

(5) Unless it specifies a shorter period, a family assistance order shall have effect for a period of six months beginning with the day on which it is made.

(6) Where—

(a)   a family assistance order is in force with respect to a child; and

(b)   a section 8 order is also in force with respect to the child, the officer concerned may refer to the court the question whether the section 8 order should be varied or discharged.

(7) A family assistance order shall not be made so as to require a local authority to make an officer of theirs available unless—

(a)   the authority agree; or

(b)   the child concerned lives or will live within their area.

(8) Where a family assistance order requires a probation officer to be made available, the officer shall be selected in accordance with arrangements made by the probation committee for the area in which the child lives or will live.

(9) If the selected probation officer is unable to carry out his duties, or dies, another probation officer shall be selected in the same manner.

PART III   LOCAL AUTHORITY SUPPORT FOR CHILDREN AND FAMILIES

Provision of services for children and their families

Provision of services for children in need, their families and others.
17.—(1) It shall be the general duty of every local authority (in addition to the other duties imposed on them by this Part)—

(a)   to safeguard and promote the welfare of children within their area who are in need; and

(b)   so far as is consistent with that duty, to promote the upbringing of such children by their families, by providing a range and level of services appropriate to those children's needs.

(2) For the purpose principally of facilitating the discharge of their general duty under this section, every local authority shall have the specific duties and powers set out in Part 1 of Schedule 2.

(3) Any service provided by an authority in the exercise of functions conferred on them by this section may be provided for the family of a particular

child in need or for any member of his family, if it is provided with a view to safeguarding or promoting the child's welfare.

(4) The Secretary of State may by order amend any provision of Part I of Schedule 2 or add any further duty or power to those for the time being mentioned there.

(5) Every local authority—

(a) shall facilitate the provision by others (including in particular voluntary organisations) of services which the authority have power to provide by virtue of this section, or section 18, 20, 23 or 24; and

(b) may make such arrangements as they see fit for any person to act on their behalf in the provision of any such service.

(6) The services provided by a local authority in the exercise of functions conferred on them by this section may include giving assistance in kind or, in exceptional circumstances, in cash.

(7) Assistance may be unconditional or subject to conditions as to the repayment of the assistance or of its value (in whole or in part).

(8) Before giving any assistance or imposing any conditions, a local authority shall have regard to the means of the child concerned and of each of his parents.

(9) No person shall be liable to make any repayment of assistance or of its value at any time when he is in receipt of income support or family credit under the Social Security Act 1986.

(10) For the purposes of this Part a child shall be taken to be in need if—

(a) he is unlikely to achieve or maintain, or to have the opportunity of achieving or maintaining, a reasonable standard of health or development without the provision for him of services by a local authority under this Part;

(b) his health or development is likely to be significantly impaired, or further impaired, without the provision for him of such services; or

(c) he is disabled,

and "family", in relation to such a child, includes any person who has parental responsibility for the child and any other person with whom he has been living.

(11) For the purposes of this Part, a child is disabled if he is blind, deaf or dumb or suffers from mental disorder of any kind or is substantially and permanently handicapped by illness, injury or congenital deformity or such other disability as may be prescribed; and in this Part—

"development" means physical, intellectual, emotional, social or behavioural development; and

"health" means physical or mental health.

Day care for pre-school and other children.

18.—(1) Every local authority shall provide such day care for children in need within their area who are—

(a) aged five or under; and

(b) not yet attending schools,

as is appropriate.

(2) A local authority may provide day care for children within their area who satisfy the conditions mentioned in subsection (1)(a) and (b) even though they are not in need.

(3)   A local authority may provide facilities (including training, advice, guidance and counselling) for those—

    (a)   caring for children in day care; or

    (b)   who at any time accompany such children while they are in day care.

(4)   In this section "day care" means any form of care or supervised activity provided for children during the day (whether or not it is provided on a regular basis).

(5)   Every local authority shall provide for children in need within their area who are attending any school such care or supervised activities as is appropriate—

    (a)   outside school hours; or

    (b)   during school holidays.

(6)   A local authority may provide such care or supervised activities for children within their area who are attending any school even though those children are not in need.

(7)   In this section "supervised activity" means an activity supervised by a responsible person.

Review of provision for day care, child minding etc.

19.—(1)   Every local authority in England and Wales shall review—

    (a)   the provision which they make under section 18;

    (b)   the extent to which the services of child minders are available within their area with respect to children under the age of eight; and

    (c)   the provision for day care within their area made for children under the age of eight by persons other than the authority required to register under section 71(1)(b).

(2)   A review under subsection (1) shall be conducted—

    (a)   together with the appropriate local education authority; and

    (b)   at least once in every review period.

(3)   Every local authority in Scotland shall, at least once in every review period, review—

    (a)   the provision for day care within their area made for children under the age of eight by the local authority and by persons required to register under section 71(1)(b); and

    (b)   the extent to which the services of child minders are available within their area with respect to children under the age of eight.

(4)   In conducting any such review the two authorities or, in Scotland, the authority shall have regard to the provision made with respect to children under the age of eight in relevant establishments within their area.

(5)   In this section—

"relevant establishment" means any establishment which is mentioned in paragraphs 3 and 4 of Schedule 9 (hospitals, schools and other establishments exempt from the registration requirements which apply in relation to the provision of day care); and

"review period" means the period of one year beginning with the commencement of this section and each subsequent period of three years beginning with an anniversary of that commencement.

(6)   Where a local authority have conducted a review under this section they shall publish the result of the review—

(a) as soon as is reasonably practicable;

(b) in such form as they consider appropriate; and

(c) together with any proposals they may have with respect to the matters reviewed.

(7) The authorities conducting any review under this section shall have regard to—

(a) any representations made to any one of them by any relevant health authority or health board; and

(b) any other representations which they consider to be relevant.

(8) In the application of this section to Scotland, "day care" has the same meaning as in section 79 and "health board" has the same meaning as in the National Health Service (Scotland) Act 1978.

Provision of accommodation for children

Provision of accommodation for children: general.

20.—(1) Every local authority shall provide accommodation for any child in need within their area who appears to them to require accommodation as a result of—

(a) there being no person who has parental responsibility for him;

(b) his being lost or having been abandoned; or

(c) the person who has been caring for him being prevented (whether or not permanently, and for whatever reason) from providing him with suitable accommodation or care.

(2) Where a local authority provide accommodation under subsection (1) for a child who is ordinarily resident in the area of another local authority, that other local authority may take over the provision of accommodation for the child within—

(a) three months of being notified in writing that the child is being provided with accommodation; or

(b) such other longer period as may be prescribed.

(3) Every local authority shall provide accommodation for any child in need within their area who has reached the age of sixteen and whose welfare the authority consider is likely to be seriously prejudiced if they do not provide him with accommodation.

(4) A local authority may provide accommodation for any child within their area (even though a person who has parental responsibility for him is able to provide him with accommodation) if they consider that to do so would safeguard or promote the child's welfare.

(5) A local authority may provide accommodation for any person who has reached the age of sixteen but is under twenty-one in any community home which takes children who have reached the age of sixteen if they consider that to do so would safeguard or promote his welfare.

(6) Before providing accommodation under this section, a local authority shall, so far as is reasonably practicable and consistent with the child's welfare—

(a) ascertain the child's wishes regarding the provision of accommodation; and

(b) give due consideration (having regard to his age and understanding) to such wishes of the child as they have been able to ascertain.

(7)   A local authority may not provide accommodation under this section for any child if any person who—
    (a)   has parental responsibility for him;
    (b)   is willing and able to—
        (i)   provide accommodation for him; or
        (ii)   arrange for accommodation to be provided for him,
objects.

(8)   Any person who has parental responsibility for a child may at any time remove the child from accommodation provided by or on behalf of the local authority under this section.

(9)   Subsections (7) and (8) do not apply while any person—
    (a)   in whose favour a residence order is in force with respect to the child; or
    (b)   who has care of the child by virtue of an order made in the exercise of the High Court's inherent jurisdiction with respect to children,
agrees to the child being looked after in accommodation provided by or on behalf of the local authority.

(10)   Where there is more than one such person as is mentioned in subsection (9), all of them must agree.

(11)   Subsections (7) and (8) do not apply where a child who has reached the age of sixteen agrees to being provided with accommodation under this section.

Provision of accommodation for children in police protection or detention or on remand, etc.

21.—(1)   Every local authority shall make provision for the reception and accommodation of children who are removed or kept away from home under Part V.

(2)   Every local authority shall receive, and provide accommodation for, children—
    (a)   in police protection whom they are requested to receive under section 46(3)(f);
    (b)   whom they are requested to receive under section 38(6) of the Police and Criminal Evidence Act 1984;
    (c)   who are—
        (i)   on remand under section 23(1) of the Children and Young Persons Act 1969; or
        (ii)   the subject of a supervision order imposing a residence requirement under section 12AA of that Act,
and with respect to whom they are the designated authority.

(3)   Where a child has been—
    (a)   removed under Part V; or
    (b)   detained under section 38 of the Police and Criminal Evidence Act 1984,
and he is not being provided with accommodation by a local authority or in a hospital vested in the Secretary of State, any reasonable expenses of accommodating him shall be recoverable from the local authority in whose area he is ordinarily resident.

Duties of local authorities in relation to children looked after by them

General duty of local authority in relation to children looked after by them.

22.—(1)   In this Act, any reference to a child who is looked after by a local authority is a reference to a child who is—

(a)   in their care; or

(b)   provided with accommodation by the authority in the exercise of any functions (in particular those under this Act) which stand referred to their social services committee under the Local Authority Social Services Act 1970.

(2)   In subsection (1) "accommodation" means accommodation which is provided for a continuous period of more than 24 hours.

(3)   It shall be the duty of a local authority looking after any child—

(a)   to safeguard and promote his welfare; and

(b)   to make such use of services available for children cared for by their own parents as appears to the authority reasonable in his case.

(4)   Before making any decision with respect to a child whom they are looking after, or proposing to look after, a local authority shall, so far as is reasonably practicable, ascertain the wishes and feelings of—

(a)   the child;

(b)   his parents;

(c)   any person who is not a parent of his but who has parental responsibility for him; and

(d)   any other person whose wishes and feelings the authority consider to be relevant,

regarding the matter to be decided.

(5)   In making any such decision a local authority shall give due consideration—

(a)   having regard to his age and understanding, to such wishes and feelings of the child as they have been able to ascertain;

(b)   to such wishes and feelings of any person mentioned in subsection (4)(b) to (d) as they have been able to ascertain; and

(c)   to the child's religious persuasion, racial origin and cultural and linguistic background.

(6)   If it appears to a local authority that it is necessary, for the purpose of protecting members of the public from serious injury, to exercise their powers with respect to a child whom they are looking after in a manner which may not be consistent with their duties under this section, they may do so.

(7)   If the Secretary of State considers it necessary, for the purpose of protecting members of the public from serious injury, to give directions to a local authority with respect to the exercise of their powers with respect to a child whom they are looking after, he may give such directions to the authority.

(8)   Where any such directions are given to an authority they shall comply with them even though doing so is inconsistent with their duties under this section.

Provision of accommodation and maintenance by local authority for children whom they are looking after.

23.—(1)   It shall be the duty of any local authority looking after a child—

(a)   when he is in their care, to provide accommodation for him; and

(b) to maintain him in other respects apart from providing accommodation for him.

(2) A local authority shall provide accommodation and maintenance for any
child whom they are looking after by—

    (a) placing him (subject to subsection (5) and any regulations made by the
Secretary of State) with—

        (i) a family;

        (ii) a relative of his; or

        (iii) any other suitable person,

on such terms as to payment by the authority and otherwise as the authority may
determine;

    (b) maintaining him in a community home;

    (c) maintaining him in a voluntary home;

    (d) maintaining him in a registered children's home;

    (e) maintaining him in a home provided by the Secretary of State under
section 82(5) on such terms as the Secretary of State may from time to time
determine; or

    (f) making such other arrangements as—

        (i) seem appropriate to them; and

        (ii) comply with any regulations made by the Secretary of State.

(3) Any person with whom a child has been placed under subsection (2)(a) is
referred to in this Act as a local authority foster parent unless he falls within
subsection (4).

(4) A person falls within this subsection if he is—

    (a) a parent of the child;

    (b) a person who is not a parent of the child but who has parental
responsibility for him; or

    (c) where the child is in care and there was a residence order in force with
respect to him immediately before the care order was made, a person in whose
favour the residence order was made.

(5) Where a child is in the care of a local authority, the authority may only
allow him to live with a person who falls within subsection (4) in accordance with
regulations made by the Secretary of State.

(6) Subject to any regulations made by the Secretary of State for the purposes
of this subsection, any local authority looking after a child shall make
arrangements to enable him to live with—

    (a) a person falling within subsection (4); or

    (b) a relative, friend or other person connected with him,

unless that would not be reasonably practicable or consistent with his welfare.

(7) Where a local authority provide accommodation for a child whom they
are looking after, they shall, subject to the provisions of this Part and so far as is
reasonably practicable and consistent with his welfare, secure that—

    (a) the accommodation is near his home; and

    (b) where the authority are also providing accommodation for a sibling of
his, they are accommodated together.

(8) Where a local authority provide accommodation for a child whom they
are looking after and who is disabled, they shall, so far as is reasonably
practicable, secure that the accommodation is not unsuitable to his particular
needs.

(9) Part II of Schedule 2 shall have effect for the purposes of making further provision as to children looked after by local authorities and in particular as to the regulations that may be made under subsections (2)(a) and (f) and (5).

Advice and assistance for certain children

Advice and assistance for certain children.
24.—(1) Where a child is being looked after by a local authority, it shall be the duty of the authority to advise, assist and befriend him with a view to promoting his welfare when he ceases to be looked after by them.

(2) In this Part "a person qualifying for advice and assistance" means a person within the area of the authority who is under twenty-one and who was, at any time after reaching the age of sixteen but while still a child—

    (a) looked after by a local authority;

    (b) accommodated by or on behalf of a voluntary organisation;

    (c) accommodated in a registered chilren's home;

    (d) accommodated—

        (i) by any health authority or local education authority; or

        (ii) in any residential care home, nursing home of mental nursing home,

for a consecutive period of at least three months;

    (e) privately fostered,

but who is no longer so looked after, accommodated or fostered.

(3) Subsection (2)(d) applies even if the period of three months mentioned there began before the child reached the age of sixteen.

(4) Where—

    (a) a local authority know that there is within their area a person qualifying for advice and assistance;

    (b) the conditions in subsection (5) are satisfied; and

    (c) that person has asked them for help of a kind which they can give under this section,

they shall (if he was being looked after by a local authority or was accommodated by or on behalf of a voluntary organisation) and may (in any other case) advise and befriend him.

(5) The conditions are that—

    (a) it appears to the authority that the person concerned is in need of advice and being befriended;

    (b) where that person was not being looked after by the authority, they are satisfied that the person by whom he was being looked after does not have the necessary facilities for advising or befriending him.

(6) Where as a result of this section a local authority are under a duty, or are empowered, to advise and befriend a person, they may also give him assistance.

(7) Assistance given under subsections (1) to (6) may be in kind or, in exceptional circumstances, in cash.

(8) A local authority may give assistance to any person who qualifies for advice and assistance by virtue of subsection (2)(a) by—

    (a) contributing to expenses incurred by him in living near the place where he is, or will be—

        (i) employed or seeking employment; or

        (ii) receiving education or training; or

(b)   making a grant to enable him to meet expenses connected with his education or training.

(9)   Where a local authority are assisting the person under subsection (8) by making a contribution or grant with respect to a course of education or training, they may—

(a)   continue to do so even though he reaches the age of twenty-one before completing the course; and

(b)   disregard any interruption in his attendance on the course if he resumes it as soon as is reasonably practicable.

(10)   Subsections (7) to (9) of section 17 shall apply in relation to assistance given under this section (otherwise than under subsection (8)) as they apply in relation to assistance given under that section.

(11)   Where it appears to a local authority that a person whom they have been advising and befriending under this section, as a person qualifying for advice and assistance, proposes to live, or is living, in the area of another local authority, they shall inform that other local authority.

(12)   Where a child who is accommodated—

(a)   by a voluntary organisation or in a registered children's home;

(b)   by any health authority or local education authority; or

(c)   in any residential care home, nursing home or mental nursing home, ceases to be so accommodated, after reaching the age of sixteen, the organisation, authority or (as the case may be) person carrying on the home shall inform the local authority within whose area the child proposes to live.

(13)   Subsection (12) only applies, by virtue of paragraph (b) or (c), if the accommodation has been provided for a consecutive period of at least three months.

Secure accommodation

Use of accommodation for restricting liberty.
25.—(1)   Subject to the following provisions of this section, a child who is being looked after by a local authority may not be placed, and, if placed, may not be kept, in accommodation provided for the purpose of restricting liberty ("secure accommodation") unless it appears—

(a)   that—

(i)   he has a history of absconding and is likely to abscond from any other description of accommodation; and

(ii)   if he absconds, he is likely to suffer significant harm; or

(b)   that if he is kept in any other description of accommodation he is likely to injure himself or other persons.

(2)   The Secretary of State may by regulations—

(a)   specify a maximum period—

(i)   beyond which a child may not be kept in secure accommodation without the authority of the court; and

(ii)   for which the court may authorise a child to be kept in secure accommodation;

(b)   empower the court from time to time to authorise a child to be kept in secure accommodation for such further period as the regulations may specify; and

(c)   provide that applications to the court under this section shall be made only by local authorities.

(3)   It shall be the duty of a court hearing an application under this section to determine whether any relevant criteria for keeping a child in secure accommodation are satisfied in his case.

(4)   If a court determines that any such criteria are satisfied, it shall make an order authorising the child to be kept in secure accommodation and specifying the maximum period for which he may be so kept.

(5)   On any adjournment of the hearing of an application under this section, a court may make an interim order permitting the child to be kept during the period of the adjournment in secure accommodation.

(6)   No court shall exercise the powers conferred by this section in respect of a child who is not legally represented in that court unless, having been informed of his right to apply for legal aid and having had the opportunity to do so, he refused or failed to apply.

(7)   The Secretary of State may by regulations provide that—

(a)   this section shall or shall not apply to any description of children specified in the regulations;

(b)   this section shall have effect in relation to children of a description specified in the regulations subject to such modifications as may be so specified;

(c)   such other provisions as may be so specified shall have effect for the purpose of determining whether a child of a description specified in the regulations may be placed or kept in secure accommodation.

(8)   The giving of an authorisation under this section shall not prejudice any power of any court in England and Wales or Scotland to give directions relating to the child to whom the authorisation relates.

(9)   This section is subject to section 20(8).

Supplemental

Review of cases and inquiries into representations.
26.—(1)   The Secretary of State may make regulations requiring the case of each child who is being looked after by a local authority to be reviewed in accordance with the provisions of the regulations.

(2)   The regulations may, in particular, make provision—

(a)   as to the manner in which each case is to be reviewed;

(b)   as to the considerations to which the local authority are to have regard in reviewing each case;

(c)   as to the time when each case is first to be reviewed and the frequency of subsequent reviews;

(d)   requiring the authority, before conducting any review, to seek the views of—

(i)   the child;

(ii)   his parents;

(iii)   any person who is not a parent of his but who has parental responsibility for him; and

(iv)   any other person whose views the authority consider to be relevant, including, in particular, the views of those persons in relation to any particular matter which is to be considered in the course of the review;

(e)   requiring the authority to consider, in the case of a child who is in their care, whether an application should be made to discharge the care order;

(f)   requiring the authority to consider, in the case of a child in accommodation provided by the authority, whether the accommodation accords with the requirements of this Part;

(g)   requiring the authority to inform the child so far as is reasonably practicable of any steps he may take under this Act;

(h)   requiring the authority to make arrangements, including arrangements with such other bodies providing services as it considers appropriate, to implement any decision which they propose to make in the course, or as a result, of the review;

(i)   requiring the authority to notify details of the result of the review and of any decision taken by them in consequence of the review to—

(i)   the child;

(ii)   his parents;

(iii)   any person who is not a parent of his but who has parental responsibility for him; and

(iv)   any other person whom they consider ought to be notified;

(j)   requiring the authority to monitor the arrangements which they have made with a view to ensuring that they comply with the regulations.

(3)   Every local authority shall establish a procedure for considering any representations (including any complaint) made to them by—

(a)   any child who is being looked after by them or who is not being looked after by them but is in need;

(b)   a parent of his;

(c)   any person who is not a parent of his but who has parental responsibility for him;

(d)   any local authority foster parent;

(e)   such other person as the authority consider has a sufficient interest in the child's welfare to warrant his representations being considered by them, about the discharge by the authority of any of their functions under this Part in relation to the child.

(4)   The procedure shall ensure that at least one person who is not a member or officer of the authority takes part in—

(a)   the consideration; and

(b)   any discussions which are held by the authority about the action (if any) to be taken in relation to the child in the light of the consideration.

(5)   In carrying out any consideration of representations under this section a local authority shall comply with any regulations made by the Secretary of State for the purpose of regulating the procedure to be followed.

(6)   The Secretary of State may make regulations requiring local authorities to monitor the arrangements that they have made with a view to ensuring that they comply with any regulations made for the purposes of subsection (5).

(7)   Where any representation has been considered under the procedure established by a local authority under this section, the authority shall—

(a)   have due regard to the findings of those considering the representation; and

(b)   take such steps as are reasonably practicable to notify (in writing)—

(i)   the person making the representation;

(ii)   the child (if the authority consider that he has sufficient understanding); and

(iii)   such other persons (if any) as appear to the authority to be likely to be affected,

of the authority's decision in the matter and their reasons for taking that decision and of any action which they have taken, or propose to take.

(8)   Every local authority shall give such publicity to their procedure for considering representations under this section as they consider appropriate.

Co-operation between authorities.

27.—(1)   Where it appears to a local authority that any authority or other person mentioned in subsection (3) could, by taking any specified action, help in the exercise of any of their functions under this Part, they may request the help of that other authority or person, specifying the action in question.

(2)   An authority whose help is so requested shall comply with the request if it is compatible with their own statutory or other duties and obligations and does not unduly prejudice the discharge of any of their functions.

(3)   The persons are—

(a)   any local authority;

(b)   any local education authority;

(c)   any local housing authority;

(d)   any health authority; and

(e)   any person authorised by the Secretary of State for the purposes of this section.

(4)   Every local authority shall assist any local education authority with the provision of services for any child within the local authority's area who has special educational needs.

Consultation with local education authorities.

28.—(1)   Where—

(a)   a child is being looked after by a local authority; and

(b)   the authority propose to provide accommodation for him in an establishment at which education is provided for children who are accommodated there,

they shall, so far as is reasonably practicable, consult the appropriate local education authority before doing so.

(2)   Where any such proposal is carried out, the local authority shall, as soon as is reasonably practicable, inform the appropriate local education authority of the arrangements that have been made for the child's accommodation.

(3)   Where the child ceases to be accommodated as mentioned in subsection (1)(b), the local authority shall inform the appropriate local education authority.

(4)   In this section "the appropriate local education authority" means—

(a)   the local education authority within whose area the local authority's area falls; or

(b)   where the child has special educational needs and a statement of his needs is maintained under the Education Act 1981, the local education authority who maintain the statement.

Recoupment of cost of providing services etc.
29.—(1) Where a local authority provide any service under section 17 or 18, other than advice, guidance or counselling, they may recover from a person specified in subsection (4) such charge for the service as they consider reasonable.

(2) Where the authority are satisfied that that person's means are insufficient for it to be reasonably practicable for him to pay the charge, they shall not require him to pay more than he can reasonably be expected to pay.

(3) No person shall be liable to pay any charge under subsection (1) at any time when he is in receipt of income support or family credit under the Social Security Act 1986.

(4) The persons are—

(a) where the service is provided for a child under sixteen, each of his parents;

(b) where it is provided for a child who has reached the age of sixteen, the child himself; and

(c) where it is provided for a member of the child's family, that member.

(5) Any charge under subsection (1) may, without prejudice to any other method of recovery, be recovered summarily as a civil debt.

(6) Part III of Schedule 2 makes provision in connection with contributions towards the maintenance of children who are being looked after by local authorities and consists of the re-enactment with modifications of provisions in Part V of the Child Care Act 1980.

(7) Where a local authority provide any accommodation under section 20(1) for a child who was (immediately before they began to look after him) ordinarily resident within the area of another local authority, they may recover from that other authority any reasonable expenses incurred by them in providing the accommodation and maintaining him.

(8) Where a local authority provide accommodation under section 21(1) or (2)(a) or (b) for a child who is ordinarily resident within the area of another local authority and they are not maintaining him in—

(a) a community home provided by them;

(b) a controlled community home; or

(c) a hospital vested in the Secretary of State,

they may recover from that other authority any reasonable expenses incurred by them in providing the accommodation and maintaining him.

(9) Where a local authority comply with any request under section 27(2) in relation to a child or other person who is not ordinarily resident within their area, they may recover from the local authority in whose area the child or person is ordinarily resident any expenses reasonably incurred by them in respect of that person.

Miscellaneous.
30.—(1) Nothing in this Part shall affect any duty imposed on a local authority by or under any other enactment.

(2) Any question arising under section 20(2), 21(3) or 29(7) to (9) as to the ordinary residence of a child shall be determined by agreement between the local authorities concerned or, in default of agreement, by the Secretary of State.

(3) Where the functions conferred on a local authority by this Part and the

functions of a local education authority are concurrent, the Secretary of State may by regulations provide by which authority the functions are to be exercised.

(4) The Secretary of State may make regulations for determining, as respects any local education authority functions specified in the regulations, whether a child who is being looked after by a local authority is to be treated, for purposes so specified, as a child of parents of sufficient resources or as a child of parents without resources.

PART IV   CARE AND SUPERVISION

General

Care and supervision orders.

31.—(1)   On the application of any local authority or authorised person, the court may make an order—

(a)   placing the child with respect to whom the application is made in the care of a designated local authority; or

(b)   putting him under the supervision of a designated local authority or of a probation officer.

(2)   A court may only make a care order or supervision order if it is satisfied—

(a)   that the child concerned is suffering, or is likely to suffer, significant harm; and

(b)   that the harm, or likelihood of harm, is attributable to—

(i)   the care given to the child, or likely to be given to him if the order were not made, not being what it would be reasonable to expect a parent to give to him; or

(ii)   the child's being beyond parental control.

(3)   No care order or supervision order may be made with respect to a child who has reached the age of seventeen (or sixteen, in the case of a child who is married).

(4)   An application under this section may be made on its own or in any other family proceedings.

(5)   The court may—

(a)   on an application for a care order, make a supervision order;

(b)   on an application for a supervision order, make a care order.

(6)   Where an authorised person proposes to make an application under this section he shall—

(a)   if it is reasonably practicable to do so; and

(b)   before making the application,

consult the local authority appearing to him to be the authority in whose area the child concerned is ordinarily resident.

(7)   An application made by an authorised person shall not be entertained by the court if, at the time when it is made, the child concerned is—

(a)   the subject of an earlier application for a care order, or supervision order, which has not been disposed of; or

(b)   subject to—

(i)   a care order or supervision order;

(ii)   an order under section 7(7)(b) of the Children and Young Persons Act 1969; or

(iii)   a supervision requirement within the meaning of the Social Work (Scotland) Act 1968.

(8)   The local authority designated in a care order must be—

(a)   the authority within whose area the child is ordinarily resident; or

(b)   where the child does not reside in the area of a local authority, the authority within whose area any circumstances arose in consequence of which the order is being made.

(9)   In this section—

"authorised person" means—

(a)   the National Society for the Prevention of Cruelty to Children and any of its officers; and

(b)   any person authorised by order of the Secretary of State to bring proceedings under this section and any officer of a body which is so authorised.

"harm" means ill-treatment or the impairment of health or development;

"development" means physical, intellectual, emotional, social or behavioural development;

"health" means physical or mental health; and

"ill-treatment" includes sexual abuse and forms of ill-treatment which are not physical.

(10)   Where the question of whether harm suffered by a child is significant turns on the child's health or development, his health or development shall be compared with that which could reasonably be expected of a similar child.

(11)   In this Act—

"a care order" means (subject to section 105(1)) an order under subsection (1)(a) and (except where express provision to the contrary is made) includes an interim care order made under section 38; and

"a supervision order" means an order under subsection (1)(b) and (except where express provision to the contrary is made) includes an interim supervision order made under section 38.

Period within which application for order under this Part must be disposed of.
32.—(1)   A court hearing an application for an order under this Part shall (in the light of any rules made by virtue of subsection (2))—

(a)   draw up a timetable with a view to disposing of the application without delay; and

(b)   give such directions as it considers appropriate for the purpose of ensuring, so far as is reasonably practicable, that that timetable is adhered to.

(2)   Rules of court may—

(a)   specify periods within which specified steps must be taken in relation to such proceedings; and

(b)   make other provision with respect to such proceedings for the purpose of ensuring, so far as is reasonably practicable, that they are disposed of without delay.

Care orders

Effect of care order.
33.—(1)   Where a care order is made with respect to a child it shall be the duty of the local authority designated by the order to receive the child into their care and

to keep him in their care while the order remains in force.

(2) Where—

    (a)   a care order has been made with respect to a child on the application of an authorised person; but

    (b)   the local authority designated by the order was not informed that that person proposed to make the application,

the child may be kept in the care of that person until received into the care of the authority.

(3) While a care order is in force with respect to a child, the local authority designated by the order shall—

    (a)   have parental responsibility for the child; and

    (b)   have the power (subject to the following provisions of this section) to determine the extent to which a parent or guardian of the child may meet his parental responsibility for him.

(4) The authority may not exercise the power in subsection (3)(b) unless they are satisfied that it is necessary to do so in order to safeguard or promote the child's welfare.

(5) Nothing in subsection (3)(b) shall prevent a parent or guardian of the child who has care of him from doing what is reasonable in all the circumstances of the case for the purpose of safeguarding or promoting his welfare.

(6) While a care order is in force with respect to a child, the local authority designated by the order shall not—

    (a)   cause the child to be brought up in any religious persuasion other than that in which he would have been brought up if the order had not been made; or

    (b)   have the right—

        (i)   to consent or refuse to consent to the making of an application with respect to the child under section 18 of the Adoption Act 1976;

        (ii)   to agree or refuse to agree to the making of an adoption order, or an order under section 55 of the Act of 1976 with respect to the child; or

        (iii)   to appoint a guardian for the child.

(7) While a care order is in force with respect to a child, no person may—

    (a)   cause the child to be known by a new surname; or

    (b)   remove him from the United Kingdom,

without either the written consent of every person who has parental responsibility for the child or the leave of the court.

(8) Subsection (7)(b) does not—

    (a)   prevent the removal of such a child, for a period of less than one month, by the authority in whose care he is; or

    (b)   apply to arrangements for such a child to live outside England and Wales (which are governed by paragraph 19 of Schedule 2).

(9) The power in subsection (3)(b) is subject (in addition to being subject to the provisions of this section) to any right, duty, power, responsibility or authority which a parent or guardian of the child has in relation to the child and his property by virtue of any other enactment.

Parental contact etc. with children in care.

34.—(1)   Where a child is in the care of a local authority, the authority shall (subject to the provisions of this section) allow the child reasonable contact with—

   (a)   his parents;

   (b)   any guardian of his;

   (c)   where there was a residence order in force with respect to the child immediately before the care order was made, the person in whose favour the order was made; and

   (d)   where, immediately before the care order was made, a person had care of the child by virtue of an order made in the exercise of the High Court's inherent jurisdiction with respect to children, that person.

   (2)   On the application made by the authority or the child, the court may make such order as it considers appropriate with respect to the contact which is to be allowed between the child and any named person.

   (3)   On an application made by—

   (a)   any person mentioned in paragraphs (a) to (d) of subsection (1); or

   (b)   any person who has obtained the leave of the court to make the application,

the court may make such order as it considers appropriate with respect to the contract which is to be allowed between the child and that person.

   (4)   On an application made by the authority or the child, the court may make an order authorising the authority to refuse to allow contact between the child and any person who is mentioned in paragraphs (a) to (d) of subsection (1) and named in the order.

   (5)   When making a care order with respect to a child, or in any family proceedings in connection with a child who is in the care of a local authority, the court may make an order under this section, even though no application for such an order has been made with respect to the child, if it considers that the order should be made.

   (6)   An authority may refuse to allow the contact that would otherwise be required by virtue of subsection (1) or an order under this section if—

   (a)   they are satisfied that it is necessary to do so in order to safeguard or promote the child's welfare; and

   (b)   the refusal—

      (i)   is decided upon as a matter of urgency; and

      (ii)   does not last for more than seven days.

   (7)   An order under this section may impose such conditions as the court considers appropriate.

   (8)   The Secretary of State may by regulations make provision as to—

   (a)   the steps to be taken by a local authority who have exercised their powers under subsection (6);

   (b)   the circumstances in which, and conditions subject to which, the terms of any order made under this section may be departed from by agreement between the local authority and the person in relation to whom this order is made;

   (c)   notification by a local authority of any variation or suspension of arrangements made (otherwise than under an order under this section) with a view to affording any person contact with a child to whom this section applies.

   (9)   The court may vary or discharge any order made under this section on the application of the authority, the child concerned or the prson named in the order.

(10)　An order under this section may be made either at the same time as the care order itself or later.

(11)　Before making a care order with respect to any child the court shall—

　　(a)　consider the arrangements which the authority have made, or propose to make, for affording any person contact with a child to whom this section applies; and

　　(b)　invite the parties to the proceedings to comment on those arrangements.

Supervision orders

Supervision orders.

35.—(1)　While a supervision order is in force it shall be the duty of the supervisor—

　　(a)　to advise, assist and befriend the supervised child;

　　(b)　to take such steps as are reasonably necessary to give effect to the order; and

　　(c)　where—

　　　　(i)　the order is not wholly complied with; or

　　　　(ii)　the supervisor considers that the order may no longer be necessary, to consider whether or not to apply to the court for its variation or discharge.

(2)　Parts I and II of Schedule 3 make further provision with respect to supervision orders.

Education supervision orders.

36.—(1)　On the application of any local education authority, the court may make an order putting the child with respect to whom the application is made under the supervision of a designated local education authority.

(2)　In this Act "an education supervision order" means an order under subsection (1).

(3)　A court may only make an education supervision order if it is satisfied that the child concerned is of compulsory school age and is not being properly educated.

(4)　For the purposes of this section, a child is being properly educated only if he is receiving efficient full-time education suitable to his age, ability and aptitude and any special educational needs he may have.

(5)　Where a child is—

　　(a)　the subject of a school attendance order which is in force under section 37 of the Education Act 1944 and which has not been complied with; or

　　(b)　a registered pupil at a school which he is not attending regularly within the meaning of section 39 of that Act,

then, unless it is proved that he is being properly educated, it shall be assumed that he is not.

(6)　An education supervision order may not be made with respect to a child who is in the care of a local authority.

(7)　The local education authority designated in an education supervision order must be—

　　(a)　the authority within whose area the child concerned is living or will live; or

(b)   where—
    (i)   the child is a registered pupil at a school; and
    (ii)   the authority mentioned in paragraph (a) and the authority within whose area the school is situated agree,
the latter authority.

(8)   Where a local education authority propose to make an application for an education supervision order they shall, before making the application, consult the social services committee (within the meaning of the Local Authority Social Services Act 1970) of the appropriate local authority.

(9)   The appropriate local authority is—
    (a)   in the case of a child who is being provided with accommodation by, or on behalf of, a local authority, that authority; and
    (b)   in any other case, the local authority within whose area the child concerned lives, or will live.

(10)   Part III of Schedule 3 makes further provision with respect to education supervision orders.

Powers of court

Powers of court in certain family proceedings.
37.—(1)   Where, in any family proceedings in which a question arises with respect to the welfare of any child, it appears to the court that it may be appropriate for a care or supervision order to be made with respect to him, the court may direct the appropriate authority to undertake an investigation of the child's circumstances.

(2)   Where the court gives a direction under this section the local authority concerned shall, when undertaking the investigation, consider whether they should—
    (a)   apply for a care order or for a supervision order with respect to the child;
    (b)   provide services or assistance for the child or his family; or
    (c)   take any other action with respect to the child.

(3)   Where a local authority undertake an investigation under this section, and decide not to apply for a care order or supervision order with respect to the child concerned, they shall inform the court of—
    (a)   their reasons for so deciding;
    (b)   any service or assistance which they have provided, or intend to provide, for the child and his family; and
    (c)   any other action which they have taken, or propose to take, with respect to the child.

(4)   The information shall be given to the court before the end of the period of eight weeks beginning with the date of the direction, unless the court otherwise directs.

(5)   The local authority named in a direction under subsection (1) must be—
    (a)   the authority in whose area the child is ordinarily resident; or
    (b)   where the child does not reside in the area of a local authority, the authority within whose area any circumstances arose in consequence of which the direction is being given.

(6)   If, on the conclusion of any investigation or review under this section, the

authority decide not to apply for a care order or supervision order with respect to the child—

(a)   they shall consider whether it would be appropriate to review the case at a later date; and

(b)   if they decide that it would be, they shall determine the date on which that review is to begin.

Interim orders.

38.—(1)   Where—

(a)   in any proceedings on an application for a care order or supervision order, the proceedings are adjourned; or

(b)   the court gives a direction under section 37(1),

the court may make an interim care order or an interim supervision order with respect to the child concerned.

(2)   A court shall not make an interim care order or interim supervision order under this section unless it is satisfied that there are reasonable grounds for believing that the circumstances with respect to the child are as mentioned in section 31(2).

(3)   Where, in any proceedings on an application for a care order or supervision order, a court makes a residence order with respect to the child concerned, it shall also make an interim supervision order with respect to him unless satisfied that his welfare will be satisfactorily safeguarded without an interim order being made.

(4)   An interim order made under or by virtue of this section shall have effect for such period as may be specified in the order, but shall in any event cease to have effect on whichever of the following events first occurs—

(a)   the expiry of the period of eight weeks beginning with the date on which the order is made;

(b)   if the order is the second or subsequent such order made with respect to the same child in the same proceedings, the expiry of the relevant period;

(c)   in a case which falls within subsection (1)(a), the disposal of the application;

(d)   in a case which falls within subsection (1)(b), on the disposal of an application for a care order or supervision order made by the authority with respect to the child;

(e)   in a case which falls within subsection (1)(b) and in which—

(i)   the court has given a direction under section 37(4), but

(ii)   no application for a care order or supervision order has been made with respect to the child,

the expiry of the period fixed by that direction.

(5)   In subsection (4)(b) "the relevant period" means—

(a)   the period of four weeks beginning with the date on which the order in question is made; or

(b)   the period of eight weeks beginning with the date on which the first order was made if that period ends later than the period mentioned in paragraph (a).

(6)   Where the court makes an interim care order, or interim supervision order, it may give such directions (if any) as it considers appropriate with regard

to the medical or psychiatric examination or other assessment of the child; but if the child is of sufficient understanding to make an informed decision he may refuse to submit to the examination or other assessment.

(7) A direction under subsection (6) may be to the effect that there is to be—

(a) no such examination or assessment; or

(b) no such examination or assessment unless the court directs otherwise.

(8) A direction under subsection (6) may be—

(a) given when the interim order is made or at any time while it is in force; and

(b) varied at any time on the application of any person falling within any class of person prescribed by rules of court for the purposes of this subsection.

(9) Paragraphs 4 and 5 of Schedule 3 shall not apply in relation to an interim supervision order.

(10) Where a court makes an order under or by virtue of this section it shall, in determining the period for which the order is to be in force, consider whether any party who was, or might have been, opposed to the making of the order was in a position to argue his case against the order in full.

Discharge and variation etc. of care orders and supervision orders.

39.—(1) A care order may be discharged by the court on the application of—

(a) any person who has parental responsibility for the child;

(b) the child himself; or

(c) the local authority designated by the order.

(2) A supervision order may be varied or discharged by the court on the application of—

(a) any person who has parental responsibility for the child;

(b) the child himself; or

(c) the supervisor.

(3) On the application of a person who is not entitled to apply for the order to be discharged, but who is a person with whom the child is living, a supervision order may be varied by the court in so far as it imposes a requirement which affects that person.

(4) Where a care order is in force with respect to a child the court may, on the application of any person entitled to apply for the order to be discharged, substitute a supervision order for the care order.

(5) When a court is considering whether to substitute one order for another under subsection (4) any provision of this Act which would otherwise require section 31(2) to be satisfied at the time when the proposed order is substituted or made shall be disregarded.

Orders pending appeals in cases about care or supervision orders.

40.—(1) Where—

(a) a court dismisses an application for a care order; and

(b) at the time when the court dismisses the application, the child concerned is the subject of an interim care order,

the court may make a care order with respect to the child to have effect subject to such directions (if any) as the court may see fit to include in the order.

(2) Where—

(a) a court dismisses an application for a care order, or an application for a supervision order; and

(b) at the time when the court dismisses the application, the child concerned is the subject of an interim supervision order,
the court may make a supervision order with respect to the child to have effect subject to such directions (if any) as the court may see fit to include in the order.

(3) Where a court grants an application to discharge a care order or supervision order, it may order that—

(a) its decision is not to have effect; or

(b) the care order, or supervision order, is to continue to have effect but subject to such directions as the court sees fit to include in the order.

(4) An order made under this section shall only have effect for such period, not exceeding the appeal period, as may be specified in the order.

(5) Where—

(a) an appeal is made against any decision of a court under this section; or

(b) any application is made to the appellate court in connection with a proposed appeal against that decision,
the appellate court may extend the period for which the order in question is to have effect, but not so as to extend it beyond the end of the appeal period.

(6) In this section "the appeal period" means—

(a) where an appeal is made against the decision in question, the period between the making of that decision and the determination of the appeal; and

(b) otherwise, the period during which an appeal may be made against the decision.

Guardians ad litem

Representation of child and of his interests in certain proceedings.
41.—(1) For the purpose of any specified proceedings, the court shall appoint a guardian ad litem for the child concerned unless satisfied that it is not necessary to do so in order to safeguard his interests.

(2) The guardian ad litem shall—

(a) be appointed in accordance with rules of court; and

(b) be under a duty to safeguard the interests of the child in the manner prescribed by such rules.

(3) Where—

(a) the child concerned is not represented by a solicitor; and

(b) any of the conditions mentioned in subsection (4) is satisfied,
the court may appoint a solicitor to represent him.

(4) The conditions are that—

(a) no guardian ad litem has been appointed for the child;

(b) the child has sufficient understanding to instruct a solicitor and wishes to do so;

(c) it appears to the court that it would be in the child's best interests for him to be represented by a solicitor.

(5) Any solicitor appointed under or by virtue of this section shall be appointed, and shall represent the child, in accordance with rules of court.

(6) In this section "specified proceedings" means any proceedings—

(a) on an application for a care order or supervision order;

(b) in which the court has given a direction under section 37(1) and has made, or is considering whether to make, an interim care order;

(c)   on an application for the discharge of a care order or the variation or discharge of a supervision order;

(d)   on an application under section 39(4);

(e)   in which the court is considering whether to make a residence order with respect to a child who is the subject of a care order;

(f)   with respect to contact between a child who is the subject of a care order and any other person;

(g)   under Part V;

(h)   on an appeal against—

(i)   the making of, or refusal to make, a care order, supervision order or any order under section 34;

(ii)   the making of, or refusal to make, a residence order with respect to a child who is the subject of a care order; or

(iii)   the variation or discharge, or refusal of an application to vary or discharge, an order of a kind mentioned in subparagraph (i) or (ii);

(iv)   the refusal of an application under section 39(4);

(v)   the making of, or refusal to make, an order under Part V; or

(i)   which are specified for the time being, for the purposes of this section, by rules of court.

(7)   The Secretary of State may by regulations provide for the establishment of panels of persons from whom guardians ad litem appointed under this section must be selected.

(8)   Subsection (7) shall not be taken to prejudice the power of the Lord Chancellor to confer or impose duties on the Official Solicitor under section 90(3) of the Supreme Court Act 1981.

(9)   The regulations may, in particular, make provision—

(a)   as to the constitution, administration and procedures of panels;

(b)   requiring two or more specified local authorities to make arrangements for the joint management of a panel;

(c)   for the defrayment by local authorities of expenses incurred by members of panels;

(d)   for the payment by local authorities of fees and allowances for members of panels;

(e)   as to the qualifications for membership of a panel;

(f)   as to the training to be given to members of panels;

(g)   as to the co-operation required of specified local authorities in the provision of panels in specified areas; and

(h)   for monitoring the work of guardians ad litem.

(10)   Rules of court may make provision as to—

(a)   the assistance which any guardian ad litem may be required by the court to give to it;

(b)   the consideration to be given by any guardian ad litem, where an order of a specified kind has been made in the proceedings in questions, as to whether to apply for the variation or discharge of the order;

(c)   the participation of guardians ad litem in reviews, of a kind specified in the rules, which are conducted by the court.

(11)   Regardless of any enactment or rule of law which would otherwise prevent it from doing so, the court may take account of—

(a)   any statement contained in a report made by a guardian ad litem who is appointed under this section for the purpose of the proceedings in question; and

(b)   any evidence given in respect of the matters referred to in the report, in so far as the statement or evidence is, in the opinion of the court, relevant to the question which the court is considering.

Right of guardian ad litem to have access to local authority records.
42.—(1)   Where a person has been appointed as a guardian ad litem under this Act he shall have the right at all reasonable times to examine and take copies of—

(a)   any records of, or held by, a local authority which were compiled in connection with the making, or proposed making, by any person of any application under this Act with respect to the child concerned; or

(b)   any other records of, or held by, a local authority which were compiled in connection with any functions which stand referred to their social services committee under the Local Authority Social Services Act 1970, so far as those records relate to that child.

(2)   Where a guardian ad litem takes a copy of any record which he is entitled to examine under this section, that copy or any part of it shall be admissible as evidence of any matter referred to in any—

(a)   report which he makes to the court in the proceedings in question; or

(b)   evidence which he gives in those proceedings.

(3)   Subsection (2) has effect regardless of any enactment or rule of law which would otherwise prevent the record in question being admissible in evidence.

PART V   PROTECTION OF CHILDREN

Child assessment orders.
43.—(1)   On the application of a local authority or authorised person for an order to be made under this section with respect to a child, the court may make the order if, but only if, it is satisfied that—

(a)   the applicant has reasonable cause to suspect that the child is suffering, or is likely to suffer, significant harm;

(b)   an assessment of the state of the child's health or development, or of the way in which he has been treated, is required to enable the applicant to determine whether or not the child is suffering, or is likely to suffer, significant harm; and

(c)   it is unlikely that such an assessment will be made, or be satisfactory, in the absence of an order under this section.

(2)   In this Act "a child assessment order" means an order under this section.

(3)   A court may treat an application under this section as an application for an emergency protection order.

(4)   No court shall make a child assessment order if it is satisfied—

(a)   that there are grounds for making an emergency protection order with respect to the child; and

(b)   that it ought to make such an order rather than a child assessment order.

(5)   A child assessment order shall—

(a)   specify the date by which the assessment is to begin; and

(b) have effect for such period, not exceeding 7 days beginning with that date, as may be specified in the order.

(6) Where a child assessment order is in force with respect to a child it shall be the duty of any person who is in a position to produce the child—

(a) to produce him to such person as may be named in the order; and

(b) to comply with such directions relating to the assessment of the child as the court thinks fit to specify in the order.

(7) A child assessment order authorises any person carrying out the assessment, or any part of the assessment, to do so in accordance with the terms of the order.

(8) Regardless of subsection (7), if the child is of sufficient understanding to make an informed decision he may refuse to submit to a medical or psychiatric examination or other assessment.

(9) The child may only be kept away from home—

(a) in accordance with directions specified in the order;

(b) if it is necessary for the purposes of the assessment; and

(c) for such period or periods as may be specified in the order.

(10) Where the child is to be kept away from home, the order shall contain such directions as the court thinks fit with regard to the contact that he must be allowed to have with other persons while away from home.

(11) Any person making an application for a child assessment order shall take such steps as are reasonably practicable to ensure that notice of the application is given to—

(a) the child's parents;

(b) any person who is not a parent of his but who has parental responsibility for him;

(c) any other person caring for the child;

(d) any person in whose favour a contact order is in force with respect to the child;

(e) any person who is allowed to have contact with the child by virtue of an order under section 34; and

(f) the child,

before the hearing of the application.

(12) Rules of court may make provision as to the circumstances in which—

(a) any of the persons mentioned in subsection (11); or

(b) such other person as may be specified in the rules,

may apply to the court for a child assessment order to be varied or discharged.

(13) In this section "authorised person" means a person who is an authorised person for the purposes of section 31.

Orders for emergency protection of children.

44.—(1) Where any person ("the applicant") applies to the court for an order to be made under this section with respect to a child, the court may make the order if, but only if, it is satisfied that—

(a) there is reasonable cause to believe that the child is likely to suffer significant harm if—

(i) he is not removed to accommodation provided by or on behalf of the applicant; or

(ii) he does not remain in the place in which he is then being accommodated;

(b) in the case of an application made by a local authority—

(i) enquires are being made with respect to the child under section 47(1)(b); and

(ii) those enquiries are being frustrated by access to the child being unreasonably refused to a person authorised to seek access and that the applicant has reasonable cause to believe that access to the child is required as a matter of urgency; or

(c) in the case of an application made by an authorised person—

(i) the applicant has reasonable cause to suspect that a child is suffering, or is likely to suffer, significant harm;

(ii) the applicant is making enquiries with respect to the child's welfare; and

(iii) those enquiries are being frustrated by access to the child being unreasonably refused to a person authorised to seek access and the applicant has reasonable cause to believe that access to the child is required as a matter of urgency.

(2) In this section—

(a) "authorised person" means a person who is an authorised person for the purposes of section 31; and

(b) "a person authorised to seek access" means—

(i) in the case of an application by a local authority, an officer of the local authority or a person authorised by the authority to act on their behalf in connection with the enquiries; or

(ii) in the case of an application by an authorised person, that person.

(3) Any person—

(a) seeking access to a child in connection with enquiries of a kind mentioned in subsection (1); and

(b) purporting to be a person authorised to do so,

shall, on being asked to do so, produce some duly authenticated document as evidence that he is such a person.

(4) While an order under this section ("an emergency protection order") is in force it—

(a) operates as a direction to any person who is in a position to do so to comply with any request to produce the child to the applicant;

(b) authorises—

(i) the removal of the child at any time to accommodation provided by or on behalf of the applicant and his being kept there; or

(ii) the prevention of the child's removal from any hospital, or other place, in which he was being accommodated immediately before the making of the order; and

(c) gives the applicant parental responsibility for the child.

(5) Where an emergency protection order is in force with respect to a child, the applicant—

(a) shall only exercise the power given by virtue of subsection (4)(b) in order to safeguard the welfare of the child;

(b) shall take, and shall only take, such action in meeting his parental responsibility for the child as is reasonably required to safeguard or promote the welfare of the child (having regard in particular to the duration of the order); and

(c)   shall comply with the requirements of any regulations made by the Secretary of State for the purposes of this subsection.

(6)   Where the court makes an emergency protection order, it may give such directions (if any) as it considers appropriate with respect to—

(a)   the contact which is, or is not, to be allowed between the child and any named person;

(b)   the medical or psychiatric examination or other assessment of the child.

(7)   Where any direction is given under subsection (6)(b), the child may, if he is of sufficient understanding to make an informed decision, refuse to submit to the examination or other assessment.

(8)   A direction under subsection (6)(a) may impose conditions and one under subsection (6)(b) may be to the effect that there is to be—

(a)   no such examination or other assessment; or

(b)   no such examination or assessment unless the court directs otherwise.

(9)   A direction under subsection (6) may be—

(a)   given when the emergency protection order is made or at any time while it is in force; and

(b)   varied at any time on the application of any person falling within any class of person prescribed by rules of court for the puposes of this subsection.

(10) Where an emergency protection order is in force with respect to a child and—

(a)   the applicant has exercised the power given by subsection (4)(b)(i) but it appears to him that it is safe for the child to be returned; or

(b)   the applicant has exercised the power given by subsection (4)(b)(ii) but it appears to him that it is safe for the child to be allowed to be removed from the place in question,

he shall return the child or (as the case may be) allow him to be removed.

(11)   Where he is required by subsection (10) to return the child the applicant shall—

(a)   return him to the care of the person from whose care he was removed; or

(b)   if that is not reasonably practicable, return him to the care of—

(i)   a parent of his;

(ii)   any person who is not a parent of his but who has parental responsibility for him; or

(iii)   such other person as the applicant (with the agreement of the court) considers appropriate.

(12)   Where the applicant has been required by subsection (10) to return the child, or to allow him to be removed, he may again exercise his powers with respect to the child (at any time while the emergency protection order remains in force) if it appears to him that a change in the circumstances of the case makes it necessary for him to do so.

(13)   Where an emergency protection order has been made with respect to a child, the applicant shall, subject to any direction given under subsection (6), allow the child reasonable contact with—

(a)   his parents;

(b)   any person who is not a parent of his but who has parental responsibility for him;

(c)   any person with whom he was living immediately before the making of the order;

(d)   any person in whose favour a contact order is in force with respect to him;

(e)   any person who is allowed to have contact with the child by virtue of an order under section 34; and

(f)   any person acting on behalf of any of those persons.

(14)   Wherever it is reasonably practicable to do so, an emergency protection order shall name the child; and where it does not name him it shall describe him as clearly as possible.

(15)   A person shall be guilty of an offence if he intentionally obstructs any person exercising the power under subsection (4)(b) to remove, or prevent the removal of, a child.

(16)   A person guilty of an offence under subsection (15) shall be liable on summary conviction to a fine not exceeding level 3 on the standard scale.

Duration of emergency protection orders and other supplemental provisions.
45.—(1)   An emergency protection order shall have effect for such period, not exceeding eight days, as may be specified in the order.

(2)   Where—

(a)   the court making an emergency protection order would, but for this subsection, specify a period of eight days as the period for which the order is to have effect; but

(b)   the last of those eight days is a public holiday (that is to say, Christmas Day, Good Friday, a bank holiday or a Sunday),

the court may specify a period which ends at noon on the first later day which is not such a holiday.

(3)   Where an emergency protection order is made on an application under section 46(7), the period of eight days mentioned in subsection (1) shall begin with the first day on which the child was taken into police protection under section 46.

(4)   Any person who—

(a)   has parental responsibility for a child as the result of an emergency protection order; and

(b)   is entitled to apply for a care order with respect to the child,

may apply to the court for the period during which the emergency protection order is to have effect to be extended.

(5)   On an application under subsection (4) the court may extend the period during which the order is to have effect by such period, not exceeding seven days, as it thinks fit, but may do so only if it has reasonable cause to believe that the child concerned is likely to suffer significant harm if the order is not extended.

(6)   An emergency protection order may only be extended once.

(7)   Regardless of any enactment or rule of law which would otherwise prevent it from doing so, a court hearing an application for, or with respect to, an emergency protection order may take account of—

(a) any statement contained in any report made to the court in the course of, or in connection with, the hearing; or

(b) any evidence given during the hearing,

which is, in the opinion of the court, relevant to the application.

(8) Any of the following may apply to the court for an emergency protection order to be discharged—

(a) the child;

(b) a parent of his;

(c) any person who is not a parent of his but who has parental responsibility for him; or

(d) any person with whom he was living immediately before the making of the order.

(9) No application for the discharge of an emergency protection order shall be heard by the court before the expiry of the period of 72 hours beginning with the making of the order.

(10) No appeal may be made against the making of, or refusal to make, an emergency protection order or against any direction given by the court in connection with such an order.

(11) Subsection (8) does not apply—

(a) where the person who would otherwise be entitled to apply for the emergency protection order to be discharged—

(i) was given notice (in accordance with rules of court) of the hearing at which the order was made; and

(ii) was present at that hearing; or

(b) to any emergency protection order the effective period of which has been extended under subsection (5).

(12) A court making an emergency protection order may direct that the applicant may, in exercising any powers which he has by virtue of the order, be accompanied by a registered medical practitioner, registered nurse or registered health visitor, if he so chooses.

Removal and accommodation of children by police in cases of emergency.
46.—(1) Where a constable has reasonable cause to believe that a child would otherwise be likely to suffer significant harm, he may—

(a) remove the child to suitable accommodation and keep him there; or

(b) take such steps as are reasonable to ensure that the child's removal from any hospital, or other place, in which he is then being accommodated is prevented.

(2) For the purposes of this Act, a child with respect to whom a constable has exercised his powers under this section is referred to as having been taken into police protection.

(3) As soon as is reasonably practicable after taking a child into police protection, the constable concerned shall—

(a) inform the local authority within whose area the child was found of the steps that have been, and are proposed to be, taken with respect to the child under this section and the reasons for taking them;

(b) give details to the authority within whose area the child is ordinarily resident ("the appropriate authority") of the place at which the child is being accommodated;

(c)   inform the child (if he appears capable of understanding)—

    (i)   of the steps that have been taken with respect to him under this section and of the reasons for taking them; and

    (ii)   of the further steps that may be taken with respect to him under this section;

(d)   take such steps as are reasonably practicable to discover the wishes and feelings of the child;

(e)   secure that the case is inquired into by an officer designated for the purposes of this section by the chief officer of the police area concerned; and

(f)   where the child was taken into police protection by being removed to accommodation which is not provided—

    (i)   by or on behalf of a local authority; or

    (ii)   as a refuge, in compliance with the requirements of section 51, secure that he is moved to accommodation which is so provided.

(4)   As soon as is reasonably practicable after taking a child into police protection, the constable concerned shall take such steps as are reasonably practicable to inform—

(a)   the child's parents;

(b)   every person who is not a parent of his but who has parental responsibility for him; and

(c)   any other person with whom the child was living immediately before being taken into police protection,
of the steps that he has taken under this section with respect to the child, the reasons for taking them and the further steps that may be taken with respect to him under this section.

(5)   On completing any inquiry under subsection (3)(e), the officer conducting it shall release the child from police protection unless he considers that there is still reasonable cause for believing that the child would be likely to suffer significant harm if released.

(6)   No child may be kept in police protection for more than 72 hours.

(7)   While a child is being kept in police protection, the designated officer may apply on behalf of the appropriate authority for an emergency protection order to be made under section 44 with respect to the child.

(8)   An application may be made under subsection (7) whether or not the authority know of it or agree to its being made.

(9)   While a child is being kept in police protection—

(a)   neither the constable concerned nor the designated officer shall have parental responsibility for him; but

(b)   the designated officer shall do what is reasonable in all the circumstances of the case for the purpose of safeguarding or promoting the child's welfare (having regard in particular to the length of the period during which the child will be so protected).

(10)   Where a child has been taken into police protection, the designated officer shall allow—

(a)   the child's parents;

(b)   any person who is not a parent of the child but who has parental responsibility for him;

(c)   any person with whom the child was living immediately before he was taken into police protection;

(d)   any person in whose favour a contact order is in force with respect to the child;

(e)   any person who is allowed to have contact with the child by virtue of an order under section 34; and

(f)   any person acting on behalf of any of those persons,

to have such contact (if any) with the child as, in the opinion of the designated officer, is both reasonable and in the child's best interests.

(11)   Where a child who has been taken into police protection is in accommodation provided by, or on behalf of, the appropriate authority, subsection (10) shall have effect as if it referred to the authority rather than to the designated officer.

Local authority's duty to investigate.

47.—(1)   Where a local authority—

(a)   are informed that a child who lives, or is found, in their area—

(i)   is the subject of an emergency protection order; or

(ii)   is in police protection; or

(b)   have reasonable cause to suspect that a child who lives, or is found, in their area is suffering, or is likely to suffer, significant harm,

the authority shall make, or cause to be made, such enquiries as they consider necessary to enable them to decide whether they should take any action to safeguard or promote the child's welfare.

(2)   Where a local authority have obtained an emergency protection order with respect to a child, they shall make, or cause to be made, such enquiries as they consider necessary to enable them to decide what action they should take to safeguard or promote the child's welfare.

(3)   The enquiries shall, in particular, be directed towards establishing—

(a)   whether the authority should make any application to the court, or exercise any of their other powers under this Act, with respect to the child;

(b)   whether, in the case of a child—

(i)   with respect to whom an emergency protection order has been made; and

(ii)   who is not in accommodation provided by or on behalf of the authority,

it would be in the child's best interests (while an emergency protection order remains in force) for him to be in such accommodation; and

(c)   whether, in the case of a child who has been taken into police protection, it would be in the child's best interests for the authority to ask for an application to be made under section 46(7).

(4)   Where enquiries are being made under subsection (1) with respect to a child, the local authority concerned shall (with a view to enabling them to determine what action, if any, to take with respect to him) take such steps as are reasonably practicable—

(a)   to obtain access to him; or

(b)   to ensure that access to him is obtained, on their behalf, by a person authorised by them for the purpose, unless they are satisfied that they already have sufficient information with respect to him.

(5)   Where, as a result of any such enquiries, it appears to the authority that there are matters connected with the child's education which should be investigated, they shall consult the relevant local education authority.

(6)   Where, in the course of enquiries made under this section—

    (a)   any officer of the local authority concerned; or

    (b)   any person authorised by the authority to act on their behalf in connection with those enquiries—

        (i)   is refused access to the child concerned; or

        (ii)   is denied information as to his whereabouts,

the authority shall apply for an emergency protection order, a child assessment order, a care order or a supervision order with respect to the child unless they are satisfied that his welfare can be satisfactorily safeguarded without their doing so.

(7)   If, on the conclusion of any enquries or review made under this section, the authority decide not to apply for an emergency protection order, a child assessment order, a care order or a supervision order they shall—

    (a)   consider whether it would be appropriate to review the case at a later date; and

    (b)   if they decide that it would be, determine the date on which that review is to begin.

(8)   Where, as a result of complying with this section, a local authority conclude that they should take action to safeguard or promote the child's welfare they shall take that action (so far as it is both within their power and reasonably practicable for them to do so).

(9)   Where a local authority are conducting enquiries under this section, it shall be the duty of any person mentioned in subsection (11) to assist them with those enquiries (in particular by providing relevant information and advice) if called upon by the authority to do so.

(10)   Subsection (9) does not oblige any person to assist a local authority where doing so would be unreasonable in all the circumstances of the case.

(11)   The persons are—

    (a)   any local authority;

    (b)   any local education authority;

    (c)   any local housing authority;

    (d)   any health authority; and

    (e)   any person authorised by the Secretary of State for the purposes of this section.

(12)   Where a local authority are making enquiries under this section with respect to a child who appears to them to be ordinarily resident within the area of another authority, they shall consult that other authority, who may undertake the necessary enquiries in their place.

Powers to assist in discovery of children who may be in need of emergency protection.

48.—(1)   Where it appears to a court making an emergency protection order that adequate information as to the child's whereabouts—

    (a)   is not available to the applicant for the order; but

(b)   is available to another person,
it may include in the order a provision requiring that other person to disclose, if asked to do so by the applicant, any information that he may have as to the child's whereabouts.

(2)   No person shall be excused from complying with such a requirement on the ground that complying might incriminate him or his spouse of an offence; but a statement or admission made in complying shall not be admissible in evidence against either of them in proceedings for any offence other than perjury.

(3)   An emergency protection order may authorise the appliant to enter premises specified by the order and search for the child with respect to whom the order is made.

(4)   Where the court is satisfied that there is reasonable cause to believe that there may be another child on those premises with respect to whom an emergency protection order ought to be made, it may make an order authorising the applicant to search for that other child on those premises.

(5)   Where—

(a)   an order has been made under subsection (4);

(b)   the child concerned has been found on the premises; and

(c)   the applicant is satisfied that the grounds for making an emergency protection order exist with respect to him,
the order shall have effect as if it were an emergency protection order.

(6)   Where an order has been made under subsection (4), the applicant shall notify the court of its effect.

(7)   A person shall be guilty of an offence if he intentionally obstructs any person exercising the power of entry and search under subsection (3) or (4).

(8)   A person guilty of an offence under subsection (7) shall be liable on summary conviction to a fine not exceeding level 3 on the standard scale.

(9)   Where, on an application made by any person for a warrant under this section, it appears to the court—

(a)   that a person attempting to exercise powers under an emergency protection order has been prevented from doing so by being refused entry to the premises concerned or access to the child concerned; or

(b)   that any such person is likely to be so prevented from exercising any such powers,
it may issue a warrant authorising any constable to assist the person mentioned in paragraph (a) or (b) in the exercise of those powers using reasonable force if necessary.

(10)   Every warrant issued under this section shall be addressed to, and executed by, a constable who shall be accompanied by the person applying for the warrant if—

(a)   that person so desires; and

(b)   the court by whom the warrant is issued does not direct otherwise.

(11)   A court granting an application for a warrant under this section may direct that the constable conerned may, in executing the warrant, be accompanied by a registered medical practitioner, registered nurse or registered health visitor if he so chooses.

(12)   An application for a warrant under this section shall be made in the manner and form prescribed by rules of court.

(13) Wherever it is reasonably practicable to do so, an order under subsection (4), an application for a warrant under this section and any such warrant shall name the child; and where it does not name him it shall describe him as clearly as possible.

Abduction of children in care etc.

49.—(1) A person shall be guilty of an offence if, knowingly and without lawful authority or reasonable excuse, he—

(a) takes a child to whom this section applies away from the responsible person;

(b) keeps such a child away from the responsible person; or

(c) induces, assists or incites such a child to run away or stay away from the responsible person.

(2) This section applies in relation to a child who is—

(a) in care;

(b) the subject of an emergency protection order; or

(c) in police protection,

and in this section "the responsible person" means any person who for the time being has care of him by virtue of the care order, the emergency protection order, or section 46, as the case may be.

(3) A person guilty of an offence under this section shall be liable on summary conviction to imprisonment for a term not exceeding six months, or to a fine not exceeding level 5 on the standard scale, or to both.

Recovery of abducted children etc.

50.—(1) Where it appears to the court that there is reason to believe that a child to whom this section applies—

(a) has been unlawfully taken away or is being unlawfully kept away from the responsible person;

(b) has run away or is staying away from the responsible person; or

(c) is missing,

the court may make an order under this section ("a recovery order").

(2) This section applies to the same children to whom section 49 applies and in this section "the responsible person" has the same meaning as in section 49.

(3) A recovery order—

(a) operates as a direction to any person who is in a position to do so to produce the child on request to any authorised person;

(b) authorises the removal of the child by any authorised person;

(c) requires any person who has information as to the child's whereabouts to disclose that information, if asked to do so, to a constable or an officer of the court;

(d) authorises a constable to enter any premises specified in the order and search for the child, using reasonable force if necessary.

(4) The court may make a recovery order only on the application of—

(a) any person who has parental responsibility for the child by virtue of a care order or emergency protection order; or

(b) where the child is in police protection, the designated officer.

(5) A recovery order shall name the child and—

(a)   any person who has parental responsibility for the child by virtue of a care order or emergency protection order; or

(b)   where the child is in police protection, the designated officer.

(6)   Premises may only be specified under subsection (3)(d) if it appears to the court that there are reasonable grounds for believing the child to be on them.

(7)   In this section—

"an authorised person" means—

(a)   any person specified by the court;

(b)   any constable;

(c)   any person who is authorised—

(i)   after the recovery order is made; and

(ii)   by a person who has parental responsibility for the child by virtue of a care order or an emergency protection order,

to exercise any power under a recovery order; and

"the designated officer" means the officer designated for the purposes of section 46.

(8)   Where a person is authorised as mentioned in subsection (7)(c)—

(a)   the authorisation shall indentify the recovery order; and

(b)   any person claiming to be so authorised shall, if asked to do so, produce some duly authenticated document showing that he is so authorised.

(9)   A person shall be guilty of an offence if he intentionally obstructs an authorised person exercising the power under subsection (3)(b) to remove a child.

(10)   A person guilty of an offence under this section shall be liable on summary conviction to a fine not exceeding level 3 on the standard scale.

(11)   No person shall be excused from complying with any request made under subsection (3)(c) on the ground that complying with it might incriminate him or his spouse of an offence; but a statement or admission made in complying shall not be admissible in evidence against either of them in proceedings for an offence other than perjury.

(12)   Where a child is made the subject of a recovery order whilst being looked after by a local authority, any reasonable expenses incurred by an authorised person in giving effect to the order shall be recoverable from the authority.

(13)   A recovery order shall have effect in Scotland as if it had been made by the Court of Session and as if that court had had jurisdiction to make it.

(14)   In this section "the court", in relation to Northern Ireland, means a magistrates' court within the meaning of the Magistrates' Courts (Northern Ireland) Order 1981.

Refuges for children at risk.
51.—(1)   Where it is proposed to use a voluntary home or registered children's home to provide a refuge for children who appear to be at risk of harm, the Secretary of State may issue a certificate under this section with respect to that home.

(2)   Where a local authority or voluntary organisation arrange for a foster parent to provide such a refuge, the Secretary of State may issue a certificate under this section with respect to that foster parent.

(3)   In subsection (2) "foster parent" means a person who is, or who from time to time is, a local authority foster parent or a foster parent with whom children are placed by a voluntary organisation.

(4)   The Secretary of State may by regulations—

(a)   make provision as to the manner in which certificates may be issued;

(b)   impose requirements which must be complied with while any certificate is in force; and

(c)   provide for the withdrawal of certificates in prescribed circumstances.

(5)   Where a certificate is in force with respect to a home, none of the provisions mentioned in subsection (7) shall apply in relation to any person providing a refuge for any child in that home.

(6)   Where a certificate is in force with respect to a foster parent, none of those provisions shall apply in relation to the provision by him of a refuge for any child in accordance with arrangements made by the local authority or voluntary organisation.

(7)   The provisions are—

(a)   section 49;

(b)   section 71 of the Social Work (Scotland) Act 1968 (harbouring children who have absconded from residential establishments etc.), so far as it applies in relation to anything done in England and Wales;

(c)   section 32(3) of the Children and Young Persons Act 1969 (compelling, persuading, inciting or assisting any person to be absent from detention, etc.), so far as it applies in relation to anything done in England and Wales;

(d)   section 2 of the Child Abduction Act 1984.

Rules and regulations.

52.—(1)   Without prejudice to section 93 or any other power to make such rules, rules of court may be made with respect to the procedure to be followed in connection with proceedings under this Part.

(2)   The rules may, in particular make provision—

(a)   as to the form in which any application is to be made or direction is to be given;

(b)   prescribing the persons who are to be notified of—

(i)   the making, or extension, of an emergency protection order; or

(ii)   the making of an application under section 45(4) or (8) or 46(7); and

(c)   as to the content of any such notification and the manner in which, and person by whom, it is to be given.

(3)   The Secretary of State may by regulations provide that, where—

(a)   an emergency protection order has been made with respect to a child;

(b)   the applicant for the order was not the local authority within whose area the child is ordinarily resident; and

(c)   that local authority are of the opinion that it would be in the child's best interests for the applicant's responsibilities under the order to be transferred to them,

that authority shall (subject to their having complied with any requirements imposed by the regulations) be treated, for the purposes of this Act, as though they and not the original applicant had applied for, and been granted, the order.

(4)   Regulations made under subsection (3) may, in particular, make provision as to—

(a)   the considerations to which the local authority shall have regard in forming an opinion as mentioned in subsection (3)(c); and

(b)   the time at which responsibility under any emergency protection order is to be treated as having been transfered to a local authority.

PART VI   COMMUNITY HOMES

Provision of community homes by local authorities.
53.—(1)   Every local authority shall make such arrangements as they consider appropriate for securing that homes ("community homes") are available—
(a)   for the care and accommodation of children looked after by them; and
(b)   for purposes connected with the welfare of children (whether or not looked after by them),
and may do so jointly with one or more other local authorities.

(2)   In making such arrangements, a local authority shall have regard to the need for ensuring the availability of accommodation—
(a)   of different descriptions; and
(b)   which is suitable for different purposes and the requirements of different descriptions of children.

(3)   A community home may be a home—
(a)   provided, managed, equipped and maintained by a local authority; or
(b)   provided by a voluntary organisation but in respect of which a local authority and the organisation—
(i)   propose that, in accordance with an instrument of management, the management, equipment and maintenance of the home shall be the responsibility of the local authority; or
(ii)   so propose that the management, equipment and maintenance of the home shall be the responsibility of the voluntary organisation.

(4)   Where a local authority are to be responsible for the management of a community home provided by a voluntary organisation, the authority shall designate the home as a controlled community home.

(5)   Where a voluntary organisation are to be responsible for the management of a community home provided by the organisation, the local authority shall designate the home as an assisted community home.

(6)   Schedule 4 shall have effect for the purpose of supplementing the provisions of this Part.

Directions that premises be no longer used for community home.
54.—(1)   Where it appears to the Secretary of State that—
(a)   any premises used for the purposes of a community home are unsuitable for those purposes; or
(b)   the conduct of a community home—
(i)   is not in accordance with regulations made by him under paragraph 4 of Schedule 4; or
(ii)   is otherwise unsatisfactory,
he may, by notice in writing served on the responsible body, direct that as from such date as may be specified in the notice the premises shall not be used for the purposes of a community home.

(2)   Where—
(a)   the Secretary of State has given a direction under subsection (1); and

(b)   the direction has not been revoked,
he may at any time by order revoke the instrument of management for the home concerned.

(3)   For the purposes of subsection (1), the responsible body—

(a)   in relation to a community home provided by a local authority, is that local authority;

(b)   in relation to a controlled community home, is the local authority specified in the home's instrument of management; and

(c)   in relation to an assisted community home, is the voluntary organisation by which the home is provided.

Determination of disputes relating to controlled and assisted community homes.
55.—(1)   Where any dispute relating to a controlled community home arises between the local authority specified in the home's instrument of management and—

(a)   the voluntary organisation by which the home is provided; or

(b)   any other local authority who have placed, or desire or are required to place, in the home a child who is looked after by them,
the dispute may be referred by either party to the Secretary of State for his determination.

(2)   Where any dispute relating to an assisted community home arises between the voluntary organisation by which the home is provided and any local authority who have placed, or desire to place, in the home a child who is looked after by them, the dispute may be referred by either party to the Secretary of State for his determination.

(3)   Where a dispute is referred to the Secretary of State under this section he may, in order to give effect to his determination of the dispute, give such directions as he thinks fit to the local authority or voluntary organisation concerned.

(4)   This section applies even though the matter in dispute may be one which, under or by virtue of Part II of Schedule 4, is reversed for the decision, or is the responsibility, of—

(a)   the local authority specified in the home's instrument of management; or

(b)   (as the case may be) the voluntary organisation by which the home is provided.

(5)   Where any trust deed relating to a controlled or assisted community home contains provision whereby a bishop or any other ecclesiastical or denominational authority has power to decided questions relating to religious instruction given in the home, no dispute which is capable of being dealt with in accordance with that provision shall be referred to the Secretary of State under this section.

(6)   In this Part "trust deed", in relation to a voluntary home, means any instrument (other than an instrument of management) regulating—

(a)   the maintenance, management or conduct of the home; or

(b)   the constitution of a body of managers or trustees of the home.

Discontinuance by voluntary organisation of controlled or assisted community home.

56.—(1)   The voluntary organisation by which a controlled or assisted community home is provided shall not cease to provide the home except after giving to the Secretary of State and the local authority specified in the home's instrument of management not less than two years' notice in writing of their intention to do so.

(2)   A notice under subsection (1) shall specify the date from which the voluntary organisation intend to cease to provide the home as a community home.

(3)   Where such a notice is given and is not withdrawn before the date specified in it, the home's instrument of management shall cease to have effect on that date and the home shall then cease to be a controlled or assisted community home.

(4)   Where a notice is given under subsection (1) and the home's managers give notice in writing to the Secretary of State that they are unable or unwilling to continue as its managers until the date specified in the subsection (1) notice, the Secretary of State may by order—

(a)   revoke the home's instrument of management; and

(b)   require the local authority who were specified in that instrument to conduct the home until—

(i)   the date specified in the subsection (1) notice; or

(ii)   such earlier date (if any) as may be specified for the purposes of this paragraph in the order,

as if it were a community home provided by the local authority.

(5)   Where the Secretary of State imposes a requirement under subsection (4)(b)—

(a)   nothing in the trust deed for the home shall affect the conduct of the home by the local authority;

(b)   the Secretary of State may by order direct that for the purposes of any provision specified in the direction and made by or under any enactment relating to community homes (other than this section) the home shall, until the date or earlier date specified as mentioned in subsection (4)(b), be treated as a controlled or assisted community home;

(c)   except in so far as the Secretary of State so directs, the home shall until that date be treated for the purposes of any such enactment as a community home provided by the local authority; and

(d)   on the date or earlier date specified as mentioned in subsection (4)(b) the home shall cease to be a community home.

Closure by local authority of controlled or assisted community home.

57.—(1)   The local authority specified in the instrument of management for a controlled or assisted community home may give—

(a)   the Secretary of State; and

(b)   the voluntary organisation by which the home is provided,

not less than two years' notice in writing of their intention to withdraw their designation of the home as a controlled or assisted community home.

(2)   A notice under subsection (1) shall specify the date ("the specified date") on which the designation is to be withdrawn.

(3) Where—

    (a) a notice is given under subsection (1) in respect of a controlled or assisted community home;

    (b) the home's managers give notice in writing to the Secretary of State that they are unable or unwilling to continue as managers until the specified date; and

    (c) the managers' notice is not withdrawn,

the Secretary of State may by order revoke the home's instrument of management from such date earlier than the specified date as may be specified in the order.

(4) Before making an order under subsection (3), the Secretary of State shall consult the local authority and the voluntary organisation.

(5) Where a notice has been given under subsection (1) and is not withdrawn, the home's instrument of management shall cease to have effect on—

    (a) the specified date; or

    (b) where an earlier date has been specified under subsection (3), that earlier date,

and the home shall then cease to be a community home.

Financial provisions applicable on cessation of controlled or assisted community home or disposal etc. of premises.

58.—(1) Where—

    (a) the instrument of management for a controlled or assisted community home is revoked or otherwise ceases to have effect under section 54(2), 56(3) or (4)(a) or 57(3) or (5); or

    (b) any premises used for the purposes of such a home are (at any time after 13th January 1987) disposed of, or put to use otherwise than for those purposes,

the proprietor shall become liable to pay compensation ("the appropriate compensation") in accordance with this section.

(2) Where the instrument of management in force at the relevant time relates—

    (a) to a controlled community home; or

    (b) to an assisted community home which, at any time before the instrument came into force, was a controlled community home,

the appropriate compensation is a sum equal to that part of the value of any premises which is attributable to expenditure incurred in relation to the premises, while the home was a controlled community home, by the authority who were then the responsible authority.

(3) Where the instrument of management in force at the relevant time relates—

    (a) to an assisted community home; or

    (b) to a controlled community home which, at any time before the instrument came into force, was an assisted community home,

the appropriate compensation is a sum equal to that part of the value of the premises which is attributable to the expenditure of money provided by way of grant under section 82, section 65 of the Children and Young Persons Act 1969 or section 82 of the Child Care Act 1980.

(4) Where the home is, at the relevant time, conducted in premises which formerly were used as an approved school or were an approved probation hostel or home, the appropriate compensation is a sum equal to that part of the value of the premises which is attributable to the expenditure—

(a) of sums paid towards the expenses of the managers of an approved school under section 104 of the Children and Young Persons Act 1933; or

(b) of sums paid under section 51(3)(c) of the Powers of Criminal Courts Act 1973 in relation to expenditure on approved probation hostels or homes.

(5) The appropriate compensation shall be paid—

(a) in the case of compensation payable under subsection (2), to the authority who were the responsible authority at the relevant time; and

(b) in any other case, to the Secretary of State.

(6) In this section—

"disposal" includes the grant of a tenancy and any other conveyance, assignment, transfer, grant, variation or extinguishment of an interest in or right over land, whether made by instrument or otherwise;

"premises" means any premises or part of premises (including land) used for the purposes of the home and belonging to the proprietor;

"the proprietor" means—

(a) the voluntary organisation by which the home is, at the relevant time, provided; or

(b) if the premises are not, at the relevant time, vested in that organisation, the persons in whom they are vested;

"the relevant time" means the time immediately before the liability to pay arises under subsection (1); and

"the responsible authority" means the local authority specified in the instrument of management in question.

(7) For the purposes of this section an event of a kind mentioned in subsection (1)(b) shall be taken to have occurred—

(a) in the case of a disposal, on the date on which the disposal was completed or, in the case of a disposal which is effected by a series of transactions, the date on which the last of those transactions was completed;

(b) in the case of premises which are put to different use, on the date on which they first begin to be put to their new use.

(8) The amount of any sum payable under this section shall be determined in accordance with such arrangements—

(a) as may be agreed between the voluntary organisation by which the home is, at the relevant time, provided and the responsible authority or (as the case may be) the Secretary of State; or

(b) in default of agreement, as may be determined by the Secretary of State.

(9) With the agreement of the responsible authority or (as the case may be) the Secretary of State, the liability to pay any sum under this section may be discharged, in whole or in part, by the transfer of any premises.

(10) This section has effect regardless of—

(a) anything in any trust deed for a controlled or assisted community home;

(b)   the provisions of any enactment or instrument governing the disposition of the property of a voluntary organisation.

PART VII   VOLUNTARY HOMES AND VOLUNTARY ORGANISATIONS

Provision of accommodation by voluntary organisations.
59.—(1)   Where a voluntary organisation provide accommodation for a child,
they shall do so by—
(a)   placing him (subject to subsection (2)) with—
  (i)   a family;
  (ii)   a relative of his; or
  (iii)   any other suitable person,
on such terms as to payment by the organisation and otherwise as the
organisation may determine;
(b)   maintaining him in a voluntary home;
(c)   maintaining him in a community home;
(d)   maintaining him in a registered children's home;
(e)   maintaining him in a home provided by the Secretary of State under
section 82(5) on such terms as the Secretary of State may from time to time
determine; or
(f)   making such other arrangements (subject to subsection (3)) as seem
appropriate to them.
(2)   The Secretary of State may make regulations as to the placing of children
with foster parents by voluntary organisations and the regulations may, in
particular, make provision which (with any necessary modifications) is similar to
the provision that may be made under section 23(2)(a).
(3)   The Secretary of State may make regulations as to the arrangements
which may be made under subsection (1)(f) and the regulations may in particular
make provision which (with any necessary modifications) is similar to the
provision that may be made under section 23(2)(f).
(4)   The Secretary of State may make regulations requiring any voluntary
organisation who are providing accommodation for a child—
(a)   to review his case; and
(b)   to consider any representations (including any complaint) made to
them by any person falling within a prescribed class of person,
in accordance with the provisions of the regulations.
(5)   Regulations under subsection (4) may in particular make provision which
(with any necessary modifications) is similar to the provision that may be made
under section 26.
(6)   Regulations under subsections (2) to (4) may provide that any person
who, without reasonable excuse, contravenes or fails to comply with a regulation
shall be guilty of an offence and liable on summary conviction to a fine not
exceeding level 4 on the standard scale.

Registration and regulation of voluntary homes.
60.—(1)   No voluntary home shall be carried on unless it is registered in a
register to be kept for the purposes of this section by the Secretary of State.

(2) The register may be kept by means of a computer.

(3) In this Act "voluntary home" means any home or other institution providing care and accommodation for children which is carried on by a voluntary organisation but does not include—

    (a) a nursing home, mental nursing home or residential care home;

    (b) a school;

    (c) any health service hospital;

    (d) any community home;

    (e) any home or other institution provided, equipped and maintained by the Secretary of State; or

    (f) any home which is exempted by regulations made for the purposes of this section by the Secretary of State.

(4) Schedule 5 shall have effect for the purpose of supplementing the provisions of this Part.

Duties of voluntary organisations.

61.—(1) Where a child is accommodated by or on behalf of a voluntary organisation, it shall be the duty of the organisation—

    (a) to safeguard and promote his welfare;

    (b) to make such use of the services and facilities available for children cared for by their own parents as appears to the organisation reasonable in his case; and

    (c) to advise, assist and befriend him with a view to promoting his welfare when he ceases to be so accommodated.

(2) Before making any decision with respect to any such child the organisation shall, so far as is reasonably practicable, ascertain the wishes and feelings of—

    (a) the child;

    (b) his parents;

    (c) any person who is not a parent of his but who has parental responsibility for him; and

    (d) any other person whose wishes and feelings the organisation consider to be relevant,

regarding the matter to be decided.

(3) In making any such decision the organisation shall give due consideration—

    (a) having regard to the child's age and understanding, to such wishes and feelings of his as they have been able to ascertain;

    (b) to such other wishes and feelings mentioned in subsection (2) as they have been able to ascertain; and

    (c) to the child's religious persuasion, racial origin and cultural and linguistic background.

Duties of local authorities.

62.—(1) Every local authority shall satisfy themselves that any voluntary organisation providing accommodation—

    (a) within the authority's area for any child; or

    (b) outside that area for any child on behalf of the authority,

are satisfactorily safeguarding and promoting the welfare of the children so provided with accommodation.

(2)　Every local authority shall arrange for children who are accommodated within their area by or on behalf of voluntary organisations to be visited, from time to time, in the interests of their welfare.

(3)　The Secretary of State may make regulations—

(a)　requiring every child who is accommodated within a local authority's area, by or on behalf of a voluntary organisation, to be visited by an officer of the authority—

(i)　in prescribed circumstances; and

(ii)　on specified occasions or within specified periods; and

(b)　imposing requirements which must be met by any local authority, or officer of a local authority, carrying out functions under this section.

(4)　Subsection (2) does not apply in relation to community homes.

(5)　Where a local authority are not satisfied that the welfare of any child who is accommodated by or on behalf of a voluntary organisation is being satisfactorily safeguarded or promoted they shall—

(a)　unless they consider that it would not be in the best interests of the child, take such steps as are reasonably practicable to secure that the care and accommodation of the child is undertaken by—

(i)　a parent of his;

(ii)　any person who is not a parent of his but who has parental responsibility for him; or

(iii)　a relative of his; and

(b)　consider the extent to which (if at all) they should exercise any of their functions with respect to the child.

(6)　Any person authorised by a local authority may, for the purpose of enabling the authority to discharge their duties under this section—

(a)　enter, at any reasonable time, and inspect any premises in which children are being accommodated as mentioned in subsection (1) or (2);

(b)　inspect any children there;

(c)　require any person to furnish him with such records of a kind required to be kept by regulations made under paragraph 7 of Schedule 5 (in whatever form they are held), or allow him to inspect such records, as he may at any time direct.

(7)　Any person exercising the power conferred by subsection (6) shall, if asked to do so, produce some duly authenticated document showing his authority to do so.

(8)　Any person authorised to exercise the power to inspect records conferred by subsection (6)—

(a)　shall be entitled at any reasonable time to have access to, and inspect and check the operation of, any computer and any associated apparatus or material which is or has been in use in connection with the records in question; and

(b)　may require—

(i)　the person by whom or on whose behalf the computer is or has been so used; or

(ii)　any person having charge of, or otherwise concerned with the operation of, the computer, apparatus or material,

to afford him such assistance as he may reasonably require.

(9)   Any person who intentionally obstructs another in the exercise of any power conferred by subsection (6) or (8) shall be guilty of an offence and liable on summary conviction to a fine not exceeding level 3 on the standard scale.

PART VIII   REGISTERED CHILDREN'S HOMES

Children not to be cared for and accommodated in unregistered children's homes.
63.—(1)   No child shall be cared for and provided with accommodation in a children's home unless the home is registered under this Part.

(2)   The register may be kept by means of a computer.

(3)   For the purposes of this Part, "a children's home"—

(a)   means a home which provides (or usually provides or is intended to provide) care and accommodation wholly or mainly for more than three children at any one time; but

(b)   does not include a home which is exempted by or under any of the following provisions of this section or by regulations made for the purposes of this subsection by the Secretary of State.

(4)   A child is not cared for and accommodated in a children's home when he is cared for and accommodated by—

(a)   a parent of his;

(b)   a person who is not a parent of his but who has parental responsibility for him; or

(c)   any relative of his.

(5)   A home is not a children's home for the purposes of this Part if it is—

(a)   a community home;

(b)   a voluntary home;

(c)   a residential care home, nursing home or mental nursing home;

(d)   a health service hospital;

(e)   a home provided, equipped and maintained by the Secretary of State; or

(f)   a school (but subject to subsection (6)).

(6)   An independent school is a children's home if—

(a)   it provides accommodation for not more than fifty children; and

(b)   it is not approved by the Secretary of State under section 11(3)(a) of the Education Act 1981.

(7)   A child shall not be treated as cared for and accommodated in a children's home when—

(a)   any person mentioned in subsection (4)(a) or (b) is living at the home; or

(b)   the person caring for him is doing so in his personal capacity and not in the course of carrying out his duties in relation to the home.

(8)   In this Act "a registered children's home" means a children's home registered under this Part.

(9)   In this section "home" includes any institution.

(10)   Where any child is at any time cared for and accommodated in a children's home which is not a registered children's home, the person carrying on the home shall be—

(a)   guilty of an offence; and

(b)   liable to a fine not exceeding level 5 on the standard scale,
unless he has a reasonable excuse.

(11)   Schedule 6 shall have effect with respect to children's homes.

(12)   Schedule 7 shall have effect for the purpose of setting out the circumstances in which a person may foster more than three children without being treated as carrying on a children's home.

Welfare of children in children's homes.

64.—(1)   Where a child is accommodated in a children's home, it shall be the duty of the person carrying on the home to—

(a)   safeguard and promote the child's welfare;

(b)   make such use of the services and facilities available for children cared for by their own parents as appears to that person reasonable in the case of the child; and

(c)   advise, assist and befriend him with a view to promoting his welfare when he ceases to be so accommodated.

(2)   Before making any decision with respect to any such child the person carrying on the home shall, so far as is reasonably practicable, ascertain the wishes and feelings of—

(a)   the child;

(b)   his parents;

(c)   any other person who is not a parent of his but who has parental responsibility for him; and

(d)   any person whose wishes and feelings the person carrying on the home considers to be relevant,

regarding the matter to be decided.

(3)   In making any such decision the person concerned shall give due consideration—

(a)   having regard to the child's age and understanding, to such wishes and feelings of his as he has been able to ascertain;

(b)   to such other wishes and feelings mentioned in subsection (2) as he has been able to ascertain; and

(c)   to the child's religious persuasion, racial origin and cultural and linguistic background.

(4)   Section 62, except subsection (4), shall apply in relation to any person who is carrying on a children's home as it applies in relation to any voluntary organisation.

Persons disqualified from carrying on, or being employed in, children's homes.

65.—(1)   A person who is disqualified (under section 68) from fostering a child privately shall not carry on, or be otherwise concerned in the management of, or have any financial interest in, a children's home unless he has—

(a)   disclosed to the responsible authority the fact that he is so disqualified; and

(b)   obtained their written consent.

(2)   No person shall employ a person who is so disqualified in a children's home unless he has—

(a)   disclosed to the responsible authority the fact that that person is so disqualified; and

(b)   obtained their written consent.

(3)   Where an authority refuse to give their consent under this section, they shall inform the applicant by a written notice which states—

(a)   the reason for the refusal;

(b)   the applicant's right to appeal against the refusal to a Registered Homes Tribunal under paragraph 8 of Schedule 6; and

(c)   the time within which he may do so.

(4)   Any person who contravenes subsection (1) or (2) shall be guilty of an offence and liable on summary conviction to imprisonment for a term not exceeding six months or to a fine not exceeding level 5 on the standard scale or to both.

(5)   Where a person contravenes subsection (2) he shall not be guilty of an offence if he proves that he did not know, and had no reasonable grounds for believing, that the person whom he was employing was disqualified under section 68.

PART IX   PRIVATE ARRANGEMENTS FOR FOSTERING CHILDREN

Privately fostered children.

66.—(1)   In this Part—

(a)   "a privately fostered child" means a child who is under the age of sixteen and who is cared for, and provided with accommodation by, someone other than—

(i)   a parent of his;

(ii)   a person who is not a parent of his but who has parental responsibility for him; or

(iii)   a relative of his; and

(b)   "to foster privately" means to look after the child in circumstances in which he is a privately fostered child as defined by this section.

(2)   A child is not a privately fostered child if the person caring for and accommodating him—

(a)   has done so for a period of less than 28 days; and

(b)   does not intend to do so for any longer period.

(3)   Subsection (1) is subject to—

(a)   the provisions of section 63; and

(b)   the exceptions made by paragraphs 1 to 5 of Schedule 8.

(4)   In the case of a child who is disabled, subsection (1)(a) shall have effect as if for "sixteen" there were substituted "eighteen".

(5)   Schedule 8 shall have effect for the purposes of supplementing the provision made by this Part.

Welfare of privately fostered children.

67.—(1)   It shall be the duty of every local authority to satisfy themselves that the welfare of children who are privately fostered within their area is being satisfactorily safeguarded and promoted and to secure that such advice is given to those caring for them as appears to the authority to be needed.

(2)   The Secretary of State may make regulations—

(a)   requiring every child who is privately fostered within a local authority's area to be visited by an officer of the authority—

    (i) in prescribed circumstances; and

    (ii) on specified occasions or within specified periods; and

  (b) imposing requirements which are to be met by any local authority, or officer of a local authority, in carrying out functions under this section.

(3) Where any person who is authorised by a local authority to visit privately fostered children has reasonable cause to believe that—

  (a) any privately fostered child is being accommodated in premises within the authority's area; or

  (b) it is proposed to accommodate any such child in any such premises, he may at any reasonable time inspect those premises and any children there.

(4) Any person exercising the power under subsection (3) shall, if so required, produce some duly authenticated document showing his authority to do so.

(5) Where a local authority are not satisfied that the welfare of any child who is privately fostered within their area is being satisfactorily safeguarded or promoted they shall—

  (a) unless they consider that it would not be in the best interests of the child, take such steps as are reasonably praticable to secure that the care and accommodation of the child is undertaken by—

    (i) a parent of his;

    (ii) any person who is not a parent of his but who has parental responsibility for him; or

    (iii) a relative of his; and

  (b) consider the extent to which (if at all) they should exercise any of their functions under this Act with respect to the child.

Persons disqualified from being private foster parents.

68.—(1) Unless he has disclosed the fact to the appropriate local authority and obtained their written consent, a person shall not foster a child privately if he is disqualified from doing so by regulations made by the Secretary of State for the purposes of this section.

(2) The regulations may, in particular, provide for a person to be so disqualified where—

  (a) an order of a kind specified in the regulations has been made at any time with respect to him;

  (b) an order of a kind so specified has been made at any time with respect to any child who has been in his care;

  (c) a requirement of a kind so specified has been imposed at any time with respect to any such child, under or by virtue of any enactment;

  (d) he has been convicted of any offence of a kind so specified, or has been placed on probation or discharged absolutely or conditionally for any such offence;

  (e) a prohibition has been imposed on him at any time under section 69 or under any other specified enactment;

  (f) his rights and powers with respect to a child have at any time been vested in a specified authority under a specified enactment.

(3) Unless he has disclosed the fact to the appropriate local authority and obtained their written consent, a person shall not foster a child privately if—

  (a) he lives in the same household as a person who is himself prevented from fostering a child by subsection (1); or

(b)   he lives in a household at which any such person is employed.

(4)   Where an authority refuse to give their consent under this section, they shall inform the applicant by a written notice which states—

(a)   the reason for the refusal;

(b)   the applicant's right under paragraph 8 of Schedule 8 to appeal against the refusal; and

(c)   the time within which he may do so.

(5)   In this section—

"the appropriate authority" means the local authority within whose area it is proposed to foster the child in question; and

"enactment" means any enactment having effect, at any time, in any part of the United Kingdom.

Power to prohibit private fostering.

69.—(1)   This section applies where a person—

(a)   proposes to foster a child privately; or

(b)   is fostering a child privately.

(2)   Where the local authority for the area within which the child is proposed to be, or is being, fostered are of the opinion that—

(a)   he is not a suitable person to foster a child;

(b)   the premises in which the child will be, or is being, accommodated are not suitable; or

(c)   it would be prejudicial to the welfare of the child for him to be, or continue to be, accommodated by that person in those premises,

the authority may impose a prohibition on him under subsection (3).

(3)   A prohibition imposed on any person under this subsection may prohibit him from fostering privately—

(a)   any child in any premises within the area of the local authority; or

(b)   any child in premises specified in the prohibition;

(c)   a child identified in the prohibition, in premises specified in the prohibition—

(4)   A local authority who have imposed a prohibition on any person under subsection (3) may, if they think fit, cancel the prohibition—

(a)   of their own motion; or

(b)   on an application made by that person,

if they are satisfied that the prohibition is no longer justified.

(5)   Where a local authority impose a requirement on any person under paragraph 6 of Schedule 8, they may also impose a prohibition on him under subsection (3).

(6)   Any prohibition imposed by virtue of subsection (5) shall not have effect unless—

(a)   the time specified for compliance with the requirement has expired; and

(b)   the requirement has not been complied with.

(7)   A prohibition imposed under this section shall be imposed by notice in writing addressed to the person on whom it is imposed and informing him of—

(a)   the reason for imposing the prohibition;

(b)   his right under paragraph 8 of Schedule 8 to appeal against the prohibition; and

(c)   the time within which he may do so.

Offences.
70.—(1)   A person shall be guilty of an offence if—
(a)   being required, under any provision made by or under this Part, to give any notice or information—
(i)   he fails without reasonable excuse to give the notice within the time specified in that provision; or
(ii)   he fails without reasonable excuse to give the information within a reasonable time; or
(iii)   he makes, or causes or procures another person to make, any statement in the notice or information which he knows to be false or misleading in a material particular;
(b)   he refuses to allow a privately fostered child to be visited by a duly authorised officer of a local authority;
(c)   he intentionally obstructs another in the exercise of the power conferred by section 67(3);
(d)   he contravenes section 68;
(e)   he fails without reasonable excuse to comply with any requirement imposed by a local authority under this Part;
(f)   he accommodates a privately fostered child in any premises in contravention of a prohibition imposed by a local authority under this Part;
(g)   he knowingly causes to be published, or publishes, an advertisement which he knows contravenes paragraph 10 of Schedule 8.

(2)   Where a person contravenes section 68(3), he shall not be guilty of an offence under this section if he proves that he did not know, and had no reasonable ground for believing, that any person to whom section 68(1) applied was living or employed in the premises in question.

(3)   A person guilty of an offence under subsection (1)(a) shal be liable on summary conviction to a fine not exceeding level 5 on the standard scale.

(4)   A person guilty of an offence under subsection (1)(b), (c) or (g) shall be liable on summary conviction to a fine not exceeding level 3 on the standard scale.

(5)   A person guilty of a offence under subsection 1(d) or (f) shall be liable on summary conviction to imprisonment for a term not exceeding six months, or to a fine not exceeding level 5 on the standard scale, or to both.

(6)   A person guilty of an offence under subsection (1)(e) shall be liable on summary conviction to a fine not exceeding level 4 on the standard scale.

(7)   If any person who is required, under any provision of this Part, to give a notice fails to give the notice within the time specified in that provision, proceedings for the offence may be brought at any time within six months from the date when evidence of the offence came to the knowledge of the local authority.

(8)   Subsection (7) is not affected by anything in section 127(1) of the Magistrates' Courts Act 1980 (time limit for proceedings).

PART X   CHILD MINDING AND DAY CARE FOR YOUNG CHILDREN

Registration.
71.—(1)   Every local authority shall keep a register of—
(a)   persons who act as child minders on domestic premises within the authority's area; and

(b) persons who provide day care for children under the age of eight on premises (other than domestic premises) within that area.

(2) For the purposes of this Part—

(a) a person acts as a child minder if—

(i) he looks after one or more children under the age of eight, for reward; and

(ii) the period, or the total of the periods, which he spends so looking after children in any day exceeds two hours; and

(b) a person does not provide day care for children unless the period, or the total of the periods, during which children are looked after exceeds two hours in any day.

(3) Where a person provides day care for children under the age of eight on different premises situated within the area of the same local authority, that person shall be separately registered with respect to each of those premises.

(4) A person who—

(a) is the parent, or a relative, of a child;

(b) has parental responsibility for a child; or

(c) is a foster parent of a child,

does not act as a child minder for the purposes of this Part when looking after that child.

(5) Where a person is employed as a nanny for a child, she does not act as a child minder when looking after that child wholly or mainly in the home of the person so employing her.

(6) Where a person is so employed by two different employers, she does not act as a child minder when looking after any of the children concerned wholly or mainly in the home of either of her employers.

(7) A local authority may refuse to register an applicant for registration under subsection (1)(a) if they are satisfied that—

(a) the applicant; or

(b) any person looking after, or likely to be looking after, any children on any premises on which the applicant is, or is likely to be, child minding, is not fit to look after children under the age of eight.

(8) A local authority may refuse to register an applicant for registration under subsection (1)(a) if they are satisfied that—

(a) any person living, or likely to be living, at any premises on which the applicant is, or is likely to be, child minding; or

(b) any person employed, or likely to be employed, on those premises, is not fit to be in the proximity of children under the age of eight.

(9) A local authority may refuse to register an applicant for registration under subsection (1)(b) if they are satisfied that any person looking after, or likely to be looking after, any children on the premises to which the application relates is not fit to look after children under the age of eight.

(10) A local authority may refuse to register an applicant for registration under subsection (1)(b) if they are satisfied that—

(a) any person living, or likely to be living, at the premises to which the application relates; or

(b) any person employed, or likely to be employed, on those premises, is not fit to be in the proximity of children under the age of eight.

(11)   A local authority may refuse to register an applicant for registration under this section if they are satisfied—

(a)   in the case of an application under subsection (1)(a), that any premises on which the applicant is, or is likely to be, child minding; or

(b)   in the case of an application under subsection (1)(b), that the premises to which the application relates,

are not fit to be used for looking after children under the age of eight, whether because of their condition or the condition of any equipment used on the premises or for any reason connected with their situation, construction or size.

(12)   In this section—

"domestic premises" means any premises which are wholly or mainly used as a private dwelling;

"premises" includes any vehicle.

(13)   For the purposes of this Part a person acts as a nanny for a child if she is employed to look after the child by—

(a)   a parent of the child;

(b)   a person who is not a parent of the child but who has parental responsibility for him; or

(c)   a person who is a relative of the child and who has assumed responsibility for his care.

(14)   For the purposes of this section, a person fosters a child if—

(a)   he is a local authority foster parent in relation to the child;

(b)   he is a foster parent with whom the child has been placed by a voluntary organisation; or

(c)   he fosters the child privately.

(15)   Any register kept under this section—

(a)   shall be open to inspection by members of the public at all reasonable times; and

(b)   may be kept by means of a computer.

(16)   Schedule 9 shall have effect for the purpose of making further provision with respect to registration under this section including, in particular, further provision for exemption from the requirement to be registered and provision for disqualification.

Requirements to be complied with by child minders.

72.—(1)   Where a local authority register a person under section 71(1)(a), they shall impose such reasonable requirements on him as they consider appropriate in his case.

(2)   In imposing requirements on him, the authority shall—

(a)   specify the maximum number of children, or the maximum number of children within specified age groups, whom he may look after when acting as a child minder;

(b)   require him to secure that any premises on which he so looks after any child, and the equipment used in those premises, are adequately maintained and kept safe;

(c)   require him to keep a record of the name and address of—

(i)   any child so looked after by him on any premises within the authority's area;

    (ii)   any person who assists in looking after any such child; and

    (iii)   any person living, or likely at any time to be living, at those premises;

    (d)   require him to notify the authority in writing of any change in the persons mentioned in paragraph (c)(ii) and (iii).

    (3)   The Secretary of State may by regulations make provision as to—

    (a)   requirements which must be imposed by local authorities under this section in prescribed circumstances;

    (b)   requirements of such descriptions as may be prescribed which must not be imposed by local authorities under this section.

    (4)   In determining the maximum number of children to be specified under subsection (2)(a), the authority shall take account of the number of other children who may at any time be on any premises on which the person concerned acts, or is likely to act, as a child minder.

    (5)   Where, in addition to the requirements mentioned in subsection (2), a local authority impose other requirements, those other requirements must not be incompatible with any of the subsection (2) requirements.

    (6)   A local authority may at any time vary any requirement imposed under this section, impose any additional requirement or remove any requirement.

Requirements to be complied with by persons providing day care for young children.
73.—(1)   Where a local authority register a person under section 71(1)(b) they shall impose such reasonable requirements on him as they consider appropriate in his case.

    (2)   Where a person is registered under section 71(1)(b) with respect to different premises within the area of the same authority, this section applies separately in relation to each registration.

    (3)   In imposing requirements on him, the authority shall—

    (a)   specify the maximum number of children, or the maximum number of children within specified age groups, who may be looked after on the premises;

    (b)   require him to secure that the premises, and the equipment used in them, are adequately maintained and kept safe;

    (c)   require him to notify the authority of any change in the facilities which he provides or in the period during which he provides them;

    (d)   specify the number of persons required to assist in looking after children on the premises;

    (e)   require him to keep a record of the name and address of—

    (i)   any child looked after on the registered premises;

    (ii)   any person who assists in looking after any such child; and

    (iii)   any person who lives, or is likely at any time to be living, at those premises;

    (f)   require him to notify the authority of any change in the persons mentioned in paragraph (e)(ii) and (iii).

    (4)   The Secretary of State may by regulations make provision as to—

    (a)   requirements which must be imposed by local authorities under this section in prescribed circumstances;

    (b)   requirements of such descriptions as may be prescribed which must not be imposed by local authorities under this section.

(5)   In subsection (3), references to children looked after are to children looked after in accordance with the provision of day care made by the registered person.

(6)   In determining the maximum number of children to be specified under subsection (3)(a), the authority shall take account of the number of other children who may at any time be on the premises.

(7)   Where, in addition to the requirements mentioned in subsection (3), a local authority impose other requirements, those other requirements must not be incompatible with any of the subsection (3) requirements.

(8)   A local authority may at any time vary any requirement imposed under this section, impose any additional requirement or remove any requirement.

Cancellation of registration.

74.—(1)   A local authority may at any time cancel the registration of any person under section 71(1)(a) if—

(a)   it appears to them that the circumstances of the case are such that they would be justified in refusing to register that person as a child minder;

(b)   the care provided by that person when looking after any child as a child minder is, in the opinion of the authority, seriously inadequate having regard to the needs of that child; or

(c)   that person has—

(i)   contravened, or failed to comply with, any requirement imposed on him under section 72; or

(ii)   failed to pay any annual fee under paragraph 7 of Schedule 9 within the prescribed time.

(2)   A local authority may at any time cancel the registration of any person under section 71(1)(b) with respect to particular premises if—

(a)   it appears to them that the circumstances of the case are such that they would be justified in refusing to register that person with respect to those premises;

(b)   the day care provided by that person on those premises is, in the opinion of the authority, seriously inadequate having regard to the needs of the children concerned; or

(c)   that the person has—

(i)   contravened, or failed to comply with, any requirement imposed on him under section 73; or

(ii)   failed to pay any annual fee under paragraph 7 of Schedule 9 within the prescribed time.

(3)   A local authority may at any time cancel all registrations of any person under section 71(1)(b) if it appears to them that the circumstances of the case are such that they would be justified in refusing to register that person with respect to any premises.

(4)   Where a requirement to carry out repairs or make alterations or additions has been imposed on a registered person under section 72 or 73, his registration shall not be cancelled on the ground that the premises are not fit to be used for looking after children if—

(a)   the time set for complying with the requirements has not expired, and

(b)   it is shown that the condition of the premises is due to the repairs not having been carried out or the alterations or additions not having been made.

(5) Any cancellation under this section must be in writing.

(6) In considering the needs of any child for the purposes of subsection (1)(b) or (2)(b), a local authority shall, in particular, have regard to the child's religious persuasion, racial origin and cultural and linguistic background.

Protection of children in an emergency.
75.—(1) If—

   (a) a local authority apply to the court for an order—

      (i) cancelling a registered person's registration;

      (ii) varying any requirement imposed on a registered person under section 72 or 73; or

      (iii) removing a requirement or imposing an additional requirement on such a person; and

   (b) it appears to the court that a child who is being, or may be, looked after by that person, or (as the case may be) in accordance with the provision for day care made by that person, is suffering, or is likely to suffer, significant harm,

the court may make the order.

(2) Any such cancellation, variation, removal or imposition shall have effect from the date on which the order is made.

(3) An application under subsection (1) may be made *ex parte* and shall be supported by a written statement of the authority's reasons for making it.

(4) Where an order is made under this section, the authority shall serve on the registered person, as soon as is reasonably practicable after the making of the order—

   (a) notice of the order and of its terms; and

   (b) a copy of the statement of the authority's reasons which supported their application for the order.

(5) Where the court imposes or varies any requirement under subsection (1), the requirement, or the requirement as varied, shall be treated for all purposes, other than those of section 77, as if it had been imposed under section 72 or (as the case may be) 73 by the authority concerned.

Inspection.
76.—(1) Any person authorised to do so by a local authority may at any reasonable time enter—

   (a) any domestic premises within the authority's area on which child minding is at any time carried on; or

   (b) any premises within their area on which day care for children under the age of eight is at any time provided.

(2) Where a local authority have reasonable cause to believe that a child is being looked after on any premises within their area in contravention of this Part, any person authorised to do so by the authority may enter those premises at any reasonable time.

(3) Any person entering premises under this section may inspect—

   (a) the premises;

   (b) any children being looked after on the premises;

   (c) the arrangements made for their welfare; and

   (d) any records relating to them which are kept as a result of this Part.

(4)   Every local authority shall exercise their power to inspect the premises mentioned in subsection (1) at least once every year.

(5)   Any person inspecting any records under this section—

(a)   shall be entitled at any reasonable time to have access to, and inspect and check the operation of, any computer and any associated apparatus or material which is or has been in use in connection with the records in question; and

(b)   may require—

(i)   the person by whom or on whose behalf the computer is or has been so used; or

(ii)   any person having charge of, or otherwise concerned with the operation of, the computer, apparatus or material,

to afford him such reasonable assistance as he may require.

(6)   A person exercising any power conferred by this section shall, if so required, produce some duly authenticated document showing his authority to do so.

(7)   Any person who intentionally obstructs another in the exercise of any such power shall be guilty of an offence and liable on summary conviction to a fine not exceeding level 3 on the standard scale.

Appeals.

77.—(1)   Not less than 14 days before—

(a)   refusing an application for registration under section 71;

(b)   cancelling any such registration;

(c)   refusing consent under paragraph 2 of Schedule 9;

(d)   imposing, removing or varying any requirement under section 72 or 73; or

(e)   refusing to grant any application for the variation or removal of any such requirement,

the authority concerned shall send to the applicant, or (as the case may be) registered person, notice in writing of their intention to take the step in question ("the step").

(2)   Every such notice shall—

(a)   give the authority's reasons for proposing to take the step; and

(b)   inform the person concerned of his rights under this section.

(3)   Where the recipient of such a notice informs the authority in writing of his desire to object to the step being taken, the authority shall afford him an opportunity to do so.

(4)   Any objection made under subsection (3) may be made in person or by a representative.

(5)   If the authority, after giving the person concerned an opportunity to object to the step being taken, decide nevertheless to take it they shall send him written notice of their decision.

(6)   A person aggrieved by the taking of any step mentioned in subsection (1) may appeal against it to the court.

(7)   Where the court imposes or varies any requirement under subsection (8) or (9) the requirement, or the requirement as varied, shall be treated for all purposes (other than this section) as if it had been imposed by the authority concerned.

(8)   Where the court allows an appeal against the refusal or cancellation of any registration under section 71 it may impose requirements under section 72 or (as the case may be) 73.

(9)   Where the court allows an appeal against such a requirement it may, instead of cancelling the requirement, vary it.

(10)   In Scotland, an appeal under subsection (6) shall be by summary application to the sherrif and shall be brought within 21 days from the date of the step to which the appeal relates.

(11)   A step of a kind mentioned in subsection (1)(b) or (c) shall not take effect until the expiry of the time within which an appeal may be brought under this section or, where such an appeal is brought, before its determination.

Offences.

78.—(1)   No person shall provide day care for children under the age of eight on any premises within the area of a local authority unless he is registered by the authority under section 71(1)(b) with respect to those premises.

(2)   If any person contravenes subsection (1) without reasonable excuse, he shall be guilty of an offence.

(3)   No person shall act as a child minder on domestic premises within the area of a local authority unless he is registered by the authority under section 71(1)(a).

(4)   Where it appears to a local authority that a person has contravened subsection (3), they may serve a notice ("an enforcement notice") on him.

(5)   An enforcement notice shall have effect for a period of one year beginning with the date on which it is served.

(6)   If a person with respect to whom an enforcement notice is in force contravenes subsection (3) without reasonable excuse, he shall be guilty of an offence.

(7)   Subsection (6) applies whether or not the subsequent contravention occurs within the area of the authority who served the enforcement notice.

(8)   Any person who without reasonable excuse contravenes, or otherwise fails to comply with, any requirement imposed on him under section 72 or 73 shall be guilty of an offence.

(9)   If any person—

(a)   acts as a child minder on domestic premises at any time when he is disqualified by regulations made under paragraph 2 of Schedule 9; or

(b)   contravenes any of sub-paragraphs (3) to (5) of paragraph 2, he shall be guilty of an offence.

(10)   Where a person contravenes sub-paragraph (3) or paragraph 2 he shall not be guilty of an offence under this section if he proves that he did not know, and had no reasonable ground for believing, that the person in question was living or employed in the household.

(11)   Where a person contravenes sub-paragraph (5) of paragraph 2 he shall not be guilty of an offence under this section if he proves that he did not know, and had no reasonable grounds for believing, that the person whom he was employing was disqualified.

(12)   A person guilty of an offence under this section shall be liable on summary conviction—

(a)   in the case of an offence under subsection (8), to a fine not exceeding level 4 on the standard scale;

(b)   in the case of an offence under subsection (9), to imprisonment for a term not exceeding six months, or to a fine not exceeding level 5 on the standard scale, or to both; and

(c)   in the case of any other offence, to a fine not exceeding level 5 on the standard scale.

Application of this Part to Scotland.
79.—(1)   In the application to Scotland of this Part—

(a)   "the court" means the sheriff;

(b)   "day care" means any form of care or of activity supervised by a responsible person provided for children during the day (whether or not it is provided on a regular basis);

(c)   "education authority" has the same meaning as in the Education (Scotland) Act 1980;

(d)   "local authority foster parent" means a foster parent with whom a child is placed by a local authority;

(e)   for references to a person having parental responsibility for a child there shall be substituted references to a person in whom parental rights and duties relating to the child are vested; and

(f)   for references to fostering a child privately there shall be substituted references to maintaining a foster child within the meaning of the Foster Children (Scotland) Act 1984.

PART XI   SECRETARY OF STATE'S SUPERVISORY FUNCTIONS AND RESPONSIBILITIES

Inspection of children's homes etc. by persons authorised by Secretary of State.
80.—(1)   The Secretary of State may cause to be inspected from time to time any—

(a)   children's home;

(b)   premises in which a child who is being looked after by a local authority is living;

(c)   premises in which a child who is being accommodated by or on behalf of a local education authority or voluntary organisation is living;

(d)   premises in which a child who is being accommodated by or on behalf of a health authority is living;

(e)   premises in which a child is living with a person with whom he has been placed by an adoption agency;

(f)   premises in which a child who is a protected child is, or will be, living;

(g)   premises in which a privately fostered child, or child who is treated as a foster child by virtue of paragraph 9 of Schedule 8, is living or in which it is proposed that he will live;

(h)   premises on which any person is acting as a child minder;

(i)   premises with respect to which a person is registered under section 71(1)(b);

(j)   residential care home, nursing home or mental nursing home required to be registered under the Registered Homes Act 1984 and used to accommodate children;

(k)   premises which are provided by a local authority and in which any service is provided by that authority under Part III;

(l)   independent school providing accommodation for any child.

(2)   An inspection under this section shall be conducted by a person authorised to do so by the Secretary of State.

(3)   An officer of a local authority shall not be so authorised except with the consent of that authority.

(4)   The Secretary of State may require any person of a kind mentioned in subsection (5) to furnish him with such information, or allow him to inspect such records (in whatever form they are held), relating to—

(a)   any premises to which subsection (1) or, in relation to Scotland, subsection (l) (h) or (i) applies;

(b)   any child who is living in any such premises; or

(c)   the discharge by the Secretary of State of any of his functions under this Act; or

(d)   the discharge by any local authority of any of their functions under this Act,

as the Secretary of State may at any time direct.

(5)   The persons are any—

(a)   local authority;

(b)   voluntary organisation;

(c)   person carrying on a children's home;

(d)   proprietor of an independent school;

(e)   person fostering any privately fostered child or providing accommodation for a child on behalf of a local authority, local education authority, health authority or voluntary organisation;

(f)   local education authority providing accommodation for any child;

(g)   person employed in a teaching or administrative capacity at any educational establishment (whether or not maintained by a local education authority) at which a child is accommodated on behalf of a local authority or local education authority;

(h)   person who is the occupier of any premises in which any person acts as a child minder (within the meaning of Part X) or provides day care for young children (within the meaning of that Part);

(i)   person carrying on any home of a kind mentioned in subsection (1)(j).

(6)   Any person inspecting any home or other premises under this section may—

(a)   inspect the children there; and

(b)   make such examination into the state and management of the home or premises and the treatment of the children there as he thinks fit.

(7)   Any person authorised by the Secretary of State to exercise the power to inspect records conferred by subsection (4)—

(a)   shall be entitled at any reasonable time to have access to, and inspect and check the operation of, any computer and any associated apparatus or material which is or has been in use in connection with the records in question; and

(b) may require—

(i) the person by whom or on whose behalf the computer is or has been so used; or

(ii) any person having charge of, or otherwise concerned with the operation of, the computer, apparatus or material,

to afford him such reasonable assistance as he may require.

(8) A person authorised to inspect any premises under this section shall have a right to enter the premises for that purpose, and for any purpose specified in subsection (4), at any reasonable time.

(9) Any person exercising that power shall, if so required, produce some duly authenticated document showing his authority to do so.

(10) Any person who intentionally obstructs another in the exercise of that power shall be guilty of an offence and liable on summary conviction to a fine not exceeding level 3 on the standard scale.

(11) The Secretary of State may by order provide for subsections (1), (4) and (6) not to apply in relation to such homes, or other premises, as may be specified in the order.

(12) Without prejudice to section 104, any such order may make different provision with respect to each of those subsections.

Inquiries.

81.—(1) The Secretary of State may cause a inquiry to be held into any matter connected with—

(a) the functions of the social services committee of a local authority, in so far as those functions relate to children;

(b) the functions of an adoption agency;

(c) the functions of a voluntary organisation, in so far as those functions relate to children;

(d) a registered children's home or voluntary home;

(e) a residential care home, nursing home or mental nursing home, so far as it provides accommodation for children;

(f) a home provided by the Secretary of State under section 82(5);

(g) the detention of a child under section 53 of the Children and Young Persons Act 1933.

(2) Before an inquiry is begun, the Secretary of State may direct that it shall be held in private.

(3) Where no direction has been given, the person holding the inquiry may if he thinks fit hold it, or any part of it, in private.

(4) Subsections (2) to (5) of section 250 of the Local Government Act 1972 (powers in relation to local inquiries) shall apply in relation to an inquiry under this section as they apply in relation to a local inquiry under that section.

(5) In this section "functions" includes powers and duties which a person has otherwise than by virtue of any enactment.

Financial support by Secretary of State.

82.—(1) The Secretary of State may (with the consent of the Treasury) defray or contribute towards—

(a) any fees or expenses incurred by any person undergoing approved child care training; or

(b) any fees charged, or expenses incurred, by any person providing approved child care training or preparing material for use in connection with such training; or

(c) the cost of maintaining any person undergoing such training.

(2) The Secretary of State may make grants to local authorities in respect of expenditure incurred by them in providing secure accommodation in community homes other than assisted community homes.

(3) Where—

(a) a grant has been made under subsection (2) with respect to any secure accommodation; but

(b) the grant is not used for the purpose for which it was made or the accommodation is not used as, or ceases to be used as, secure accommodation, the Secretary of State may (with the consent of the Treasury) require the authority concerned to repay the grant, in whole or in part.

(4) The Secretary of State may make grants to voluntary organisations towards—

(a) expenditure incurred by them in connection with the establishment, maintenance or improvement of voluntary homes which, at the time when the expenditure was incurred—

(i)   were assisted community homes; or

(ii) were designated as such; or

(b) expenses incurred in respect of the borrowing of money to defray any such expenditure.

(5) The Secretary of State may arrange for the provision, equipment and maintenance of homes for the accommodation of children who are in need of particular facilities and services which—

(a) are or will be provided in those home; and

(b) in the opinion of the Secretary of State, are unlikely to be readily available in community homes.

(6) In this Part—

"child care training" means training undergone by any person with a view to, or in the course of—

(a) his employment for the purposes of any of the functions mentioned in section 83(9) or in connection with adoption ,of children or with the accommodation of children in a residential care home, nursing home or mental nursing home; or

(b) his employment by a voluntary organisation for similar purposes;

"approved child care training" means child care training which is approved by the Secretary of State; and

"secure accommodation" means accommodation provided for the purpose of restricting the liberty of children.

(7) Any grant made under this section shall be of such amount, and shall be subject to such conditions, as the Secretary of State may (with the consent of the Treasury) determine.

Research and returns of information.

83.—(1) The Secretary of State may conduct, or assist other persons in conducting, research into any matter connected with—

(a)   his functions, or the functions of local authorities, under the enactments mentioned in subsection (9);

(b)   the adoption of children; or

(c)   the accommodation of children in a residential care home, nursing home or mental nursing home.

(2)   Any local authority may conduct, or assist other persons in conducting, research into any matter connected with—

(a)   their functions under the enactments mentioned in sbsection (9);

(b)   the adoption of children; or

(c)   the accommodation of children in a residential care home, nursing home or mental nursing home.

(3)   Every local authority shall, at such times and in such form as the Secretary of State may direct, transmit to him such particulars as he may require with respect to—

(a)   the performance by the local authority of all or any of their functions—

(i)   under the enactments mentioned in subsection (9); or

(ii)   in connection with the accommodation of children in a residential care home, nursing home or mental nursing home; and

(b)   the children in relation to whom the authority have exercised those functions.

(4)   Every voluntary organisation shall, at such times and in such form as the Secretary of State may direct, transmit to him such particulars as he may require with respect to children accommodated by them or on their behalf.

(5)   The Secretary of State may direct the clerk of each magistrates' court to which the direction is expressed to relate to transmit—

(a)   to such person as may be specified in the direction; and

(b)   at such times and in such form as he may direct,

such particulars as he may require with respect to proceedings of the court which relate to children.

(6)   The Secretary of State shall in each year lay before Parliament a consolidated and classified abstract of the information transmitted to him under sbsections (3) to (5).

(7)   The Secretary of State may institute research designed to provide information on which requests for information under this section may be based.

(8)   The Secretary of State shall keep under review the adequacy of the provision of child care training and for that purpose shall receive and consider any information from or representations made by—

(a)   the Central Council for Education and Training in Social Work;

(b)   such representatives of local authorities as appear to him to be appropriate; or

(c)   such other persons or organisations as appear to him to be appropriate, concerning the provision of such training.

(9)   The enactments are—

(a)   this Act;

(b)   the Children and Young Persons Acts 1933 to 1969;

(c)   section 116 of the Mental Health Act 1983 (so far as it relates to children looked after by local authorities);

(d)   section 10 of the Mental Health (Scotland) Act 1984 (so far as it relates to children for whom local authorities have responsibility).

Local authority failure to comply with statutory duty: default power of Secretary of State.
84.—(1) If the Secretary of State is satisfied that any local authority has failed, without reasonable excuse, to comply with any of the duties imposed on them by or under this Act he may make an order declaring that authority to be in default with respect to that duty.

(2) An order under subsection (1) shall give the Secretary of State's reasons for making it.

(3) An order under subsection (1) may contain such directions for the purpose of ensuring that the duty is complied with, within such period as may be specified in the order, as appear to the Secretary of State to be necessary.

(4) Any such direction shall, on the application of the Secretary of State, be enforceable by mandamus.

PART XII MISCELLANEOUS AND GENERAL

Notification of children accommodated in certain establishments

Children accommodated by health authorities and local education authorities.
85.—(1) Where a child is provided with accommodation by any health authority or local education authority ("the accommodating authority")—

(a) for a consecutive period of at least three months; or

(b) with the intention, on the part of that authority, of accommodating him for such a period,
the accommodating authority shall notify the responsible authority.

(2) Where subsection (1) applies with respect to a child, the accommodating authority shall also notify the responsible authority when they cease to accommodate the child.

(3) In this section "the responsible authority" means—

(a) the local authority appearing to the accommodating authority to be the authority within whose area the child was ordinarily resident immediately before being accommodated; or

(b) where it appears to the accommodating authority that a child was not ordinarily resident within the area of any local authority, the local authority within whose area the accommodation is situated.

(4) Where a local authority have been notified under this section, they shall—

(a) take such steps as are reasonably practicable to enable them to determine whether the child's welfare is adequately safeguarded and promoted while he is accommodated by the accommodating authority; and

(b) consider the extent to which (if at all) they should exercise any of their functions under this Act with respect to the child.

Children accommodated in residential care, nursing or mental nursing homes.
86.—(1) Where a child is provided with accommodation in any residential care home, nursing home or mental nursing home—

(a) for a consecutive period of at least three months; or

(b) with the intention, on the part of the person taking the decision to accommodate him, of accommodating him for such period, the person carrying on the home shall notify the local authority within whose area the home is carried on.

(2)   Where subsection (1) applies with respect to a child, the person carrying on the home shall also notify that authority when he ceases to accommodate the child in the home.

(3)   Where a local authority have been notified under this section, they shall—

(a)   take such steps as are reasonably practicable to enable them to determine whether the child's welfare is adequately safeguarded and promoted while he is accommodated in the home; and

(b)   consider the extent to which (if at all) they should exercise any of their functions under this Act with respect to the child.

(4)   If the person carrying on any home fails, without reasonable excuse, to comply with this section he shall be guilty of an offence.

(5)   A person authorised by a local authority may enter any residential care home, nursing home or mental nursing home within the authority's area for the purpose of establishing whether the requirements of this section have been complied with.

(6)   Any person who intentionally obstructs another in the exercise of the power of entry shall be guilty of an offence.

(7)   Any person exercising the power of entry shall, if so required, produce some duly authenticated document showing his authority to do so.

(8)   Any person committing an offence under this section shall be liable on summary conviction to a fine not exceeding level 3 on the standard scale.

Welfare of children accommodated in independent schools.
87.—(1)   It shall be the duty of—

(a)   the proprietor of any independent school which provides accommodation for any child; and

(b)   any person who is not the proprietor of such a school but who is responsible for conducting it,
to safeguard and promote the child's welfare.

(2)   Subsection (1) does not apply in relation to a school which is a children's home or a residential care home.

(3)   Where accommodation is provided for a child by an independent school within the area of a local authority, the authority shall take such steps as are reasonably practicable to enable them to determine whether the child's welfare is adequately safeguarded and promoted while he is accommodated by the school.

(4)   Where a local authority are of the opinion that there has been a failure to comply with subsection (1) in relation to a child provided with accommodation by a school within their area, they shall notify the Secretary of State.

(5)   Any person authorised by a local authority may, for the purpose of enabling the authority to discharge their duty under this section, enter at any reasonable time any independent school within their area which provides accommodation for any child.

(6)   Any person entering an independent school in exercise of the power conferred by subsection (5) may carry out such inspection of premises, children and records as is prescribed by regulations made by the Secretary of State for the purposes of this section.

(7)   Any person exercising that power shall, if asked to do so, produce some duly authenticated document showing his authority to do so.

(8)   Any person authorised by the regulations to inspect records—

(a)   shall be entitled at any reasonable time to have access to, and inspect and check the operation of, any computer and any associated apparatus or material which is or has been in use in connection with the records in question; and

(b)   may require—

(i)   the person by whom or on whose behalf the computer is or has been so used; or

(ii)   any person having charge of, or otherwise concerned with the opration of, the computer, apparatus or material,

to afford him such assistance as he may reasonably require.

(9)   Any person who intentionally obstructs another in the exercise of any power conferred by this section of the regulations shall be guilty of an offence and liable on summary conviction to a fine not exceeding level 3 on the standard scale.

(10)   In this section "proprietor" has the same meaning as in the Education Act 1944.

Adoption

Amendments of adoption legislation.

88.—(1)   The Adoption Act 1976 shall have effect subject to the amendments made by Part I of Schedule 10.

(2)   The Adoption (Scotland) Act 1978 shall have effect subject to the amendments made by Part II of Schedule 10.

Paternity tests

Tests to establish paternity.

89.—In section 20 of the Family Law Reform Act 1969 (power of court to require use of tests to determine paternity), the following subsections shall be inserted after subsection (1)—

"(1A)   Where—

(a)   an application is made for a direction under this section; and

(b)   the person whose paternity is in issue is under the age of eighteen when the application is made,

the application shall specify who is to carry out the tests.

(1B)   In the case of a direction made on an application to which subsection (1A) applies the court shall—

(a)   specify, as the person who is to carry out the tests, the person specified in the application; or

(b)   where the court considers that it would be inappropriate to specify that person (whether because to specify him would be incompatible with any provision made by or under regulations made under section 22 of this Act or for any other reason), decline to give the direction applied for."

Criminal care and supervision orders

Care and supervision orders in criminal proceedings.

90.—(1)   The power of a court to make an order under subsection (2) of section

Text of the Children Act 1989
1 of the Children and Young Persons Act 1969 (care proceedings in juvenile courts) where it is of the opinion that the condition mentioned in paragraph (f) of that subsection ("the offence condition") is satisfied is hereby abolished.

(2) The powers of the court to make care orders—

(a) under section 7(7)(a) of the Children and Young Persons Act 1969 (alteration in treatment of young offenders etc.); and

(b) under section 15(1) of that Act, on discharging a supervision order made under section 7(7)(b) of that Act,

are hereby abolished.

(3) The powers given by that Act to include requirements in supervision orders shall have effect subject to amendments made by Schedule 12.

Effect and duration of orders etc.

Effect and duration of orders etc.

91.—(1) The making of a residence order with respect to a child who is the subject of a care order discharges the care order.

(2) The making of a care order with respect to a child who is the subject of any section 8 order discharges that order.

(3) The making of a care order with respect to a child who is the subject of a supervision order discharges that other order.

(4) The making of a care order with respect to a child who is a ward of court brings that wardship to an end.

(5) The making of a care order with respect to a child who is the subject of a school attendance order made under section 37 of the Education Act 1944 discharges the school attendance order.

(6) Where an emergency protection order is made with respect to a child who is in care, the care order shall have effect subject to the emergency protection order.

(7) Any order made under section 4(1) or 5(1) shall continue in force until the child reaches the age of eighteen, unless it is brought to an end earlier.

(8) Any—

(a) agreement under section 4; or

(b) appointment under section 5(3) or (4),

shall continue in force until the child reaches the age of eighteen, unless it is brought to an end earlier.

(9) An order under Schedule 1 has effect as specified in that Schedule.

(10) A section 8 order shall, if it would otherwise still be in force, cease to have effect when the child reaches the age of sixteen, unless it is to have effect beyond that age by virtue of section 9(6).

(11) Where a section 8 order has effect with respect to a child who has reached the age of sixteen, it shall, if it would otherwise still be in force, cease to have effect when he reaches the age of eighteen.

(12) Any care order, other than an interim care order, shall continue in force until the child reaches the age of eighteen, unless it is brought to an end earlier.

(13) Any order made under any other provision of this Act in relation to a child shall, if it would otherwise still be in force, cease to have effect when he reaches the age of eighteen.

(14) On disposing of any application for an order under this Act, the court

may (whether or not it makes any other order in response to the application) order that no application for an order under this Act of any specified kind may be made with respect to the child concerned by any person named in the order without leave of the court.

(15) Where an application ("the previous application") has been made for—

    (a) the discharge of a care order;

    (b) the discharge of a supervision order;

    (c) the discharge of an education supervision order;

    (d) the substitution of a supervision order for a care order; or

    (e) a child assessment order,

no further application of a kind mentioned in paragraphs (a) to (e) may be made with respect to the child concerned, without leave of the court, unless the period between the disposal of the previous application and the making of the further application exceeds six months.

(16) Subsection (15) does not apply to applications made in relation to interim orders.

(17) Where—

    (a) a person has made an application for an order under section 34;

    (b) the application has been refused; and

    (c) a period of less than six months has elapsed since the refusal,

that person may not make a further application for such an order with respect to the same child, unless he has obtained the leave of the court.

Jurisdiction and procedure etc.

Jurisdiction of courts.

92.—(1) The name "domestic proceedings", given to certain proceedings in magistrates' courts, is hereby changed to "family proceedings" and the names "domestic court" and "domestic court panel" are hereby changed to "family proceedings court" and "family panel", respectively.

(2) Proceedings under this Act shall be treated as family proceedings in relation to magistrates' courts.

(3) Subsection (2) is subject to the provisions of section 65(1) and (2) of the Magistrates' Courts Act 1980 (proceedings which may be treated as not being family proceedings), as amended by this Act.

(4) A magistrates' court shall not be competent to entertain any application, or make any order, involving the administration or application of—

    (a) any property belonging to or held in trust for a child; or

    (b) the income of any such property.

(5) The powers of a magistrates' court under section 63(2) of the Act of 1980 to suspend or rescind orders shall not apply in relation to any order made under this Act.

(6) Part I of Schedule 11 makes provision, including provision for the Lord Chancellor to make orders, with respect to the jurisdiction of courts and justices of the peace in relation to—

    (a) proceedings under this Act; and

    (b) proceedings under certain other enactments.

(7) For the purposes of this Act "the court" means the High Court, a county court or a magistrates' court.

(8)   Subsection (7) is subject to the provision made by or under Part I of Schedule 11 and to any express provision as to the jurisdiction of any court made by any other provision of this Act.

(9)   The Lord Chancellor may by order make provision for the principal registry of the Family Division of the High Court to be treated as if it were a county court for such purposes of this Act, or of any provision made under this Act, as may be specified in the order.

(10)   Any order under subsection (9) may make such provision as the Lord Chancellor thinks expedient for the purpose of applying (with or without modifications) provisions which apply in relation to the procedure in county courts to the principal registry when it acts as if it were a county court.

(11)   Part II of Schedule 11 makes amendments consequential on this section.

Rules of Court.
93.—(1)   An authority having power to make rules of court may make such provision for giving effect to—
  (a)   this Act;
  (b)   the provisions of any statutory instrument made under this Act; or
  (c)   any amendment made by this Act in any other enactment,
as appears to that authority to be necessary or expedient.

(2)   The rules may, in particular, make provision—
  (a)   with respect to the procedure to be followed in any relevant proceedings (including the manner in which any application is to be made or other proceedings commenced);
  (b)   as to the persons entitled to participate in any relevant proceedings, whether as parties to the proceedings or by being given the opportunity to make representations to the court;
  (c)   with respect to the documents and information to be furnished, and notices to be given, in connection with any relevant proceedings;
  (d)   applying (with or without modification) enactments which govern the procedure to be followed with respect to proceedings brought on a complaint made to a magistrates' court to relevant proceedings in such a court brought otherwise than on a complaint;
  (e)   with respect to preliminary hearings;
  (f)   for the service outside the United Kingdom, in such circumstances and in such manner as may be prescribed, of any notice of proceedings in a magistrates' court;
  (g)   for the exercise by magistrates' courts, in such circumstances as may be prescribed, of such powers as may be prescribed (even though a party to the proceedings in question is outside England and Wales);
  (h)   enabling the court, in such circumstances as may be prescribed, to proceed on any application even though the respondent has not been given notice of the proceedings;
  (i)   authorising a single justice to discharge the functions of a magistrates' court with respect to such relevant proceedings as may be prescribed;
  (j)   authorising a magistrates' court to order any of the parties to such relevant proceedings as may be prescribed, in such circumstances as may be prescribed, to pay the whole or part of the costs of all or any of the other parties.

(3) In subsection (2)—
"notice of proceedings" means a summons or such other notice of proceedings as is required; and "given", in relation to a summons, means "served";
"prescribed" means prescribed by the rules; and
"relevant proceedings" means any application made, or proceedings brought, under any of the provisions mentioned in paragraphs (a) to (c) of subsection (1) and any part of such proceedings.

(4) This section and any other power in this Act to make rules of court are not to be taken as in any way limiting any other power of the authority in question to make rules of court.

(5) When making any rules under this section an authority shall be subject to the same requirements as to consultation (if any) as apply when the authority makes rules under its general rule making power.

Appeals.
94.—(1) An appeal shall lie to the High Court against—
(a) the making by a magistrates' court of any order under this Act; or
(b) any refusal by a magistrates' court to make such an order.

(2) Where a magistrates' court has power, in relation to any proceedings under this Act, to decline jurisdiction because it considers that the case can more conveniently be dealt with by another court, no appeal shall lie against any exercise by that magistrates' court of that power.

(3) Subsection (1) does not apply in relation to an interim order for periodical payments made under Schedule 1.

(4) On an appeal under this section, the High Court may make such orders as may be necessary to give effect to its determination of the appeal.

(5) Where an order is made under subsection (4) the High Court may also make such incidental or consequential orders as appear to it to be just.

(6) Where an appeal from a magistrates' court relates to an order for the making of periodical payments, the High Court may order that its determination of the appeal shall have effect from such date as it thinks fit to specify in the order.

(7) The date so specified must not be earlier than the earliest date allowed in accordance with rules of court made for the purposes of this section.

(8) Where, on an appeal under this section in respect of an order requiring a person to make periodical payments, the High Court reduces the amount of those payments or discharges the order—
(a) it may order the person entitled to the payments to pay to the person making them such sum in respect of payments already made as the High Court thinks fit; and
(b) if any arrears are due under the order for periodical payments, it may remit payment of the whole, or part, of those arrears.

(9) Any order of the High Court made on an appeal under this section (other than one directing that an application be re-heard by a magistrates' court) shall, for the purposes—
(a) of the enforcement of the order; and
(b) of any power to vary, revive or discharge orders,
be treated as if it were an order of the magistrates' court from which the appeal was brought and not an order of the High Court.

(10)   The Lord Chancellor may by order make provision as to the circumstances in which appeals may be made against decisions taken by courts on questions arising in connection with the transfer, or proposed transfer, of proceedings by virtue of any order under paragraph 2 of Schedule 11.

(11)   Except to the extent provided for in any order made under subsection (10), no appeal may be made against any decision of a kind mentioned in that subsection.

Attendance of child at hearing under Part IV or V.
95.—(1)   In any proceedings in which a court is hearing an application for an order under Part IV or V, or is considering whether to make any such order, the court may order the child concerned to attend such stage or stages of the proceedings as may be specified in the order.

(2)   The power conferred by subsection (1) shall be exercised in accordance with rules of court.

(3)   Subsections (4) to (6) apply where—
  (a)   an order under subsection (1) has not been complied with; or
  (b)   the court has reasonable cause to believe that it will not be complied with.

(4)   The court may make an order authorising a constable, or such person as may be specified in the order—
  (a)   to take charge of the child and to bring him to the court; and
  (b)   to enter and search any premises specified in the order if he has reasonable cause to believe that the child may be found on the premises.

(5)   The court may order any person who is in a position to do so to bring the child to the court.

(6)   Where the court has reason to believe that a person has information about the whereabouts of the child it may order him to disclose it to the court.

Evidence given by, or with respect to, children.
96.—(1)   Subsection (2) applies in any civil proceedings where a child who is called as a witness in any civil proceedings does not, in the opinion of the court, understand the nature of an oath.

(2)   The child's evidence may be heard by the court if, in its opinion—
  (a)   he understands that it is his duty to speak the truth; and
  (b)   he has sufficient understanding to justify his evidence being heard.

(3)   The Lord Chancellor may by order make provision for the admissibility of evidence which would otherwise be inadmissible under any rule of law relating to hearsay.

(4)   An order under subsection (3) may only be made with respect to—
  (a)   civil proceedings in general or such civil proceedings, or class of civil proceedings, as may be prescribed; and
  (b)   evidence in connection with the upbringing, maintenance or welfare of a child.

(5)   An order under subsection (3)—
  (a)   may, in particular, provide for the admissibility of statements which are made orally or in a prescribed form or which are recorded by any prescribed method of recording;

(b)   may make different provision for different purposes and in releation to different descriptions of court; and

(c)   may make such amendments and repeals in any enactment relating to evidence (other than in this Act) as the Lord Chancellor considers necessary or expedient in consequence of the provision made by the order.

(6)   Subsection (5)(b) is without prejudice to section 104(4):

(7)   In this section—

"civil proceedings" and "court" have the same meaning as they have in the Civil Evidence Act 1968 by virtue of section 18 of that Act; and

"prescribed" means prescribed by an order under subsection (3).

Privacy for children involved in certain proceedings.

97.—(1)   Rules made under section 144 of the Magistrates' Courts Act 1980 may make provision for a magistrates' court to sit in private in proceedings in which any powers under this Act may be exercised by the court with respect to any child.

(2)   No person shall publish any material which is intended, or likely, to identify—

(a)   any child as being involved in any proceedings before a magistrates' court in which any power under this Act may be exercised by the court with respect to that or any other child; or

(b)   an address or school as being that of a child involved in any such proceedings.

(3)   In any proceedings for an offence under this section it shall be a defence for the accused to prove that he did not know, and had no reason to suspect, that the published material was intended, or likely, to identify the child.

(4)   The court or the Secretary of State may, if satisfied that the welfare of the child requires it, by order dispense with the requirements of subsection (2) to such extent as may be specified in the order.

(5)   For the purposes of this section—

"publish" includes—

(a)   broadcast by radio, television or cable television; or

(b)   cause to be published; and

"material" includes any picture or representation.

(6)   Any person who contravenes this section shall be guilty of an offence and liable, on summary conviction, to a fine not exceeding level 4 on the standard scale.

(7)   Subsection (1) is without prejudice to—

(a)   the generality of the rule making power in section 144 of the Act of 1980; or

(b)   any other power of a magistrates' court to sit in private.

(8)   Section 71 of the Act of 1980 (newspaper reports of certain proceedings) shall apply in relation to any proceedings to which this section applies subject to the provisions of this section.

Self-incrimination.

98.—(1)   In any proceedings in which a court is hearing an application for an order under Part IV or V, no person shall be excused from—

(a)   giving evidence on any matter; or

(b)   answering any question put to him in the course of his giving evidence, on the ground that doing so might incriminate him or his spouse of an offence.

(2)   A statement or admission made in such proceedings shall not be admissible in evidence against the person making it or his spouse in proceedings for an offence other than perjury.

Legal aid.

99.—(1)   The Legal Aid Act 1988 is amended as mentioned in subsections (2) to (4).

(2)   In section 15 (availability of, and payment for, representation under provisions relating to civil legal aid), for the words "and (3)" in subsection (1) there shall be substituted "to (3B)"; and the following subsections shall be inserted after subsection (3)—

"(3A)   Representation under this Part shall not be available—
(a)   to any local authority; or
(b)   to any other body which falls within a prescribed description,
for the purposes of any proceedings under the Children Act 1989.

(3B)   Regardless of subsection (2) or (3), representation under this Part must be granted where a child who is brought before a court under section 25 of the 1989 Act (use of accommodation for restricting liberty) is not, but wishes to be, legally represented before the court."

(3)   In section 19(5) (scope of provisions about criminal legal aid), at the end of the definition of "criminal proceedings" there shall be added "and also includes proceedings under section 15 of the Children and Young Persons Act 1969 (variation and discharge of supervision orders) and section 16(8) of that Act (appeals in such proceedings)".

(4)   Sections 27, 28 and 30(1) and (2) (provisions about legal aid in care, and other, proceedings in relation to children) shall cease to have effect.

(5)   The Lord Chancellor may by order make such further amendments in the Legal Aid Act 1988 as he considers necessary or expedient in consequence of any provision made by or under this Act.

Restrictions on use of wardship jurisdiction.

100.—(1)   Section 7 of the Family Law Reform Act 1969 (which gives the High Court power to place a ward of court in the care, or under the supervision, of a local authority) shall cease to have effect.

(2)   No court shall exercise the High Court's inherent jurisdiction with respect to children—

(a)   so as to require a child to be placed in the care, or put under the supervision, of a local authority;

(b)   so as to require a child to be accommodated by or on behalf of a local authority; or

(c)   so as to make a child who is the subject of a care order a ward of court; or

(d)   for the purpose of conferring on any local authority power to determine any question which has arisen, or which may arise, in connection with any aspect of parental responsibility for a child.

(3)   No application for any exercise of the court's inherent jurisdiction with respect to children may be made by a local authority unless the authority have obtained the leave of the court.

(4)   The court may only grant leave if it is satisfied that—
    (a)   the result which the authority wish to achieve could not be achieved through the making of any order of a kind to which subsection (5) applies; and
    (b)   there is reasonable cause to believe that if the court's inherent jurisdiction is not exercised with respect to the child he is likely to suffer significant harm.

(5)   This subsection applies to any order—
    (a)   made otherwise than in the exercise of the court's inherent jurisdiction; and
    (b)   which the local authority is entitled to apply for (assuming, in the case of any application which may only be made with leave, that leave is granted).

Effect of orders as between England and Wales and Northern Ireland, the Channel Islands or the Isle of Man.

101.—(1)   The Secretary of State may make regulations providing—
    (a)   for prescribed orders which—
        (i)   are made by a court in Northern Ireland; and
        (ii)   appear to the Secretary of State to correspond in their effect to orders which may be made under any provision of this Act,
to have effect in prescribed circumstances, for prescribed purposes of this Act, as if they were orders of a prescribed kind made under this Act;
    (b)   for prescribed orders which—
        (i)   are made by a court in England and Wales; and
        (ii)   appear to the Secretary of State to correspond in their effect to orders which may be made under any provision in force in Northern Ireland,
to have effect in prescribed circumstances, for prescribed purposes of the law of Northern Ireland, as if they were orders of a prescribed kind made in Northern Ireland.

(2)   Regulations under subsection (1) may provide for the order concerned to cease to have effect for the purposes of the law of Northern Ireland, or (as the case may be) the law of England and Wales, if prescribed conditions are satisfied.

(3)   The Secretary of State may make regulations providing for prescribed orders which—
    (a)   are made by a court in the Isle of Man or in any of the Channel Islands; and
    (b)   appear to the Secretary of State to correspond in their effect to orders which may be made under this Act,
to have effect in prescribed circumstances for prescribed purposes of this Act, as if they were orders of a prescribed kind made under this Act.

(4)   Where a child who is in the care of a local authority is lawfully taken to live in Northern Ireland, the Isle of Man or any of the Channel Islands, the care order in question shall cease to have effect if the conditions prescribed in regulations by the Secretary of State are satisfied.

(3)   Any regulations made under this secton may—
    (a)   make such consequential amendments (including repeals) in—
        (i)   section 25 of the Children and Young Persons Act 1969 (transfers between England and Wales and Northern Ireland); or
        (ii)   section 26 (transfers between England and Wales and Channel Islands or Isle of Man) of that Act,

as the Secretary of State considers necessary or expedient; and

    (b)   modify any provisions of this Act, in its application (by virtue of the regulations) in relation to an order made otherwise than in England and Wales.

Search warrants

Power of constable to assist in exercise of certain powers to search for children or inspect premises.

102.—(1)   Where, on an application made by any person for a warrant under this section, it appears to the court—

    (a)   that a person attempting to exercise powers under any enactment mentioned in subsection (6) has been prevented from doing so by being refused entry to the premises concerned or refused access to the child concerned; or

    (b)   that any such person is likely to be so prevented from exercising any such powers,

it may issue a warrant authorising any constable to assist that person in the exercise of those powers, using reasonable force if necessary.

    (2)   Every warrant issued under this section shall be addressed to, and executed by, a constable who shall be accompanied by the person applying for the warrant if—

    (a)   that person so desires; and

    (b)   the court by whom the warrant is issued does not direct otherwise.

    (3)   A court granting an application for a warrant under this section may direct that the constable concerned may, in executing the warrant, be accompanied by a registered medical practitioner, registered nurse or registered health visitor if he so chooses.

    (4)   An application for a warrant under this section shall be made in the manner and form prescribed by rules of court.

    (5)   Where—

    (a)   an application for a warrant under this section relates to a particular child; and

    (b)   it is reasonably practicable to do so,

the application and any warrant granted on the application shall name the child; and where it does not name him it shall describe him as clearly as possible.

    (6)   The enactments are—

    (a)   sections 62, 64, 67, 76, 80, 86 and 87;

    (b)   paragraph 8(1)(b) and (2)(b) of Schedule 3;

    (c)   section 33 of the Adoption Act 1976 (duty of local authority to secure that protected children are visited from time to time).

General

Offences by bodies corporate.

103.—(1)   This section applies where any offence under this Act is committed by a body corporate.

    (2)   If the offence is proved to have been committed with the consent or connivance of or to be attributable to any neglect on the part of any director, manager, secretary or other similar officer of the body corporate, or any person who was purporting to act in any such capacity, he (as well as the body corporate) shall be guilty of the offence and shall be liable to be proceeded against and punished accordingly.

Regulations and orders.

104.—(1)   Any power of the Lord Chancellor or the Secretary of State under this Act to make an order, regulations, or rules, except an order under section 54(2), 56(4)(a), 57(3), 84 or 97(4) or paragraph 1(1) of Schedule 4, shall be exercisable by statutory instrument.

(2)   Any such statutory instrument, except one made under section 17(4), 107 or 108(2), shall be subject to annulment in pursuance of a resolution of either House of Parliament.

(3)   An order under section 17(4) shall not be made unless a draft of it has been laid before, and approved by a resolution of, each House of Parliament.

(4)   Any statutory instrument made under this Act may—

    (a)   make different provisions for different cases;

    (b)   provide for exemptions from any of its provisions; and

    (c)   contain such incidental, supplemental and transitional provisions as the person making it considers expedient.

Interpretation.

105.—(1)   In this Act—

"adoption agency" means a body which may be referred to as an adoption agency by virtue of section 1 of the Adoption Act 1976;

"bank holiday" means a day which is a bank holiday under the Banking and Financial Dealings Act 1971;

"care order" has the meaning given by section 31(11) and also includes any order which by or under any enactment has the effect of, or is deemed to be, a care order for the purposes of this Act; and any reference to a child who is in the care of an authority is a reference to a child who is in their care by virtue of a care order;

"child" means, subject to paragraph 16 of Schedule 1, a person under the age of eighteen;

"child assessment order" has the meaning given by section 43(2);

"child minder" has the meaning given by section 71;

"child of the family", in relation to the parties to a marriage, means—

    (a)   a child of both of those parties;

    (b)   any other child, not being a child who is placed with those parties as foster parents by a local authority or voluntary organisation, who has been treated by both of those parties as a child of their family;

"children's home", has the same meaning as in section 63;

"community home" has the meaning given by section 53;

"contact order" has the meaning given by section 8(1);

"day care" has the same meaning given by section 18;

"disabled", in relation to a child, has the same meaning as in section 17(11);

"district health authority" has the same meaning as in the National Health Service Act 1977;

"domestic premises" has the meaning given by section 71(12);

"education supervision order" has the meaning given in section 36;

"emergency protection order" means an order under section 44;

"family assistance order" has the meaning given in section 16(2);

"family proceedings" has the meaning given by section 8(3);

"functions" includes powers and duties;

"guardian of a child" means a guardian (other than a guardian of the estate of a child) appointed in accordance with the provisions of section 5;

"harm" has the same meaning as in section 31(9) and the question of whether harm is significant shall be determined in accordance with section 31(10);

"health authority" means any district health authority and any special health authority established under the National Health Service Act 1977;

"health service hospital" has the same meaning as in the National Health Service Act 1977;

"hospital" has the same meaning as in the Mental Health Act 1983, except that it does not include a special hospital within the meaning of the Act;

"ill-treatment" has the same meaning as in section 31(9);

"independent school" has the same meaning as in the Education Act 1944;

"local authority" means, in relation to England and Wales, the council of a county, a metropolitan district, a London Borough or the Common Council of the City of London and, in relation to Scotland, a local authority within the meaning of section 1(2) of the Social Work (Scotland) Act 1968;

"local authority foster parent" has the same meaning as in section 23(3);

"local education authority" has the same meaning as in the Education Act 1944;

"local housing authority" has the same meaning as in the Housing Act 1985;

"mental nursing home" has the same meaning as in the Registered Homes Act 1984;

"nursing home" has the same meaning as in the Act of 1984;

"parental responsibility" has the meaning given in section 3;

"parental responsibility agreement" has the meaning given in section 4(1);

"prescribed" means prescribed by regulations made under this Act;

"privately fostered child" and "to foster a child privately" have the same meaning as in section 66;

"prohibited steps order" has the meaning given by section 8(1);

"protected child" has the same meaning as in Part III of the Adoption Act 1976;

"registered children's home" has the same meaning as in section 63;

"registered pupil" has the same meaning as in the Education Act 1944;

"relative", in relation to a child, means a grandparent, brother, sister, uncle or aunt (whether of full blood or half blood or by affinity) or step-parent;

"residence order" has the meaning given by section 8(1);

"residential care home" has the same meaning as in the Registered Homes Act 1984;

"responsible person", in relation to a child who is the subject of a supervision order, has the meaning given in paragraph 1 of Schedule 3;

"school" has the same meaning as in the Education Act 1944 or, in relation to Scotland, in the Education (Scotland) Act 1980;

"service", in relation to any provision, made under Part III, includes any facility;

"signed", in relation to any person, includes the making by that person of his mark;

"special educational needs" has the same meaning as in the Education Act 1981;

"special health authority" has the same meaning as in the National Health Service Act 1977;

"specific issue order" has the meaning given by section 8(1);

"supervision order" has the meaning given by section 31(11);

"supervised child" and "supervisor", in relation to a supervision order or an education supervision order, mean respectively the child who is (or is to be) under supervision and the person under whose supervision he is (or is to be) by virtue of the order;

"upbringing", in relation to any child, includes the care of the child but not his maintenance;

"voluntary home" has the meaning given by section 60;

"voluntary organisation" means a body (other than a public or local authority) whose activities are not carried on for profit.

(2)   References in this Act to a child whose father and mother were, or (as the case may be) were not, married to each other at the time of his birth must be read with section 1 of the Family Law Reform Act 1987 (which extends the meaning of such references).

(3)   References in this Act to—

(a)   a person with whom a child lives, or is to live, as the result of a residence order; or

(b)   a person in whose favour a residence order is in force,

shall be construed as references to the person named in the order as the person with whom the child is to live.

(4)   References in this Act to a child who is looked after by a local authority have the same meaning as they have (by virtue of section 22) in Part III.

(5)   References in this Act to accommodation provided by or on behalf of a local authority are references to accommodation so provided in the exercise of functions which stand referred to the social services committee of that or any other local authority under the Local Authority Social Services Act 1970.

(6)   In determining the "ordinary residence" of a child for any purpose of this Act, there shall be disregarded any period in which he lives in any place—

(a)   which is a school or other institution;

(b)   in accordance with the requirements of a supervision order under this Act or an order under section 7(7)(b) of the Children and Young Persons Act 1969; or

(c)   while he is being provided with accommodation by or on behalf of a local authority.

(7)   References in this Act to children who are in need shall be construed in accordance with section 17.

(8)   Any notice or other document required under this Act to be served on any person may be served on him by being delivered personally to him, or being sent by post to him in a registered letter or by the recorded delivery service at his proper address.

(9)   Any such notice or other document required to be served on a body corporate or a firm shall be duly served if it is served on the secretary or clerk of that body or a partner of that firm.

(10)   For the purposes of this section, and of section 7 of the Interpretation Act 1978 in its application to this section, the proper address of a person—

(a)   in the case of a secretary or clerk of a body corporate, shall be that of the registered or principal office of that body;

(b)   in the case of a partner of a firm, shall be that of the principal office of the firm; and

(c)   in any other case, shall be last known address of the person to be served.

Financial provisions.

106.—(1)   Any—

(a)   grants made by the Secretary of State under this Act; and

(b)   any other expenses incurred by the Secretary of State under this Act, shall be payable out of money provided by Parliament.

(2)   Any sums received by the Secretary of State under section 58, or by way of the repayment of any grant made under section 82(2) or (4) shall be paid into the Consolidated Fund.

Application to Channel Islands.

107.—Her Majesty may by Order in Council direct that any of the provisions of this Act shall extend to any of the Channel Islands with such exceptions and modifications as may be specified in the Order.

Short title, commencement, extent etc.

108.—(1)   This Act may be cited as the Children Act 1989.

(2)   Sections 89 and 96(3) to (7), and paragraph 35 of Schedule 12, shall come into force on the passing of this Act and paragraph 36 of Schedule 12 shall come into force at the end of the period of two months beginning with the day on which this Act is passed but otherwise this Act shall come into force on such date as may be appointed by order made by the Lord Chancellor or the Secretary of State, or by both acting jointly.

(3)   Different dates may be appointed for different provisions of this Act and in relation to different cases.

(4)   The minor amendments set out in Schedule 12 shall have effect.

(5)   The consequential amendments set out in Schedule 13 shall have effect.

(6)   The transitional provisions and savings set out in Schedule 14 shall have effect.

(7)   The repeals set out in Schedule 15 shall have effect.

(8)   An order under subsection (2) may make such transitional provisions or savings as appear to the person making the order to be necessary or expedient in connection with the provisions brought into force by the order, including—

(a)   provisions adding to or modifying the provisions of Schedule 14; and

(b)   such adaptations—

(i)   of the provisions brought into force by the order; and

(ii)   of any provisions of this Act then in force,

as appear to him necessary or expedient in consequence of the partial operation of this Act.

(9)   The Lord Chancellor may by order make such amendments or repeals, in such enactments as may be specified in the order, as appear to him to be necessary or expedient in consequence of any provision of this Act.

(10)   This Act shall, in its application to the Isles of Scilly, have effect subject to such exceptions, adaptations and modifications as the Secretary of State may by order prescribe.

(11)   The following provisions of this Act extend to Scotland—

section 19;

section 25(8);

section 50(13);

Part X;

section 80(1)(h) and (i), (2) to (4), (5)(a), (b) and (h) and (6) to (12);

section 88;

section 104 (so far as necessary);

section 105 (so far as necessary);

subsections (1) to (3), (8) and (9) and this subsection;

in Schedule 2, paragraph 24;

in Schedule 12, paragraphs 1, 7 to 10, 18, 27, 30(a) and 41 to 44;

in Schedule 13, paragraphs 18 to 23, 32, 46, 47, 50, 57, 62, 63, 68(a) and (b) and 71;

in Schedule 14, paragraphs 1, 33 and 34;

in Schedule 15, the entries relating to—

(a)   the Custody of Children Act 1891;

(b)   the Nurseries and Child Minders Regulation Act 1948;

(c)   section 53(3) of the Children and Young Persons Act 1963;

(d)   section 60 of the Health Services and Public Health Act 1968;

(e)   the Social Work (Scotland) Act 1968;

(f)   the Adoption (Scotland) Act 1978;

(g)   the Child Care Act 1980;

(h)   the Foster Children (Scotland) Act 1984;

(i)   the Child Abduction and Custody Act 1985; and

(j)   the Family Law Act 1986.

(12)   The following provisions of this Act extend to Northern Ireland—

section 50;

section 101(1)(b), (2) and 5(a)(i);

subsections (1) to (3), (8) and (9) and this subsection;

in Schedule 2, paragraph 24;

in Schedule 12, paragraphs 7 to 10, 18 and 27;

in Schedule 13, paragraphs 21, 22, 46, 47, 57, 62, 63, 68(c) to (e) and 69 to 71;

in Schedule 14, paragraphs 18, 28 to 30 and 38(a); and

in Schedule 15, the entries relating to the Guardianship of Minors Act 1971, the Children Act 1975, the Child Care Act 1980 and the Family Law Act 1986.

SCHEDULES

Section 15(1).   **SCHEDULE 1**
FINANCIAL PROVISION FOR CHILDREN

Orders for financial relief against parents

1.—(1) On an application made by a parent or guardian of a child, or by any person in whose favour a residence order is in force with respect to a child, the court may—

(a) in the case of an application to the High Court or a county court, make one or more of the orders mentioned in sub-paragraph (2);

(b) in the case of an application to a magistrates' court, make one or both of the orders mentioned in paragraphs (a) and (c) of that sub-paragraph.

(2) The orders referred to in sub-paragraph (1) are—

(a) an order requiring either or both parents of a child—

(i) to make to the applicant for the benefit of the child; or

(ii) to make to the child himself,

such periodical payments, for such terms, as may be specified in the order;

(b) an order requiring either or both parents of a child—

(i) to secure to the applicant for the benefit of the child; or

(ii) to secure to the child himself,

such periodical payments, for such terms, as may be so specified;

(c) an order requiring either or both parents of a child—

(i) to pay to the applicant for the benefit of the child; or

(ii) to pay to the child himself,

such lump sum as may be so specified;

(d) an order requiring a settlement to be made for the benefit of the child, and to the satisfaction of the court, of property—

(i) to which either parent is entitled (either in possession or in reversion); and

(ii) which is specified in the order;

(e) an order requiring either or both parents of a child—

(i) to transfer to the applicant, for the benefit of the child; or

(ii) to transfer to the child himself,

such property to which the parent is, or the parents are, entitled (either in possession or in reversion) as may be specified in the order.

(3) The powers conferred by this paragraph may be exercised at any time.

(4) An order under sub-paragraph (2)(a) or (b) may be varied or discharged by a subsequent order made on the application of any person by or to whom payments were required to be made under the previous order.

(5) Where a court makes an order under this paragraph—

(a) it may at any time make a further such order under sub-paragraph (2)(a), (b) or (c) with respect to the child concerned if he has not reached the age of eighteen;

(b) it may not make more than one order under sub-paragraph (2)(d) or (e) against the same person in respect of the same child.

(6) On making, varying or discharging a residence order the court may exercise any of its powers under this Schedule even though no application has been made to it under this Schedule.

Orders for financial relief for persons over eighteen

2.—(1) If, on an application by a person who has reached the age of eighteen, it appears to the court—

(a) that the applicant is, will be or (if an order were made under this paragraph) would be receiving instruction at an educational establishment or undergoing training for a trade, profession or vocation, whether or not while in gainful employment; or

(b) that there are special circumstances which justify the making of an order under this paragraph,

the court may make one or both of the orders mentioned in sub-paragraph (2).

(2) The orders are—

(a) an order requiring either or both of the applicant's parents to pay to the applicant such periodical payments, for such term, as may be specified in the order;

(b) an order requiring either or both of the applicant's parents to pay to the applicant such lump sum as may be so specified.

(3) An application may not be made under this paragraph by any person if, immediately before he reached the age of sixteen, a periodical payments order was in force with respect to him.

(4) No order shall be made under this paragraph at a time when the parents of the applicant are living with each other in the same household.

(5) An order under sub-paragraph (2)(a) may be varied or discharged by a subsequent order made on the application of any person by or to whom payments were required to be made under the previous order.

(6) In sub-paragraph (3) "periodical payments order" means an order made under—

(a) this Schedule;

(b) section 6(3) of the Family Law Reform Act 1969;

(c) section 23 or 27 of the Matrimonial Causes Act 1973;

(d) Part I of the Domestic Proceedings and Magistrates' Courts Act 1978,

for the making or securing of periodical payments.

(7) The powers conferred by this paragraph shall be exercisable at any time.

(8) Where the court makes an order under this paragraph it may from time to time while that order remains in force make a further such order.

Duration of orders for financial relief

3.—(1) The term to be specified in an order for periodical payments made under paragraph 1(2)(a) or (b) in favour of a child may begin with the date of the making of an application for the order in question or any later date but—

(a) shall not in the first instance extend beyond the child's seventeenth birthday unless the court thinks it right in the circumstances of the case to specify a later date; and

(b) shall not in any event extend beyond the child's eighteenth birthday.

(2)   Paragraph (b) of sub-paragraph (1) shall not apply in the case of a child if it appears to the court that—

(a)   the child is, or will be or (if an order were made without complying with that paragraph) would be receiving instruction at an educational establishment or undergoing training for a trade, profession or vocation, whether or not while in gainful employment; or

(b)   there are special circumstances which justify the making of an order without complying with that paragraph.

(3)   An order for periodical payments made under paragraph 1(2)(a) or 2(2)(a) shall, notwithstanding anything in the order, cease to have effect on the death of the person liable to make payments under the order.

(4)   Where an order is made under paragraph 1(2)(a) or (b) requiring periodical payments to be made or secured to the parent of a child, the order shall cease to have effect if—

(a)   any parent making or securing the payments; and

(b)   any parent to whom the payments are made or secured,

live together for a period of more than six months.

Matters to which court is to have regard in making orders for financial relief

4.—(1)   In deciding whether to exercise its powers under paragraph 1 or 2, and if so in what manner, the court shall have regard to all the circumstances including—

(a)   the income, earning capacity, property and other financial resources which each person mentioned in sub-paragraph (3) has or is likely to have in the forseeable future;

(b)   the financial needs, obligations and responsibilities which each person mentioned in sub-paragraph (3) has or is likely to have in the forseeable future;

(c)   the financial needs of the child;

(d)   the income, earning capacity (if any), property and other financial resources of the child;

(e)   any physical or mental disability of the child;

(f)   the manner in which the child was being, or was expected to be, educated or trained.

(2)   In deciding whether to exercise its powers under paragraph 1 against a person who is not the mother or father of the child, and if so in what manner, the court shall in addition have regard to—

(a)   whether that person had assumed responsibility for the maintenance of the child and, if so, the extent to which and basis on which he assumed that responsibility and the length of the period during which he met that responsibility;

(b)   whether he did so knowing that the child was not his child;

(c)   the liability of any other person to maintain the child.

(3)   Where the court makes an order under paragraph 1 against a person who is not the father of the child, it shall record in the order that the order is made on the basis that the person against whom the order is made is not the child's father.

(4)   The persons mentioned in sub-paragraph (1) are—

(a)   in relation to a decision whether to exercise its powers under paragraph 1, any parent of the child;

(b)   in relation to a decision whether to exercise its powers under paragraph 2, the mother and father of the child;

(c)   the applicant for the order;

(d)   any other person in whose favour the court proposes to make the order.

Provisions relating to lump sums

5.—(1)   Without prejudice to the generality of paragraph 1, an order under that paragraph for the payment of a lump sum may be made for the purpose of enabling any liabilities or expenses—

(a)   incurred in connection with the birth of the child or in maintaining the child; and

(b)   reasonably incurred before the making of the order,

to be met.

(2)   The amount of any lump sum required to be paid by an order made by a magistrates' court under paragraph 1 or 2 shall not exceed £1000 or such larger amount as the Secretary of State may from time to time by order fix for the purposes of this sub-paragraph.

(3)   The power of the court under paragraph 1 or 2 to vary or discharge an order for the making or securing of periodical payments by a parent shall include power to make an order under that provision for the payment of a lump sum by that parent.

(4)   The amount of any lump sum which a parent may be required to pay by virtue of sub-paragraph (3) shall not, in the case of an order made by a magistrates' court, exceed the maximum amount that may at the time of the making of the order be required to be paid under sub-paragraph (2), but a magistrates' court may make an order for the payment of a lump sum not exceeding that amount even though the parent was required to pay a lump sum by a previous order under this Act.

(5)   An order made under paragraph 1 or 2 for the payment of a lump sum may provide for the payment of that sum by instalments.

(6)   Where the court provides for the payment of a lump sum by instalments the court, on an application made either by the person liable to pay or the person entitled to receive that sum, shall have power to vary that order by varying—

(a)   the number of instalments payable;

(b)   the amount of any instalment payable;

(c)   the date on which any instalment becomes payable.

Variation etc. of orders for periodical payments

6.—(1)   In exercising its powers under paragraph 1 or 2 to vary or discharge an order for the making or securing of periodical payments the court shall have regard to all the circumstances of the case, including any change in any of the matters to which the court was required to have regard when making the order.

(2)   The power of the court under paragraph 1 or 2 to vary an order for the making or securing of periodical payments shall include power to suspend any provision of the order temporarily and to revive any provision so suspended.

(3)   Where on an application under paragraph 1 or 2 for the variation or discharge of an order for the making or securing of periodical payments the court

varies the payments required to be made under that order, the court may provide that the payments as so varied shall be made from such date as the court may specify, not being earlier than the date of the making of the application.

(4)   An application for the variation of an order made under paragraph 1 for the making or securing of periodical payments to or for the benefit of a child may, if the child has reached the age of sixteen, be made by the child himself.

(5)   Where an order for the making or securing of periodical payments made under paragraph 1 ceases to have effect on the date on which the child reaches the age of sixteen, or at any time after that date but before or on the date on which he reaches the age of eighteen, the child may apply to the court which made the order for an order for its revival.

(6)   If on such an application it appears to the court that—

(a)   the child is, will be or (if an order were made under this sub-paragraph) would be receiving instruction at an educational establishment or undergoing training for a trade, profession or vocation, whether or not while in gainful employment; or

(b)   there are special circumstances which justify the making of an order under this paragraph,

the court shall have power by order to revive the order from such date as the court may specify, not being earlier than the date of the making of the application.

(7)   Any order which is revived by an order under sub-paragraph (5) may be varied or discharged under that provision, on the application of any person by whom or to whom payments are required to be made under the revived order.

(8)   An order for the making or securing of periodical payments made under paragraph 1 or 2 may be varied or discharged, after the death of either parent, on the application of a guardian of the child concerned.

Variation of orders for secured periodical payments after death of parent

7.—(1)   Where the parent liable to make payments under a secured periodical payments order has died, the persons who may apply for the variation or discharge of the order shall include the personal representatives of the deceased parent.

(2)   No application for the variation of the order shall, except with the permission of the court, be made after the end of the period of six months from the date on which representation in regard to the estate of that parent is first taken out.

(3)   The personal representatives of a deceased person against whom a secured periodical payments order was made shall not be liable for having distributed any part of the estate of the deceased after the end of the period of six months referred to in sub-paragraph (2) on the ground that they ought to have taken into account the possibility that the court might permit an application for variation to be made after that period by the person entitled to payments under the order.

(4)   Sub-paragraph (3) shall not prejudice any power to recover any part of the estate so distributed arising by virtue of the variation of an order in accordance with this paragraph.

(5)   Where an application to vary a secured periodical payments order is made after the death of the parent liable to make payments under the order, the

circumstances to which the court is required to have regard under paragraph 6(1) shall include the changed circumstances resulting from the death of the parent.

(6)   In considering for the purposes of sub-paragraph (2) the question when representation was first taken out, a grant limited to settled land or to trust property shall be left out of account and a grant limited to real estate or to personal estate shall be left out of account unless a grant limited to the remainder of the estate has previously been made or is made at the same time.

(7)   In this paragraph "secured periodical payments order" means an order for secured periodical payments under paragraph 1(2)(b).

Financial relief under other enactments

8.—(1)   This paragraph applies where a residence order is made with respect to a child at a time when there is in force an order ("the financial relief order") made under any enactment other than this Act and requiring a person to contribute to the child's maintenance.

(2)   Where this paragraph applies, the court may, on the application of—

(a)   any person required by the financial relief order to contribute to the child's maintenance; or

(b)   any person in whose favour a residence order with respect to the child is in force,

make an order revoking the financial relief order, or varying it by altering the amount of any sum payable under that order or by substituting the applicant for the person to whom any such sum is otherwise payable under that order.

Interim orders

9.—(1)   Where an application is made under paragraph 1 or 2 the court may, at any time before it disposes of the application, make an interim order—

(a)   requiring either or both parents to make such periodical payments, at such times and for such term as the court thinks fit; and

(b)   giving any direction which the court thinks fit.

(2)   An interim order made under this paragraph may provide for payments to be made from such date as the court may specify, not being earlier than the date of the making of the application under paragraph 1 or 2.

(3)   An interim order made under this paragraph shall cease to have effect when the application is disposed of or, if earlier, on the date specified for the purposes of this paragraph in the interim order.

(4)   An interim order in which a date has been specified for the purposes of sub-paragraph (3) may be varied by substituting a later date.

Alteration of maintenance agreements

10.—(1)   In this paragraph and in paragraph 11 "maintenance agreement" means any agreement in writing made with respect to a child, whether before or after the commencement of this paragraph, which—

(a)   is or was made between the father and mother of the child; and

(b)   contains provision with respect to the making or securing of payments, or the disposition or use of any property, for the maintenance or education of the child, and any such provisions are in this paragraph, and paragraph 11, referred to as "financial arrangements".

(2) Where a maintenance agreement is for the time being subsisting and each of the parties to the agreement is for the time being either domiciled or resident in England and Wales, then, either party may apply to the court for an order under this paragraph.

(3) If the court to which the application is made is satisfied either—

(a) that, by reason of a change in the circumstances in the light of which any financial arrangements contained in the agreement were made (including a change foreseen by the parties when making the agreement), the agreement should be altered so as to make different financial arrangements; or

(b) that the agreement does not contain proper financial arrangements with respect to the child,

then that court may by order make such alterations in the agreement by varying or revoking any financial arrangements contained in it as may appear to it to be just having regard to all the circumstances.

(4) If the maintenance agreement is altered by an order under this paragraph, the agreement shall have effect thereafter as if the alteration had been made by agreement between the parties and for valuable consideration.

(5) Where a court decides to make an order under this paragraph altering the maintenance agreement—

(a) by inserting provision for the making or securing by one of the parties to the agreement of periodical payments for the maintenance of the child; or

(b) by increasing the rate of periodical payments required to be made or secured by one of the parties for the maintenance of the child,

then, in deciding the term for which under the agreement as altered by the order the payments or (as the case may be) the additional payments attributable to the increase are to be made or secured for the benefit of the child, the court shall apply the provisions of sub-paragraphs (1) and (2) of paragraph 3 as if the order were an order under paragraph 1(2)(a) or (b).

(6) A magistrates' court shall not entertain an application under sub-paragraph (2) unless both the parties to the agreement are resident in England and Wales and at least one of the parties is resident in the commission area (within the meaning of the Justices of the Peace Act 1979) for which the court is appointed, and shall not have power to make any order on such an application except—

(a) in a case where the agreement contains no provision for periodical payments by either of the parties, an order inserting provision for the making by one of the parties of periodical payments for the maintenance of the child;

(b) in a case where the agreement includes provision for the making by one of the parties of periodical payments, an order increasing or reducing the rate of, or terminating, any of those payments.

(7) For the avoidance of doubt it is hereby declared that nothing in this paragraph affects any power of a court before which any proceedings between the parties to a maintenance agreement are brought under any other enactment to make an order containing financial arrangements or any right of either party to apply for such an order in such proceedings.

11.—(1) Where a maintenance agreement provides for the continuation, after the death of one of the parties, of payments for the maintenance of a child and that party dies domiciled in England and Wales, the surviving party or the personal representatives of the deceased party may apply to the High Court or a county court for an order under paragraph 10.

(2) If a maintenance agreement is altered by a court on an application under this paragraph, the agreement shall have effect thereafter as if the alteration had been made, immediately before the death, by agreement between the parties and for valuable consideration.

(3) An application under this paragraph shall not, except with leave of the High Court or a county court, be made after the end of the period of six months beginning with the day on which representation in regard to the estate of the deceased is first taken out.

(4) In considering for the purposes of sub-paragraph (3) the question when representation was first taken out, a grant limited to settled land or to trust property shall be left out of account and a grant limited to real estate or to personal estate shall be left out of account unless a grant limited to the remainder of the estate has previously been made or is made at the same time.

(5) A county court shall not entertain an application under this paragraph, or an application for leave to make an application under this paragraph, unless it would have jurisdiction to hear and determine proceedings for an order under section 2 of the Inheritance (Provision for Family and Dependants) Act 1975 in relation to the deceased's estate by virtue of section 25 of the County Courts Act 1984 (jurisdiction under the Act of 1975).

(6) The provisions of this paragraph shall not render the personal representatives of the deceased liable for having distributed any part of the estate of the deceased after the expiry of the period of six months referred to in sub-paragraph (3) on the ground that they ought to have taken into account the possibility that a court might grant leave for an application by virtue of this paragraph to be made by the surviving party after that period.

(7) Sub-paragraph (6) shall not prejudice any power to recover any part of the estate so distributed arising by virtue of the making of an order in pursuance of this paragraph.

Enforcement of orders for maintenance

12.—(1) Any person for the time being under an obligation to make payments in pursuance of any order for the payment of money made by a magistrates' court under this Act shall give notice of any change of address to such person (if any) as may be specified in the order.

(2) Any person failing without reasonable excuse to give such a notice shall be guilty of an offence and liable on summary conviction to a fine not exceeding level 2 on the standard scale.

(3) An order for the payment of money made by a magistrates' court under this Act shall be enforceable as a magistrates' court maintenance order within the meaning of section 150(1) of the Magistrates' Courts Act 1980.

Direction for settlement of instrument by conveyancing counsel

13.   Where the High Court or a county court decides to make an order under this Act for the securing of periodical payments or for the transfer or settlement of property, it may direct that the matter be referred to one of the conveyancing counsel of the court to settle a proper instrument to be executed by all necessary parties.

Financial provision for child resident in country outside England and Wales

14.—(1)   Where one parent of a child lives in England and Wales and the child lives outside England and Wales with—

(a)   another parent of his;

(b)   a guardian of his; or

(c)   a person in whose favour a residence order is in force with respect to the child,

the court shall have power, on an application made by any of the persons mentioned in paragraphs (a) to (c), to make one or both of the orders mentioned in paragraph 1(2)(a) and (b) against the parent living in England and Wales.

(2)   Any reference in this Act to the powers of the court under paragraph 1(2) or to an order made under paragraph 1(2) shall include a reference to the powers which the court has by virtue of sub-paragraph (1) or (as the case may be) to an order made by virtue of sub-paragraph (1).

Local authority contribution to child's maintenance

15.—(1)   Where a child lives, or is to live, with a person as the result of a residence order, a local authority may make contributions to that person towards the cost of the accommodation and maintenance of the child.

(2)   Sub-paragraph (1) does not apply where the person with whom the child lives, or is to live, is a parent of the child or the husband or wife of a parent of the child.

Interpretation

16.—(1)   In this Schedule "child" includes, in any case where an application is made under paragraph 2 or 6 in relation to a person who has reached the age of eighteen, that person.

(2)   In this Schedule, except paragraphs 2 and 15, "parent" includes any party to a marriage (whether or not subsisting) in relation to whom the child concerned is a child of the family; and for this purpose any reference to either parent or both parents shall be construed as references to any parent of his and to all of his parents.

Sections 17, 23 and 29.   **SCHEDULE 2**
LOCAL AUTHORITY SUPPORT FOR CHILDREN AND FAMILIES

PART I   PROVISION OF SERVICES FOR FAMILIES

Identification of children in need and provision of information

1.—(1)   Every local authority shall take reasonable steps to identify the extent to which there are children in need within their area.

(2) Every local authority shall—
  (a) publish information—
      (i) about services provided by them under sections 17, 18, 20 and 24; and
      (ii) where they consider it appropriate, about the provision by others (including, in particular, voluntary organisations) of services which the authority have power to provide under those sections; and
  (b) take such steps as are reasonably practicable to ensure that those who might benefit from the services receive the information relevant to them.

Maintenance of a register of disabled children

2.—(1) Every local authority shall open and maintain a register of disabled children within their area.

(2) The register may be kept by means of a computer.

Assessment of children's needs

3. Where it appears to a local authority that a child within their area is in need, the authority may assess his needs for the purposes of this Act at the same time as any assessment of his needs is made under—
  (a) the Chronically Sick and Disabled Persons Act 1970;
  (b) the Education Act 1981;
  (c) the Disabled Persons (Services, Consultation and Representation) Act 1986; or
  (d) any other enactment.

Prevention of neglect and abuse

4.—(1) Every local authority shall take reasonable steps, through the provision of services under Part III of this Act, to prevent children within their area suffering ill-treatment or neglect.

(2) Where a local authority believe that a child who is at any time within their area—
  (a) is likely to suffer harm; but
  (b) lives or proposes to live in the area of another local authority
they shall inform that other local authority.

(3) When informing that other local authority they shall specify—
  (a) the harm that they believe he is likely to suffer; and
  (b) (if they can) where the child lives or proposes to live.

Provision of accommodation in order to protect child

5.—(1) Where—
  (a) it appears to a local authority that a child who is living on particular premises is suffering, or is likely to suffer, ill treatment at the hands of another person who is living on those premises; and
  (b) that other person proposes to move from the premises,
the authority may assist that other person to obtain alternative accommodation.

(2) Assistance given under this paragraph may be in cash.

(3) Subsections (7) to (9) of section 17 shall apply in relation to assistance given under this paragraph as they apply in relation to assistance given under that section.

Provision for disabled children

6. Every local authority shall provide services designed—
   (a) to minimise the effect on disabled children within their area of their disabilities; and
   (b) to give such children the opportunity to lead lives which are as normal as possible.

Provision to reduce need for care proceedings etc.

7. Every local authority shall take reasonable steps designed—
   (a) to reduce the need to bring—
       (i) proceedings for care or supervision orders with respect to children within their area;
       (ii) criminal proceedings against such children;
       (iii) any family or other proceedings with respect to such children which might lead to them being placed in the authority's care; or
       (iv) proceedings under the inherent jurisdiction of the High Court with respect to children;
   (b) to encourage children within their area not to commit criminal offences; and
   (c) to avoid the need for children within their area to be placed in secure accommodation.

Provision for children living with their families

8. Every local authority shall make such provision as they consider appropriate for the following services to be available with respect to children in need within their area while they are living with their families—
   (a) advice, guidance and counselling;
   (b) occupational, social, cultural or recreational activities;
   (c) home help (which may include laundry facilities);
   (d) facilities for, or assistance with, travelling to and from home for the purpose of taking advantage of any other service provided under this Act or of any similar service;
   (e) assistance to enable the child concerned and his family to have a holiday.

Family centres

9.—(1) Every local authority shall provide such family centres as they consider appropriate in relation to children within their area.
   (2) "Family centre" means a centre at which any of the persons mentioned in sub-paragraph (3) may—
   (a) attend for occupational, social, cultural or recreational activities;
   (b) attend for advice, guidance and counselling; or
   (c) be provided with accommodation while he is receiving advice, guidance or counselling.
   (3) The persons are—
   (a) a child;
   (b) his parents;

(c) any person who is not a parent of his but who has parental responsibility for him;

(d) any other person who is looking after him.

Maintenance of the family home

10. Every local authority shall take such steps as are reasonably practicable, where any child within their area who is in need and whom they are not looking after is living apart from his family—

(a) to enable him to live with his family; or

(b) to promote contact between him and his family,

if, in their opinion, it is necessary to do so in order to safeguard or promote his welfare.

Duty to consider racial groups to which children in need belong

11. Every local authority shall, in making any arrangements—

(a) for the provision of day care within their area; or

(b) designed to encourage persons to act as local authority foster parents,

have regard to the different racial groups to which children within their area who are in need belong.

PART II   CHILDREN LOOKED AFTER BY LOCAL AUTHORITIES

Regulations as to placing of children with local authority foster parents

12. Regulations under section 23(2)(a) may, in particular, make provision—

(a) with regard to the welfare of children placed with local authority foster parents;

(b) as to the arrangements to be made by local authorities in connection with the health and education of such children;

(c) as to the records to be kept by local authorities;

(d) for securing that a child is not placed with a local authority foster parent unless that person is for the time being approved as a local authority foster parent by such local authority as may be prescribed;

(e) for securing that where possible the local authority foster parent with whom a child is to be placed is—

(i) of the same religious persuasion as the child; or

(ii) gives an undertaking that the child will be brought up in that religious persuasion;

(f) for securing that children placed with local authority foster parents, and the premises in which they are accommodated, will be supervised and inspected by a local authority and that the children will be removed from those premises if their welfare appears to require it;

(g) as to the circumstances in which local authorities may make arrangements for duties imposed on them by the regulations to be discharged, on their behalf.

Regulations as to arrangements under section 23(2)(f)

13. Regulations under section 23(2)(f) may, in particular, make provision as to—

(a)   the persons to be notified of any proposed arrangements;

(b)   the opportunities such persons are to have to make representations in relation to the arrangements proposed;

(c)   the persons to be notified of any proposed changes in arrangements;

(d)   the records to be kept by local authorities;

(e)   the supervision by local authorities of any arrangements made.

Regulations as to conditions under which child in care is allowed to live with parent, etc.

14.   Regulations under section 23(5) may, in particular, impose requirements on a local authority as to—

(a)   the making of any decision by a local authority to allow a child to live with any person falling within of section 23(4) (including requirements as to those who must be consulted before the decision is made, and those who must be notified when it has been made);

(b)   the supervision or medical examination of the child concerned;

(c)   the removal of the child, in such circumstances as may be prescribed, from the care of the person with whom he has been allowed to live.

Promotion and maintenance of contact between child and family

15.—(1)   Where a child is being looked after by a local authority, the authority shall, unless it is not reasonably practicable or consistent with his welfare, endeavour to promote contact between the child and—

(a)   his parents;

(b)   any person who is not a parent of his but who has parental responsibility for him; and

(c)   any relative, friend or other person connected with him.

(2)   Where a child is being looked after by a local authority—

(a)   the authority shall take steps as are reasonably practicable to secure that—

(i)   his parents; and

(ii)   any person who is not a parent of his but who has parental responsibility for him,

are kept informed of where he is being accommodated; and

(b)   every such person shall secure that the authority are kept informed of his or her address.

(3)   Where a local authority ("the receiving authority") take over the provision of accommodation for a child from another local authority ("the transferring authority") under section 20(2)—

(a)   the receiving authority shall (where reasonably praticable) inform—

(i)   the child's parents; and

(ii)   any person who is not a parent of his but who has parental responsibility for him;

(b)   sub-paragraph (2)(a) shall apply to the transferring authority, as well as the receiving authority, until at least one such person has been informed of the change; and

(c)   sub-paragraph (2)(b) shall not require any person to inform the receiving authority of his address until he has been so informed.

(4)   Nothing in this paragraph requires a local authority to inform any person
of the whereabouts of a child if—
    (a)   the child is in the care of the authority; and
    (b)   the authority has reasonable cause to believe that informing the person
would prejudice the child's welfare.
(5)   Any person who fails (without reasonable excuse) to comply with sub-
paragraph (2)(b) shall be guilty of an offence and liable on summary conviction
to a fine not exceeding level 2 on the standard scale.
(6)   It shall be a defence in any proceedings under sub-paragraph (5) to prove
that the defendant was residing at the same address as another person who was
the child's parent or had parental responsibility for the child and had reasonable
cause to believe that the other person had informed the appropriate authority
that both of them were residing at that address.

Visits to or by, children: expenses

16.—(1)   This paragraph applies where—
    (a)   a child is being looked after by a local authority; and
    (b)   the conditions mentioned in sub-paragraph (3) are satisfied.
(2)   The authority may—
    (a)   make payments to—
        (i)   a parent of the child;
        (ii)   any person who is not a parent of his but who has parental
responsibility for him; or
        (iii)   any relative, friend or other person connected with him,
in respect of travelling, subsistence or other expenses incurred by that person in
visiting the child; or
    (b)   make payments to the child, or to any person on his behalf, in respect
of travelling, subsistence or other expenses incurred by or on behalf of the child in
his visiting—
        (i)   a parent of his;
        (ii)   any person who is not a parent of his but who has parental
responsibility for him; or
        (iii)   any relative, friend or other person connected with him.
(3)   The conditions are that—
    (a)   it appears to the authority that the visit in question could not otherwise
be made without undue financial hardship; and
    (b)   the circumstances warrant the making of the payments.

Appointment of visitor for child who is not being visited

17.—(1)   Where it appears to a local authority in relation to any child that
they are looking after that—
    (a)   communication between the child and—
        (i)   a parent of his; or
        (ii)   any person who is not a parent of his but who has parental
responsibility for him,
has been infrequent; or
    (b)   he has not visited or been visited by (or lived with) any such person
during the preceeding twelve months,

and that it would be in the child's best interests for an independent person to be appointed to be his visitor for the purposes of this paragraph, they shall appoint such a visitor.

(2)   A person so appointed shall—

(a)   have the duty of visiting, advising and befriending the child; and

(b)   be entitled to recover from the authority who appointed him any reasonable expenses incurred by him for the purposes of his functions under this paragraph.

(3)   A person's appointment as a visitor in pursuance of this paragraph shall be determined if—

(a)   he gives notice in writing to the authority who appointed him that he resigns the appointment; or

(b)   the authority give him notice in writing that they have terminated it.

(4)   The determination of such an appointment shall not prejudice any duty under this paragraph to make a further appointment.

(5)   Where a local authority propose to appoint a visitor for a child under this paragraph, the appointment shall not be made if—

(a)   the child objects to it; and

(b)   the authority are satisfied that he has sufficient understanding to make an informed decision.

(6)   Where a visitor has been appointed for a child under this paragraph, the local authority shall determine the appointment if—

(a)   the child objects to its continuing; and

(b)   the authority are satisfied that he has sufficient understanding to make an informed decision.

(7)   The Secretary of State may make regulations as to the circumstances in which a person appointed as a visitor under this paragraph is to be regarded as independent of the local authority appointing him.

Power to guarantee apprenticeship deeds etc.

18.—(1)   While a child is being looked after by a local authority, or is a person qualifying for advice and assistance, the authority may undertake any obligation by way of guarantee under any deed of apprenticeship or articles of clerkship which he enters into.

(2)   Where a local authority have undertaken any such obligation under any deed or articles they may at any time (whether or not they are still looking after the person concerned) undertake the like obligation under any supplemental deed or articles.

Arrangements to assist children to live abroad

19.—(1)   A local authority may only arrange for, or assist in arranging for, any child in their care to live outside England and Wales with the approval of the court.

(2)   A local authority may, with the approval of every person who has parental responsibility for the child arrange for, or assist in arranging for, any other child looked after by them to live outside England and Wales.

(3)   The court shall not give its approval under sub-paragraph (1) unless it is satisfied that—

    (a)   living outside England and Wales would be in the child's best interests;

    (b)   suitable arrangements have been, or will be, made for his reception and welfare in the country in which he will live;

    (c)   the child has consented to living in that country; and

    (d)   every person who has parental responsibility for the child has consented to his living in that country.

    (4)   Where the court is satisfied that the child does not have sufficient understanding to give or withhold his consent, it may disregard sub-paragraph (3)(c) and give its approval if the child is to live in the country concerned with a parent, guardian, or other suitable person.

    (5)   Where a person whose consent is required by sub-paragraph (3)(d) fails to give his consent, the court may disregard that provision and give its approval if it is satisfied that that person—

    (a)   cannot be found;

    (b)   is incapable of consenting; or

    (c)   is withholding his consent unreasonably.

    (6)   Section 56 of the Adoption Act 1976 (which requires authority for the taking or sending abroad for adoption of a child who is a British subject) shall not apply in the case of any child who is to live outside England and Wales with the approval of the court given under this paragraph.

    (7)   Where a court decides to give its approval under this paragraph it may order that its decision is not to have effect during the appeal period.

    (8)   In sub-paragraph (7) "the appeal period" means—

    (a)   where an appeal is made against the decision, the period between the making of the decision and the determination of the appeal; and

    (b)   otherwise, the period during which an appeal may be made against the decision.

Death of children being looked after by local authorities

    20.—(1)   If a child who is being looked after by a local authority dies, the authority—

    (a)   shall notify the Secretary of State;

    (b)   shall, so far as is reasonably practicable, notify the child's parents and every person who is not a parent of his but who has parental responsibility for him;

    (c)   may, with the consent (so far as it is reasonably practicable to obtain it) of every person who has parental responsibility for the child, arrange for the child's body to be buried or cremated; and

    (d)   may, if the conditions mentioned in sub-paragraph (2) are satisfied, make payments to any person who has parental responsibility for the child, or any relative, friend or other person connected with the child, in respect of travelling, subsistence or other expenses incurred by that person in attending the child's funeral.

    (2)   The conditions are that—

    (a)   it appears to the authority that the person concerned could not otherwise attend the child's funeral without undue financial hardship; and

    (b)   that the circumstances warrant the making of the payments.

(3)   Sub-paragraph (1) does not authorise cremation where it does not accord with the practice of the child's religious persuasion.

(4)   Where a local authority have exercised their power under sub-paragraph (1)(c) with respect to a child who was under sixteen when he died, they may recover from any parent of the child any expenses incurred by them.

(5)   Any sums so recoverable shall, without prejudice to any other method of recovery, be recoverable summarily as a civil debt.

(6)   Nothing in this paragraph affects any enactment regulating or authorising the burial, cremation or anatomical examination of the body of a deceased person.

PART III   CONTRIBUTIONS TOWARDS MAINTENANCE OF CHILDREN LOOKED AFTER BY LOCAL AUTHORITIES

Liability to contribute

21.—(1)   Where a local authority are looking after a child (other than in the cases mentioned in sub-paragraph (7)) they shall consider whether they should recover contributions towards the child's maintenance from any person liable to contribute ("a contributor").

(2)   An authority may only recover contributions from a contributor if they consider it reasonable to do so.

(3)   The persons liable to contribute are—
    (a)   where the child is under sixteen, each of his parents;
    (b)   where he has reached the age of sixteen, the child himself.

(4)   A parent is not liable to contribute during any period when he is in receipt of income support or family credit under the Social Security Act 1986.

(5)   A person is not liable to contribute towards the maintenance of a child in the care of a local authority in respect of any period during which the child is allowed by the authority (under section 23(5)) to live with a parent of his.

(6)   A contributor is not obliged to make any contribution towards a child's maintenance except as agreed or determined in accordance with this Part of this Schedule.

(7)   The cases are where the child is looked after by a local authority under—
    (a)   section 21;
    (b)   an interim care order;
    (c)   section 53 of the Children and Young Persons Act 1933.

Agreed contributions

22.—(1)   Contributions towards a child's maintenance may only be recovered if the local authority have served a notice ("a contribution notice") on the contributor specifying—
    (a)   the weekly sum which they consider that he should contribute; and
    (b)   arrangements for payment.

(2)   The contribution notice must be in writing and dated.

(3)   Arrangements for payment shall, in particular, include—
    (a)   the date on which liability to contribute begins (which must not be earlier than the date of the notice);

(b)   the date on which liability under the notice will end (if the child has not before that date ceased to be looked after by the authority); and

(c)   the date on which the first payment is to be made.

(4)   The authority may specify in a contribution notice a weekly sum which is a standard contribution determined by them for all children looked after by them.

(5)   The authority may not specify in a contribution notice a weekly sum greater than that which they consider—

(a)   they would normally be prepared to pay if they had placed a similar child with local authority foster parents; and

(b)   it is reasonably practicable for the contributor to pay (having regard to his means).

(6)   An authority may at any time withdraw a contribution notice (without prejudice to their power to serve another).

(7)   Where the authority and the contributor agree—

(a)   the sum which the contributor is to contribute; and

(b)   arrangements for payment,

(whether as specified in the contribution notice or otherwise) and the contributor notifies the authority in writing that he so agrees, the authority may recover summarily as a civil debt any contribution which is overdue and unpaid.

(8)   A contributor may, by serving a notice in writing on the authority, withdraw his agreement in relation to any period of liability falling after the date of service of the notice.

(9)   Sub-paragraph (7) is without prejudice to any other method of recovery.

Contribution orders

23.—(1)   Where a contributor has been served with a contribution notice and has—

(a)   failed to reach any agreement with the local authority as mentioned in paragraph 22(7) within the period of one month beginning with the day on which the contribution notice was served; or

(b)   served a notice under paragraph 22(8) withdrawing his agreement, the authority may apply to the court for an order under this paragraph.

(2)   On such an application the court may make an order ("a contribution order") requiring the contributor to contribute a weekly sum towards the child's maintenance in accordance with arrangements for payment specified by the court.

(3)   A contribution order—

(a)   shall not specify a weekly sum greater than that specified in the contribution notice; and

(b)   shall be made with due regard to the contributor's means

(4)   A contribution order shall not—

(a)   take effect before the date specified in the contribution notice; or

(b)   have effect while the contributor is not liable to contribute (by virtue of paragraph 21); or

(c)   remain in force after the child has ceased to be looked after by the authority who obtained the order.

(5)　An authority may not apply to the court under sub-paragraph (1) in relation to a contribution notice which they have withdrawn.

(6)　Where—

(a)　a contribution order is in force;

(b)　the authority serve another contribution notice; and

(c)　the contributor and the authority reach an agreement under paragraph 22(7) in respect of that other contribution notice,

the effect of the agreement shall be to discharge the order from the date on which it is agreed that the agreement shall take effect.

(7)　Where an agreement is reached under sub-paragraph (6) the authority shall notify the court—

(a)　of the agreement; and

(b)　of the date on which it took effect.

(8)　A contribution order may be varied or revoked on the application of the contributor or the authority.

(9)　In proceedings for the variation of a contribution order, the authority shall specify—

(a)　the weekly sum which, having regard to paragraph 22, they propose that the contributor should contribute under the order as varied; and

(b)　the proposed arrangements for payment.

(10)　Where a contribution order is varied, the order—

(a)　shall not specify a weekly sum greater than that specified by the authority in the proceedings for variation; and

(b)　shall be made with due regard to the contributor's means.

(11)　An appeal shall lie in accordance with rules of court from any order made under this paragraph.

Enforcement of contribution orders etc.

24.—(1)　A contribution order made by a magistrates' court shall be enforceable as a magistrates' court maintenance order (within the meaning of section 150(1) of the Magistrates' Courts Act 1980).

(2)　Where a contributor has agreed, or has been ordered, to make contributions to a local authority, any other local authority within whose area the contributor is for the time being living may—

(a)　at the request of the local authority who served the contribution notice; and

(b)　subject to agreement as to any sum to be deducted in respect of services rendered,

collect from the contributor any contributions due on behalf of the authority who served the notice.

(3)　In sub-paragraph (2) the reference to any other local authority includes a reference to—

(a)　a local authority within the meaning of section 1(2) of the Social Work (Scotland) Act 1968; and

(b)　a Health and Social Services Board established under Article 16 of the Health and Personal Social Services (Northern Ireland) Order 1972.

(4)　The power to collect sums under sub-paragraph (2) includes the power to—

(a)   receive and give a discharge for any contributions due; and

(b)   (if necessary) enforce payment of any contributions,
even though those contributions may have fallen due at a time when the contributor was living elsewhere.

(5)   Any contribution collected under sub-paragraph (2) shall be paid (subject to any agreed deduction) to the local authority who served the contribution notice.

(6)   In any proceedings under this paragraph, a document which purports to be—

(a)   a copy of an order made by a court under or by virtue of paragraph 23; and

(b)   certified as a true copy by the clerk of the court,
shall be evidence of the order.

(7)   In any proceedings under this paragraph, a certificate which—

(a)   purports to be signed by the clerk or some other duly authorised officer of the local authority who obtained the contribution order; and

(b)   states that any sum due to the authority under the order is overdue and unpaid,
shall be evidence that the sum is overdue and unpaid.

Regulations

25.   The Secretary of State may make regulations—

(a)   as to the considerations which a local authority must take into account in deciding—

(i)   whether it is reasonable to recover contributions; and

(ii)   what the arrangements for payment should be;

(b)   as to the procedures they must follow in reaching agreements with—

(i)   contributors (under paragraphs 22 and 23); and

(ii)   any other local authority (under paragraph 23).

Sections 35 and 36.   **SCHEDULE 3**
                    SUPERVISION ORDERS

PART I   GENERAL

Meaning of "responsible person"

1.   In this Schedule, "the responsible person", in relation to a supervised child, means—

(a)   any person who has parental responsibility for the child; and

(b)   any other person with whom the child is living.

Power of supervisor to give directions to supervised child

2.—(1)   A supervision order may require the supervised child to comply with any directions given from time to time by the supervisor which require him to do all or any of the following things—

(a)   to live at a place or places specified in the directions for a period or periods so specified;

(b)   to present himself to a person or persons specified in the directions at a place or places and on a day or days so specified;

(c)   to participate in activities specified in the directions on a day or days so specified.

(2)   It shall be for the supervisor to decide whether, and to what extent, he exercises his power to give directions and to decide the form of any directions which he gives.

(3)   Sub-paragraph (1) does not confer on a supervisor power to give directions in respect of any medical or psychiatric examination or treatment (which are matters dealt with in paragraphs 4 and 5).

Imposition of obligations on responsible person

3.—(1)   With the consent of any responsible person, a supervision order may include a requirement—

(a)   that he take all reasonable steps to ensure that the supervised child complies with any direction given by the supervisor under paragraph 2;

(b)   that he take all reasonable steps to ensure that the supervised child complies with any requirement included in the order under paragraph 4 or 5;

(c)   that he comply with any directions given by the supervisor requiring him to attend at a place specified in the directions for the purpose of taking part in activities so specified.

(2)   A direction given under sub-paragraph (1)(c) may specify the time at which the responsible person is to attend and whether or not the supervised child is required to attend with him.

(3)   A supervision order may require any person who is a responsible person in relation to the supervised child to keep the supervisor informed of his address, if it differs from the child's.

Psychiatric and medical examinations

4.—(1)   A supervision order may require the supervised child—

(a)   to submit to a medical or psychiatric examination; or

(b)   to submit to any such examination from time to time as directed by the supervisor.

(2)   Any such examination shall be required to be conducted—

(a)   by, or under the direction of, such registered medical practitioner as may be specified in the order;

(b)   at a place specified in the order and at which the supervised child is to attend as a non-resident patient; or

(c)   at—

(i)   a health service hospital; or

(ii)   in the case of a psychiatric examination, a hospital or mental nursing home,

at which the supervised child is, or is to attend as, a resident patient.

(3)   A requirement of a kind mentioned in sub-paragraph (2)(c) shall not be included unless the court is satisfied, on the evidence of a registered medical practitioner, that—

(a)   the child may be suffering from a physical or mental condition that requires, and may be susceptible to, treatment; and

(b)   a period as a resident patient is necessary if the examination is to be carried out properly.

(4)   No court shall include a requirement under this paragraph in a supervision order unless it is satisfied that—

(a)   where the child has sufficient understanding to make an informed decision, he consents to its inclusion; and

(b)   satisfactory arrangements have been, or can be, made for the examination.

Psychiatric and medical treatment

5.—(1)   Where a court which proposes to make or vary a supervision order is satisfied, on the evidence of a registered medical practitioner approved for the purposes of section 12 of the Mental Health Act 1983, that the mental condition of the supervised child—

(a)   is such as requires, and may be susceptible to, treatment; but

(b)   is not such as to warrant his detention in pursuance of a hospital order under Part III of that Act,

the court may include in the order a requirement that the supervised child shall, for a period specified in the order, submit to such treatment as is so specified.

(2)   The treatment specified in accordance with sub-paragraph (1) must be—

(a)   by, or under the direction of, such registered medical practitioner as may be specified in the order;

(b)   as a non-resident patient at such a place as may be so specified; or

(c)   as a resident patient in a hospital or mental nursing home.

(3)   Where a court which proposes to make or vary a supervision order is satisfied, on the evidence of a registered medical practitioner, that the physical condition of the supervised child is such as requires, and may be susceptible to, treatment, the court may include in the order a requirement that the supervised child shall, for a period specified in the order, submit to such treatment as is so specified.

(4)   The treatment specified in accordance with sub-paragraph (3) must be—

(a)   by, or under the direction of, such registered medical practitioner as may be specified in the order;

(b)   as a non-resident patient at such place as may be so specified; or

(c)   as a resident patient in a health service hospital.

(5)   No court shall include a requirement under this paragraph in a supervision order unless it is satisfied—

(a)   where the child has sufficient understanding to make an informed decision, that he consents to its inclusion; and

(b)   that satisfactory arrangements have been, or can be, made for the treatment.

(6)   If a medical practitioner by whom or under whose direction a supervised person is being treated in pursuance of a requirement included in a supervision order by virtue of this paragraph is unwilling to continue to treat or direct the treatment of the supervised child or is of the opinion that—

(a)   the treatment should be continued beyond the period specified in the order;

(b)   the supervised child needs different treatment;

  (c)   he is not susceptible to treatment; or
  (d)   he does not require further treatment,
the practitioner shall make a report in writing to that effect to the supervisor.

  (7)   On receiving a report under this paragraph the supervisor shall refer it to the court, and on such a reference the court may make an order cancelling or varying the requirement.

PART II   MISCELLANEOUS

Life of supervision order

  6.—(1)   Subject to sub-paragraph (2) and section 91, a supervision order shall cease to have effect at the end of the period of one year beginning with the date on which it was made.

  (2)   A supervision order shall also cease to have effect if an event mentioned in section 25(1)(a) or (b) of the Child Abduction and Custody Act 1985 (termination of existing orders) occurs with respect to the child.

  (3)   Where the supervisor applies to the court to extend, or further extend, a supervision order the court may extend the order for such period as it may specify.

  (4)   A supervision order may not be extended so as to run beyond the end of the period of three years beginning with the date on which it was made.

Limited life of directions

  7.—(1)   The total number of days in respect of which a supervised child or (as the case may be) responsible person may be required to comply with directions given under paragraph 2 or 3 shall not exceed 90 or such lesser number (if any) as the supervision order may specify.

  (2)   For the purpose of calculating that total number of days, the supervisor may disregard any day in respect of which directions previously given in pursuance of the order were not complied with.

Information to be given to supervisor etc.

  8.—(1)   A supervision order may require the supervised child—
  (a)   to keep the supervisor informed of any change in his address; and
  (b)   to allow the supervisor to visit him at the place where he is living.

  (2)   The responsible person in relation to any child with respect to whom a supervision order is made shall—
  (a)   if asked by the supervisor, inform him of the child's address (if it is known to him); and
  (b)   if he is living with the child, allow the supervisor reasonable contact with the child.

Selection of supervisor

  9.—(1)   A supervision order shall not designate a local authority as the supervisor unless—
  (a)   the authority agree; or
  (b)   the supervised child lives or will live within their area.

(2)   A court shall not place a child under the supervision of a probation officer unless—

  (a)   the appropriate authority so request; and

  (b)   a probation officer is already exercising or has exercised, in relation to another member of the household to which the child belongs, duties imposed on probation officers—

    (i)   by paragraph 8 of Schedule 3 to the Powers of Criminal Courts Act 1973; or

    (ii)   by rules under paragraph 18(1)(b) of that Schedule.

(3)   In sub-paragraph (2) "the appropriate authority" means the local authority appearing to the court to be the authority in whose area the supervised child lives or will live.

(4)   Where a supervision order places a person under the supervision of a probation officer, the officer shall be selected in accordance with arrangements made by the probation committee for the area in question.

(5)   If the selected probation officer is unable to carry out his duties, or dies, another probation officer shall be selected in the same manner.

Effect of supervision order on earlier orders

10.   The making of a supervision order with respect to any child brings to an end any earlier care or supervision order which—

  (a)   was made with respect to that child; and

  (b)   would otherwise continue in force.

Local authority functions and expenditure

11.—(1)   The Secretary of State may make regulations with respect to the exercise by a local authority of their functions where a child has been placed under their supervision by a supervision order.

(2)   Where a supervision order requires compliance with directions given by virtue of this section, any expenditure incurred by the supervisor for the purposes of the directions shall be defrayed by the local authority designated in the order.

PART III   EDUCATION SUPERVISION ORDERS

Effect of orders

12—(1)   Where an education supervision order is in force with respect to a child, it shall be the duty of the supervisor—

  (a)   to advise, assist and befriend, and give directions to—

    (i)   the supervised child; and

    (ii)   his parents,

in such a way as will, in the opinion of the supervisor, secure that he is properly educated;

  (b)   where any such directions given to—

    (i)   the supervised child; or

    (ii)   a parent of his,

have not been complied with, to consider what further steps to take in the exercise of the supervisor's powers under this Act.

(2)   Before giving any directions under sub-paragraph (1) the supervisor shall, so far as is reasonably practicable, ascertain the wishes and feelings of—
    (a)   the child; and
    (b)   his parents,
including, in particular, their wishes as to the place at which the child should be educated.

(3)   When settling the terms of any such directions, the supervisor shall give due consideration—
    (a)   having regard to the child's age and understanding, to such wishes and feelings of his as the supervisor has been able to ascertain; and
    (b)   to such wishes and feelings of the child's parents as he has been able to ascertain.

(4)   Directions may be given under this paragraph at any time while the education supervision order is in force.

13.—(1)   Where an education supervision order is in force with respect to a child, the duties of the child's parents under sections 36 and 39 of the Education Act 1944 (duty to secure education of children and to secure regular attendance of registered pupils) shall be superseded by their duty to comply with any directions in force under the education supervision order.

(2)   Where an education supervision order is made with respect to a child—
    (a)   any school attendance order—
      (i)   made under section 37 of the Act of 1944 with respect to the child; and
      (ii)   in force immediately before the making of the education supervision order,
shall cease to have effect; and
    (b)   while the education supervision order remains in force, the following provisions shall not apply with respect to the child—
      (i)   section 37 of that Act (school attendance orders);
      (ii)   section 76 of that Act (pupils to be educated in accordance with wishes of their parents);
      (iii)   sections 6 and 7 of the Education Act 1980 (parental preference and appeals against admission decisions);
    (c)   a supervision order made with respect to the child in criminal proceedings, while the education supervision order is in force, may not include an education requirement of the kind which could otherwise be included under section 12C of the Children and Young Persons Act 1969;
    (d)   any education requirement of a kind mentioned in paragraph (c), which was in force with respect to the child immediately before the making of the education supervision order, shall cease to have effect.

Effect where child also subject to supervision order

14.—(1)   This paragrah applies where an education supervision order and a supervision order, or order under section 7(7)(b) of the Children and Young Persons Act 1969, are in force at the same time with respect to the same child.

(2)   Any failure to comply with a direction given by the supervisor under the education supervision order shall be disregarded if it would not have been

reasonably practicable to comply with it without failing to comply with a direction given under the other order.

Duration of orders

15.—(1)   An education supervision order shall have effect for a period of one year, beginning with the date on which it is made.

(2)   An education supervision order shall not expire if, before it would otherwise have expired, the court has (on the application of the authority in whose favour the order was made) extended the period during which it is in force.

(3)   Such an application may not be made earlier than three months before the date on which the order would otherwise expire.

(4)   The period during which an education supervision order is in force may be extended under sub-paragraph (2) on more than one occasion.

(5)   No one extension may be for a period of more than three years.

(6)   An education supervision order shall cease to have effect on—
  (a)   the child's ceasing to be of compulsory school age; or
  (b)   the making of a care order with respect to the child;
and sub-paragraphs (1) to (4) are subject to this sub-paragraph.

Information to be given to supervisor etc.

16.—(1)   An education supervision order may require the child—
  (a)   to keep the supervisor informed of any change in his address; and
  (b)   to allow the supervisor to visit him at the place where he is living.

(2)   A person who is the parent of a child with respect to whom an education supervision order has been made shall—
  (a)   if asked by the supervisor, inform him of the child's address (if it is known to him); and
  (b)   if he is living with the child, allow the supervisor reasonable contact with the child.

Discharge of orders

17.—(1)   The court may discharge any education supervision order on the application of—
  (a)   the child concerned;
  (b)   a parent of his; or
  (c)   the local education authority concerned.

(2)   On discharging an education supervision order, the court may direct the local authority within whose area the child lives, or will live, to investigate the circumstances of the child.

Offences

18.—(1)   If a parent of a child with respect to whom an education supervision order is in force persistently fails to comply with a direction given under the order he shall be guilty of an offence.

(2)   It shall be a defence for any person charged with such an offence to prove that—
  (a)   he took all reasonable steps to ensure that the direction was complied with:

(b)   the direction was unreasonable; or

(c)   he had complied with—

(i)   a requirement included in a supervision order made with respect to the child; or

(ii)   directions given under such a requirement,

and that it was not reasonably practicable to comply both with the direction and with the requirement or directions mentioned in this paragraph.

(3)   A person guilty of an offence under this paragraph shall be liable on summary conviction to a fine not exceeding level 3 on the standard scale.

Persistent failure of child to comply with directions

19.—(1)   Where a child with respect to whom an education supervision order is in force persistently fails to comply with any direction given under the order, the local education authority concerned shall notify the appropriate local authority.

(2)   Where a local authority have been notified under sub-paragraph (1) they shall investigate the circumstances of the child.

(3)   In this paragraph "the appropriate local authority" has the same meaning as in section 36.

Miscellaneous

20.   The Secretay of State may by regulations make provision modifying, or displacing, the provisions of any enactment about education in relation to any child with respect to whom an education supervision order is in force to such extent as appears to the Secretary of State to be necessary or expedient in consequence of the provision made by this Act with respect to such orders.

Interpretation

21.   In this Part of this Schedule "parent" has the same meaning as in the Education Act 1944 (as amended by Schedule 13).

Section 53(6).   **SCHEDULE 4**

MANAGEMENT AND CONDUCT OF COMMUNITY HOMES

PART I   INSTRUMENTS OF MANAGEMENT

Instruments of management for controlled and assisted community homes

1.—(1)   The Secretary of State may by order make an instrument of management providing for the constitution of a body of managers for any voluntary home which is designated as a controlled or assisted community home.

(2)   Sub-paragraph (3) applies where two or more voluntary homes are designated as controlled community homes or as assisted community homes.

(3)   If—

(a)   those homes are, or are to be, provided by the same voluntary organisation; and

(b)   the same local authority is to be represented on the body of managers for those homes, a single instrument of management may be made by the Secretary of State under this paragraph constituting one body of managers for those homes or for any two or more of them.

(4) The number of persons who, in accordance with an instrument of management, constitute the body of managers for a voluntary home shall be such number (which must be a multiple of three) as may be specified in the instrument.

(5) The instrument shall provide that the local authority specified in the instrument shall appoint—

(a) in the case of a voluntary home which is designated as a controlled community home, two-thirds of the managers; and

(b) in the case of a voluntary home which is designated as an assisted community home, one-third of them.

(6) An instrument of management shall provide that the foundation managers shall be appointed, in such manner and by such persons as may be specified in the instrument—

(a) so as to represent the interests of the voluntary organisation by which the home is, or is to be, provided; and

(b) for the purpose of securing that—

(i) so far as is practicable, the character of the home as a voluntary home will be preserved; and

(ii) subject to paragraph 2(3), the terms of any trust deed relating to the home are observed.

(7) An instrument of management shall come into force on such date as it may specify.

(8) If an instrument of management is in force in relation to a voluntary home the home shall be (and be known as) a controlled community home or an assisted community home, according to its designation.

(9) In this paragraph—

"foundation managers", in relation to a voluntary home, means those of the managers of the home who are not appointed by a local authority in accordance with sub-paragraph (5); and

"designated" means designated in accordance with section 53.

2.—(1) An instrument of management shall contain such provisions as the Secretary of State considers appropriate.

(2) Nothing in the instrument of management shall affect the purposes for which the premises comprising the home are held.

(3) Without prejudice to the generality of sub-paragraph (1), an instrument of management may contain provisions—

(a) specifying the nature and purpose of the home (or each of the homes) to which it relates;

(b) requiring a specified number or proportion of the places in that home (or those homes) to be made available to local authorities and to any other body specified in the instrument; and

(c) relating to the management of that home (or those homes) and the charging of fees with respect to—

(i) children placed there; or

(ii) places made available to any local authority or other body.

(4)   Subject to sub-paragraphs (1) and (2), in the event of any inconsistency between the provisions of any trust deed and an instrument of management, the instrument of management shall prevail over the provisions of the trust deed in so far as they relate to the home concerned.

(5)   After consultation with the voluntary organisation concerned and with the local authority specified in its instrument of management, the Secretary of State may by order vary or revoke any provisions of the instrument.

PART II MANAGEMENT OF CONTROLLED AND ASSISTED COMMUNITY HOMES

3.—(1)   The management, equipment and maintenance of a controlled community home shall be the responsibility of the local authority specified in its instrument of management.

(2)   The management, equipment and maintenance of an assisted community home shall be the responsibility of the voluntary organisation by which the home is provided.

(3)   In this paragraph—
"home" means a controlled community home or (as the case may be) assisted community home; and
"the managers", in relation to a home, means the managers constituted by its instrument of management; and
"the responsible body", in relation to a home, means the local athority or (as the case may be) voluntary organisation responsible for its management, equipment and maintenance.

(4)   The functions of a home's responsible body shall be exercised through the managers.

(5)   Anything done, liability incurred or property acquired by a home's managers shall be done, incurred or acquired by them as agents of the responsible body.

(6)   In so far as any matter is reserved for the decision of a home's responsible body by
(a)   sub-paragraph (8);
(b)   the instrument of management;
(c)   the service by the body on the managers, or any of them, of a notice reserving any matter,
that matter shall be dealt with by the body and not by the managers.

(7)   In dealing with any matter so reserved, the responsible body shall have regard to any representations made to the body by the managers.

(8)   The employment of persons at a home shall be a matter reserved for the decision of the responsible body.

(9)   Where the instrument of management of a controlled community home so provides, the responsible body may enter into arrangements with the voluntary organisation by which that home is provided whereby, in accordance with such terms as may be agreed between them and the voluntary organisation, persons who are not in the employment of the responsible body shall undertake duties at that home.

(10)   Subject to sub-paragraph (11)—

(a)   where the responsible body for an assisted community home proposes to engage any person to work at that home or to terminate without notice the employment of any person at that home, it shall consult the local authority specified in the instrument of management and, if that authority so direct, the responsible body shall not carry out its proposal without their consent; and

(b)   that local authority may, after consultation with the responsible body, require that body to terminate the employment of any person at that home.

(11)   Paragraphs (a) and (b) of sub-pragraph (10) shall not apply—

(a)   in such cases or circumstances as may be specified by notice in writing given by the local authority to the responsible body; and

(b)   in relation to the employment of any persons or class of persons specified in the home's instrument of management.

(12)   The accounting year of the managers of a home shall be such as may be specified by the responsible body.

(13)   Before such date in each accounting year as may be so specified, the managers of a home shall submit to the responsible body estimates, in such form as the body may require, of expenditure and receipts in respect of the next accounting year.

(14)   Any expenses incurred by the managers of a home with the approval of the responsible body shall be defrayed by that body.

(15)   The managers of a home shall keep—

(a)   proper accounts with respect to the home; and

(b)   proper records in relation to the accounts.

(16)   Where an instrument of management relates to more than one home, one set of accounts and records may be kept in respect of all the homes to which it relates.

PART III   REGULATIONS

4.—(1)   The Secretary of State may make regulations—

(a)   as to the placing of children in community homes;

(b)   as to the conduct of such homes; and

(c)   for securing the welfare of children in such homes.

(2)   The regulations may, in particular—

(a)   prescribe standards to which the premises used for such homes are to conform;

(b)   impose requirements as to the accommodation, staff and equipment to be provided in such homes, and as to the arrangements to be made for protecting the health of children in such homes;

(c)   provide for the control and discipline of children in such homes;

(d)   impose requirements as to the keeping of records and giving of notices in respect of children in such homes;

(e)   impose requirements as to the facilities which are to be provided for giving religious instruction to children in such homes;

(f)   authorise the Secretary of State to give and revoke directions requiring—

(i)   the local authority by whom a home is provided or who are specified in the instrument of management for a controlled community home, or

(ii)   the voluntary organisation by which an assisted community home is provided,
to accommodate in the home a child looked after by a local authority for whom no places are made available in that home or to take such action in relation to a child accommodated in the home as may be specified in the directions;

(g)   provide for consultation with the Secretary of State as to applicants for appointment to the charge of a home;

(h)   empower the Secretary of State to prohibit the appointment of any particular applicant except in the cases (if any) in which the regulations dispense with such consultation by reason that the person to be appointed possesses such qualifications as may be prescribed;

(i)   require the approval of the Secretary of State for the provision and use of accommodation for the purpose of restricting the liberty of children in such homes and impose other requirements (in addition to those imposed by section 25) as to the placing of a child in accommodation provided for that purpose, including a requirement to obtain the permission of any local authority who are looking after the child;

(j)   provide that, to such extent as may be provided for in the regulations, the Secretary of State may direct that any provision of regulations under this paragraph which is specified in the direction and makes any such provision as is referred to in paragraph (a) or (b) shall not apply in relation to a particular home or the premises used for it, and may provide for the variation or revocation of any such direction by the Secretary of State.

(3)   Without prejudice to the power to make regulations under this paragraph conferring functions on—

(a)   the local authority or voluntary organisation by which a community home is provided; or

(b)   the managers of a controlled or assisted community home,
regulations under this paragraph may confer functions in relation to a controlled or assisted community home on the local authority named in the instrument of management for the home.

Section 60(4).   **SCHEDULE 5**
VOLUNTARY HOMES AND VOLUNTARY ORGANISATIONS

PART I   REGISTRATION OF VOLUNTARY HOMES

General

1.—(1)   An application for registration under this paragraph shall—

(a)   be made by the persons intending to carry on the home to which the application relates; and

(b)   be made in such a manner, and be accompanied by such particulars, as the Secretary of State may prescribe.

(2)   On an application duly made under sub-paragraph (1) the Secretary of State may—

(a)   grant or refuse the application, as he thinks fit; or

(b)   grant the application subject to such conditions as he considers appropriate.

(3) The Secretary of State may from time to time—

(a) vary any condition for the time being in force with respect to a voluntary home by virtue of this paragraph; or

(b) impose an additional condition,

either on the application of the person carrying on the home or without such an application.

(4) Where at any time it appears to the Secretary of State that the conduct of any voluntary home—

(a) is not in accordance with regulations made under paragraph 7; or

(b) is otherwise unsatisfactory,

he may cancel the registration of the home and remove it from the register.

(5) Any person who, without reasonable excuse, carries on a voluntary home in contravention of—

(a) section 60; or

(b) a condition to which the registration of the home is for the time being subject by virtue of this Part,

shall be guilty of an offence.

(6) Any person guilty of such an offence shall be liable on summary conviction to a fine not exceeding—

(a) level 5 on the standard scale, if his offence is under sub-paragraph (5)(a); or

(b) level 4, if it is under sub-paragraph (5)(b).

(7) Where the Secretary of State registers a home under this paragraph, or cancels the registration of a home, he shall notify the local authority within whose area the home is situated.

Procedure

2.—(1) Where—

(a) a person applies for registration of a voluntary home; and

(b) the Secretary of State proposes to grant his application,

the Secretary of State shall give hime written notice of his proposal and of the conditions subject to which he proposes to grant the application.

(2) The Secretary of State need not give notice if he proposes to grant the application subject only to conditions which—

(a) the applicant specified in the application; or

(b) the Secretary of State and the applicant have subsequently agreed.

(3) Where the Secretary of State proposes to refuse such an application he shall give notice of his proposal to the applicant.

(4) The Secretary of State shall give any person carrying on a voluntary home notice of a proposal to—

(a) cancel the registration of the home;

(b) vary any condition for the time being in force with respect to the home by virtue of paragraph 1; or

(c) impose any additional condition.

(5) A notice under this paragraph shall give the Secretary of State's reasons for his proposal.

Right to make representations

3.—(1)   A notice under paragraph 2 shall state that within 14 days of service of the notice any person on whom it is served may (in writing) require the Secretary of State to give him an opportunity to make representations to the Secretary of State concerning the matter.

(2)   Where a notice has been served under paragraph 2, the Secretary of State shall not determine the matter until either—

(a)   any person on whom the notice was served has made representations to him concerning the matter; or

(b)   the period during which any such person could have required the Secretary of State to give him an opportunity to make representations has elapsed without the Secretary of State being required to give such an opportunity; or

(c)   the conditions specified in sub-paragraph (3) are satisfied.

(3)   The conditions are that—

(a)   a person on whom the notice was served has required the Secretary of State to give him an opportunity to make representations to the Secretary of State;

(b)   the Secretary of State has allowed him a reasonable period to make his representations; and

(c)   he has failed to make them within that period.

(4)   The representations may be made, at the option of the person making them, either in writing or orally.

(5)   If he informs the Secretary of State that he desires to make oral representations, the Secretary of State shall give him an opportunity of appearing before, and of being heard by, a person appointed by the Secretary of State.

Decision of Secretary of State

4.—(1)   If the Secretary of State decides to adopt the proposal, he shall serve notice in writing of his decision on any person on whom he was required to serve notice of his proposal.

(2)   A notice under this paragraph shall be accompanied by a notice explaining the right of appeal conferred by paragraph 5.

(3)   A decision of the Secretary of State, other than a decision to grant an application for registration subject only to such conditions as are mentioned in paragraph 2(2) or to refuse an application for registration, shall not take effect—

(a)   if no appeal is brought, until the end of the period of 28 days referred to in paragraph 5(3); and

(b)   if an appeal is brought, until it is determined or abandoned.

Appeals

5.—(1)   An appeal against a decision of the Secretary of State under Part VII shall lie to a Registered Homes Tribunal.

(2)   An appeal shall be brought by notice in writing given to the Secretary of State.

(3)   No appeal may be brought by a person more than 28 days after service on him of notice of the decision.

(4)   On an appeal, the Tribuanl may confirm the Secretary of State's decision or direct that it shall not have effect.

(5)   A Tribunal shall also have power on an appeal to—

(a)   vary any condition for the time being in force by virtue of Part VII with respect to the home to which the appeal relates;

(b)   direct that any such condition shall cease to have effect; or

(c)   direct that any such condition as it thinks fit shall have effect with respect to the home.

Notification of particulars with respect to voluntary homes

6.—(1)   It shall be the duty of the person in charge of any voluntary home established after the commencement of this Act to send to the Secretary of State within three months from the establishment of the home such particulars with respect to the home as the Secretary of State may prescribe.

(2)   It shall be the duty of the person in charge of any voluntary home (whether established before or after the commencement of this Act) to send to the Secretary of State such particulars with respect to the home as may be prescribed.

(3)   The particulars must be sent—

(a)   in the case of a home established before the commencement of this Act, in every year, or

(b)   in the case of a home established after the commencement of this Act, in every year subsequent to the year in which particulars are sent under sub-paragraph (1),

by such date as the Secretary of State may prescribe.

(4)   Where the Secretary of State by regulations varies the particulars which are to be sent to him under sub-paragraph (1) or (2) by the person in charge of a voluntary home—

(a)   that person shall send to the Secretary of State the prescribed particulars within three months from the date of the making of the regulations;

(b)   where any such home was established before, but not more than three months before, the making of the regulations, compliance with paragraph (a) shall be sufficient compliance with the requirement of sub-paragraph (1) to send the prescribed particulars within three months from the establishment of the home;

(c)   in the year in which the particulars are varied, compliance with paragraph (a) by the person in charge of any voluntary home shall be sufficient compliance with the requirement of sub-paragraph (2) to send the prescribed particulars before the prescribed date in that year.

(5)   If the person in charge of a voluntary home fails, without reasonable excuse, to comply with any of the requirements of this paragraph he shall be guilty of an offence.

(6)   Any person guilty of such an offence shall be liable on summary conviction to a fine not exceeding level 2 on the standard scale.

PART II   REGULATIONS AS TO VOLUNTARY HOMES

Regulations as to conduct of voluntary homes

7.—(1)   The Secretary of State may make regulations—

(a)   as to the placing of children in voluntary homes;
(b)   as to the conduct of such homes; and
(c)   for securing the welfare of children in such homes.

(2)   The regulations may, in particular—

(a)   prescribe standards to which the premises used for such homes are to conform;

(b)   impose requirements as to the accommodation, staff and equipment to be provided in such homes, and as to the arrangements to be made for protecting the health of children in such homes;

(c)   provide for the control and discipline of children in such homes;

(d)   require the furnishing to the Secretary of State of information as to the facilities provided for—

(i)   the parents of children in the homes; and

(ii)   persons who are not parents of such children but who have parental responsibility for them; and

(iii)   other persons connected with such children, to visit and communicate with the children;

(e)   authorise the Secretary of State to limit the number of children who may be accommodated in any particular voluntary home;

(f)   prohibit the use of accommodation for the purpose of restricting the liberty of children in such homes;

(g)   impose requirements as to the keeping of records and giving of notices with respect to children in such homes;

(h)   impose requirements as to the facilities which are to be provided for giving religious instruction to children in such homes;

(i)   require notice to be given to the Secretary of State of any change of the person carrying on or in charge of a voluntary home or of the premises used by such a home.

(3)   The regulations may provide that a contravention of, or failure to comply with, any specified provision of the regulations without reasonable excuse shall be an offence against the regulations.

(4)   Any person guilty of such an offence shall be liable to a fine not exceeding level 4 on the standard scale.

Disqualification

8.   The Secretary of State may by regulation make provision with respect to the disqualification of persons in relation to voluntary homes of a kind similar to that made in relation to children's homes by section 65.

Section 63(11).   **SCHEDULE 6**
REGISTERED CHILDREN'S HOMES

PART I   REGISTRATION

Application for registration

1.—(1)   An application for the registration of a children's home shall be made—

    (a) by the person carrying on, or intending to carry on, the home; and

    (b) to the local authority for the area in which the home is, or is to be, situated.

(2) The application shall be made in the prescribed manner and shall be accompanied by—

    (a) such particulars as may be prescribed; and

    (b) such reasonable fee as the local authority may determine.

(3) In this Schedule "prescribed" means prescribed by regulations made by the Secretary of State.

(4) If a local authority are satisfied that a children's home with respect to which an application has been made in accordance with this Schedule complies or (as the case may be) will comply—

    (a) with such requirements as may be prescribed, and

    (b) with such other requirements (if any) as appear to them to be appropriate,

they shall grant the application, either unconditionally or subject to conditions imposed under paragraph 2.

(5) Before deciding whether or not to grant an application a local authority shall comply with any prescribed requirements.

(6) Regulations made for the purposes of sub-paragraph (5) may, in particular, make provision as to the inspection of the home in question.

(7) Where an application is granted, the authority shall notify the applicant that the home has been registered under this Act as from such date as may be specified in the notice.

(8) If the authority are not satisfied as mentioned in sub-paragraph (4), they shall refuse the application.

(9) For the purposes of this Act, an application which has not been granted or refused within the period of twelve months beginning with the date when it is served on the authority shall be deemed to have been refused by them, and the applicant shall be deemed to have been notified of their refusal at the end of that period.

(10) Where a school to which section 63(1) applies is registered it shall not cease to be a registered children's home by reason only of a subsequent change in the number of children for whom it provides accommodation.

Conditions imposed on registration

2.—(1) A local authority may grant an application for registration subject to such conditions relating to the conduct of the home as they think fit.

(2) A local authority may from time to time—

    (a) vary any condition for the time being in force with respect to a home by virtue of this paragraph; or

    (b) impose an additional condition,

either on the application of the person carrying on the home or without such an application.

(3) If any condition imposed or varied under this paragraph is not complied with, the person carrying on the home shall, if he has no reasonable excuse, be guilty of an offence and liable on summary conviction to a fine not exceeding level 4 on the standard scale.

Annual review of registration

3.—(1) In this Part "the responsible authority", in relation to a registered children's home means the local authority who registered it.

(2) The responsible authority for a registered children's home shall, at the end of the period of twelve months beginning with the date of registration, and annually thereafter, review its registration for the purpose of determining whether the registration should continue in force or be cancelled under paragraph 4(3).

(3) If on any such annual review the responsible authority are satisfied that the home is being carried on in accordance with the relevant requirements they shall determine that, subject to sub-paragraph (4), the registration should continue in force.

(4) The responsible authority shall give to the person carrying on the home notice of their determination under sub-paragraph (3) above and the notice shall require him to pay to the authority with respect to the review such reasonable fee as the authority may determine.

(5) It shall be a condition of the home's continued registration that the fee is so paid before the expiry of the period of twenty-eight days beginning with the date on which the notice is received by the person carrying on the home.

(6) In this Schedule "the relevant requirements" means any requirements of Part VIII and of any regulations made under paragraph 10, and any conditions imposed under paragraph 2.

Cancellation of registration

4.—(1) The person carrying on a registered children's home may at any time make an application, in such manner and including such particulars as may be prescribed, for the cancellation by the responsible authority of the registration of the home.

(2) If the authority are satisfied, in the case of a school registered by virtue of section 63(6), that it is no longer a school to which that provision applies, the authority shall give to the person carrying on the home notice that the registration of the home has been cancelled as from the date of the notice.

(3) If on any annual review under paragraph 3, or at any other time, it appears to the responsible authority that a registered home is being carried on otherwise than in accordance with the relevant requirements, they may determine that the registration of the home should be cancelled.

(4) The responsible authority may at any time determine that the registration of a home should be cancelled on the ground—

(a) that the person carrying on the home has been convicted of an offence under this Part or any regulations made under paragraph 10; or

(b) that any other person has been convicted of such an offence in relation to the home.

Procedure

5.—(1) Where—

(a) a person applies for the registration of a children's home; and

(b) the local authority propose to grant his application,

they shall give him written notice of their proposal and of the conditions (if any) subject to which they propose to grant his application.

(2)   The authority need not give notice if they propose to grant the application subject only to conditions which—

(a)   the applicant specified in the application; or

(b)   the authority and the applicant have subsequently agreed.

(3)   The authority shall give an applicant notice of a proposal to refuse his application.

(4)   The authority shall give any person carrying on a registered children's home notice of a proposal—

(a)   to cancel the registration;

(b)   to vary any condition for the time being in force with respect to the home by virtue of Part VIII; or

(c)   to impose any additional condition.

(5)   A notice under this paragraph shall give the local authority's reasons for their proposal.

Right to make representations

6.—(1)   A notice under paragraph 5 shall state that within 14 days of service of the notice any person on whom it is served may in writing require the local authority to give him an opportunity to make representations to them concerning the matter.

(2)   Where a notice has been served under paragraph 5, the local authority shall not determine the matter until—

(a)   any person on whom the notice was served has made representations to them concerning the matter;

(b)   the period during which any such person could have required the local authority to give him an opportnity to make representations has elapsed without their being required to give such an opportunity; or

(c)   the conditions specified in sub-paragraph (3) below are satisfied.

(3)   The conditions are—

(a)   that a person on whom the notice was served has required the local authority to give him an opportunity to make representations to them concerning the matter;

(b)   that the authority have allowed him a reasonable period to make his representations; and

(c)   that he has failed to make them within that period.

(4)   The representations may be made, at the option of the person making them, either in writing or orally.

(5)   If he informs the local authority that he desires to make oral representations, the authority shall give him an opportunity of appearing before and of being heard by a committee or sub-committee of theirs.

Decision of local authority

7.—(1)   If the local authority decide to adopt a proposal of theirs to grant an application, they shall serve notice in writing of their decision on any person on whom they were required to serve notice of their proposal.

(2)   A notice under this paragraph shall be accompanied by an explanation of the right of appeal conferred by paragraph 8.

(3)   A decision of a local authority, other than a decision to grant an application for registration subject only to such conditions as are mentioned in paragraph 5(2) or to refuse an application for registration, shall not take effect—

(a)   if no appeal is brought, until the end of the period of 28 days referred to in paragraph 8(3); and

(b)   if an appeal is brought, until it is determined or abandoned.

Appeals

8.—(1)   An appeal against a decision of a local authority under Part VIII shall lie to a Registered Homes Tribunal.

(2)   An appeal shall be brought by notice in writing given to the local authority.

(3)   No appeal shall be brought by a person more than 28 days after service on him of notice of the decision.

(4)   On an appeal the Tribunal may confirm the local authority's decision or direct that it shall not have effect.

(5)   A Tribunal shall also have power on an appeal—

(a)   to vary any condition in force with respect to the home to which the appeal relates by virtue of paragraph 2;

(b)   to direct that any such condition shall cease to have effect; or

(c)   to direct that any such condition as it thinks fit shall have effect with respect to the home.

(6)   A local authority shall comply with any direction given by a Tribunal under this paragraph.

Prohibition on further applications

9.—(1)   Where an application for the registration of a home is refused, no further application may be made within the period of six months beginning with the date when the applicant is notified of the refusal.

(2)   Sub-paragraph (1) shall have effect, where an appeal against the refusal of an application is determined or abandoned, as if the reference to the date when the applicant is notified of the refusal were a reference to the date on which the appeal is determined or abandoned.

(3)   Where the registration of a home is cancelled, no application for the registration of the home shall be made within a period of six months beginning with the date of cancellation.

(4)   Sub-paragraph (3) shall have effect, where an appeal against the cancellation of the registration of a home is determined or abandoned, as if the reference to the date of cancellation were a reference to the date on which the appeal is determined or abandoned.

PART II   REGULATIONS

10.—(1)   The Secretary of State may make regulations—

(a)   as to the placing of children in registered children's homes;

(b)   as to the conduct of such homes; and

(c)   for securing the welfare of the children in such homes.

(2)   The regulations may in particular—

(a)   prescribe standards to which the premises used for such homes are to conform;

(b)   impose requirements as to the accommodation, staff and equipment to be provided in such homes;

(c)   impose requirements as to the arrangements to be made for protecting the health of children in such homes;

(d)   provide for the control and discipline of children in such homes;

(e)   require the furnishing to the responsible authority of information as to the facilities provided for—

(i)   the parents of children in such homes;

(ii)   persons who are not parents of such children but who have parental responsibility for them; and

(iii)   other persons connected with such children,

to visit and communicate with the children;

(f)   impose requirements as to the keeping of records and giving of notices with respect to children in such homes;

(g)   impose requirements as to the facilities which are to be provided for giving religious instruction to children in such homes;

(h)   make provision as to the carrying out of annual reviews under paragraph 3;

(i)   authorise the responsible authority to limit the number of children who may be accommodated in any particular registered home;

(j)   prohibit the use of accommodation for the purpose of restricting the liberty of children in such homes;

(k)   require notice to be given to the responsible authority of any change of the person carrying on or in charge of a registered home or of the premises used by such a home;

(l)   make provision similar to that made by regulations under section 26.

(3)   The regulations may provide that a contravention of or a failure to comply with any specified provision of the regulations, without reasonable excuse, shall be an offence against the regulations.

(4)   Any person guilty of such an offence shall be liable on summary conviction to a fine not exceeding level 4 on the standard scale.

Section 63(12).   **SCHEDULE 7**
FOSTER PARENTS: LIMITS ON NUMBER OF FOSTER CHILDREN

Interpretation

1.   For the purposes of this Schedule, a person fosters a child if—

(a)   he is a local authority foster parent in relation to the child;

(b)   he is a foster parent with whom the child has been placed by a voluntary organisation; or

(c)   he fosters the child privately.

The usual fostering limit

2.   Subject to what follows, a person may not foster more than three children ("the usual fostering limit").

Siblings

3.   A person may exceed the usual fostering limit if the children concerned are all siblings with respect to each other.

Exemption by local authority

4.—(1)   A person may exceed the usual fostering limit if he is exempted from it by the local authority within whose area he lives.

(2)   In considering whether to exempt a person, a local authority shall have regard, in particular, to—

(a)   the number of children whom the person proposes to foster;

(b)   the arrangements which the person proposes for the care and accommodation of the fostered children;

(c)   the intended and likely relationship between the person and the fostered children;

(d)   the period of time for which he proposes to foster the children; and

(e)   whether the welfare of the fostered children (and of any other children who are or will be living in the accommodation) will be safeguarded and promoted.

(3)   Where a local authority exempt a person, they shall inform him by notice in writing—

(a)   that he is so exempted;

(b)   of the children, described by name, whom he may foster; and

(c)   of any condition to which the exemption is subject.

(4)   A local authority may at any time by notice in writing—

(a)   vary or cancel an exemption; or

(b)   impose, vary or cancel a condition to which the exemption is subject,

and, in considering whether to do so, they shall have regard in particlar to the considerations mentioned in sub-paragraph (2).

(5)   The Secretary of State may make regulations amplifying or modifying the provisions of this paragraph in order to provide for cases where children need to be placed with foster parents as a matter of urgency.

Effect of exceeding fostering limit

5.—(1)   A person shall cease to be treated as fostering and shall be treated as carrying on a children's home if—

(a)   he exceeds the usual fostering limit; or

(b)   where he is exempted under paragraph 4,—

(i)   he fosters any child not named in the exemption; and

(ii)   in so doing, he exceeds the usual fostering limit.

(2)   Sub-paragraph (1) does not apply if the children concerned are all siblings in respect of each other.

Complaints etc.

6.—(1) Every local authority shall establish a procedure for considering any representations (including any complaint) made to them about the discharge of their functions under paragraph 4 by a person exempted or seeking to be exempted under that paragraph.

(2) In carrying out any consideration of representations under sub-paragraph (1), a local authority shall comply with any regulations made by the Secretary of State for the purposes of this paragraph.

Section 66(5).   **SCHEDULE 8**
                        PRIVATELY FOSTERED CHILDREN

Exemptions

1. A child is not a privately fostered child while he is being looked after by a local authority.

2.—(1) A child is not a privately fostered child while he is in the care of any person—
    (a) in premises in which any—
      (i) parent of his;
      (ii) person who is not a parent of his but who has parental responsibility for him; or
      (iii) person who is a relative of his and who has assumed responsibility for his care,
is for the time being living;
    (b) in any children's home;
    (c) in accommodation provided by or on behalf of any voluntary organisation;
    (d) in any school in which he is receiving full-time education;
    (e) in any health service hospital;
    (f) in any residential care home, nursing home or mental nursing home; or
    (g) in any home or institution not specified in this paragraph but provided, equipped and maintained by the Secretary of State.

(2) Sub-paragraph (1)(b) to (g) does not apply where the person caring for the child is doing so in his personal capacity and not in the course of carrying out his duties in relation to the establishment mentioned in the paragraph in question.

3. A child is not a privately fostered child while he is in the care of any person in compliance with—
    (a) an order under section 7(7)(b) of the Children and Young Persons Act 1969; or
    (b) a supervision requirement within the meaning of the Social Work (Scotland) Act 1968.

4. A child is not a privately fostered child while he is liable to be detained, or subject to guardianship, under the Mental Health Act 1983.

5. A child is not a privately fostered child while—

(a)   he is placed in the care of a person who proposes to adopt him under arrangements made by an adoption agency within the meaning of—
> (i)   section 1 of the Adoption Act 1976;
> (ii)   section 1 of the Adoption (Scotland) Act 1978; or
> (iii)   Article 3 of the Adoption (Northern Ireland) Order 1987; or
(b)   he is a protected child.

Power of local authority to impose requirements

6.—(1)   Where a person is fostering any child privately, or proposes to foster any child privately, the appropriate local authority may impose on him requirements as to—
(a)   the number, age and sex of the children who may be privately fostered by him;
(b)   the standard of the accommodation and equipment to be provided for them;
(c)   the arrangements to be made with respect to their health and safety; and
(d)   particular arrangements which must be made with respect to the provision of care for them,
and it shall be his duty to comply with any such requirement before the end of such period as the authority may specify unless, in the case of a proposal, the proposal is not carried out.

(2)   A requirement may be limited to a particular child, or class of child.

(3)   A requirement (other than one imposed under sub-paragraph (1)(a)) may be limited by the authority so as to apply only when the number of children fostered by the person exceeds a specified number.

(4)   A requirement shall be imposed by notice in writing addressed to the person on whom it is imposed and informing him of—
(a)   the reason for imposing the requirement;
(b)   his right under paragraph 8 to appeal against it; and
(c)   the time within which he may do so.

(5)   A local authority may at any time vary any requirement, impose any additional requirement or remove any requirement.

(6)   In this Schedule—
(a)   "the appropriate local authority" means—
> (i)   the local authority within whose area the child is being fostered; or
> (ii)   in the case of a proposal to foster a child, the local authority within whose area it is proposed that he will be fostered; and
(b)   "requirement", in relation to any person, means a requirement imposed on him under this paragraph.

Regulations requiring notification of fostering etc.

7.—(1)   The Secretary of State may by regulations make provision as to—
(a)   the circumstances in which notification is required to be given in connection with children who are, have been or are proposed to be fostered privately; and
(b)   the manner and form in which such notification is to be given.

(2)   The regulations may, in particular—

(a) require any person who is, or proposes to be, involved (whether or not directly) in arranging for a child to be fostered privately to notify the appropriate authority;

(b) require any person who is—

(i) a parent of a child; or

(ii) a person who is not a parent of his but who has parental responsibility for a child,

and who knows that it is proposed that the child should be fostered privately, to notify the appropriate authority;

(c) require any parent of a privately fostered child, or person who is not a parent of such a child but who has parental responsibility for him, to notify the appropriate authority of any change in his address;

(d) require any person who proposes to foster a child privately, to notify the appropriate authority of his proposal;

(e) require any person who is fostering a child privately, or proposes to do so, to notify the appropriate authority of—

(i) any offence of which he has been convicted;

(ii) any disqualification imposed on him under section 68; or

(iii) any prohibition imposed on him under section 69;

(f) require any person who is fostering a child privately, to notify the appropriate authority of any change in his address;

(g) require any person who is fostering a child privately to notify the appropriate authority in writing of any person who begins, or ceases, to be part of his household;

(h) require any person who has been fostering a child privately, but has ceased to do so, to notify the appropriate authority (indicating, where the child has died, that this is the reason).

Appeals

8.—(1) A person aggrieved by—

(a) a requirement imposed under paragraph 6;

(b) a refusal of consent under section 68;

(c) a prohibition imposed under section 69;

(d) a refusal to cancel such a prohibition;

(e) a refusal to make an exemption under paragraph 4 of Schedule 7;

(f) a condition imposed in such an exemption; or

(g) a variation or cancellation of such an exemption,

may appeal to the court.

(2) The appeal must be made within fourteen days from the date on which the person appealing is notified of the requirement, refusal, prohibition, condition, variation or cancellation.

(3) Where the appeal is against—

(a) a requirement imposed under paragraph 6;

(b) a condition of an exemption imposed under paragraph 4 of Schedule 7; or

(c) a variation or cancellation of such an exemption,

the requirement, condition, variation or cancellation shall not have effect while the appeal is pending.

(4)   Where it allows an appeal against a requirement or prohibition, the court may, instead of cancelling the requirement or prohibition—

(a)   vary the requirement, or allow more time for compliance with it; or

(b)   if an absolute prohibition has been imposed, substitute for it a prohibition on using the premises after such time as the court may specify unless such specified requirements as the local authority had power to impose under paragraph 6 are complied with.

(5)   Any requirement or prohibition specified or substituted by a court under this paragraph shall be deemed for the purposes of Part IX (other than this paragraph) to have been imposed by the local authority under paragraph 6 or (as the case may be) section 69.

(6)   Where it allows an appeal against a refusal to make an exemption, a condition imposed in such an exemption or a variation or cancellation of such an exemption, the court may—

(a)   make an exemption;

(b)   impose a condition; or

(c)   vary the exemption.

(7)   Any exemption made or varied under sub-paragraph (6), or any condition imposed under that sub-paragraph, shall be deemed for the purposes of Schedule 7 (but not for the purposes of this paragraph) to have been made, varied or imposed under that Schedule.

(8)   Nothing in sub-paragraph (1)(e) to (g) confers any right of appeal on—

(a)   a person who is, or would be if exempted under Schedule 7, a local authority foster parent; or

(b)   a person who is, or would be if so exempted, a person with whom a child is placed by a voluntary organisation.

Extension of Part IX to certain school children during holidays

9.—(1)   Where a child under sixteen who is a pupil at a school which is not maintained by a local education authority lives at the school during school holidays for a period of more than two weeks, Part IX shall apply in relation to the child as if—

(a)   while living at the school, he were a privately fostered child; and

(b)   paragraphs 2(1)(d) and 6 were omitted.

(2)   Sub-paragraph (3) applies to any person who proposes to care for and accommodate one or more children at a school in circumstances in which some or all of them will be treated as private foster children by virtue of this paragraph.

(3)   That person shall, not less than two weeks before the first of those children is treated as a private foster child by virtue of this paragraph during the holiday in question, give written notice of his proposal to the local authority within whose area the child is ordinarily resident ("the appropriate authority"), stating the estimated number of the children.

(4)   A local authority may exempt any person from the duty of giving notice under sub-paragraph (3).

(5)   Any such exemption may be granted for a special period or indefinitely and may be revoked at any time by notice in writing given to the person exempted.

(6)   Where a child who is treated as a private foster child by virtue of this

paragraph dies, the person caring for him at the school shall, not later than 48 hours after his death, give written notice of it—

(a) to the appropriate authority; and

(b) where reasonably practicable, to each parent of the child and to every person who is not a parent of is but who has parental responsibility for him.

(7) Where a child who is treated as a foster child by virtue of this paragraph ceases for any other reason to be such a child, the person caring for him at the school shall give written notice of the fact to the appropriate local authority.

Prohibition of advertisements relating to fostering

10. No advertisement indicating that a person will undertake, or will arrange for, a child to be privately fostered shall be published, unless it states that person's name and address.

Avoidance of insurances on lives of privately fostered children

11. A person who fosters a child privately and for reward shall be deemed for the purposes of the Life Assurance Act 1774 to have no interest in the life of the child.

Section 71(16).   **SCHEDULE 9**
CHILD MINDING AND DAY CARE FOR YOUNG CHILDREN

Applications for registration

1.—(1) An application for registration under section 71 shall be of no effect unless it contains—

(a) a statement with respect to the applicant which complies with the requirements of regulations made for the purposes of this paragraph by the Secretary of State; and

(b) a statement with respect to any person assisting or likely to be assisting in looking after children on the premises in question, or living or likely to be living there, which complies with the requirements of such regulations.

(2) Where a person provides, or proposes to provide, day care for children under the age of eight on different premises situated within the area of the same local authority, he shall make a separate application with respect to each of those premises.

(3) An application under section 71 shall be accompanied by such fee as may be prescribed.

(4) On receipt of an application for registration under section 71 from any person who is acting, or proposes to act, in any way which requires him to be registered under that section, a local authority shall register him if the application is properly made and they are not otherwise entitled to refuse to do so.

Disqualification from registration

2.—(1) A person may not be registered under section 71 if he is disqualified by regulations made by the Secretary of State for the purposes of this paragraph.

(2) The regulations may, in particular, provide for a person to be disqualified where—

(a)   an order of a prescribed kind has been made at any time with respect to him;

(b)   an order of a prescribed kind has been made at any time with respect to any child who has been in his care;

(c)   a requirement of a prescribed kind has been imposed at any time with respect to such a child, under or by virtue of any enactment;

(d)   he has at any time been refused registration under Part X or any other prescribed enactment or had any such registration cancelled;

(e)   he has been convicted of any offence of a prescribed kind, or has been placed on probation or discharged absolutely or conditionally for any such offence;

(f)   he has at any time been disqualified from fostering a child privately;

(g)   a prohibition has been imposed on him at any time under section 61, section 10 of the Foster Children (Scotland) Act 1984 or any other prescribed enactment;

(h)   his rights and powers with respect to a child have at any time been vested in a prescribed authority under a prescribed enactment.

(3)   A person who lives—

(a)   in the same household as a person who is himself disqualified by the regulations; or

(b)   in a household at which any such person is employed,

shall be disqualified unless he has disclosed the fact to the appropriate local authority and obtained their written consent.

(4)   A person who is disqualified shall not provide day care, or be concerned in the management of, or have any financial interest in, any provision of day care unless he has—

(a)   disclosed the fact to the appropriate local authority; and

(b)   obtained their written consent.

(5)   No person shall employ, in connection with the provision of day care, a person who is disqualified, unless he has—

(a)   disclosed to the appropriate local authority the fact that the person is so disqualified; and

(b)   obtained their written consent.

(6)   In this paragraph "enactment" means any enactment having effect, at any time, in any part of the United Kingdom.

Exemption of certain schools

3.—(1)   Section 71 does not apply in relation to any child looked after in any—

(a)   school maintained or assisted by a local education authority;

(b)   school under the management of an education authority;

(c)   school in respect of which payments are made by the Secretary of State under section 100 of the Education Act 1944;

(d)   independent school;

(e)   grant-aided school;

(f)   grant maintained school;

(g)   self-governing school;

(h)   play centre maintained or assisted by a local education authority under section 53 of the Act of 1944, or by an education authority under section 6 of the Education (Scotland) Act 1980.

(2)   The exemption provided by sub-paragraph (1) only applies where the child concerned is being looked after in accordance with provision for day care made by—

(a)   the person carrying on the establishment in question as part of the establishment's activities; or

(b)   a person employed to work at that establishment and authorised to make that provision as part of the establishment's activities.

(3)   In sub-paragraph (1)—

"assisted" and "maintained" have the same meanings as in the Education Act 1944;

"grant maintained" has the same meaning as in section 52(3) of the Education Reform Act 1988; and

"grant-aided school", "self-governing school" and (in relation to Scotland) "independent school" have the same meanining as in the Education (Scotland) Act 1980.

Exemption for other establishments

4.—(1)   Section 71(1)(b) does not apply in relation to any child looked after in—

(a)   a registered children's home;

(b)   a voluntary home;

(c)   a community home;

(d)   a residential care home, nursing home or mental nursing home required to be registered under the Registered Homes Act 1984;

(e)   a health service hospital;

(f)   a home provided, equipped and maintained by the Secretary of State; or

(g)   an establishment which is required to be registered under section 61 of the Social Work (Scotland) Act 1968.

(2)   The exemption provided by sub-paragraph (1) only applies where the child concerned is being looked after in accordance with provision for day care made by—

(a)   the department, authority or other person carrying on the establishment in question as part of the establishment's activities; or

(b)   a person employed to work at that establishment and authorised to make that provision as part of the establishment's activities.

(3)   In this paragraph "a health service hospital" includes a health service hospital within the meaning of the National Health Service (Scotland) Act 1978.

Exemption for occasional facilities

5.—(1)   Where day care for children under the age of eight is provided in particular premises on less than six days in any year, that provision shall be disregarded for the purposes of section 71 if the person making it has notified the appropriate local authority in writing before the first occasion on which the premises concerned are so used in that year.

(2)   In sub-paragraph (1) "year" means the year beginning with the day on

which the day care in question is (after the commencement of this paragraph) first provided in the premises concerned and any subsequent year.

Certificates of registration

6.—(1)   Where a local authority register a person under section 71 they shall issue him with a certificate of registration.

(2)   The certificate shall specify—

(a)   the registered person's name and address;

(b)   in a case falling within section 71(1)(b), the address or situation of the premises concerned; and

(c)   any requirements imposed under section 72 or 73.

(3)   Where, due to a change of circumstances, any part of the certificate requires to be amended, the authority shall issue an amended certificate.

(4)   Where the authority are satisfied that the certificate has been lost or destroyed, they shall issue a copy, on payment by the registered person of such fee as may be prescribed.

Fees for annual inspection of premises

7.—(1)   Where—

(a)   a person is registered under section 71, and

(b)   the local authority concerned make an annual inspection of the premises in question under section 76,

they shall serve on that person a notice informing him that the inspection is to be carried out and requiring him to pay to them such fee as may be prescribed.

(2)   It shall be a condition of the continued registration of that person under section 71 that the fee is so paid before the expiry of the period of twenty-eight days beginning with the date on which the inspection is carried out.

Co-operation between authorities

8.—(1)   Where it appears to a local authority that any local education authority or, in Scotland, education authority could, by taking any specified action, help in the exercise of any of their functions under Part X, they may request the help of that local education authority, or education authority, specifying the action in question.

(2)   An authority whose help is so requested shall comply with the request if it is compatible with their own statutory or other duties and obligations and does not unduly prejudice the discharge of any of their functions.

Section 88.   **SCHEDULE 10**
              AMENDMENTS OF ADOPTION LEGISLATION

PART I   AMENDMENTS OF ADOPTION ACT 1976 (c. 36)

1.   In section 2 (local authorities' social services) for the words from "relating to" to the end there shall be substituted—

"(a)   under the Children Act 1989, relating to family assistance orders, local authority support for children and families, care and supervision and emergency protection of children, community homes, voluntary homes and organisations, registered children's homes, private arrangements for fostering children, child minding and day care for young children and children accommodated by health authorities and local education authorities or in residential care, nursing or mental nursing homes or in independent schools; and

(b) under the National Health Service Act 1977, relating to the provision of care for expectant and nursing mothers."

2. In section 11 (restrictions on arranging adoptions and placing of children) for subsection (2) there shall be substituted—

"(2) An adoption society which is—

(a) approved as respects Scotland under section 3 of the Adoption (Scotland) Act 1978; or

(b) registered as respects Northern Ireland under Article 4 of the Adoption (Northern Ireland) Order 1987,

but which is not approved under section 3 of this Act, shall not act as an adoption society in England and Wales except to the extent that the society considers it necessary to do so in the interests of a person mentioned in section 1 of the Act of 1978 or Article 3 of the Order of 1987."

3.—(1) In section 12 (adoption orders), in subsection (1) for the words "vesting the parental rights and duties relating to a child in" there shall be substituted "giving parental responsibility for a child to".

(2) In subsection (2) of that section for the words "the parental rights and duties so far as they relate" there shall be substituted "parental responsibility so far as it relates".

(3) In subsection (3) of that section for paragraph (a) there shall be substituted—

"(a) the parental responsibility which any person has for the child immediately before the making of the order;

(aa) any order under the Children Act 1989";

and in paragraph (b) for the words from "for any period" to the end there shall be substituted "or upbringing for any period after the making of the order."

4. For section 14(1) (adoption by married couple) there shall be substituted—

"(1) An adoption order shall not be made on the application of more than one person except in the circumstances specified in subsections (1A) and (1B).

(1A) An adoption order may be made on the application of a married couple where both the husband and the wife have attained the age of 21 years.

(1B) An adoption order may be made on the application of a married couple where—

(a) the husband or the wife—

(i) is the father or mother of the child; and

(ii) has attained the age of 18 years;

and

(b) his or her spouse has attained the age of 21 years."

5.—(1)   In section 16 (parental agreement), in subsection (1) for the words
from "in England" to "Scotland)" there shall be substituted—
     "(i)   in England and Wales, under section 18;
     (ii)   in Scotland, under section 18 of the Adoption (Scotland) Act
1978; or
     (iii)   in Northern Ireland, under Article 17(1) or 18(1) of the
Adoption (Northern Ireland) Order 1987."
(2)   In subsection (2)(c) of that section for the words "the parental duties in
relation to" there shall be substituted "his parental responsibility for".
6.—(1)   In section 18 (freeing child for adoption), after subsection (2) there
shall be inserted—
     "(2A)   For the purposes of subsection (2) a child is in the care of an
adoption agency if the adoption agency is a local authority and he is in their
care."
(2)   In subsection (5) of that section, for the words from "the parental rights"
to "vest in" there shall be substituted "parental responsibility for the child is
given to", and for the words "and (3)" there shall be substituted "to (4)".
(3)   For subsections (7) and (8) of that section there shall be substituted—
     "(7)   Before making an order under this section in the case of a child
whose father does not have parental responsibility for him, the court shall
satisfy itself in relation to any person claiming to be the father that—
     (a)   he has no intention of applying for—
       (i)   an order under section 4(1) of the Children Act 1989, or
       (ii)   a residence order under section 10 of that Act, or
     (b)   if he did make any such application, it would be likely to be
refused.
     (8)   Subsections (5) and (7) of section 12 apply in relation to the making
of an order under this section as they apply in relation to the making of an
order under that section."

7.   In section 19(2) (progress reports to former parents) for the words "in
which the parental rights and duties were vested" there shall be substituted "to
which parental responsibility was given".

8.—(1)   In section 20 (revocation of section 18 order), in subsections (1) and
(2) for the words "the parental rights and duties", in both places where they
occur, there shall be substituted "parental responsibility".
(2)   For subsection (3) of that section there shall be substituted—
     "(3)   The revocation of an order under section 18 ("a section 18 order")
operates—
     (a)   to extinguish the parental responsibility given to the adoption
agency under the section 18 order;
     (b)   to give parental responsibility for the child to—
       (i)   the child's mother; and
       (ii)   where the child's father and mother were married to each other
at the time of his birth, the father; and
     (c)   to revive—
       (i)   any parental responsibility agreement,
       (ii)   any order under section 4(1) of the Children Act 1989, and

(iii)   any appointment of a guardian in respect of the child (whether made by a court or otherwise),
extinguished by the making of the section 18 order.

(3A)   Subject to subsection (3)(c), the revocation does not—
(a)   operate to revive—
(i)   any order under the Children Act 1989, or
(ii)   any duty referred to in section 12(3)(b),
extinguished by the making of the section 18 order; or
(b)   affect any person's parental responsibility so far as it relates to the period between the making of the section 18 order and the date of revocation of that order."

9.   For section 21 (transfer of parental rights and duties between adoption agencies) there shall be substituted—

"21. Variation of section 18 order so as to substitute one adoption agency for another.

(1)   On an application to which this section applies, an authorised court may vary an order under section 18 so as to give parental responsibility for the child to another adoption agency ('the substitute agency') in place of the agency for the time being having parental responsibility for the child under the order ('the existing agency').

(2)   This section applies to any application made jointly by—
(a)   the existing agency; and
(b)   the would-be substitute agency.

(3)   Where an order under section 18 is varied under this section, section 19 shall apply as if the substitute agency had been given responsibility for the child on the making of the order."

10.   In section 22 (notification to local authority of adoption application), after subsection (1) there shall be inserted the following subsections—

"(1A)   An application for such an adoption order shall not be made unless the person wishing to make the application has, within the period of two years preceding the making of the application, given notice as mentioned in subsection (1).

(1B)   In subsections (1) and (1A) the references to the area in which the applicant or person has his home are references to the area in which he has his home at the time of giving the notice."

(2)   In subsection (4) of the section for the word "receives" there shall be substituted "receive" and for the words "in the care of" there shall be substituted "looked after by".

11.   In section 25(1) (interim orders) for the words "vesting the legal custody of the child in" there shall be substituted "giving parental responsibility for the child to".

12.   In—
(a)   section 27(1) and (2) (restrictions on removal where adoption agreed or application made under section 18); and
(b)   section 28(1) and (2) (restrictions on removal where applicant has provided home for 5 years),

for the words "actual custody", in each place where they occur, there shall be substituted "home".

13.   After section 27(2) there shall be inserted—
   "(2A)   For the purposes of subsection (2) a child is in the care of an adoption agency if the adoption agency is a local authority and he is in their care."

14.—(1)   After section 28(2) there shall be inserted—
   "(2A)   The reference in subsections (1) and (2) to any enactment does not include a reference to section 20(8) of the Children Act 1989".
(2)   For subsection (3) of that section there shall be substituted—
   "(3)   In any case where subsection (1) or (2) applies and—
      (a)   the child was being looked after by a local authority before he began to have his home with the applicant or, as the case may be, the prospective adopter, and
      (b)   the child is still being looked after by a local authority,
the authority which are looking after the child shall not remove him from the home of the applicant or the prospective adopter except in accordance with section 30 or 31 or with the leave of a court."
(3)   In subsection (5) of that section—
      (a)   for the word "receives" there shall be substituted "receive"; and
      (b)   for the words "in the care of another local authority or of a voluntary organisation" there shall be substituted "looked after by another local authority".

15.   In section 29 (return of child taken away in breach of section 27 or 28) for subsections (1) and (2) there shall be substituted—
   "(1)   An authorised court may, on the application of a person from whose home a child has been removed in breach of—
      (a)   section 27 or 28,
      (b)   section 27 or 28 of the Adoption (Scotland) Act 1978, or
      (c)   Article 28 or 29 of the Adoption (Northern Ireland) Order 1987,
order the person who has so removed the child to return the child to the applicant.
   (2)   An authorised court may, on the application of a person who has reasonable grounds for believing that another person is intending to remove a child from his home in breach of—
      (a)   section 27 or 28,
      (b)   section 27 or 28 of the Adoption (Scotland) Act 1978, or
      (c)   Article 28 or 29 of the Adoption (Northern Ireland) Order 1987,
by order direct that other person not to remove the child from the applicant's home in breach of any of those provisions."

16.—(1)   In section 30 (return of children placed for adoption by adoption agencies), in subsection (1) there shall be substituted—
      (a)   for the words "delivered into the actual custody of" the words "placed with";
      (b)   in paragraph (a) for the words "retain the actual custody of the child" the words "give the child a home"; and

(c)   in paragraph (b) for the words "actual custody" the word "home".
(2)   In subsection (3) of that section for the words "in his actual custody" there shall be substituted "with him".

17.—(1)   In section 31 (application of section 30 where child not placed for adoption), in subsection (1) for the words from "child", where it first occurs, to "except" there shall be substituted "child—
    (a)   who is (when the notice is given) being looked after by a local authority; but
    (b)   who was placed with that person otherwise than in pursuance of such arrangements as are mentioned in section 30(1),
that section shall apply as if the child had been placed in pursuance of such arrangements".
(2)   In subsection (2) of that section for the words "for the time being in the care of" there shall be substituted "(when the notice is given) being looked after by".
(3)   In subsection (3) of that section—
    (a)   for the words "remains in the actual custody of" there shall be substituted "has his home with"; and
    (b)   for the words "section 45 of the Child Care Act 1980" there shall be substituted "Part III of Schedule 2 to the Children Act 1989".
(4)   At the end of that section there shall be added—
    "(4)   Nothing in this section affects the right of any person who has parental responsibility for a child to remove him under section 20(8) of the Children Act 1989".

18.—(1)   In section 32 (meaning of "protected child"), in subsection (2) for the words "section 37 of the Adoption Act 1958" there shall be substituted—
    "(a)   section 32 of the Adoption (Scotland) Act 1978; or
    (b)   Article 33 of the Adoption (Northern Ireland) Order 1987."
(2)   In subsection (3) of that section for paragraph (a) there shall be substituted—
    "(a)   he is in the care of any person—
        (i)   in any community home, voluntary home or registered children's home;
        (ii)   in any school in which he is receiving full-time education;
        (iii)   in any health service hospital";
and at the end of that subsection there shall be added—
    "(d)   he is in the care of any person in any home or institution not specified in this subsection but provided, equipped and maintained by the Secretary of State."
(3)   After that subsection there shall be inserted—
    "(3A)   In subsection (3) 'community home', 'voluntary home', 'registered children's home', 'school' and 'health service hospital' have the same meaning as in the Children Act 1989."
(4)   For subsection (4) of that section there shall be substituted—
    "(4)   A protected child ceases to be a protected child—
        (a)   on the grant or refusal of the application for an adoption order;
        (b)   on the notification to the local authority for the area where the

child has his home that the application for an adoption order has been withdrawn;

(c) in a case where no application is made for an adoption order, on the expiry of the period of two years from the giving of the notice;

(d) on the making of a residence order, a care order or a supervision order under the Children Act 1989 in respect of the child;

(e) on the appointment of a guardian for him under that Act;

(f) on his attaining the age of 18 years; or

(g) on his marriage,

whichever first occurs.

(5) In subsection (4)(d) the references to a care order and a supervision order do not include references to an interim care order or interim supervision order."

19.—(1) In section 35 (notices and information to be given to local authorities), in subsection (1) for the words "who has a protected child in his actual custody" there shall be substituted "with whom a protected child has his home".

(2) In subsection (2) of that section for the words "in whose actual custody he was" there shall be substituted "with whom he had his home".

20.—(1) In section 51 (disclosure of birth records of adopted children), in subsection (1) for the words "subsections (4) and (6)" there shall be substituted "what follows".

(2) For subsections (3) to (7) of that section there shall be substituted—

"(3) Before supplying any information to an applicant under subsection (1), the Registrar General shall inform the applicant that counselling services are available to him—

(a) if he is in England and Wales—

(i) at the General Register Office;

(ii) from the local authority in whose area he is living;

(iii) where the adoption order relating to him was made in England and Wales, from the local authority in whose area the court which made the order sat; or

(iv) from any other local authority;

(b) if he is in Scotland—

(i) from the regional or islands council in whose area he is living;

(ii) where the adoption order relating to him was made in Scotland, from the council in whose area the court which made the order sat; or

(iii) from any other regional or islands council;

(c) if he is Northern Ireland—

(i) from the Board in whose area he is living;

(ii) where the adoption order relating to him was made in Northern Ireland, from the Board in whose area the court which made the order sat; or

(iii) from any other Board;

(d) if he is in the United Kingdom and his adoption was arranged by an adoption society—

(i) approved under section 3,

(ii) approved under section 3 of the Adoption (Scotland) Act 1978,

(iii) registered under Article 4 of the Adoption (Northern Ireland) Order 1987,
from that society.

(4) Where an adopted person who is in England and Wales—

    (a) applies for information under—

        (i) subsection (1), or

        (ii) Article 54 of the Adoption (Northern Ireland) Order 1987, or

    (b) is supplied with information under section 45 of the Adoption (Scotland) Act 1978,
it shall be the duty of the persons and bodies mentioned in subsection (5) to provide counselling for him if asked by him to do so.

(5) The persons and bodies are—

    (a) the Registrar General;

    (b) any local authority falling within subsection (3)(a)(ii) to (iv);

    (c) any adoption society falling within subsection (3)(d) in so far as it is acting as an adoption society in England and Wales.

(6) If the applicant choses to receive counselling from a person or body falling within subsection (3), the Registrar General shall send to the person or body the information to which the applicant is entitled under subsection (1).

(7) Where a person—

    (a) was adopted before 12th November 1975, and

    (b) applies for information under subsection (1),
the Registrar General shall not supply the information to him unless he has attended an interview with a counsellor arranged by a person or body from whom counselling services are available as mentioned in subsection (3).

(8) Where the Registrar General is prevented by subsection (7) from supplying information to a person who is not living in the United Kingdom, he may supply the information to any body which—

    (a) the Registrar General is satisfied is suitable to provide counselling to that person, and

    (b) has notified the Registrar General that it is prepared to provide such counselling.

(9) In this section—
"a Board" means a Health and Social Services Board established under Article 16 of the Health and Personal Social Services (Northern Ireland) Order 1972; and
"prescribed" means prescribed by regulations made by the Registrar General."

21. After section 51 there shall be inserted—

"51A Adoption Contact Register.
(1) The Registrar General shall maintain at the General Register Office a register to be called the Adoption Contact Register.

(2) The register shall be in two parts—

    (a) Part I: Adopted Persons; and

    (b) Part II: Relatives.

(3) The Registrar General shall, on payment of such fee as may be

prescribed, enter in Part I of the register the name and address of any adopted person who fulfils the conditions in subsection (4) and who gives notice that he wishes to contact any relative of his.

(4)   The conditions are that—

(a)   a record of the adopted person's birth is kept by the Registrar General; and

(b)   the adopted person has attained the age of 18 years and—

(i)   has been supplied by the Registrar General with information under section 51; or

(ii)   has satisfied the Registrar General that he has such information as is necessary to obtain a certified copy of the record of his birth.

(5)   The Registrar General shall, on payment of such fee as may be prescribed, enter in Part II of the register the name and address of any person who fulfils the conditions in subsection (6) and who gives notice that he wishes to contact an adopted person.

(6)   The conditions are that—

(a)   a record of the adopted person's birth is kept by the Registrar General; and

(b)   the person giving notice under subsection (5) has attained the age of 18 years and has satisfied the Registrar General that—

(i)   he is a relative of the adopted person; and

(ii)   he has such information as is necessary to enable him to obtain a certified copy of the record of the adopted person's birth.

(7)   The Registrar General shall, on receiving notice from any person named in an entry in the register that he wishes the entry to be cancelled, cancel the entry.

(8)   Any notice given under this section must be in such form as may be determined by the Registrar General.

(9)   The Registrar General shall transmit to an adopted person whose name is entered in Part I of the register the name and address of any relative in respect of whom there is an entry in Part II of the register.

(10)   Any entry cancelled under subsection (7) ceases from the time of cancellation to be an entry for the purposes of subsection (9).

(11)   The register shall not be open to public inspection or search and the Registrar General shall not supply any person with information entered in the register (whether in an uncancelled or a cancelled entry) except in accordance with this section.

(12)   The register may be kept by means of a computer.

(13)   In this section—

(a)   "relative" means any person (other than an adoptive relative) who is related to the adopted person by blood (including half-blood) or marriage;

(b)   "address" includes any address at or through which the person concerned may be contacted; and

(c)   "prescribed" means prescribed by the Secretary of State."

22.—(1)   In section 55 (adoption of children abroad), in subsection (1) after the word "Scotland" there shall be inserted "or Northern Ireland" and for the words "vesting in him the parental rights and duties relating to the child" there shall be substituted "giving him parental responsibility for the child".

(2)   In subsection (3) of that section for the words "word '(Scotland)'" there shall be substituted "words '(Scotland)' or '(Northern Ireland'."

23.—(1)   In section 56 (restriction on removal of children for adoption outside Great Britain),—

(a)   in subsections (1) and (3) for the words "transferring the actual custody of a child to", in both places where they occur, there shall be substituted "placing a child with"; and

(b)   in subsection (3)(a) for the words "in the actual custody of" there shall be substituted "with".

(2)   In subsection (1) of that section—

(a)   for the words from "or under" to "abroad)" there shall be substituted "section 49 of the Adoption (Scotland) Act 1978 or Article 57 of the Adoption (Northern Ireland) Order 1987"; and

(b)   for the words "British Islands" there shall be substituted "United Kingdom, the Channel Islands and the Isle of Man".

24.—(1)   In section 57 (prohibition on certain payments) in subsection (1)(c), for the words "transfer by that person of the actual custody of a child" there shall be substituted "handing over of a child by that person".

(2)   In subsection (3A)(b) of that section, for the words "in the actual custody of" there shall be substituted "with".

25.   After section 57 there shall be inserted—

"57A. Permitted allowances.

(1)   The Secretary of State may make regulations for the purpose of enabling adoption agencies to pay allowances to persons who have adopted, or intend to adopt, children in pursuance of arrangements made by the agencies.

(2)   Section 57(1) shall not apply to any payment made by an adoption agency in accordance with the regulations.

(3)   The regulations may, in particular, make provision as to—

(a)   the procedure to be followed by any agency in determining whether a person should be paid an allowance;

(b)   the circumstances in which an allowance may be paid;

(c)   the factors to be taken into account in determining the amount of an allowance;

(d)   the procedure for review, variation and termination of allowances; and

(e)   the information about allowances to be supplied by any agency to any person who is intending to adopt a child.

(4)   Any scheme approved under section 57(4) shall be revoked as from the coming into force of this section.

(5)   Section 57(1) shall not apply in relation to any payment made—

(a)   in accordance with a scheme revoked under subsection (4) or section 57(5)(b); and

(b)   to a person to whom such payments were made before the revocation of the scheme.

(6)   Subsection (5) shall not apply where any person to whom any

payments may lawfully be made by virtue of subsection (5) agrees to receive (instead of such payments) payments complying with regulations made under this section."

26.—(1)   In section 59 (effect of determination and orders made in Scotland and overseas in adoption proceedings), in subsection (1) for the words "Great Britain" there shall be substituted "the United Kingdom".

(2)   For subsection (2) of that section there shall be substituted—

"(2)   Subsections (2) to (4) of section 12 shall apply in relation to an order freeing a child for adoption (other than an order under section 18) as if it were an adoption order; and, on the revocation in Scotland or Northern Ireland of an order freeing a child for adoption, subsections (3) and (3A) of section 20 shall apply as if the order had been revoked under that section."

27.   In section 60 (evidence of adoption in Scotland and Northern Ireland), in paragraph (a) for the words "section 22(2) of the Adoption Act 1958" there shall be substituted "section 45(2) of the Adoption (Scotland) Act 1978" and in paragraph (b) for the words from "section 23(4)" to "in force" there shall be substituted "Article 63(1) of the Adoption (Northern Ireland) Order 1987".

28.   In section 62(5)(b) (courts), for the words from "section 8" to "child)" there shall be substituted—

"(i)   section 12 or 18 of the Adoption (Scotland) Act 1978; or
(ii)   Article 12, 17 or 18 of the Adoption (Northern Ireland) Order 1987".

29.   After section 65 (guardians ad litem and reporting officers) there shall be inserted—

"65A. Panels for selection of guardians ad litem and reporting officers.

(1)   The Secretary of State may by regulations provide for the establishment of panels of persons from whom guardians ad litem and reporting officers appointed under rules made under section 65 must be selected.

(2)   The regulations may, in particlular, make provision—

(a)   as to the constitution, administration and procedures of panels;

(b)   requiring two or more specified local authorities to make arrangements for the joint management of a panel;

(c)   for the defrayment by local authorities of expenses incurred by members of panels;

(d)   for the payment by local authorities of fees and allowances for members of panels;

(e)   as to the qualifications for membership of a panel;

(f)   as to the training to be given to members of panels;

(g)   as to the co-operation required of specified local authorities in the provision of panels in specified areas; and

(h)   for monitoring the work of guardians ad litem and reporting officers.

(3)   Rules of court may make provision as to the assistance which any guardian ad litem or reporting officer may be required by the court to give to it."

30.—(1) Section 72(1) (interpretation) shall be amended as follows.

(2) In the definition of "adoption agency" for the words from "section 1" to the end there shall be substituted "—
   (a) section 1 of the Adoption (Scotland) Act 1978; and
   (b) Article 3 of the Adoption (Northern Ireland) Order 1987."

(3) For the definition of "adoption order" there shall be substituted—
   "'adoption order'—
      (a) means an order under section 12(1); and
      (b) in sections 12(3) and (4), 18 to 20, 27, 28 and 30 to 32 and in the definition of 'British adoption order' in this subsection includes an order under section 12 of the Adoption (Scotland) Act 1978 and Article 12 of the Adoption (Northern Ireland) Order 1987 (adoption orders in Scotland and Northern Ireland respectively); and
      (c) in sections 27, 28 and 30 to 32 includes an order under section 55, section 49 of the Adoption (Scotland) Act 1978 and Article 57 of the Adoption (Northern Ireland) Order 1987 (orders in relation to children being adopted abroad)."

(4) For the definition of "British adoption order" there shall be substituted—
   "'British adoption order' means—
      (a) an adoption order as defined in this subsection, and
      (b) an order under any provision for the adoption of a child effected under the law of any British territory outside the United Kingdom."

(5) For the definition of "guardian" there shall be substituted—
   "'guardian' has the same meaning as in the Children Act 1989."

(6) In the definition of "order freeing a child for adoption" for the words from "section 27(2)" to the end there shall be substituted "sections 27(2) and 59 includes an order under—
   (a) section 18 of the Adoption (Scotland) Act 1978; and
   (b) Article 17 or 18 of the Adoption (Northern Ireland) Order 1987".

(7) After the definition of "overseas adoption" there shall be inserted—
   "'parent' means, in relation to a child, any parent who has parental responsibility for the child under the Children Act 1989;
   'parental responsibility' and 'parental responsibility agreement' have the same meaning as in the Children Act 1989."

(8) After the definition of "United Kingdom national" there shall be inserted—
   "'upbringing' has the same meaning as in the Children Act 1989."

(9) For section 72(1A) there shall be substituted the following subsections—
   "(1A) In this Act, in determining with what person, or where, a child has his home, any absence of the child at a hospital or boarding school and any other temporary absence shall be disregarded.
   (1B) In this Act, references to a child who is in the care of or looked after by a local authority have the same meanining as in the Children Act 1989."

31. For section 74(3) and (4) (extent) there shall be substituted—
   "(3) This Act extends to England and Wales only."

PART II   AMENDMENTS OF ADOPTION (SCOTLAND) ACT 1978 (c. 28)

32.   In section 11 (restrictions on arranging of adoptions and placing of children) for subsection (2) there shall be substituted—
"(2)   An adoption society which is—
(a)   approved as respects England and Wales under section 3 of the Adoption Act 1976; or
(b)   registered as respects Northern Ireland under Article 4 of the Adoption (Northern Ireland) Order 1987,
but which is not approved under section 3 of this Act, shall not act as an adoption society in Scotland except to the extent that the society considers it necessary to do so in the interests of a person mentioned in section 1 of that Act or, as the case may be, Article 3 of that Order."

33.   For section 14(1) (adoption by married couple) there shall be substituted—
"(1)   Subject to section 53(1) of the Children Act 1975 (which provides for the making of a custody order instead of an adoption order in certain cases), an adoption order shall not be made on the application of more than one person except in the circumstances specified in subsections (1A) and (1B).
(1A)   An adoption order may be made on the application of a married couple where both the husband and the wife have attained the age of 21 years.
(1B)   An adoption order may be made on the application of a married couple where—
(a)   the husband or the wife—
(i)   is the father or mother of the child; and
(ii)   has attained the age of 18 years; and
(b)   his or her spouse has attained the age of 21 years."

34.   In section 16(1)(a) (parental agreement) for the words from "in England" to "revoked", in the second place where it occurs, there shall be substituted—
"(i)   in Scotland under section 18;
(ii)   in England and Wales under section 18 of the Adoption Act 1976; or
(iii)   in Northern Ireland under Article 17(1) or 18(1) of the Adoption (Northern Ireland) Order 1987,
and not revoked".

35.   In section 18(5) (effect of order freeing child for adoption) for the words "and (3)" there shall be substituted "to (4)".

36.   In section 20(3)(c) (revocation of section 18 order) the words "section 12(3)(b) of the Adoption Act 1976 or of" shall cease to have effect.

37.   For section 21 (transfer of parental rights and duties between adoption agencies) there shall be substituted—

"21. Variation of section 18 order so as to substitute one adoption agency for another.

(1)   On an application to which this section applies an authorised court may vary an order under section 18 so as to transfer the parental rights and duties relating to the child from the adoption agency in which they are vested under the order ('the existing agency') to another adoption agency ('the substitute agency').

(2)   This section applies to any application made jointly by the existing agency and the would-be substitute agency.

(3)   Where an order under section 18 is varied under this section, section 19 shall apply as if the parental rights and duties relating to the child had vested in the substitute agency on the making of the order."

38.   In section 22(4) (notification to local authority of adoption application) for the word "receives" there shall be substituted "receive".

39.   In section 29 (return of child taken away in breach of section 27 or 28) after the world "1976" in each place where it occurs there shall be inserted "or Article 28 or 29 of the Adoption (Northern Ireland) Order 1987".

40.   In section 32 (meaning of "protected child"), at the end of subsection (2) there shall be added "or Article 33 of the Adoption (Northern Ireland) Order 1987".

41.   In section 45 (adopted children register)—

(a)   for the words from "or an approved" in subsection (5) to the end of subsection (6) there shall be substituted—

"Board or adoption society falling within subsection (6) which is providing counselling for that adopted person.

(6)   Where the Registrar General for Scotland furnishes an adopted person with information under subsection (5), he shall advise that person that counselling services are available—

(a)   if the person is in Scotland—

(i)   from the local authority in whose area he is living;

(ii)   where the adoption order relating to him was made in Scotland, from the local authority in whose area the court which made the order sat; or

(iii)   from any other local authority in Scotland;

(b)   if the person is in England and Wales—

(i)   from the local authority in whose area he is living;

(ii)   where the adoption order relating to him was made in England and Wales, from the local authority in whose area the court which made the order sat; or

(iii)   from any other local authority in England and Wales;

(c)   if the person is in Northern Ireland—

(i)   from the Board in whose area he is living;

(ii)   where the adoption order relating to him was made in Northern Ireland, from the Board in whose area the court which made the order sat; or

(iii)   from any other Board;

(d)   if the person is in the United Kingdom and his adoption was arranged by an adoption society—

    (i)   approved under section 3;

    (ii)   approved under section 3 of the Adoption Act 1976; or

    (iii)   registered under Article 4 of the Adoption (Northern Ireland) Order 1987,

from that society.

    (6A)   Where an adopted person who is in Scotland—

    (a)   is furnished with information under subsection (5); or

    (b)   applies for information under—

        (i)   section 51(1) of the Adoption Act 1976; or

        (ii)   Article 54 of the Adoption (Northern Ireland) Order 1987,

any body mentioned in subsection (6B) to which the adopted person applies for counselling shall have a duty to provide counselling for him.

    (6B)   The bodies referred to in subsection (6A) are—

    (a)   any local authority falling within subsection (6)(a); and

    (b)   any adoption society falling within subsection (6)(d) so far as it is acting as an adoption society in Scotland.";

    (b)   in subsection (7)—

    (i)   for the word "under" there shall be substituted "from a local authority, Board or adoption society falling within";

    (ii)   for the words "or adoption society which is providing that counselling" there shall be substituted ", Board or adoption society"; and

    (iii)   after the word "authority" where it second occurs there shall be inserted ", Board"; and

    (c)   after subsection (9) there shall be inserted the following subsection—

    "(10)   In this section—

"Board" means a Health and Social Services Board established under article 16 of the Health and Personal Social Services (Northern Ireland) Order 1972; and

"local authority", in relation to England and Wales, means the council of a county (other than a metropolitan county), a metropolitan district, a London borough or the Common Council of the City of London."

42.   In section 49 (adoption of children abroad)—

    (a)   in subsection (1) after the word "Scotland" there shall be inserted "or Northern Ireland"; and

    (b)   in subsection (3) for the words "word 'England'"there shall be substituted "words '(England), or '(Northern Ireland)'".

43.   In section 50(1) (restriction on removal of children for adoption outside Great Britain) after the word "1976" there shall be inserted "or Article 57 of the Adoption (Northern Ireland) Order 1987".

44.   In section 53(1) (effect of determination and orders made in England and Wales and overseas in adoption proceedings)—

    (a)   in subsection (1) for the words "Great Britain" there shall be substituted "the United Kingdom"; and

    (b)   for subsection (2) there shall be substituted—

    "(2)   Subsections (2) to (4) of section 12 shall apply in relation to an order freeing a child for adoption (other than an order under section 18) as if it were an adoption order; and on the revocation in England and Wales or Northern Ireland of an order freeing a child for adoption subsection (3) of section 20 shall apply as if the order had been revoked under that section."

45.   In section 54(b) (evidence of adoption in Northern Ireland) for the words from "section 23(4)" to "in force" there shall be substituted "Article 63(1) of the Adoption (Northern Ireland) Order 1987".

46.   In section 65(1) (interpretation)—
(a)   in the definition of "adoption agency", at the end there shall be added "and an adoption agency within the meaning of Article 3 of the Adoption (Northern Ireland) Order 1987 (adoption agencies in Northern Ireland)";
(b)   for the definition of "adoption order" there shall be substituted—
"'adoption order'—
(a)   means an order under section 12(1); and
(b)   in sections 12(3) and (4), 18 to 20, 27, 28 and 30 to 32 and in the definition of "British adoption order" in this subsection includes an order under section 12 of the Adoption Act 1976 and Article 12 of the Adoption (Northern Ireland) Order 1987 (adoption orders in England and Wales and Northern Ireland respectively); and
(c)   in sections 27, 28 and 30 to 32 includes an order under section 49, section 55 of the Adoption Act 1976 and Article 57 of the Adoption (Northern Ireland) Order 1987 (orders in relation to children being adopted abroad);";
(c)   for the definition of "British adoption order" there shall be substituted—
"'British adoption order' means—
(a)   an adoption order as defined in this subsection; and
(b)   an order under any provision for the adoption of a child effected under the law of any British territory outside the United Kingdom;";
(d)   in the definition of "order freeing a child for adoption" for the words from "section 27(2)" to the end there shall be substituted "sections 27(2) and 53 includes an order under—
(a)   section 18 of the Adoption Act 1976; and
(b)   Article 17 or 18 of the Adoption (Northern Ireland) Order 1987;".

Section 92.   **SCHEDULE 11**
                               JURISDICTION

                          PART I   GENERAL

Commencement of proceedings

1.—(1)   The Lord Chancellor may by order specify proceedings under this Act or the Adoption Act 1976 which may only be commenced in—
(a)   a specified level of court;
(b)   a court which falls within a specified class of court; or
(c)   a particular court determined in accordance with, or specified in, the order.
(2)   The Lord Chancellor may by order specify circumstances in which

specified proceedings under this Act or the Adoption Act 1976 (which might otherwise be commenced elsewhere) may only be commenced in—

(a)   a specified level of court;

(b)   a court which falls within a specified class of court; or

(c)   a particular court determined in accordance with, or specified in, the order.

(3)   The Lord Chancellor may by order make provision by virtue of which, where specified proceedings with respect to a child under—

(a)   this Act;

(b)   the Adoption Act 1976; or

(c)   the High Court's inherent jurisdiction with respect to children,

have been commenced in or transferred to any court (whether or not by virtue of an order under this Schedule), any other specified family proceedings which may affect, or are otherwise connected with, the child may, in specified circumstances, only be commenced in that court.

(4)   A class of court specified in an order under this Schedule may be described by reference to a description of proceedings and may include different levels of court.

Transfer of proceedings

2.—(1)   The Lord Chancellor may by order provide that in specified circumstances the whole, or any specified part of, specified proceedings to which this paragraph applies shall be transferred to—

(a)   a specified level of court;

(b)   a court which falls within a specified class of court; or

(c)   a particular court determined in accordance with, or specified in, the order.

(2)   Any order under this paragraph may provide for the transfer to be made at any stage, or specified stage, of the proceedings and whether or not the proceedings, or any part of them, have already been transferred.

(3)   The proceedings to which this paragraph applies are—

(a)   any proceedings under this Act;

(b)   any proceedings under the Adoption Act 1976;

(c)   any other proceedings which—

(i)   are family proceedings for the purposes of this Act, other than proceedings under the inherent jurisdiction of the High Court; and

(ii)   may affect, or are otherwise connected with, the child concerned.

(4)   Proceedings to which this paragraph applies by virtue of sub-paragraph (3)(c) may only be transferred in accordance with the provisions of an order made under this paragraph for the purpose of consolidating them with proceedings under—

(a)   this Act;

(b)   the Adoption Act 1976; or

(c)   the High Court's inherent jurisdiction with respect to children.

(5)   An order under this paragraph may make such provision as the Lord Chancellor thinks appropriate for excluding proceedings to which this paragraph applies from the operation of any enactment which would otherwise govern the transfer of those proceedings, or any part of them.

Hearings by single justice

3.—(1) In such circumstances as the Lord Chancellor may by order specify—

(a) the jurisdiction of a magistrates' court to make an emergency protection order;

(b) any specified question with respect to the transfer of specified proceedings to or from a magistrates' court in accordance with the provisions of an order under paragraph 2,

may be exercised by a single justice.

(2) Any provision made under this paragraph shall be without prejudice to any other enactment or rule of law relating to the functions which may be performed by a single justice of the peace.

General

4.—(1) For the purposes of this Schedule—

(a) the commencement of proceedings under this Act includes the making of any application under this Act in the course of proceedings (whether or not those proceedings are proceedings under this Act); and

(b) there are three levels of court, that is to say the High Court, any county court and any magistrates' court.

(2) In this Schedule "specified" means specified by an order made under this Schedule.

(3) Any order under paragraph 1 may make provision as to the effect of commencing proceedings in contravention of any of the provisions of the order.

(4) An order under paragraph 2 may make provision as to the effect of a failure to comply with any of the provisions of the order.

(5) An order under this Schedule may—

(a) make such consequential, incidental or transitional provision as the Lord Chancellor considers expedient, including provision amending any other enactment so far as it concerns the jurisdiction of any court or justice of the peace;

(b) make provision for treating proceedings which are—

(i) in part proceedings of a kind mentioned in paragraph (a) or (b) of paragraph 2(3); and

(ii) in part proceedings of a kind mentioned in paragraph (c) of paragraph 2(3),

as consisting entirely of proceedings of one or other of those kinds, for the purposes of the application of any order made under paragraph 2.

PART II CONSEQUENTIAL AMENDMENTS

The Administration of Justice Act 1964 (c. 42)

5. In section 38 of the Administration of Justice Act 1964 (interpretation), the definition of "domestic court", which is spent, shall be omitted.

The Domestic Proceedings and Magistrates' Courts Act 1978 (c. 22)

6. In the Domestic Proceedings and Magistrates' Courts Act 1978—

(a) for the words "domestic proceedings", wherever they occur in sections

16(5)(c) and 88(1), there shall be substituted "family proceedings";

(b)   for the words "domestic court panel", wherever they occur in section 16(5)(b), there shall be substituted "family panel".

The Justices of the Peace Act 1979 (c. 55)

7.   In the Justices of the Peace Act 1979—

(a)   for the words "domestic proceedings", wherever they occur in section 16(5), there shall be substituted "family proceedings";

(b)   for the words "domestic court", wherever they occur in section 17(3), there shall be substituted "family proceedings court";

(c)   for the words "domestic courts", wherever they occur in sections 38(2) and 58(1) and (5), there shall be substituted "family proceedings courts".

The Magistrates' Courts Act 1980 (c. 43)

8.   In the Magistrates' Courts Act 1980—

(a)   in section 65(1) (meaning of family proceedings), the following paragraph shall be inserted after paragraph (m)—

"(n)   the Children Act 1989";

(b)   in section 65(2)(a) for the words "and (m)" there shall be substituted "(m) and (n)";

(c)   for the words "domestic proceedings", wherever they occur in sections 65(1), (2) and (3), 66(1) and (2), 67(1), (2) and (7), 69(1), (2), (3) and (4), 70(2) and (3), 71(1) and (2), 72(1), 73, 74(1), 121(8) and 150(1), there shall be substituted "family proceedings";

(d)   for the words "domestic court panel", wherever they occur in sections 66(2), 67(2), (4), (5), (7) and (8) and 68(1), (2) and (3), there shall be substituted "family panel";

(e)   for the words "domestic court panels", wherever they occur in section 67(3), (4), (5) and (6), there shall be substituted "family panels";

(f)   for the words "domestic courts", wherever they occur in sections 67(1) and (3) and 68(1), there shall be substituted "family proceedings courts";

(g)   for the words "domestic court", wherever they occur in section 67(2) and (5), there shall be substituted "family proceedings court".

The Supreme Court Act 1981 (c. 54)

9.   In paragraph 3 of Schedule 1 to the Supreme Court Act 1981 (distribution of business to the Family Division of the High Court), the following sub-paragraph shall be added at the end—

"(e)   proceedings under the Children Act 1989".

The Matrimonial and Family Proceedings Act 1984 (c. 42)

10.   In section 44 of the Matrimonial and Family Proceedings Act 1984 (domestic proceedings in magistrates' courts to include applications to alter maintenance agreements) for the words "domestic proceedings", wherever they occur, there shall be substituted "family proceedings".

The Insolvency Act 1986 (c. 45)

11.—(1)   In section 281(5)(b) of the Insolvency Act 1986 (discharge not to release bankrupt from bankruptcy debt arising under any order made in family proceedings or in domestic proceedings), the words "or in domestic proceedings" shall be omitted.

(2) In section 281(8) of that Act (interpretation), for the definitions of "domestic proceedings" and "family proceedings" there shall be substituted—
  "family proceedings" means—
    (a) family proceedings within the meaning of the Magistrates' Courts Act 1980 and any proceedings which would be such proceedings but for section 65(1)(ii) of that Act (proceedings for variation of order for periodical payments); and
    (b) family proceedings within the meaning of Part V of the Matrimonial and Family Proceedings Act 1984."

Section 108(4).   **SCHEDULE 12**
                             MINOR AMENDMENTS

The Custody of Children Act 1891 (c.3)

1.   The Custody of Children Act 1891 (which contains miscellaneous obsolete provisions with respect to the custody of children) shall cease to have effect.

The Children and Young Persons Act 1933 (c.12)

2.   In this section 1(2)(a) of the Children and Young Persons Act 1933 (cruelty to persons under sixteen), after the words "young person" there shall be inserted ", or the legal guardian of a child or young person,".

3.   Section 40 of that Act shall cease to have effect.

The Education Act 1944 (c. 31)

4.   In section 40(1) of the Education Act 1944 (enforcement of school attendance), the words from "or to imprisonment" to the end shall cease to have effect.

The Marriage Act 1949 (c. 76)

5.—(1) In section 3 of the Marriage Act 1949 (consent required to the marriage of a child by common licence or superintendent registrar's certificate), in subsection (1) for the words "the Second Schedule to this Act" there shall be substituted "subsection (1A) of this section".

(2) After that subsection there shall be inserted—
  "(1A) The consents are—
    (a) subject to paragraphs (b) to (d) of this subsection, the consent of—
       (i) each parent (if any) of the child who has parental responsibility for him; and
       (ii) each guardian (if any) of the child;
    (b) where a residence order is in force with respect to the child, the consent of the person or persons with whom he lives, or is to live, as a result of the order (in substitution for the consents mentioned in paragraph (a) of this subsection);

(c)   where a care order is in force with respect to the child, the consent of the local authority designated in the order (in addition to the consents mentioned in paragraph (a) of this subsection);

(d)   where neither paragraph (b) nor (c) of this subsection applies but a residence order was in force with respect to the child immediately before he reached the age of sixteen, the consent of the person or persons with whom he lived, or was to live, as a result of the order (in substitution for the consents mentioned in paragraph (a) of this subsection).

(1B)   In this section 'guardian of a child', 'parental responsibility', 'residence order' and 'care order' have the same meaning as in the Children Act 1989."

The Births and Deaths Registration Act 1953 (c. 20)

6.—(1)   Sections 10 and 10A of the Births and Deaths Registration Act 1953 (registration of father, and re-registration, where parents not married) shall be amended as follows.

(2)   In sections 10(1) and 10A(1) for paragraph (d) there shall be substituted—

"(d)   at the request of the mother or that person on production of—

(i)   a copy of a parental responsibility agreement made between them in relation to the child; and

(ii)   a declaration in the prescribed form by the person making the request stating that the agreement was made in compliance with section 4 of the Children Act 1989 and has not been brought to an end by an order of a court; or

(e)   at the request of the mother or that person on production of—

(i)   a certified copy of an order under section 4 of the Children Act 1989 giving that person parental responsibility for the child; and

(ii)   a declaration in the prescribed form by the person making the request stating that the order has not been brought to an end by an order of a court; or

(f)   at the request of the mother or that person on production of—

(i)   a certified copy of an order under paragraph 1 of Schedule 1 to the Children Act 1989 which requires that person to make any financial provision for the child and which is not an order falling within paragraph 4(3) of that Schedule; and

(ii)   a declaration in the prescribed form by the person making the request stating that the order has not been discharged by an order of a court; or

(g)   at the request of the mother or that person on production of—

(i)   a certified copy of any of the orders which are mentioned in subsection (1A) of this section which has been made in relation to the child; and

(ii)   a declaration in the prescribed form by the person making the request stating that the order has not been brought to an end or discharged by an order of a court."

(3)   After sections 10(1) and 10A(1) there shall be inserted—

"(1A)   The orders are—

      (a)   an order under section 4 of the Family Law Reform Act 1987 that that person shall have all the parental rights and duties with respect to the child;

      (b)   an order that that person shall have custody or care and control or legal custody of the child made under section 9 of the Guardianship of Minors Act 1971 at a time when such an order could only be made in favour of a parent;

      (c)   an order under section 9 or 11B of that Act which requires that person to make any financial provision in relation to the child;

      (d)   an order under section 4 of the Affiliation Proceedings Act 1957 naming that person as putative father of the child."

(4)   In section 10(2) for the words "or (d)" there shall be substituted "to (g)".

(5)   In section 10(3) for the words from "'relevant order'" to the end there shall be substituted "'parental responsibility agreement' has the same meaning as in the Children Act 1989".

(6)   In section 10A(2) in paragraphs (b) and (c) for the words "paragraph (d)" in both places where they occur there shall be substituted "any of paragraphs (d) to (g)".

The Army Act 1955 (c. 18)

7.   In section 151 of the Army Act 1955 (deductions from pay for maintenance of wife or child), in subsection (1A)(a) for the words "in the care of a local authority in England or Wales" there shall be substituted "being looked after by a local authority in England or Wales (within the meaning of the Children Act 1989)".

8.—(1)   Schedule 5A to that Act (powers of court on trial of civilian) shall be amended as follows.

(2)   For paragraphs 7(3) and (4) there shall be substituted—

   "(3)   While an authorisation under a reception order is in force the order shall (subject to sub-paragraph (4) below) be deemed to be a care order for the purposes of the Children Act 1989, and the authorised authority shall be deemed to be the authority designated in that deemed care order.

   (3A)   In sub-paragraph (3) above "care order" means a care order which is not an interim care order under section 38 of the Children Act 1989.

   (4)   The Children Act 1989 shall apply to a reception order which is deemed to be a care order by virtue of sub-paragraph (3) above as if sections 31(8) (designated local authority), 91 (duration of care order etc.) and 101 (effect of orders as between different jurisdictions) were omitted."

(3)   In sub-paragraph (5)(c) for the words from "attains" to the end there shall be substituted "attains 18 years of age".

(4)   In paragraph 8(1) for the words "Children and Young Persons Act 1969" there shall be substituted "Children Act 1989".

The Air Force Act 1955 (c. 19)

9.   Section 151(1A) of the Air Force Act 1955 (deductions from pay for maintenance of wife or child) shall have effect subject to the amendment that is set out in paragraph 7 in relation to section 151(A) of the Army Act 1955.

10.   Schedule 5A to that Act (powers of court on trial of civilian) shall have effect subject to the amendments that are set out in paragraph 8(2) to (4) in relation to Schedule 5A to the Army Act 1955.

The Sexual Offences Act 1956 (c. 69)

11.   In section 19(3) of the Sexual Offences Act 1956 (abduction of unmarried girl under eighteen from parent or guardian) for the words "the lawful care or charge of" there shall be substituted "parental responsibility for or care of".

12.   In section 20(2) of that Act (abduction of unmarried girl under sixteen from parent or guardian) for the words "the lawful care or charge of" there shall be substituted "parental responsibility for or care of".

13.   In section 21(3) of that Act (abduction of defective from parent or guardian) for the words "the lawful care or charge of" there shall be substituted "parental responsibility for or care of".

14.   In section 28 of that Act (causing or encouraging prostitution of, intercourse with, or indecent assault on, girl under sixteen) for subsections (3) and (4) there shall be substituted—

"(3)   The persons who are to be treated for the purposes of this section as responsible for a girl are (subject to subsection (4) of this section)—

(a)   her parents;

(b)   any person who is not a parent of hers but who has parental responsibility for her; and

(c)   any person who has care of her.

(4)   An individual falling within subsection (3)(a) or (b) of this section is not to be treated as responsible for a girl if—

(a)   a residence order under the Children Act 1989 is in force with respect to her and he is not named in the order as the person with whom she is to live; or

(b)   a care order under that Act is in force with respect to her."

15.   Section 38 of that Act (power of court to divest person of authority over girl or boy in case of incest) shall cease to have effect.

16.—(1)   In section 43 of that Act (power to search for and recover woman detained for immoral purposes), in subsection (5) for the words "the lawful care or charge of" there shall be substituted "parental responsibility for or care of".

(2)   In subsection (6) of that section, for the words "section forty of the Children and Young Persons Act 1933" there shall be substituted "Part V of the Children Act 1989".

17.   After section 46 of that Act there shall be inserted—

"46A. Meaning of 'parental responsibility'.
In this Act 'parental responsibility' has the same meaning as in the Children Act 1989."

The Naval Discipline Act 1957 (c. 53)

18.   Schedule 4A to the Naval Discipline Act 1957 (powers of court on trial of

civilian) shall have effect subject to the amendments that are set out in paragraph 8(2) to (4) in relation to Schedule 5A to the Army Act 1955.

The Children and Young Persons Act 1963 (c. 37)

19.   Section 3 of the Children and Young Persons Act 1963 (children and young persons beyond control) shall cease to have effect.

The Children and Young Persons Act 1969 (c. 54)

20.   In section 5 of the Children and Young Persons Act 1969 (restrictions on criminal proceedings for offences by young persons), in subsection (2), for the words "section 1 of this Act" there shall be substituted "Part IV of the Children Act 1989".

21.   After section 7(7) of that Act (alteration in treatment of young offenders, etc.) there shall be inserted—
    "(7B)   An order under subsection (7)(c) of this section shall not require a person to enter into a recognisance—
        (a)   for an amount exceeding £1,000; or
        (b)   for a period exceeding—
            (i)   three years; or
            (ii)   where the young person concerned will attain the age of eighteen in a period shorter than three years, that shorter period.
    (7C)   Section 120 of the Magistrates' Courts Act 1980 shall apply to a recognisance entered into in pursuance of an order under subsection (7)(c) of this section as it applies to a recognisance to keep the peace."

22.   In section 12A of that Act (young offenders) for subsections (1) and (2) there shall be substituted—
    "(1)   This subsection applies to any supervision order made under section 7(7) of this Act unless it requires the supervised person to comply with directions given by the supervisor under section 12(2) of this Act."

23.   After that section there shall be inserted—

"12AA. Requirement for young offender to live in local authority accommodation.
    (1)   Where the conditions mentioned in subsection (6) of this section are satisfied, a supervision order may impose a requirement ('a residence requirement') that a child or young person shall live for a specified period in local authority accommodation
    (2)   A residence requirement shall designate the local authority who are to receive the child or young person and that authority shall be the authority in whose area the child or young person resides.
    (3)   The court shall not impose a residence requirement without first consulting the designated authority.
    (4)   A residence requirement may stipulate that the child or young person shall not live with a named person.
    (5)   The maximum period which may be specified in a residence requirement is six months.
    (6)   The conditions are that—

(a)   a supervision order has previously been made in respect of the child or young person;

(b)   that order imposed—

(i)   a requirement under section 12A(3) of this Act; or

(ii)   a residence requirement;

(c)   he is found guilty of an offence which—

(i)   was committed while that order was in force;

(ii)   if it had been committed by a person over the age of twenty-one, would have been punishable with imprisonment; and

(iii)   in the opinion of the court is serious; and

(d)   the court is satisfied that the behaviour which constituted the offence was due, to a significant extent, to the circumstances in which he was living,

except that the condition in paragraph (d) of this subsection does not apply where the condition in paragraph (b)(ii) is satisfied.

(7)   For the purposes of satisfying itself as mentioned in subsection (6)(d) of this section, the court shall obtain a social inquiry report which makes particular reference to the circumstances in which the child or young person was living.

(8)   Subsection (7) of this section does not apply if the court already has before it a social inquiry report which contains sufficient information about the circumstances in which the child or young person was living.

(9)   A court shall not include a residence requirement in respect of a child or young person who is not legally represented at the relevant time in that court unless—

(a)   he has applied for legal aid for the purposes of the proceedings and the application was refused on the ground that it did not appear that his resources were such that he required assistance; or

(b)   he has been informed of his right to apply for legal aid for the purposes of the proceedings and has had the opportunity to do so, but nevertheless refused or failed to apply.

(10)   In subsection (9) of this section—

(a)   'the relevant time' means the time when the court is considering whether or not to impose the requirement; and

(b)   'the proceedings' means—

(i)   the whole proceedings; or

(ii)   the part of the proceedings relating to the imposition of the requirement.

(11)   A supervision order imposing a residence requirement may also impose any of the requirements mentioned in sections 12, 12A, 12B or 12C of this Act.

(12)   In this section 'social inquiry report' has the same meaning as in section 2 of the Criminal Justice Act 1982."

24.—(1)   In section 15 of that Act (variation and discharge of supervision orders), in subsections (1)(a), (2A), (3)(e) and (4) after the word "12A", in each place where it occurs, there shall be inserted "12AA".

(2)   In subsection (4) of that section for the words "(not being a juvenile court)" there shall be substituted "other than a juvenile court".

25.—(1) In section 16 of that Act (provisions supplementary to section 15), in subsection (3) for the words "either direct" to the end there shall be substituted—

"(i)   direct that he be released forthwith; or

(ii)   remand him."

(2)   In subsection (4) of that section—

(a)   in paragraph (a) for the words "an interim order made by virtue of" there shall be substituted "a remand under";

(b)   in paragraph (b) for the words "makes an interim order in respect of" there shall be substituted "remands", and

(c)   for the words "make an interim order in respect of" there shall be substituted "remand".

(3)   In subsections (5)(b) and (c) and (6)(a) after the word "12A", in each place where it occurs, there shall be inserted "12AA".

26.   For section 23 of that Act (remand to care of local authorities etc.) there shall be substituted—

"23. Remand to local authority accommodation, committal of young persons of unruly character, etc.

(1)   Where a court—

(a)   remands or commits for trial a child charged with homicide or remands a child convicted of homicide; or

(b)   remands a young person charged with or convicted of one or more offences or commits him for trial or sentence,

and he is not released on bail, then, unless he is a young person who is certified by the court to be of unruly character, the court shall remand him to local authority accommodation.

(2)   A court remanding a person to local authority accommodation shall designate the authority who are to receive him and that authority shall be the authority in whose area it appears to the court that—

(a)   he resides; or

(b)   the offence or one of the offences was committed.

(3)   Where a person is remanded to local authority accommodation, it shall be lawful for any person acting on behalf of the designated authority to detain him.

(4)   The court shall not certify a young person as being of unruly character unless—

(a)   he cannot safely be remanded to local authority accommodation; and

(b)   the conditions prescribed by order made by the Secretary of State under this subsection are satisfied in relation to him.

(5)   Where the court certifies that a young person is of unruly character, it shall commit him—

(a)   to a remand centre, if it has been notified that such a centre is available for the reception from the court of such persons; and

(b)   to a prison, if it has not been so notified.

(6)   Where a young person is remanded to local authority accommodation, a court may, on the application of the designated authority, certify him

to be of unruly character in accordance with subsection (4) of this section (and on so doing he shall cease to be remanded to local authority accommodation and subsection (5) of this section shall apply).

(7) For the purposes of subsection (6) of this section, "a court" means—

(a) the court which remanded the young person; or

(b) any magistrates' court having jurisdiction in the place where that person is for the time being,

and in this section "court" and "magistrates' court" include a justice.

(8) This section has effect subject to—

(a) section 37 of the Magistrates' Courts Act 1980 (committal to the Crown Court with a view to a sentence of detention in a young offender institution); and

(b) section 128(7) of that Act (remands to the custody of a constable for periods of not more than three days),

but section 128(7) shall have effect in relation to a child or young person as if for the reference to three clear days there were substituted a reference to twenty-four hours."

27.—(1) In section 32 of that Act (detention of absentees), for subsection (1A) there shall be substituted the following subsections—

"(1A) If a child or young person is absent, without the consent of the responsible person—

(a) from a place of safety to which he has been taken under section 16(3) of this Act; or

(b) from local authority accommodation—

(i) in which he is required to live under section 12AA of this Act; or

(ii) to which he has been remanded under section 23(1) of this Act,

he may be arrested by a constable anywhere in the United Kingdom or Channel Islands without a warrant.

(1B) A person so arrested shall be conducted to—

(a) the place of safety;

(b) the local authority accommodation; or

(c) such other place as the responsible person may direct,

at the responsible person's expense.

(1C) In this section 'the responsible person' means the person who made the arrangements under section 16(3) of this Act or, as the case may be, the authority designated under section 12AA or 23 of this Act."

(2) In subsection (2B) of that section for the words "person referred to in subsection (1A)(a) or (b) (as the case may be) of this section" there shall be substituted "responsible person".

28. In section 34(1) of that Act (transitional modifications of Part I for persons of specified ages)—

(a) in paragraph (a), for the words "13(2) or 28(4) or (5)" there shall be substituted "or 13(2)"; and

(b) in paragraph (e), for the words "section 23(2) or (3)" there shall be substituted "section 23(4) to (6)".

29. In section 70(1) of that Act (interpretation)—

(a) after the definition of "local authority" there shall be inserted—

"'local authority accommodation' means accommodation provided by or on behalf of a local authority (within the meaning of the Children Act 1989)"; and

(b)   in the definition of "reside" for "12(4) and (5)" there shall be substituted "12B(1) and (2)".

30.   In section 73 of that Act (extent, etc.)—

(a)   in subsection (4)(a) for "32(1), (3) and (4)" there shall be substituted "32(1) to (1C) and (2A) to (4)"; and

(b)   in subsection (6) for "32(1), (1A)" there shall be substituted "32(1) to (1C)".

The Matrimonial Causes Act 1973 (c. 18)

31.   For section 41 of the Matrimonial Causes Act 1973 (restrictions on decrees for dissolution, annulment or separation affecting children) there shall be substituted—

"41. Restrictions on decrees for dissolution, annulment or separation affecting children

(1)   In any proceedings for a decree of divorce or nullity of marriage, or a decree of judicial separation, the court shall consider—

(a)   whether there are any children of the family to whom this section applies; and

(b)   where there are any such children, whether (in the light of the arrangements which have been, or are proposed to be, made for their upbringing and welfare) it should exercise any of its powers under the Children Act 1989 with respect to any of them.

(2)   Where, in any case to which this section applies, it appears to the court that—

(a)   the circumstances of the case require it, or are likely to require it, to exercise any of its powers under the Act of 1989 with respect to any such child;

(b)   it is not in a position to exercise that power or (as the case may be) those powers without giving further consideration to the case; and

(c)   there are exceptional circumstances which make it desirable in the interests of the child that the court should give a direction under this section, it may direct that the decree of divorce or nullity is not to be made absolute, or that the decree of judicial separation is not to be granted, until the court orders otherwise.

(3)   This section applies to—

(a)   any child of the family who has not reached the age of sixteen at the date when the court considers the case in accordance with the requirements of this section; and

(b)   any child of the family who has reached that age at that date and in relation to whom the court directs that this section shall apply."

32.   In section 42 of that Act, subsection (3) (declaration by court that party to marriage unfit to have custody of children of marriage) shall cease to have effect.

33.   In section 52(1) of that Act (interpretation), in the definition of "child of the family", for the words "has been boarded-out with those parties" there shall be substituted "is placed with those parties as foster parents".

The National Health Service Act 1977 (c. 49)

34.   In Schedule 8 to the National Health Service Act 1977 (functions of local social services authorities), the following sub-paragraph shall be added at the end of paragraph 2—

"(4A)   This paragraph does not apply in relation to persons under the age of 18."

The Child Care Act 1980 (c. 5)

35.   Until the repeal of the Child Care Act 1980 by this Act takes effect, the definition of "parent" in section 87 of that Act shall have effect as if it applied only in relation to Part I and sections 13, 24, 64 and 65 of that Act (provisions excluded by section 2(1)(f) of the Family Law Reform Act 1987 from the application of the general rule in that Act governing the meaning of references to relationships between persons).

The Education Act 1981 (c. 60)

36.   The following section shall be inserted in the Education Act 1981, after section 3—

"3A. Provision outside England and Wales for certain children.

(1)   A local authority may make such arrangements as they think fit to enable any child in respect of whom they maintain a statement under section 7 to attend an establishment outside England and Wales which specialises in providing for children with special needs.

(2)   In subsection (1) above "children with special needs" means children who have particular needs which would be special educational needs if those children were in England and Wales.

(3)   Where an authority make arrangements under this section with respect to a child, those arrangements may, in particular, include contributing to or paying—

(a)   fees charged by the establishment;

(b)   expenses reasonably incurred in maintaining him while he is the establishment or travelling to or from it;

(c)   those travelling expenses;

(d)   expenses reasonably incurred by any person accompanying him while he is travelling or staying at the establishment.

(4)   This section is not to be taken as in any way limiting any other powers of a local education authority."

The Child Abduction Act 1984 (c. 37)

37.   Section 1 of the Child Abduction Act 1984 (offence of abduction by parent, etc.) shall be amended as follows.

(2)   For subsections (2) to (4) there shall be substituted—

"(2)   A person is connected with a child for the purposes of this section if—

(a)   he is a parent of the child; or

(b)   in the case of a child whose parents were not married to each other at the time of his birth, there are reasonable grounds for believing that he is the father of the child; or

(c)   he is a guardian of the child; or

(d)   he is a person in whose favour a residence order is in force with respect to the child; or

(e)   he has custody of the child.

(3)   In this section 'the appropriate consent', in relation to a child, means—

(a)   the consent of each of the following—

(i)   the child's mother;

(ii)   the child's father, if he has parental responsibility for him;

(iii)   any guardian of the child;

(iv)   any person in whose favour a residence order is in force with respect to the child;

(v)   any person who has custody of the child; or

(b)   the leave of the court granted under or by virtue of any provision of Part II of the Children Act 1989; or

(c)   if any person has custody of the child, the leave of the court which awarded custody to him.

(4)   A person does not commit an offence under this section by taking or sending a child out of the United Kingdom without obtaining the appropriate consent if—

(a)   he is a person in whose favour there is a residence order in force with respect to the child, and

(b)   he takes or sends him out of the United Kingdom for a period of less than one month.

(4A)   Subsection (4) above does not apply if the person taking or sending the child out of the United Kingdom does so in breach of an order under Part II of the Children Act 1989."

(3)   In subsection (5) for the words from "but" to the end there shall be substituted—

"(5A)   Subsection (5)(c) above does not apply if—

(a)   the person who refused to consent is a person—

(i)   in whose favour there is a residence order in force with respect to the child; or

(ii)   who has custody of the child; or

(b)   the person taking or sending the child out of the United Kingdom is, by so acting, in breach of an order made by a court in the United Kingdom."

(4)   For subsection (7) there shall be substituted—

"(7)   For the purposes of this section—

(a)   'guardian of a child', 'residence order' and 'parental responsibility' have the same meaning as in the Children Act 1989; and

(b)   a person shall be treated as having custody of a child if there is in force an order of a court in the United Kingdom awarding him (whether solely or jointly with another person) custody, legal custody or care and control of the child."

(5) In subsection (8) for the words from "or voluntary organisation" to "custodianship proceedings or" there shall be substituted "detained in a place of safety, remanded to a local authority accommodation or the subject of".

38.—(1) In section 2 of that Act (offence of abduction of child by other persons), in subsection (1) for the words from "Subject" to "above" there shall be substituted "Subject to subsection (3) below, a person, other than one mentioned in subsection (2) below."

(2) For subsection (2) of that section there shall be substituted—
"(2) The persons are—
(a) where the father and mother of the child in question were married to each other at the time of his birth, the child's father and mother;
(b) where the father and mother of the child in question were not married to each other at the time of his birth, the child's mother; and
(c) any other person mentioned in section 1(2)(c) to (e) above.

(3) In proceedings against any person for an offence under this section, it shall be a defence for that person to prove—
(a) where the father and mother of the child in question were not married to each other at the time of his birth—
(i) that he is the child's father; or
(ii) that, at the time of the alleged offence, he believed, on reasonable grounds, that he was the child's father; or
(b) that, at the time of the alleged offence, he believed that the child had attained the age of sixteen."

39. At the end of section 3 of that Act (construction of references to taking, sending and detaining) there shall be added "and
(d) references to a child's parents and to a child whose parents were (or were not) married to each other at the time of his birth shall be construed in accordance with section 1 of the Family Law Reform Act 1987 (which extends their meaning)."

40.—(1) The Schedule to that Act (modifications of section 1 for children in certain cases) shall be amended as follows.

(2) In paragraph 1(1) for the words "or voluntary organisation" there shall be substituted "within the meaning of the Children Act 1989".

(3) For paragraph 2(1) there shall be substituted—
"(1) This paragraph applies in the case of a child who is—
(a) detained in a place of safety under section 16(3) of the Children and Young Persons Act 1969; or
(b) remanded to local authority accommodation under section 23 of that Act."

(4) In paragraph 3(1)—
(a) in paragraph (a) for the words "section 14 of the Children Act 1975" there shall be substituted "section 18 of the Adoption Act 1976"; and
(b) in paragraph (d) for the words "section 25 of the Children Act 1975 or section 53 of the Adoption Act 1958" there shall be substituted "section 55 of the Adoption Act 1976".

(5)   In paragraph 3(2)(a)—

(a)   in sub-paragraph (i), for the words from "order or," to "Children Act 1975" there shall be substituted "section 18 order or, if the section 18 order has been varied under section 21 of that Act so as to give parental responsibility to another agency", and

(b)   in sub-paragraph (ii), for the words "(c) or (e)" there shall be substituted "or (c)".

(6)   At the end of paragraph 3 there shall be added—

"(3)   Sub-paragraph (2) above shall be construed as if the references to the court included, in any case where the court is a magistrates' court, a reference to any magistrates' court acting for the same area as that court".

(7)   For paragraph 5 there shall be substituted—

"5.   In this Schedule—

(a)   'adoption agency' and 'adoption order' have the same meaning as in the Adoption Act 1976; and

(b)   'area', in relation to a magistrates' court, means the petty sessions area (within the meaning of the Justices of the Peace Act 1979) for which the court is appointed."

The Foster Children (Scotland) Act 1984 (c. 56)

41.   In section 1 of the Foster Children (Scotland) Act 1984 (definition of foster child)—

(a)   for the words "he is— (a)" there shall be substituted "(a) he is"; and

(b)   the words "for a period of more than 6 days" and the words from "The period" to the end shall cease to have effect.

42.   In section 2(2) of that Act (exceptions to section 1), for paragraph (f) there shall be substituted—

"(f)   if he has been in that person's care for a period of less than 28 days and that person does not intend to undertake his care for any longer period."

43.   In section 7(1) of that Act (persons disqualified from keeping foster children)—

(a)   the word "or" at the end of paragraph (e) shall be omitted; and

(b)   after paragraph (f) there shall be inserted "or

(g)   he is disqualified from fostering a child privately (within the meaning of the Children Act 1989) by regulations made under section 68 of that Act,".

The Disabled Persons (Services, Consultation and Representation) Act 1986 (c. 33)

44.   In section 2(5) of the Disabled Persons (Services, Consultation and Representation) Act 1986 (circumstances in which authorised representative has right to visit etc. disabled person), after paragraph (d) there shall be inserted—

"(dd)   in accommodation provided by any educational establishment."

The Legal Aid Act 1988 (c. 34)

45.   In paragraph 2 of Part I of Schedule 2 to the Legal Aid Act 1988 (proceedings in magistrates' courts to which the civil legal aid provisions of Part IV of the Act apply), the following sub-paragraph shall be added at the end—
"(g)   proceedings under the Children Act 1989."

Section 108(5).   **SCHEDULE 13**
                               CONSEQUENTIAL AMENDMENTS

The Wills Act 1837 (c. 26)

1.   In section 1 of the Wills Act 1837 (interpretation), in the definition of "will", for the words "and also to a disposition by will and testament or devise of the custody and tuition of any child" there shall be substituted "and also to an appointment by will of a guardian of a child".

The Children and Young Persons Act 1933 (c. 12)

2.   In section 1(1) of the Children and Young Persons Act 1933 (cruelty to persons under sixteen) for the words "has the custody, charge or care of" there shall be substituted "has responsibility for".

3.   In the following sections of that Act—
   (a)   3(1) (allowing persons under sixteen to be in brothels);
   (b)   4(1) and (2) (causing or allowing persons under sixteen to be used for begging);
   (c)   11 (exposing children under twelve to risk of burning); and
   (d)   25(1) (restrictions on persons under eighteen going abroad for the purpose of performing for profit),
for the words "the custody, charge or care of" there shall, in each case, be substituted "responsibility for".

4.   In section 10(1A) of that Act (vagrants preventing children from receiving education), for the words from "to bring the child" to the end there shall be substituted "to make an application in respect of the child or young person for an education supervision order under section 36 of the Children Act 1989".

5.   For section 17 of that Act (interpretation of Part I) there shall be substituted the following section—
"17. Interpretation of Part I
   (1)   For the purposes of this Part of this Act, the following shall be presumed to have responsibility for a child or young person—
      (a)   any person who—
         (i)   has parental responsibility for him (within the meaning of the Children Act 1989); or
         (ii)   is otherwise legally liable to maintain him; and
      (b)   any person who has care of him.
   (2)   A person who is presumed to be responsible for a child or young person by virtue of subsection (1)(a) shall not be taken to have ceased to be responsible for him by reason only that he does not have care of him."

6.—(1) In section 34 of that Act (attendance at court of parent of child or young person charged with an offence etc.), in subsection (1) after the word "offence" there shall be inserted "is the subject of an application for a care or supervision order under Part IV of the Children Act 1989".

(2) In subsection (7) of that section after the words "Children and Young Persons Act 1969" there shall be inserted "or Part IV of the Children Act 1989".

(3) After subsection (7) of that section there shall be inserted—

"(7A) If it appears that at the time of his arrest the child or young person is being provided with accommodation by or on behalf of a local authority under section 20 of the Children Act 1989, the local authority shall also be informed as described in subsection (3) above as soon as it is reasonably practicable to do so."

7. In section 107(1) of that Act (interpretation)—

(a) in the definition of "guardian", for the words "charge of or control over" there shall be substituted "care of";

(b) in the definition of "legal guardian" there shall be substituted—

"'legal guardian', in relation to a child or young person, means a guardian of a child as defined in the Children Act 1989".

The Education Act 1944 (c. 31)

8.—(1) Section 40 of the Education Act 1944 (enforcement of school attendance) shall be amended as follows.

(2) For subsection (2) there shall be substituted—

"(2) Proceedings for such offences shall not be instituted except by a local education authority.

(2A) Before instituting such proceedings the local education authority shall consider whether it would be appropriate, instead of or as well as instituting the proceedings, to apply for an education supervision order with respect to the child."

(3) For subsections (3) and (4) there shall be substituted—

"(3) The court—

(a) by which a person is convicted of an offence against section 37 of this Act; or

(b) before which a person is charged with an offence under section 39 of this Act,

may direct the local education authority instituting the proceedings to apply for an education supervision order with respect to the child unless the authority, having consulted the appropriate local authority, decide that the child's welfare will be satisfactorily safeguarded even though no education supervision order is made.

(3A) Where, following such a direction, a local education authority decide not to apply for an education supervision order they shall inform the court of the reasons for their decision.

(3B) Unless the court has directed otherwise, the information required under subsection (3A) shall be given to the court before the end of the period of eight weeks beginning with the date on which the direction was given.

(4) Where—

(a) a local education authority apply for an education supervision order with respect to a child who is the subject of a school attendance order; and

(b)   the court decides that section 36(3) of the Children Act 1989 prevents it from making the order; the court may direct that the school attendance order shall cease to be in force."

(4)   After subsection (4) there shall be inserted—

"(5)   In this section—

'appropriate local authority' has the same meaning as in section 36(9) of the Children Act 1989; and

'education supervision order' means an education supervision order under that Act."

9.   In section 71 of that Act (complaints with respect to independent schools), the following paragraph shall be added after paragraph (d), in subsection (1)—

"(e)   there has been a failure, in relation to a child provided with accommodation by the school, to comply with the duty imposed by section 87 of the Children Act 1989 (welfare of children accommodated in independent schools);".

10.   After section 114(1C) of that Act (interpretation) there shall be inserted the following subsections—

"(1D)   In this Act, unless the context otherwise requires, 'parent', in relation to a child or young person, includes any person—

(a)   who is not a parent of his but who has parental responsibility for him, or

(b)   who has care of him,

except for the purposes of the enactments mentioned in subsection (1E) of this section, where it only includes such a person if he is an individual.

(1E)   The enactments are—

(a)   sections 5(4), 15(2) and (6), 31 and 65(1) of, and paragraph 7(6) of Schedule 2 to, the Education (No. 2) Act 1986; and

(b)   sections 53(8), 54(2), 58(5)(k), 60 and 61 of the Education Reform Act 1988.

(1F)   For the purposes of subsection (1D) of this section—

(a)   'parental responsibility' has the same meaning as in the Children Act 1989; and

(b)   in determining whether an individual has care of a child or young person any absence of the child or young person at a hospital or boarding school and any other temporary absence shall be disregarded."

The National Assistance Act 1948 (c. 29)

11.—(1)   In section 21(1)(a) of the National Assistance Act 1948 (persons for whom local authority is to provide residential accommodation) after the word "persons" there shall be inserted "aged eighteen or over".

(2)   In section 29(1) of that Act (welfare arrangements for blind, deaf, dumb and crippled persons) after the words "that is to say persons" and after the words "and other persons" there shall, in each case, be inserted "aged eighteen or over".

The Reserve and Auxiliary Forces (Protection of Civil Interests) Act 1951
(c. 65)

12.   For section 2(1)(d) of the Reserve and Auxiliary Forces (Protection of Civil Interests) Act 1951 (cases in which leave of the appropriate court is required before enforcing certain orders for the payment of money), there shall be substituted—

> "(d)   an order for alimony, maintenance or other payment made under sections 21 to 33 of the Matrimonial Causes Act 1973 or made, or having effect as if made, under Schedule 1 to the Children Act 1989."

The Mines and Quarries Act 1954 (c. 70)

13.   In section 182(1) of the Mines and Quarries Act 1954 (interpretation), in the definition of "parent", for the words from "or guardian" to first "young person" there shall be substituted "of a young person or any person who is not a parent of his but who has parental responsibility for him (within the meaning of the Children Act 1989)".

The Administration of Justice Act 1960 (c. 65)

14.   In section 12 of the Administration of Justice Act 1960 (publication of information relating to proceedings in private), in subsection (1) for paragraph (a) there shall be substituted—

> "(a)   where the proceedings—
> (i)   relate to the exercise of the inherent jurisdiction of the High Court with respect to minors;
> (ii)   are brought under the Children Act 1989; or
> (iii)   otherwise relate wholly or mainly to the maintenance or upbringing of a minor;".

The Factories Act 1961 (c. 34)

15.   In section 176(1) of the Factories Act 1961 (interpretation), in the definition of "parent", for the words from "or guardian" to first "young person" there shall be substituted "of a child or young person or any person who is not a parent of his but who has parental responsibility for him (within the meaning of the Children Act 1989)".

The Criminal Justice Act 1967 (c. 80)

16.   In section 67(1A)(c) of the Criminal Justice Act 1967 (computation of sentences of imprisonment passed in England and Wales) for the words "in the care of a local authority" there shall be substituted "remanded to local authority accommodation."

The Health Services and Public Health Act 1968 (c. 46)

17.—(1)   In section 64(3)(a) of the Health Services and Public Health Act 1968 (meaning of "relevant enactments" in relation to power of Minister of Health or Secretary of State to provide financial assistance), for sub-paragraph (xix) inserted by paragraph 19 of Schedule 5 to the Child Care Act 1980 there shall be substituted—

"(xx) the Children Act 1989."

(2) In section 65(3)(b) of that Act (meaning of "relevant enactments" in relation to power of local authority to provide financial and other assistance), for sub-paragraph (xx) inserted by paragraph 20 of Schedule 5 to the Child Care Act 1980 there shall be substituted—

"(xxi) the Children Act 1989."

The Social Work (Scotland) Act 1968 (c. 49)

18. In section 2(2) of the Social Work (Scotland) Act 1968 (matters referred to social work committee) after paragraph (j) there shall be inserted—

"(k) section 19 and Part X of the Children Act 1989,".

19. In section 5(2)(c) of that Act (power of Secretary of State to make regulations) for the words "and (j)" there shall be substituted "to (k)".

20. In section 21(3) of that Act (mode of provision of accommodation and maintenance) for the words "section 21 of the Child Care Act 1980" there shall be substituted "section 23 of the Children Act 1989".

21. In section 74(6) of that Act (parent of child in residential establishment moving to England or Wales) for the words from "Children and Young Persons Act 1969" to the end there shall be substituted "Children Act 1989, but as if section 31(8) were omitted".

22. In section 75(2) of that Act (parent of child subject to care order etc. moving to Scotland), for the words "Children and Young Persons Act 1969" there shall be substituted "Children Act 1989".

23. In section 86(3) of that Act (meaning of ordinary residence for purpose of adjustments between authority providing accommodation and authority of area of residence), the words "the Child Care Act 1980 or" shall be omitted and after the words "education authority" there shall be inserted "or placed with local authority foster parents under the Children Act 1989".

The Civil Evidence Act 1968 (c. 64)

24. In section 12(5)(b) of the Civil Evidence Act 1968 (findings of paternity etc. as evidence in civil proceedings — meaning of "relevant proceedings") for sub-paragraph (iv) there shall be substituted—

"(iv) paragraph 23 of Schedule 2 to the Children Act 1989."

The Administration of Justice Act 1970 (c. 31)

25.—(1) In Schedule 8 to the Administration of Justice Act 1970 (maintenance orders for purposes of Maintenance Orders Act 1958 and the 1970 Act), in paragraph 6 for the words "section 47 or 51 of the Child Care Act 1980" there shall be substituted "paragraph 23 of Schedule 2 to the Children Act 1989".

The Local Authority Social Services Act 1970 (c. 42)

26.—(1) In Schedule 1 to the Local Authority Social Services Act 1970 (enactments conferring functions assigned to social service committee)—

(a) in the entry relating to the Mental Health Act 1959, for the words "sections 8 and 9" there shall be substituted "section 8"; and

(b)   in the entry relating to the Children and Young Persons Act 1969, for the words "sections 1, 2 and 9" there shall be substituted "section 9".

(2)   At the end of that Schedule there shall be added—

"Children Act 1989.	Welfare reports.
The whole Act, in so far as it confers functions on a local authority within the meaning of that Act.	Consent to application for residence order in respect of child in care.
	Family assistance orders.
	Functions under Part III of the Act (local authority support for children and families).
	Care and supervision.
	Protection of children.
	Functions in relation to community homes, voluntary homes and voluntary organisations, registered children's homes, private arrangements for fostering children, child minding and day care for young children.
	Inspection of children's homes on behalf of the Secretary of State.
	Research and returns of information.
	Functions in relation to children accommodated by health authorities and local education authorities or in residential care, nursing or mental nursing homes or in independent schools."

The Chronically Sick and Disabled Persons Act 1970 (c. 44)

27.   After section 28 of the Chronically Sick and Disabled Persons Act 1970 there shall be inserted—

"**28A. "Application of Act to authorities having functions under the Children Act 1989.**

This Act applies with respect to disabled children in relation to whom a local authority have functions under Part III of the Children Act 1989 as it applies in relation to persons to whom section 29 of the National Assistance Act 1948 applies."

The Courts Act 1971 (c. 23)

28.   In Part I of Schedule 9 to the Courts Act 1971 (substitution of references to Crown Court), in the entry relating to the Children and Young Persons Act 1969, for the words "Sections 2(12), 3(8), 16(8), 21(4)(5)" there shall be substituted "Section 16(8).".

The Attachment of Earnings Act 1971 (c. 32)

29.   In Schedule 1 to the Attachment of Earnings Act 1971 (maintenance

orders to which that Act applies), in paragraph 7, for the words "section 47 or 51 of the Child Care Act 1980" there shall be substituted "paragraph 23 of Schedule 2 to the Children Act 1989".

The Tribunals and Inquiries Act 1971 (c. 62)

30.   In Schedule 1 to the Tribunals and Inquiries Act 1971 (tribunals under direct supervision of the Council on Tribunals), for paragraph 4 there shall be substituted—

"Registration of voluntary homes and children's homes under the Children Act 1989.	4. Registered Homes Tribunals constituted under Part III of the Registered Homes Act 1984."

The Local Government Act 1972 (c. 70)

31.—(1)   In section 102(1) of the Local Government Act 1972 (appointment of committees) for the words "section 31 of the Child Care Act 1980" there shall be substituted "section 53 of the Children Act 1989".

(2)   In Schedule 12A to that Act (access to information: exempt information), in Part III (interpretation), in paragraph 1(1)(b) for the words "section 20 of the Children and Young Persons Act 1969" there shall be substituted "section 31 of the Children Act 1989".

The Employment of Children Act 1973 (c. 24)

32.—(1)   In section 2 of the Employment of Children Act 1973 (supervision by education authorities), in subsection (2)(a) for the words "guardian or a person who has actual custody of" there shall be substituted "any person responsible for".

(2)   After that subsection there shall be inserted—

"(2A)   For the purposes of subsection (2)(a) above a person is responsible for a child—

(a)   in England and Wales, if he has parental responsibility for the child or care of him; and

(b)   in Scotland, if he is his guardian or has actual custody of him.".

The Domicile and Matrimonial Proceedings Act 1973 (c. 45)

33.—(1)   In Schedule 1 to the Domicile and Matrimonial Proceedings Act 1973 (proceedings in divorce etc. stayed by reference to proceedings in other jurisdiction), paragraph 11(1) shall be amended as follows—

(a)   at the end of the definition of "lump sum" there shall be added "or an order made in equivalent circumstances under Schedule 1 to the Children Act 1989 and of a kind mentioned in paragraph 1(2)(c) of that Schedule";

(b)   in the definition of "relevant order", at the end of paragraph (b), there shall be added "or an order made in equivalent circumstances under Schedule 1 to the Children Act 1989 and of a kind mentioned in paragraph 1(2)(a) or (b) of that Schedule";

(c)   in paragraph (c) of that definition, after the word "children)" there shall be inserted "or a section 8 order under the Children Act 1989"; and

(d)   in paragraph (d) of that definition for the words "the custody, care or control" there shall be substituted "care".

(2)   In paragraph 11(3) of that Schedule—
(a)   the word "four" shall be omitted; and
(b)   for the words "the custody of a child and the education of a child" there shall be substituted "or any provision which could be made by a section 8 order under the Children Act 1989".

The Powers of Criminal Courts Act 1973 (c. 62)

34.   In Schedule 3 to the Powers of Criminal Courts Act 1973 (the probation and after-care service and its functions), in paragraph 3(2A) after paragraph (b) there shall be inserted—
"and
(c)   directions given under paragraph 2 or 3 of Schedule 3 to the Children Act 1989".

The Rehabilitation of Offenders Act 1974 (c. 53)

35.—(1)   Section 7(2) of the Rehabilitation of Offenders Act 1974 (limitations on rehabilitation under the Act) shall be amended as follows.
(2)   For paragraph (c) there shall be substituted—
"(c)   in any proceedings relating to adoption, the marriage of any minor, the exercise of the inherent jurisdiction of the High Court with respect to minors or the provision by any person of accommodation, care or schooling for minors;
(cc)   in any proceedings brought under the Children Act 1989;"
(3)   For paragraph (d) there shall be substituted—
"(d)   in any proceedings relating to the variation or discharge of a supervision order under the Children and Young Persons Act 1969, or on appeal from any such proceedings".

The Domestic Proceedings and Magistrates' Courts Act 1978 (c. 22)

36.   For section 8 of the Domestic Proceedings and Magistrates' Courts Act 1978 (orders for the custody of children) there shall be substituted—

"8. Restrictions on making of orders under this Act: welfare of children.
Where an application is made by a party to a marriage for an order under section 2, 6 or 7 of this Act, then, if there is a child of the family who is under the age of eighteen, the court shall not dismiss or make a final order on the application until it has decided whether to exercise any of its powers under the Children Act 1989 with respect to the child."

37.   In section 19(3A)(b) (interim orders) for the words "subsections (2) and" there shall be substituted "subsection".

38.   For section 20(12) of that Act (variation and revocation of orders for periodical payments) there shall be substituted—
"(12)   An application under this section may be made—
(a)   where it is for the variation or revocation of an order under section 2, 6, 7 or 19 of this Act for periodical payments, by either party to the marriage in question; and
(b)   where it is for the variation of an order under section 2(1)(c), 6 or 7

of this Act for periodical payments to or in respect of a child, also by the child himself, if he has attained the age of sixteen."

39.—(1)   For section 20A of that Act (revival of orders for periodical payments) there shall be substituted—

"20A. Revival of orders for periodical payments.
   (1)   Where an order made by a magistrates' court under this Part of this Act for the making of periodical payments to or in respect of a child (other than an interim maintenance order) ceases to have effect—
   (a)   on the date on which the child attains the age of sixteen, or
   (b)   at any time after that date but before or on the date on which he attains the age of eighteen,
the child may apply to the court which made the order for an order for its revival.
   (2)   If on such an application it appears to the court that—
   (a)   the child is, will be or (if an order were made under this subsection) would be receiving instruction at an educational establishment or undergoing training for a trade, profession or vocation, whether or not while in gainful employment, or
   (b)   there are special circumstances which justify the making of an order under this subsection,
the court shall have power by order to revive the order from such date as the court may specify, not being earlier than the date of the making of the application.
   (3)   Any order revived under this section may be varied or revoked under section 20 in the same way as it could have been varied or revoked had it continued in being."

40.   In section 23(1) of that Act (supplementary provisions with respect to the variation and revocation of orders) for the words "14(3), 20 or 21" there shall be substituted "20" and for the words "section 20 of this Act" there shall be substituted "that section".

41.—(1)   In section 25 of that Act (effect on certain orders of parties living together), in subsection (1)(a) for the words "6 or 11(2)" there shall be substituted "or 6".
   (2)   In subsection (2) of that section—
   (a)   in paragraph (a) for the words "6 or 11(2)" there shall be substituted "or 6"; and
   (b)   after paragraph (a) there shall be inserted "or".

42.   In section 29(5) of that Act (appeals) for the words "sections 14(3), 20 and 21" there shall be substituted "section 20".

43.   In section 88(1) of that Act (interpretation)—
   (a)   in the definition of "child", for the words from "an illegitimate" to the end there shall be substituted "a child whose father and mother were not married to each other at the time of his birth"; and
   (b)   in the definition of "child of the family", for the words "being boarded-out with those parties" there shall be substituted "placed with those parties as foster parents".

The Magistrates' Courts Act 1980 (c. 43)

44.—(1) In section 59(2) of the Magistrates' Courts Act 1980 (periodical payments through justices' clerk) for the words "the Guardianship of Minors Acts 1971 and 1973" there shall be substituted "(or having effect as if made under) Schedule 1 to the Children Act 1989".

(2) For section 62(5) of that Act (payments to children) there shall be substituted—

"(5) In this section references to the person with whom a child has his home—

(a) in the case of any child who is being looked after by a local authority (within the meaning of section 22 of the Children Act 1989), are references to that local authority; and

(b) in any other case, are references to the person who, disregarding any absence of the child at a hospital or boarding school and any other temporary absence, has care of the child.".

The Supreme Court Act 1981 (c. 54)

45.—(1) In section 18 of the Supreme Court Act 1981 (restrictions on appeals to Court of Appeal)—

(a) in subsection (1)(h)(i), for the word "custody" there shall be substituted "residence"; and

(b) in subsection (1)(h)(ii) for the words "access to", in both places, there shall be substituted "contact with".

(2) In Schedule 41 of that Act (wards of court), the following subsection shall be inserted after subsection (2)—

"(2A) Subsection (2) does not apply with respect to a child who is the subject of a care order (as defined by section 105 of the Children Act 1989)."

(3) In Schedule 1 to that Act (distribution of business in High Court), for paragraph 3(b)(ii) there shall be substituted—

"(ii) the exercise of the inherent jurisdiction of the High Court with respect to minors, the maintenance of minors and any proceedings under the Children Act 1989, except proceedings solely for the appointment of a guardian of a minor's estate;".

The Armed Forces Act 1981 (c. 55)

46. In section 14 of the Armed Forces Act 1981 (temporary removal to, and detention in, place of safety abroad or in the United Kingdom of service children in need of care and control), in subsection (9A) for the words "the Children and Young Persons Act 1933, the Children and Young Persons Act 1969" there shall be substituted "the Children Act 1989".

The Civil Jurisdiction and Judgments Act 1982 (c. 27)

47. In paragraph 5(a) of Schedule 5 to the Civil Jurisdiction and Judgments Act 1982 (maintenance and similar payments excluded from Schedule 4 to that Act) for the words "section 47 or 51 of the Child Care Act 1980" there shall be substituted "paragraph 23 of Schedule 2 to the Children Act 1989".

The Mental Health Act 1983 (c. 20)

48.—(1) For section 27 of the Mental Health Act 1983 (children and young persons in care of local authority) there shall be substituted the following section—

"27. Children and young persons in care.

Where—

(a) a patient who is a child or young person is in the care of a local authority by virtue of a care order within the meaning of the Children Act 1989; or

(b) the rights and powers of a parent of a patient who is a child or young person are vested in a local authority by virtue of section 16 of the Social Work (Scotland) Act 1968,

the authority shall be deemed to be the nearest relative of the patient in preference to any person except the patient's husband or wife (if any)."

(2) Section 28 of that Act (nearest relative of minor under guardianship, etc.) is amended as mentioned in sub-paragraphs (3) and (4).

(3) For subsection (1) there shall be substituted—

"(1) Where—

(a) a guardian has been appointed for a person who has not attained the age of eighteen years; or

(b) a residence order (as defined by section 8 of the Children Act 1989) is in force with respect to such a person,

the guardian (or guardians, where there is more than one) or the person named in the residence order shall, to the exclusion of any other person, be deemed to be his nearest relative."

(4) For subsection (3) there shall be substituted—

"(3) In this section "guardian" does not include a guardian under this Part of this Act."

(5) In section 131(2) of that Act (informal admission of patients aged sixteen or over) for the words from "notwithstanding" to the end there shall be substituted "even though there are one or more persons who have parental responsibility for him (within the meaning of the Children Act 1989).

The Registered Homes Act 1984 (c. 23)

49.—(1) In section 1(5) of the Registered Homes Act 1984 (requirement of registration) for paragraphs (d) and (e) there shall be substituted—

"(d) any community home, voluntary home or children's home within the meaning of the Children Act 1989,"

(2) In section 39 of that Act (preliminary) for paragraphs (a) and (b) there shall be substituted—

"(a) the Children Act 1989."

The Mental Health (Scotland) Act 1984 (c. 36)

50. For section 54 of the Mental Health (Scotland) Act 1984 (children and young persons in care of local authority) there shall be substituted the following section—

"54. Children and young persons in care of local authority.

Where—

    (a)   the rights and powers of a parent of a patient who is a child or young person are vested in a local authority by virtue of section 16 of the Social Work (Scotland) Act 1968; or

    (b)   a patient who is a child or young person is in the care of a local authority by virtue of a care order made under the Children Act 1989, the authority shall be deemed to be the nearest relative of the patient in preference to any person except the patient's husband or wife (if any)."

The Matrimonial and Family Proceedings Act 1984 (c. 42)

51.   In section 38(2)(b) of the Matrimonial and Family Proceedings Act 1984 (transfer of family proceedings from High Court to county court) after the words "a ward of court" there shall be inserted "or any other proceedings which relate to the exercise of the inherent jurisdiction of the High Court with respect to minors".

The Police and Criminal Evidence Act 1984 (c. 60)

52.   In section 37(14) of the Police and Criminal Evidence Act 1984 (duties of custody officer before charge) after the words "Children and Young Persons Act 1969" there shall be inserted "or in Part IV of the Children Act 1989".

53.—(1)   In section 38 of that Act (duties of custody officer after charge), in subsection (6) for the words "make arrangements" to the end there shall be substituted "secure that the arrested juvenile is moved to local authority accommodation".

(2)   After that subsection there shall be inserted—

    "(6A)   In this section 'local authority accommodation' means accommodation provided by or on behalf of a local authority (within the meaning of the Children Act 1989).

    (6B)   Where an arrested juvenile is moved to local authority accommodation under subsection (6) above, it shall be lawful for any person acting on behalf of the authority to detain him.".

(3)   In subsection (8) of that section for the words "Children and Young Persons Act 1969" there shall be substituted "Children Act 1989".

54.   In section 39(4) of that Act (responsibilities in relation to persons detained) for the words "transferred to the care of a local authority in pursuance of arrangements made" there shall be substituted "moved to local authority accommodation".

55.   In Schedule 2 to that Act (preserved powers of arrest) in the entry relating to the Children and Young Persons Act 1969 for the words "Sections 28(2) and" there shall be substituted "Section".

The Surrogacy Arrangements Act 1985 (c. 49)

56.   In section 1(2)(b) of the Surrogacy Arrangements Act 1985 (meaning of "surrogate mother", etc.) for the words "the parental rights being exercised" there shall be substituted "parental responsibility being met".

The Child Abduction and Custody Act 1985 (c. 60)

57.—(1) In section 9(a) and 20(2)(a) of the Child Abduction and Custody Act 1985 (orders with respect to which court's powers suspended), for the words "any other order under section 1(2) of the Children and Young Persons Act 1969" there shall be substituted "a supervision order under section 31 of the Children Act 1989".

(2) At the end of section 27 of that Act (interpretation, there shall be added—

"(4) In this Act a decision relating to rights of access in England and Wales means a decision as to the contact which a child may, or may not, have with any person."

(3) In Part I of Schedule 3 to that Act (orders in England and Wales which are custody orders for the purposes of the Act), for paragraph 1 there shall be substituted—

"1. The following are the orders referred to in section 27(1) of this Act—

(a) a care order under the Children Act 1989 (as defined by section 31(11) of that Act, read with section 105(1) and Schedule 14);

(b) a residence order (as defined by section 8 of the Act of 1989); and

(c) any order made by a court in England and Wales under any of the following enactments—

(i) section 9(1), 10(1)(a) or 11(a) of the Guardianship of Minors Act 1971;

(ii) section 42(1) or (2) or 43(1) of the Matrimonial Causes Act 1973;

(iii) section 2(2)(b), 4(b) or (5) of the Guardianship Act 1973 as applied by section 34(5) of the Children Act 1975;

(iv) section 8(2)(a), 10(1) or 19(1)(ii) of the Domestic Proceedings and Magistrates Courts Act 1978;

(v) section 26(1)(b) of the Adoption Act 1976."

The Disabled Persons (Services, Consultation and Representation) Act 1986 (c. 33)

58. In section 1(3) of the Disabled Persons (Services, Consultation and Representation) Act 1986 (circumstances in which regulations may provide for the appointment of authorised representatives of disabled persons)—

(a) in paragraph (a), for the words "parent or guardian of a disabled person under the age of sixteen" there shall be substituted—

"(i) the parent of a disabled person under the age of sixteen, or

(ii) any other person who is not a parent of his but who has parental responsibility for him"; and

(b) in paragraph (b), for the words "in the care of" there shall be substituted "looked after by".

59.—(1) Section 2 of that Act (circumstances in which authorised representative has right to visit etc. disabled person) shall be amended as follows.

(2) In subsection 3(a) for the words from second "the" to "by" there shall be substituted "for the words 'if so requested by the disabled person' there shall be substituted 'if so requested by any person mentioned in section 1(3)(a)(i) or (ii)'."

(3) In subsection (5) after paragraph (b) there shall be inserted—

"(bb)   in accommodation provided by or on behalf of a local authority under Part III of the Children Act 1989, or".

(4)   After paragraph (c) of subsection (5) there shall be inserted—
   "(cc)   in accommodation provided by a voluntary organisation in accordance with arrangements made by a local authority under section 17 of the Children Act 1989, or".

60.   In section 5(7)(b) of that Act (disabled persons leaving special education) for the word "guardian" there shall be substituted "other person who is not a parent of his but who has parental responsibility for him".

61.—(1)   In section 16 of that Act (interpretation) in the definition of "disabled person", in paragraph (a) for the words from "means" to "applies" there shall be substituted "means—
      "(i)   in the case of a person aged eighteen or over, a person to whom section 29 of the 1948 Act applies, and
      "(ii)   in the case of a person under the age of eighteen, a person who is disabled within the meaning of Part III of the Children Act 1989".

(2)   After the definition of "parent" in that section there shall be inserted—
   "'parental responsibility' has the same meaning as in the Children Act 1989."

(3)   In the definition of "the welfare enactments" in that section, in paragraph (a) after the words "the 1977 Act" there shall be inserted "as Part III of the Children Act 1989".

(4)   At the end of that section there shall be added—
   "(2)   In this Act any reference to a child who is looked after by a local authority has the same meaning as in the Children Act 1989."

The Family Law Act 1986 (c. 55)

62.—(1)   The Family Law Act 1986 shall be amended as follows.
(2)   Subject to paragraphs 63 to 71, in Part I—
   (a)   for the words "custody order", in each place where they occur, there shall be substituted "Part I order";
   (b)   for the words "proceedings with respect to the custody of", in each place where they occur, there shall be substituted "Part I proceedings with respect to"; and
   (c)   for the words "matters relating to the custody of", in each place where they occur, there shall be substituted "Part I matters relating to".

(3)   For section 42(7) (general interpretation of Part I) there shall be substituted—
   "(7)   In this Part—
      (a)   references to Part I proceedings in respect of a child are references to any proceedings for a Part I order or an order corresponding to a Part I order and include, in relation to proceedings outside the United Kingdom, references to proceedings before a tribunal or other authority having power under the law having effect there to determine Part I matters; and
      (b)   references to Part I matters are references to matters that might be determined by a Part I order or an order corresponding to a Part I order."

63.—(1) In section 1 (orders to which Part I of the Act of 1986 applies), in subsection (1)—

(a) for paragraph (a) there shall be substituted—

"(a) a section 8 order made by a court in England and Wales under the Children Act 1989, other than an order varying or discharging such an order"; and

(b) for paragraph (d) there shall be substituted the following paragraphs—

"(d) an order made by a court in England and Wales in the exercise of the inherent jurisdiction of the High Court with respect to children—

(i) so far as it gives care of a child to any person or provides for contact with, or the education of, a child; but

(ii) excluding an order varying or revoking such an order;

(e) an order made by the High Court in Northern Ireland in the exercise of its jurisdiction relating to wardship—

(i) so far as it gives care and control of a child to any person or provides for the education of or access to a child; but

(ii) excluding an order relating to a child of whom care or care and control is (immediately after the making of the order) vested in the Department of Health and Social Services or a Health and Social Services Board."

(2) In subsection (2) of that section, in paragraph (c) for "(d)" there shall be substituted "(e)".

(3) For subsections (3) to (5) of that section there shall be substituted—

"(3) In this Part, 'Part I order'—

(a) includes any order which would have been a custody order by virtue of this section in any form in which it was in force at any time before its amendment by the Children Act 1989; and

(b) (subject to sections 32 and 40 of this Act) excludes any order which would have been excluded from being a custody order by virtue of this section in any such form."

64. For section 2 there shall be substituted the following sections—

"2. Jurisdiction: general.

(1) A court in England and Wales shall not have jurisdiction to make a section 1(1)(a) order with respect to a child in or in connection with matrimonial proceedings in England and Wales unless the condition in section 2A of this Act is satisfied.

(2) A court in England and Wales shall not have jurisdiction to make a section 1(1)(a) order in a non-matrimonial case (that is to say, where the condition in section 2A of this Act is not satisfied) unless the condition in section 3 of this Act is satisfied.

(3) A court in England and Wales shall not have jurisdiction to make a section 1(1)(d) order unless—

(a) the condition in section 3 of this Act is satisfied, or

(b) the child concerned is present in England and Wales on the relevant date and the court considers that the immediate exercise of its powers is necessary for his protection.

2A. Jurisdiction in or in connection with matrimonial proceedings.

(1)   The condition referred to in section 2(1) of this Act is that the matrimonial proceedings are proceedings in respect of the marriage of the parents of the child concerned and—

    (a)   the proceedings—

        (i)   are proceedings for divorce or nullity of marriage, and

        (ii)   are continuing;

    (b)   the proceedings—

        (i)   are proceedings for judicial separation,

        (ii)   are continuing,

and the jurisdiction of the court is not excluded by subsection (2) below; or

    (c)   the proceedings have been dismissed after the beginning of the trial but—

        (i)   the section 1(1)(a) order is being made forthwith, or

        (ii)   the application for the order was made on or before the dismissal.

(2)   For the purposes of subsection (1)(b) above, the jurisdiction of the court is excluded if, after the grant of a decree of judicial separation, on the relevant date, proceedings for divorce or nullity in respect of the marriage are continuing in Scotland or Northern Ireland.

(3)   Subsection (2) above shall not apply if the court in which the other proceedings there referred to are continuing has made—

    (a)   an order under section 13(6) or 21(5) of this Act (not being an order made by virtue of section 13(6)(a)(i)), or

    (b)   an order under section 14(2) or 22(2) of this Act which is recorded as being made for the purpose of enabling Part I proceedings to be taken in England and Wales with respect to the child concerned.

(4)   Where a court—

    (a)   has jurisdiction to make a section 1(1)(a) order in or in connection with matrimonial proceedings, but

    (b)   considers that it would be more appropriate for Part I matters relating to the child to be determined outside England and Wales,

the court may by order direct that, while the order under this subsection is in force, no section 1(1)(a) order shall be made by any court in or in connection with those proceedings."

65.—(1)   In section 3 (habitual residence or presence of child concerned) in subsection (1) for "section 2" there shall be substituted "section 2(2)".

(2)   In subsection (2) of that section for the words "proceedings for divorce, nullity or judicial separation" there shall be substituted "matrimonial proceedings".

66.—(1)   In section 6 (duration and variation of Part I orders), for subsection (3) there shall be substituted the following subsections—

    "(3)   A court in England and Wales shall not have jurisdiction to vary a Part I order if, on the relevant date, matrimonial proceedings are continuing in Scotland or Northern Ireland in respect of the marriage of the parents of the child concerned.

    (3A)   Subsection (3) above shall not apply if—

(a)   the Part I order was made in or in connection with proceedings for divorce or nullity in England and Wales in respect of the marriage of the parents of the child concerned; and

(b)   those proceedings are continuing.

(3B)   Subsection (3) above shall not apply if—

(a)   the Part I order was made in or in connection with proceedings for judicial separation in England and Wales;

(b)   those proceedings are continuing; and

(c)   the decree of judicial separation has not yet been granted."

(2)   In subsection (5) of that section for the words from "variation of" to "if the ward" there shall be substituted "variation of a section 1(1)(d) order if the child concerned".

(3)   For subsections (6) and (7) of that section there shall be substituted the following subsections—

"(6)   Subsection (7) below applies where a Part I order which is—

(a)   a residence order (within the meaning of the Children Act 1989) in favour of a person with respect to a child,

(b)   an order made in the exercise of the High Court's inherent jurisdiction with respect to children by virtue of which a person has care of a child, or

(c)   an order—

(i)   of a kind mentioned in section 1(3)(a) of this Act,

(ii)   under which a person is entitled to the actual possession of a child,

ceases to have effect in relation to that person by virtue of subsection (1) above.

(7)   Where this subsection applies, any family assistance order made under section 16 of the Children Act 1989 with respect to the child shall also cease to have effect.

(8)   For the purposes of subsection (7) above the reference to a family assistance order under section 16 of the Children Act 1989 shall be deemed to include a reference to an order for the supervision of a child made under—

(a)   section 7(4) of the Family Law Reform Act 1969,

(b)   section 44 of the Matrimonial Causes Act 1973,

(c)   section 2(2)(a) of the Guardianship Act 1973,

(d)   section 34(5) or 36(3)(b) of the Children Act 1975, or

(e)   section 9 of the Domestic Proceedings and Magistrates' Courts Act 1978;

but this subsection shall cease to have effect once all such orders for the supervision of children have ceased to have effect in accordance with Schedule 14 to the Children Act 1989."

67.   For section 7 (interpretation of Chapter II) there shall be substituted—

"7. Interpretation of Chapter II.

In this Chapter—

(a)   'child' means a person who has not attained the age of eighteen;

(b)   'matrimonial proceedings' means proceedings for divorce, nullity of marriage or judicial separation;

(c) 'the relevant date' means, in relation to the making or variation of an order—

    (i) where an application is made for an order to be made or varied, the date of the application (or first application, if two or more are determined together), and

    (ii) where no such application is made, the date on which the court is considering whether to make or, as the case may be, vary the order; and

(d) 'section 1(1)(a) order' and 'section 1(1)(d) order' mean orders falling within section 1(1)(a) and (d) of this Act respectively."

68. In each of the following sections—

(a) section 11(2)(a) (provisions supplementary to sections 9 and 10),
(b) section 13(5)(a) (jurisdiction ancillary to matrimonial proceedings),
(c) section 20(3)(a) (habitual residence or presence of child),
(d) section 21(4)(a) (jurisdiction in divorce proceedings, etc.), and
(e) section 23(4)(a) (duration and variation of custody orders),

for "4(5)" there shall be substituted "2A(4)".

69. In each of the following sections—

(a) section 19(2) (jurisdiction in cases other than divorce, etc.),
(b) section 20(6) (habitual residence or presence of child), and
(c) section 23(5) (duration and variation of custody orders),

for "section 1(1)(d)" there shall e substituted "section 1(1)(e)".

70. In section 34(3) (power to order recovery of child) for paragraph (a) there shall be substituted—

    "(a) section 14 of the Children Act 1989".

71.—(1) In section 42 (general interpretation of Part I), in subsection (4)(a) for the words "has been boarded out with those parties" there shall be substituted "is placed with those parties as foster parents".

(2) In subsection (6) of that section, in paragraph (a) after the word "person" there shall be inserted "to be allowed contact with or".

The Local Government Act 1988 (c. 9)

72. In Schedule 1 to the Local Government Act 1988 (competition) at the end of paragraph 2(4) (cleaning of buildings: buildings to which competition provisions do not apply) for paragraph (c) there shall be substituted—

    "(c) section 53 of the Children Act 1989."

Amendments of local Acts

73.—(1) Section 16 of the Greater London Council (General Powers) Act 1981 (exemption from provisions of Part IV of the Act of certain premises) shall be amended as follows.

(2) After paragraph (g) there shall be inserted—

    "(gg) used as a children's home as defined in section 63 of the Children Act 1989".

(3) In paragraph (h)—

(a) for the words "section 56 of the Child Care Act 1980" there shall be substituted "section 60 of the Children Act 1989";

  (b)   for the words "section 57" there shall be substituted "section 60"; and
  (c)   for the words "section 32" there shall be substituted "section 53".
  (4)   In paragraph (i), for the words "section 8 of the Foster Children Act 1980" there shall be substituted "section 67 of the Children Act 1989".

  74.—(1)   Section 10(2) of the Greater London Council (General Powers) Act 1984 (exemption from provisions of Part IV of the Act of certain premises) shall be amended as follows.
  (2)   In paragraph (d)—
  (a)   for the words "section 56 of the Child Care Act 1980" there shall be substituted "section 60 of the Children Act 1989";
  (b)   for the words "section 57" there shall be substituted "section 60"; and
  (c)   for the words "section 31" there shall be substituted "section 53".
  (3)   In paragraph (e), for the words "section 8 of the Foster Children Act 1980" there shall be substituted "section 67 of the Children Act 1989".
  (4)   In paragraph (1) for the words "section 1 of the Children's Homes Act 1982" there shall be substituted "section 63 of the Children Act 1989".

Section 108(6).   **SCHEDULE 14**
                    TRANSITIONALS AND SAVINGS

Pending proceedings, etc.

  1.—(1)   Subject to sub-paragraph (4), nothing in any provision of this Act (other than the repeals mentioned in sub–paragraph (2)) shall affect any proceedings which are pending immediately before the commencement of that provision.
  (2)   The repeals are those of—
  (a)   section 42(3) of the Matrimonial Causes Act 1973 (declaration by court that party to marriage unfit to have custody of children of family); and
  (b)   section 38 of the Sexual Offences Act 1956 (power of court to divest person of authority over girl or boy in cases of incest).
  (3)   For the purposes of the following provisions of this Schedule, any referece to an order in force immediately before the commencement of a provision of this Act shall be construed as including a reference to an order made after that commencement in proceedings pending before that commencement.
  (4)   Sub–paragraph (3) is not to be read as making the order in question have effect from a date earlier than that on which it was made.
  (5)   An order under section 96(3) may make such provision with respect to the application of the order in relation to proceedings which are pending when the order comes into force as the Lord Chancellor considers appropriate.

  2.   Where, immediately before the day on which Part IV comes into force, there was in force an order under section 3(1) of the Children and Young Persons Act 1963 (order directing a local authority to bring a child or young person before a juvenile court under section 1 of the Children and Young Persons Act 1969), the order shall cease to have effect on that day.

CUSTODY ORDERS, ETC.

Cessation of declarations of unfitness, etc.

3. Where, immediately before the day on which Parts I and II come into force, there was in force—

(a) a declaration under section 42(3) of the Matrimonial Causes Act 1973 (declaration by court that party to marriage unfit to have custody of children of family); or

(b) an order under section 38(1) of the Sexual Offences Act 1956 divesting a person of authority over a girl or boy in a case of incest;

the declaration or, as the case may be, the order shall cease to have effect on that day.

The Family Law Reform Act 1987 (c. 42)

Conversion of orders under section 4

4. Where, immediately before the day on which Parts I and II come into force, there was in force an order under section 4(1) of the Family Law Reform Act 1987 (order giving father parental rights and duties in relation to a child), then, on and after that day, the order shall be deemed to be an order under section 4 of this Act giving the father parental responsibility for the child.

Orders to which paragraphs 6 to 11 apply

5.—(1) In paragraphs 6 to 11 "an existing order" means any order which—

(a) is in force immediately before the commencement of Parts I and II;

(b) was made under any enactment mentioned in sub-paragraph (2);

(c) determines all or any of the following—

(i) who is to have custody of a child;

(ii) who is to have care and control of a child;

(iii) who is to have access to a child;

(iv) any matter with respect to a child's education or upbringing; and

(d) is not an order of a kind mentioned in paragraph 15(1).

(2) The enactments are—

(a) the Domestic Proceedings and Magistrates' Courts Act 1978;

(b) the Children Act 1975;

(c) the Matrimonial Causes Act 1973;

(d) the Guardianship of Minors Acts 1971 and 1973;

(e) the Matrimonial Causes Act 1965;

(f) the Matrimonial Proceedings (Magistrates' Courts) Act 1960.

(3) For the purposes of this paragraph and paragraphs 6 to 11 "custody" includes legal custody and joint as well as sole custody but does not include access.

Parental responsibility of parents

6.—(1) Where

(a) a child's father and mother were married to each other at the time of his birth; and

(b) there is an existing order with respect to the child,

each parent shall have parental responsibility for the child in accordance with section 2 as modified by sub-paragraph (3).

(2) Where—

(a) a child's father and mother were not married to each other at the time of his birth; and

(b) there is an existing order with respect to the child,

section 2 shall apply as modified by sub-paragraphs (3) and (4).

(3) The modification is that for section 2(8) there shall be substituted—

"(8) The fact that a person has parental responsibility for a child does not entitle him to act in a way which would be incompatible with any existing order or any order made under this Act with respect to the child".

(4) The modifications are that—

(a) for the purposes of section 2(2), where the father has custody or care and control of the child by virtue of any existing order, the court shall be deemed to have made (at the commencement of that section) an order under section 4(1) giving him parental responsibility for the child; and

(b) where by virtue of paragraph (a) a court is deemed to have made an order under section 4(1) in favour of a father who has care and control of a child by virtue of an existing order, the court shall not bring the order under section 4(1) to an end at any time while has has care and control of the child by virtue of the order.

Persons who are not parents but who have custody or care and control

7.—(1) Where a person who is not the parent or guardian of a child has custody or care and control of him by virtue of an existing order, that person shall have parental responsibility for him so long as he continues to have that custody or care and control by virtue of the order.

(2) Where sub-paragraph (1) applies, Parts I and II shall have effect as modified by this paragraph.

(3) The modification are that—

(a) for section 2(8) there shall be substituted—

"(8) The fact that a person has parental responsibility for a child does not entitle him to act in a way which would be incompatible with any existing order or with any order made under this Act with respect to the child";

(b) at the end of section 10(4) there shall be inserted—

"(c) any person who has custody or care and control of a child by virtue of any existing order"; and

(c) at the end of section 34(1)(c) there shall be inserted—

"(cc) where immediately before the care order was made there was an existing order by virtue of which a person had custody or care and control of the child, that person."

Persons who have care and control

8.—(1) Sub-paragraphs (2) to (6) apply where a person has care and control of a child by virtue of an existing order, but they shall cease to apply when that order ceases to have effect.

(2) Section 5 shall have effect as if—

(a)   for any reference to a residence order in favour of a parent or guardian there were substituted a reference to any existing order by virtue of which the parent or guardian has care and control of the child; and

(b)   for subsection (9) there were substituted—

"(9)   Subsections (1) and (7) do not apply if the existing order referred to in paragraph (b) of those subsections was one by virtue of which a surviving parent of the child also had care and control of him."

(3)   Section 10 shall have effect as if for subsection (5)(c)(i) there were substituted—

"(i)   in any case where by virtue of an existing order any person or persons has or have care and control of the child, has the consent of that person or each of those persons".

(4)   Section 20 shall have effect as if for subsection (9)(a) there were substituted "who has care and control of the child by virtue of an existing order."

(5)   Section 23 shall have effect as if for subsection (4)(c) there were substituted—

"(c)   where the child is in care and immediately before the care order was made there was an existing order by virtue of which a person had care and control of the child, that person."

(6)   In Schedule 1, paragraphs 1(1) and 14(1) shall have effect as if for the words "in whose favour a residence order is in force with respect to the child" there were substituted "who has been given care and control of the child by virtue of an existing order".

Persons who have access

9.—(1)   Sub-paragraphs (2) to (4) apply where a person has access by virtue of an existing order.

(2)   Section 10 shall have effect as if after subsection (5) there were inserted—

"(5A)   Any person who has access to a child by virtue of an existing order is entitled to apply for a contact order."

(3)   Section 16(2) shall have effect as if after paragraph (b) there were inserted—

"(bb)   any person who has access to the child by virtue of an existing order."

(4)   Sections 43(11), 44(13) and 46(10), shall have effect as if in each case after paragraph (d) there were inserted—

"(dd)   any person who has been given access to him by virtue of an existing order."

Enforcement of certain existing orders

10.—(1)   Sub-paragraph (2) applies in relation to any existing order which, but for the repeal by this Act of—

(a)   section 13(1) of the Guardianship of Minors Act 1971;

(b)   section 43(1) of the Children Act 1975; or

(c)   section 33 of the Domestic Proceedings and Magistrates' Courts Act 1978,

(provisions concerning the enforcement of custody orders) might have been enforced as if it were an order requiring a person to give up a child to another person.

(2) Where this sub-paragraph applies, the existing order may, after the repeal of the enactments mentioned in sub-paragraph (1)(a) to (c), be enforced under section 14 as if—

    (a) any reference to a residence order were a reference to the existing order; and

    (b) any reference to a person in whose favour the residence order is in force were a reference to a person to whom actual custody of the child is given by an existing order which is in force.

(3) In sub-paragraph (2) "actual custody", in relation to a child, means the actual possession of his person.

Discharge of existing orders

11.—(1) The making of a residence order or a care order with respect to a child who is the subject of an existing order discharges the existing order.

(2) Where the court makes any section 8 order (other than a residence order) with respect to a child with respect to whom any existing order is in force, the existing order shall have effect subject to the section 8 order.

(3) The court may discharge an existing order which is in force with respect to a child—

    (a) in any family proceedings relating to the child or in which any question arises with respect to the child's welfare; or

    (b) on the application of—

        (i) any parent or guardian of the child;

        (ii) the child himself; or

        (iii) any person named in the order.

(4) A child may not apply for the discharge of an existing order except with the leave of the court.

(5) The power in sub-paragraph (3) to discharge an existing order includes the power to discharge any part of the order.

(6) In considering whether to discharge an order under the power conferred by sub-paragraph (3) the court shall, if the discharge of the order is opposed by any party to the proceedings, have regard in particular to the matters mentioned in section 1(3).

GUARDIANS

Existing guardians to be guardians under this Act

12.—(1) Any appointment of a person as guardian of a child which—

    (a) was made—

        (i) under sections 3 to 5 of the Guardianship of Minors Act 1971;

        (ii) under section 38(3) of the Sexual Offences Act 1956; or

        (iii) under the High Court's inherent jurisdiction with respect to children; and

    (b) has taken effect before the commencement of section 5,

shall (subject to sub-paragraph (2)) be deemed, on and after the commencement of section 5, to be an appointment made and having effect under that section.

(2) Where an appointment of a person as guardian of a child has effect under

section 5 by virtue of sub-paragraph (1)(a)(ii), the appointment shall not have effect for a period which is longer than any period specified in the order.

Appointment of guardian not yet in effect

13. Any appointment of a person to be a guardian of a child—
  (a) which was made as mentioned in paragraph 12(1)(a)(i); but
  (b) which, immediately before the commencement of section 5, had not taken effect,
shall take effect in accordance with section 5 (as modified, where it applies, by paragraph 8(2)).

Persons deemed to be appointed as guardians under existing wills

14. For the purposes of the Wills Act 1873 and of this Act any disposition by will and testament or devise of the custody and tuition of any child, made before the commencement of section 5 and paragraph 1 of Schedule 13, shall be deemed to be an appointment by will of a guardian of the child.

CHILDREN IN CARE

Children in compulsory care

15.—(1) Sub-paragraph (2) applies where, immediately before the day on which Part IV comes into force, a person was—
  (a) in care by virtue of—
    (i) a care order under section 1 of the Children and Young Person Act 1969;
    (ii) a care order under section 15 of that Act, on discharging a supervision order made under section 1 of that Act; or
    (iii) an order or authorisation under section 25 or 26 of that Act;
  (b) deemed, by virtue of—
    (i) paragraph 7(3) of Schedule 5A to the Army Act 1955;
    (ii) paragraph 7(3) of Schedule 5A to the Air Force Act 1955; or
    (iii) paragraph 7(3) of Schedule 4A to the Naval Discipline Act 1957,
to be the subject of a care order under the Children and Young Persons Act 1969;
  (c) in care—
    (i) under section 2 of the Child Care Act 1980; or
    (ii) by virtue of paragraph 1 of Schedule 4 to that Act (which extends the meaning of a child in care under section 2 to include children in care under section 1 of the Children Act 1948),
and a child in respect of whom a resolution under section 3 of the Act of 1980 or section 2 of the Act of 1948 was in force;
  (d) a child in respect of whom a resolution had been passed under section 65 of the Child Care Act 1980;
  (e) in care by virtue of an order under—
    (i) section 2(1)(e) of the Matrimonial Proceedings (Magistrates' Courts) Act 1960;
    (ii) section 7(2) of the Family Law Reform Act 1969;
    (iii) section 43(1) of the Matrimonial Causes Act 1973; or

(iv)   section 2(2)(b) of the Guardianship Act 1973;
(v)   section 10 of the Domestic Proceedings and Magistrates' Courts Act 1978,
(orders having effect for certain purposes as if the child had been received into care under section 2 of the Child Care Act 1980;
(f)   in care by virtue of an order made, on the revocation of a custodianship order, under section 36 of the Children Act 1975; or
(g)   in care by virtue of an order made, on the refusal of an adoption order, under section 26 of the Adoption Act 1976 or any order having effect (by virtue of paragraph 1 of Schedule 2 to that Act) as if made under that section.

(2)   Where this sub-paragraph applies, then, on and after the day on which Part IV commences—
(a)   the order or resolution in question shall be deemed to be a care order;
(b)   the authority in whose care the person was immediately before that commencement shall be deemed to be the authority designated in that deemed care order; and
(c)   any reference to a child in the care of a local authority shall include a reference to a person who is the subject of such a deemed care order,
and the provisions of this act shall apply accordingly, subject to paragraph 16.

Modifications

16.—(1)   Sub-paragraph (2) only applies where a person who is the subject of a care order by virtue of paragraph 15(2) is a person falling within sub-paragraph (1)(a) or (b) of that paragraph.

(2)   Where the person would otherwise have remained in care until reaching the age of nineteen, by virtue of—
(a)   section 20(3)(a) or 21(1) of the Children and Young Persons Act 1969; or
(b)   paragraph 7(5)(c)(i) of—
(i)   Schedule 5A to the Army Act 1955;
(i)   Schedule 5A to the Air Force Act 1955; or
(iii)   Schedule 4A to the Naval Discipline Act 1957,
this Act applies as if in section 91(12) for the word "eighteen" there were substituted "nineteen".

(3)   Where a person who is the subject of a care order by virtue of paragraph 15(2) is a person falling within sub-paragraph (1)(b) of that paragraph, this Act applies as if section 101 were omitted.

(4)   Sub-paragraph (5) only applies where a child who is the subject of a care order by virtue of paragraph 15(2) is a person falling within sub-paragraph (1)(e) to (g) of that paragraph.

(5)   Where a court, on making the order, or at any time thereafter, gave directions under—
(a)   section 4(4)(a) of the Guardianship Act 1973; or
(b)   section 43(5)(a) of the Matrimonial Causes Act 1973,
as to the exercise by the authority of any powers, those directions shall continue to have effect (regardless of any conflicting provision in this Act) until varied or discharged by a court under this sub-paragraph.

Children placed with parent etc. while in compulsory care

17.—(1) This paragraph applies where a child is deemed by paragraph 15 to be in the care of a local authority under an order or resolution which is deemed by that paragraph to be a care order.

(2) If, immediately before the day on which Part III comes into force, the child was allowed to be under the charge and control of—

(a) a parent or guardian under section 21(2) of the Child Care Act 1980; or

(b) a person who, before the child was in the authority's care, had care and control of the child by virtue of an order falling within paragraph 5,

on and after that day the provision made by and under section 23(5) shall apply as if the child had been placed with the person in question in accordance with that provision.

Orders for access to children in compulsory care

18.—(1) This paragraph applies to any access order—

(a) made under section 12C of the Child Care Act 1980 (access orders with respect to children in care of local authorities); and

(b) in force immediately before the commencement of Part IV.

(2) On and after the commencement of Part IV, the access order shall have effect as an order made under section 34 in favour of the person named in the order.

19.—(1) This paragraph applies where, immediately before the commencement of Part IV, an access order made under section 12C of the Act of 1980 was suspended by virtue of an order made under section 12E of that Act (suspension of access orders in emergencies).

(2) The suspending order shall continue to have effect as if this Act had not been passed.

(3) If—

(a) before the commencement of Part IV; and

(b) during the period for which the operation of the access order is suspended,

the local authority concerned made an application for its variation or discharge to an appropriate juvenile court, its operation shall be suspended until the date on which the application to vary or discharge it is determined or abandoned.

Children in voluntary care

20.—(1) This paragraph applies where, immediately before the day on which Part III comes into force—

(a) a child was in the care of a local authority—

(i) under section 2(1) of the Child Care Act 1980; or

(ii) by virtue of paragraph 1 of Schedule 4 to that Act (which extends the meaning of references to children in care under section 2 to include references to children in care under section 1 of the Children Act 1948); and

(b) he was not a person in respect of whom a resolution under section 3 of the Act of 1980 or section 2 of the Act of 1948 was in force.

(2) Where this paragraph applies, the child shall, on and after the day mentioned in sub-paragraph (1), be treated for the purposes of this Act as a child

who is provided with accommodation by the local authority under Part III, but he shall cease to be so treated once he ceases to be so accommodated in accordance with the provisions of Part III.

(3) Where—

(a) this paragraph applies; and

(b) the child, immediately before the day mentioned in sub-paragraph (1), was (by virtue of section 21(2) of the Act of 1980) under the charge and control of a person falling within paragraph 17(2)(a) or (b),

the child shall not be treated for the purposes of this Act as if he were being looked after by the authority concerned.

Boarded out children

21.—(1) Where, immediately before the day on which Part III comes into force, a child in the care of a local authority—

(a) was—

(i) boarded out with a person under section 21(1)(a) of the Child Care Act 1980; or

(ii) placed under the charge and control of a person, under section 21(2) of that Act; and

(b) the person with whom he was boarded out, or (as the case may be) placed, was not a person falling within paragraph 17(2)(a) or (b),

on and after that day, he shall be treated (subject to sub-paragraph (2)) as having been placed with a local authority foster parent and shall cease to be so treated when he ceases to be placed with that person in accordance with the provisions of this Act.

(2) Regulations made under section 23(2)(a) shall not apply in relation to a person who is a local authority foster parent by virtue of sub-paragraph (1) before the end of the period of twelve months beginning with the day on which Part III comes into force and accordingly that person shall for that period be subject—

(a) in a case falling within sub-paragraph (1)(a)(i), to terms and regulations mentioned in section 21(1)(a) of the Act of 1980; and

(b) in a case falling within sub-paragraph (1)(a)(ii), to terms fixed under section 21(2) of that Act and regulations made under section 22A of that Act, as if that Act had not been repealed by this Act.

Children in care to qualify for advice and assistance

22. Any reference in Part III to a person qualifying for advice and assistance shall be construed as including a reference to a person within the area of the local authority in question who is under twenty-one and who was, at any time after reaching the age of sixteen but while still a child—

(a) a person falling within—

(i) any of paragraphs (a) to (g) of paragraph 15(1); or

(ii) paragraph 20(1); or

(b) the subject of a criminal care order (within the meaning of paragraph 34).

Emigration of children in care

23.   Where—

(a)   the Secretary of State has received a request in writing from a local authority that he give his consent under section 24 of the Child Care Act 1980 to the emigration of a child in their care; but

(b)   immediately before the repeal of the Act of 1980 by this Act, he has not determined whether or not to give his consent,

section 24 of the Act of 1980 shall continue to apply (regardless of that repeal) until the Secretary of State has determined whether or not to give his consent to the request.

Contributions for maintenance of children in care

24.—(1)   Where, immediately before the day on which Part III of Schedule 2 comes into force, there was in force an order made (or having effect as if made) under any of the enactments mentioned in sub-paragraph (2), then, on and after that day—

(a)   the order shall have effect as if made under paragraph 23(2) of Schedule 2 against a person liable to contribute; and

(b)   Part III of Schedule 2 shall apply to the order, subject to the modifications in sub-paragraph (3).

(2)   The enactments are—

(a)   section 11(4) of the Domestic Proceedings and Magistrates' Courts Act 1978;

(b)   section 26(2) of the Adoption Act 1976;

(c)   section 36(5) of the Children act 1975;

(d)   section 2(3) of the Guardianship Act 1973;

(e)   section 2(1)(h) of the Matrimonial Proceedings (Magistrates' Courts) Act 1960,

(provisions empowering the court to make an order requiring a person to make periodical payments to a local authority in respect of a child in care).

(3)   The modifications are that, in paragraph 23 of Schedule 2—

(a)   in sub-paragraph (4), paragraph (a) shall be omitted;

(b)   for sub-paragraph (6) there shall be substituted—

"(6)   Where—

(a)   a contribution order is in force;

(b)   the authority serve a contribution notice under paragraph 22; and

(c)   the contributor and the authority reach an agreement under paragraph 22(7) in respect of the contribution notice,

the effect of the agreement shall be to discharge the order from the date on which it is agreed that the agreement shall take effect"; and

(c)   at the end of sub-paragraph (10) there shall be inserted—

"and

(c)   where the order is against a person who is not a parent of the child, shall be made with due regard to—

(i)   whether that person had assumed responsibility for the maintenance of the child, and, if so, the extent to which and basis on which he assumed that responsibility and the length of the period during which he met that responsibility;

    (ii)   whether he did so knowing that the child was not his child;

    (iii)   the liability of any other person to maintain the child."

SUPERVISION ORDERS

Orders under section 1(3)(b) or 21(2) of the 1969 Act

25.—(1)   This paragraph applies to any supervision order—

    (a)   made—

       (i)   under section 1(3)(b) of the Children and Young Persons Act 1969; or

       (ii)   under section 21(2) of that Act on the discharge of a care order made under section 1(3)(c) of that Act; and

    (b)   in force immediately before the commencement of Part IV.

(2)   On and after the commencement of Part IV, the order shall be deemed to be a supervision order made under section 31 and—

    (a)   any requirement of the order that the child reside with a named individual shall continue to have effect while the order remains in force, unless the court otherwise directs;

    (b)   any other requirement imposed by the court, or directions given by the supervisor, shall be deemed to have been imposed or given under the appropriate provisions of Schedule 3.

(3)   Where, immediately before the commencement of Part IV, the order had been in force for a period of more than six months, it shall cease to have effect at the end of the period of six months beginning with the day on which Part IV comes into force unless—

    (a)   the court directs that it shall cease to have effect at the end of a different period (which shall not exceed three years);

    (b)   it ceases to have effect earlier in accordance with section 91; or

    (c)   it would have ceased to have had effect earlier had this Act not been passed.

(4)   Where sub-paragraph (3) applies, paragraph 6 of Schedule 3 shall not apply.

(5)   Where, immediately before the commencement of Part IV, the order had been in force for less than six months it shall cease to have effect in accordance with section 91 and paragraph 6 of Schedule 3 unless—

    (a)   the court directs that it shall cease to have effect at the end of a different period (which shall not exceed three years); or

    (b)   it would have ceased to have had effect earlier had this Act not been passed.

Other supervision orders

26.—(1)   This paragraph applies to any order for the supervision of a child which was in force immediately before the commencement of Part IV and was made under—

    (a)   section 2(1)(f) of the Matrimonial Proceedings (Magistrates Courts) Act 1960;

    (b)   section 7(4) of the Family Law Reform Act 1969;

    (c)   section 44 of the Matrimonial Causes Act 1973;

    (d)   section 2(2)(a) of the Guardianship Act 1973;
    (e)   section 34(5) or 36(3)(b) of the Children Act 1975;
    (f)   section 26(1)(a) of the Adoption Act 1976; or
    (g)   section 9 of the Domestic Proceedings and Magistrates Courts Act 1978.

(2)   The order shall not be deemed to be a supervision order made under any provision of this Act but shall nevertheless continue in force for a period of one year beginning with the day on which Part IV comes into force unless—

    (a)   the court directs that it shall cease to have effect at the end of a lesser period, or
    (b)   it would have ceased to have had effect earlier had this Act not been passed.

PLACE OF SAFETY ORDERS

27.—(1)   This paragraph applies to—
    (a)   any order or warrant authorising the removal of a child to a place of safety which—
        (i)   was made, or issued, under any of the enactments mentioned in sub-paragraph (2); and
        (ii)   was in force immediately before the commencement of Part IV; and
    (b)   any interim order made under section 23(5) of the Children and Young Persons Act 1963 or section 28(6) of the Children and Young Persons Act 1969.

(2)   The enactments are—
    (a)   section 40 of the Children and Young Persons Act 1933 (warrant to search for or remove child);
    (b)   section 28(1) of the Children and Young Persons Act 1969 (detention of child in place of safety);
    (c)   section 34(1) of the Adoption Act 1976 (removal of protected children from unsuitable surroundings);
    (d)   section 12(1) of the Foster Children Act 1980 (removal of foster children kept in unsuitable surroundings).

(3)   The order or warrant shall continue to have effect as if this Act had not been passed.

(4)   Any enactment repealed by this Act shall continue to have effect in relation to the order or warrant so far as is necessary for the purposes of securing that the effect of the order is what it would have been had this Act not been passed.

(5)   Sub-paragraph (4) does not apply to the power to make an interim order or further interim order given by section 23(5) of the Children and Young Persons Act 1963 or section 28(6) of the Children and Young Persons Act 1969.

(6)   Where, immediately before section 28 of the Children and Young Persons Act 1969 is repealed by this Act, a child is being detained under the powers granted by that section, he may continue to be detained in accordance with that section but subsection (6) shall not apply.

RECOVERY OF CHILDREN

28.   The repeal by this Act of subsection (1) of section 16 of the Child Care Act 1980 (arrest of child absent from compulsory care) shall not affect the operation of that section in relation to any child arrested before the coming into force of the repeal.

29.—(1)   This paragraph applies where—

(a)   a summons has been issued under section 15 or 16 of the Child Care Act 1980 (recovery of children in voluntary or compulsory care); and

(b)   the child concerned is not produced in accordance with the summons before the repeal of that section by this Act comes into force.

(2)   The summons, any warrant issued in connection with it and section 15 or (as the case may be) section 16, shall continue to have effect as if this Act had not been passed.

30.   The amendment by paragraph 27 of Schedule 12 of section 32 of the Children and Young Persons Act 1969 (detention of absentees) shall not affect the operation of that section in relation to—

(a)   any child arrested; or

(b)   any summons or warrant issued,

under that section before the coming into force of that paragraph.

VOLUNTARY ORGANISATIONS: PARENTAL RIGHTS RESOLUTIONS

31.—(1)   This paragraph applies to a resolution—

(a)   made under section 64 of the Child Care Act 1980 (transfer of parental rights and duties to voluntary organisations); and

(b)   in force immediately before the commencement of Part IV.

(2)   The resolution shall continue to have effect until the end of the period of six months beginning with the day on which Part IV comes into force unless it is brought to an end earlier in accordance with the provisions of the Act of 1980 preserved by this paragraph.

(3)   While the resolution remains in force, any relevant provisions of, or made under, the Act of 1980 shall continue to have effect with respect to it.

(4)   Sub-paragraph (3) does not apply to—

(a)   section 62 of the Act of 1980 and any regulations made under that section (arrangements by voluntary organisations for emigration of children); or

(b)   subsection 65 of the Act of 1980 (duty of local authority to assume parental rights and duties).

(5)   Section 5(2) of the Act of 1980 (which is applied to resolutions under Part VI of that Act by section 64(7) of that Act) shall have effect with respect to the resolution as if the reference in paragraph (c) to an appointment of a guardian under section 5 of the Guardianship of Minors Act 1971 were a reference to an appointment of a guardian under section 5 of this Act.

FOSTER CHILDREN

32.—(1) This paragraph applies where—

(a) immediately before the commencement of Part VIII, a child was a foster child within the meaning of the Foster Children Act 1980; and

(b) the circumstances of the case are such that, had Parts VIII and IX then been in force, he would have been treated for the purposes of this Act as a child who was being provided with accommodation in a children's home and not as a child who was being privately fostered.

(2) If the child continues to be cared for and provided with accommodation as before, section 63(1) and (10) shall not apply in relation to him if—

(a) an application for registration of the home in question is made under

AND CHILD MINDING

33.—(1) Sub-paragraph (2) applies where, immediately before the commencement of Part X, any premises are registered under section 1(1)(a) of the Nurseries and Child-Minders Regulation Act 1948 (registration of premises, other than premises wholly or mainly used as private dwellings, where children are received to be looked after).

(2) During the transitional period, the provisions of the Act of 1948 shall continue to have effect with respect to those premises to the exclusion of Part X.

(3) Nothing in sub-paragraph (2) shall prevent the local authority concerned from registering any person under section 71(1)(b) with respect to the premises.

(4) In this paragraph "the transitional period" means the period ending with—

(a) the first anniversary of the commencement of Part X; or

(b) if earlier, the date on which the local authority concerned registers any person under section 71(1)(b) with respect to the premises.

34.—(1) Sub-paragraph (2) applies where, immediately before the commencement of Part X—

(a) a person is registered under section 1(1)(b) of the Act of 1948 (registration of persons who for reward receive into their homes children under the age of five to be looked after); and

(b) all the children looked after by him as mentioned in section 1(1)(b) of that Act are under the age of five.

(2) During the transitional period, the provisions of the Act of 1948 shall continue to have effect with respect to that person to the exclusion of Part X.

(3) Nothing in sub-paragraph (2) shall prevent the local authority concerned from registering that person under section 71(1)(a).

(4)   In this paragraph "the transitional period" means the period ending with—

(a)   the first anniversary of the commencement of Part X; or

(b)   if earlier, the date on which the local authority concerned registers that person under section 71(1)(a).

CHILDREN ACCOMMODATED IN CERTAIN ESTABLISHMENTS

35.   In calculating, for the purposes of section 85(1)(a) or 86(1)(a), the period of time for which a child has been accommodated any part of that period which fell before the day on which that section came into force shall be disregarded.

CRIMINAL CARE ORDERS

36.—(1)   This paragraph applies where, immediately before the commencement of section 90(2) there was in force an order ("a criminal care order") made—

(a)   under section 7(7)(a) of the Children and Young Persons Act 1969 (alteration in treatment of young offenders etc.); or

(b)   under section 15(1) of that Act, on discharging a supervision order made under section 7(7)(b) of that Act.

(2)   The criminal care order shall continue to have effect until the end of the period of six months beginning with the day on which section 90(2) comes into force unless it is brought to an end earlier in accordance with—

(a)   the provisions of the Act of 1969 preserved by sub-paragraph (3)(a); or

(b)   this paragraph.

(3)   While the criminal care order remains in force, any relevant provisions—

(a)   of the Act of 1969; and

(b)   of the Child Care Act 1980,

shall continue to have effect with respect to it.

(4)   While the criminal care order remains in force, a court may, on the application of the appropriate person, make—

(a)   a residence order;

(b)   a care order or a supervision order under section 31;

(c)   an education supervision order under section 36 (regardless of subsection (6) of that section); or

(d)   an order falling within sub-paragraph (5),

and shall, on making any of those orders, discharge the criminal care order.

(5)   The order mentioned in sub-paragraph (4)(d) is an order having effect as if it were a supervision order of a kind mentioned in section 12AA of the Act of 1969 (as inserted by paragraph 23 of Schedule 12), that is to say, a supervision order—

(a)   imposing a requirement that the child shall live for a specified period in local authority accommodation; but

(b)   in relation to which the conditions mentioned in subsection (4) of section 12AA are not required to be satisfied.

(6)   The maximum period which may be specified in an order made under sub-paragraph (4)(d) is six months and such an order may stipulate that the child

shall not live with a named person.

(7)   Where this paragraph applies, section 5 of the Rehabilitation of Offenders Act 1974 (rehabilitation periods for particular sentences) shall have effect regardless of the repeals in it made by this Act.

(8)   In sub-paragraph (4) "appropriate person" means—

(a)   in the case of an application for a residence order, any person (other than a local authority) who has the leave of the court;

(b)   in the case of an application for an education supervision order, a local education authority; and

(c)   in any other case, the local authority to whose care the child was committed by the order.

MISCELLANEOUS

Consents under the Marriage Act 1949 (c. 76)

37.—(1)   In the circumstances mentioned in sub-paragraph (2), section 3 of and Schedule 2 to the Marriage Act 1949 (consents to marry) shall continue to have effect regardless of the amendment of that Act by paragraph 5 of Schedule 12.

(2)   The circumstances are that—

(a)   immediately before the day on which paragraph 5 of Schedule 12 comes into force, there is in force—

(i)   an existing order, as defined in paragraph 5(1); or

(ii)   an order of a kind mentioned in paragraph 16(1); and

(b)   section 3 of and Schedule 2 to the Act of 1949 would, but for this Act, have applied to the marriage of the child who is the subject of the order.

The Children Act 1975 (c. 72)

38.   The amendments of other enactments made by the following provisions of the Children Act 1975 shall continue to have effect regardless of the repeal of the Act of 1975 by this Act—

(a)   section 68(4), (5) and (7) (amendments of section 32 of the Children and Young Persons Act 1969); and

(b)   in Schedule 3—

(i)   paragraph 13 (amendments of Births and Deaths Registration Act 1953);

(ii)   paragraph 43 (amendment of Perpetuities and Accumulations Act 1964);

(iii)   paragraphs 46 and 47 (amendments of Health Services and Public Health Act 1968); and

(iv)   paragraph 77 (amendment of Parliamentary and Other Pensions Act 1972).

The Child Care Act 1980 (c. 5)

39.   The amendment made to section 106(2)(a) of the Children and Young Persons Act 1963 by paragraph 26 of Schedule 5 to the Child Care Act 1980 shall continue to have effect regardless of the repeal of the Act of 1980 by this Act.

Legal aid

40.   The Lord Chancellor may by order make such transitional and saving provisions as appear to him to be necessary or expedient, in consequence of any provision made by or under this Act, in connection with the operation of any provisions of the Legal Aid Act 1988 (including any provision of that Act which is amended or repealed by this Act).

Section 108(7).   **SCHEDULE 15**
                                    REPEALS

Chapter	Short title	Extent of repeal
1891 c. 3.	The Custody of Children Act 1891.	The whole Act.
1933 c. 12.	The Children and Young Persons Act 1933.	In section 14(2), the words from "may also" to "together, and". In section 34(8), "(a)" and the words from "and (b)" to the end. Section 40. In section 107(1), the definitions of "care order" and "interim order".
1944 c. 31	The Education Act 1944.	In section 40(1), the words from "or to imprisonment." to the end. In section 114(1), the definition of parent.
1948 c. 53.	The Nurseries and Minders Regulation Act 1948.	The whole Act.
1949 c. 76	The Marriage Act 1949	In section 3(1), the words "unless the child is subject to a custodianship order, when the consent of the custodian and, where the custodian is the husband or wife of a parent of the child of that parent shall be required". Section 78(1A). Schedule 2.
1956 c. 69.	The Sexual Offences Act 1956.	Section 38.
1959 c. 72.	The Mental Health Act 1959.	Section 9.
1963 c. 37.	The Children and Young Persons Act 1963.	Section 3. Section 23. In section 29(1), the words "under section 1 of the Children and Young Persons Act 1969 or".

Chapter	Short title	Extent of repeal
		Section 53(3).
		In Schedule 3, paragraph 11.
1964 c. 42	The Administration of Justice Act 1964.	In section 38, the definition of "domestic court".
1968 c. 46.	The Health Services and Public Health Act 1968.	Section 60.
		In section 64(3)(a), sub-paragraphs (vi), (vii), (ix) and (xv).
		In section 65(3)(b), paragraphs (vii), (viii) and (x).
1968 c. 49.	The Social Work (Scotland) Act 1968.	Section 1(4)(a).
		Section 5(2)(d).
		In section 86(3), the words "the Child Care Act 1980 or".
		In Schedule 8, paragraph 20.
1969 c. 46.	The Family Law Reform Act 1969.	Section 7.
1969 c. 54.	The Children and Young Persons Act 1969.	Sections 1 to 3.
		In section 7, in subsection (7) the words "to subsection (7A) of this section and", paragraph (a) and the words from "and subsection (13) of section 2 of this Act" to the end; and subsection (7A).
		Section 7A.
		In section 8(3), the words from "and as if the reference to acquittal" to the end.
		In section 9(1), the words "proceedings under section 1 of this Act or".
		Section 11A.
		Section 14A.
		In section 15, in subsection (1) the words "and may on discharging the supervision order make a care order (other than an interim order) in respect of the supervised person"; in subsection (2) the words "and the supervision order was not made by virtue of section 1 of this Act or on the occasion of the discharge of a care order"; in subsection (2A), the words "or made by a court on discharging a care order made under that subsection"; and in subsection (4), the

Chapter	Short title	Extent of repeal
		words "or made by a court on discharging a care order made under that section".
		In section 16, in subsection (6)(a), the words "a care order or"; and in subsection (8) the words "or, in a case where a parent or guardian of his was a party to the proceedings on an application under the preceding section by virtue of an order under section 32A of this Act, the parent or guardian".
		In section 17, paragraphs (b) and (c).
		Sections 20 to 22.
		Section 27(4).
		Section 28.
		Sections 32A to 32C.
		In section 34(2) the words "under section 1 of this Act or", the words "2(3) or" and the words "and accordingly in the case of such a person the reference in section 1(1) of this Act to the said section 2(3) shall be construed as including a reference to this subsection".
		In section 70, in subsection (1), the definitions of "care order" and "interim order"; and in subsection (2) the words "21(2), 22(4) or (6) or 28(5)" and the words "care order or warrant".
		In Schedule 5, paragraphs 12(1), 37, 47 and 48.
1970 c. 34.	The Marriage (Registrar General's Licence) Act 1970.	In section 3(b), the words from "as amended" to "1969".
1970 c. 42.	The Local Authority Social Services Act 1970.	In Schedule 1, in the entry relating to the Children and Young Persons Act 1969, the words "welfare, etc. of foster children"; the entries relating to the Matrimonial Causes Act 1973, section 44, the Domestic Proceedings and Magistrates' Courts Act 1978, section 9, the Child Care Act 1980 and the Foster Children Act 1980.

Chapter	Short title	Extent of repeal
1971 c. 3.	The Guardianship of Minors Act 1971.	The whole Act.
1971 c. 23.	The Courts Act 1971.	In Schedule 8, paragraph 59(1).
1972 c. 18.	The Maintenance Orders (Reciprocal Enforcement) Act 1972.	Section 41.
1972 c. 70.	The Local Government Act 1972.	In Schedule 23, paragraphs 4 and 9(3).
1972 c. 71.	The Criminal Justice Act 1972.	Section 51(1).
1973 c. 18.	The Matrimonial Causes Act 1973.	Sections 42 to 44. In section 52(1), the definition of "custody". In Schedule 2, paragraph 11.
1973 c. 29.	The Guardianship Act 1973.	The whole Act.
1973 c. 45	The Domicile and Matrimonial Proceedings Act 1973.	In Schedule 1, in paragraph 11(1) the definitions of "custody" and "education" and in paragraph 11(3) the word "four".
1973 c. 62.	The Powers of Criminal Courts Act 1973.	In section 13(1), the words "and the purposes of section 1(2)(bb) of the Children and Young Persons Act 1969". In Schedule 3, in paragraph 3(2A), the word "and" immediately preceding paragraph (b).
1974 c. 53.	The Rehabilitation of Offenders Act 1974.	In section 1(4)(b) the words "or in care proceedings under section 1 of the Children and Young Persons Act 1969". In section 5, in subsection 5(e), the words "a care order or"; and in subsection (10) the words "care order or".
1975 c. 72.	The Children Act 1975.	The whole Act.
1976 c. 36.	The Adoption Act 1976.	Section 11(5). Section 14(3). In section 15, in subsection (1), the words from "subject" to "cases)" and subsection (4). Section 26.

Chapter	Short title	Extent of repeal
		In section 28(5), the words "or the organisation". Section 34. Section 36(1)(c). Section 37(1), (3) and (4). Section 55(4). In section 57, in subsection (2), the words from "and the court" to the end and subsections (4) to (10). In section 72(1), the definition of "place of safety", in the definition of "local authority" the words from " and" to the end and, in the definition of "specified order", the words "Northern Ireland or". In Schedule 3, paragraphs 8, 11, 19, 21, and 22.
1977 c. 45.	The Criminal Law Act 1977.	Section 58(3).
1977 c. 49.	The National Health Service Act 1977.	In section 21, in subsection (1)(a) the words "and young children". In Schedule 8, in paragraph 1(1), the words from "and of children" to the end; in paragraph 2(2) the words from "or (b) to persons who" to "arrangements"; and in paragraph 3(1) "(a)" and the words from "or (b) a child" to "school age". In Schedule 15, paragraphs 10 and 25.
1978 c. 22.	The Domestic Proceedings and Magistrates' Courts Act 1978.	Sections 9 to 15. In section 19, in subsection (1) the words "following powers, that is to say" and sub-paragraph (ii), subsections (2) and (4), in subsection (7) the words "and one interim custody order" and in subsection (9) the words "or 21". In section 20, subsection (4) and in subsection (9) the words "subject to the provisions of section 11(8) of this Act". Section 21. In section 24, the words "or 21" in both places where they occur. In section 25, in subsection (1) paragraph (b) and the word "or"

Chapter	Short title	Extent of repeal
		immediately preceding it and in subsection (2) paragraphs (c) and (d).
		Section 29(4).
		Sections 33 and 34.
		Sections 36 to 53.
		Sections 64 to 72.
		Sections 73(1) and 74(1) and (3).
		In section 88(1), the definition of "actual custody".
		In Schedule 2, paragraphs 22, 23, 27, 29, 31, 36, 41 to 43, 46 to 50.
1978 c. 28.	The Adoption (Scotland) Act 1978.	In section 20(3)(c), the words "section 12(3)(b) of the Adoption Act 1976 or of".
		In section 45(5), the word "approved".
		Section 49(4).
		In section 65(1), in the definition of "local authority", the words from "and" to the end and, in the definition of "specified order", the words "Northern Ireland or".
1978 c. 30.	The Interpretation Act 1978.	In Schedule 1, the entry with respect to the construction of certain expressions relating to children.
1980 c. 5.	The Child Care Act 1980.	The whole Act.
1980 c. 6.	The Foster Children Act 1980.	The whole Act.
1980 c. 43.	The Magistrates' Courts Act 1980.	In Section 65(1), paragraphs (e) and (g) and the paragraph (m) inserted in section 65 by paragraph 82 of Schedule 2 to the Family Law Reform Act 1987.
		In section 81(8), in the definition of "guardian" the words "by deed or will" and in the definition of "sums adjudged to be paid by a conviction" the words from "as applied" to the end.
		In section 143(2), paragraph (i).
		In Schedule 7, paragraphs 78, 83, 91, 92, 110, 116, 117, 138, 157, 158, 165, 166 and 199 to 210.
1981 c. 60.	The Education Act 1981.	In Schedule 3, paragraph 9.

Chapter	Short title	Extent of repeal
1982 c. 20	The Children's Homes Act 1982.	The whole Act.
1982 c. 48.	The Criminal Justice Act 1982.	Sections 22 to 25. Section 27. In Schedule 14, paragraphs 45 and 46.
1983 c. 20.	The Mental Health Act 1983.	In section 26(5), paragraph (d) and the word "or" immediately preceding it. In section 28(1), the words "(including an order under section 38 of the Sexual Offences Act 1956)". In Schedule 4, paragraphs 12, 26(a), (b) and (c) and 35, 44, 50 and 51.
1983 c. 41.	The Health and Social Services and Social Security Adjudications Act 1983.	Section 4(1). Sections 5 and 6. In section 11, in subsection (2) the words "the Child Care Act 1980 and the Children's Homes Act 1982". In section 19, subsections (1) to (5). Schedule 1. In Schedule 2, paragraphs 3, 9 to 14, 20 to 24, 27, 28, 34, 37 and 46 to 62. In Schedule 4, paragraphs 38 to 48. In Schedule 9, paragraphs 5, 16 and 17.
1984 c. 23.	The Registered Homes Act 1984.	In Schedule 1, in paragraph 5, sub-paragraph (a) and paragraphs 6, 7 and 8.
1984 c. 28.	The County Courts Act 1984.	In Schedule 2, paragraph 56.
1984 c. 37.	The Child Abduction Act 1984.	In section 3, the word "and" immediately preceding paragraph (c). In the Schedule, in paragraph 1(2) the words "or voluntary organisation" and paragraph 3(1)(e).
1984 c. 42.	The Matrimonial and Family Proceedings Act 1984.	In Schedule 1, paragraphs 19 and 23.
1984 c. 56.	The Foster Children (Scotland) Act 1984.	In section 1, the words "for a period of more than 6 days" and the words from "The period" to the end. In section 7(1), the word "or" at the end of paragraph (e). In Schedule 2, paragraphs 1 to 3 and 8.

Chapter	Short title	Extent of repeal
1984 c. 60.	The Police and Criminal Evidence Act 1984.	In section 37(15), the words "and is not excluded from this Part of this Act by section 52 below". Section 39(5). Section 52. In section 118(1), in the definition of parent or guardian, paragraph (b) and the word "and" immediately preceeding it. In Schedule 2, the entry relating to section 16 of the Child Care Act 1980. In Schedule 6, paragraphs 19(a) and 22.
1985 c. 23.	The Prosecutions of Offences Act 1985.	Section 27.
1985 c. 60.	The Child Abduction and Custody Act 1985.	Section 9(c). Section 20(2)(b) and (c). Section 25(3) and (5). In Schedule 3, paragraph 1(2).
1986 c. 28.	The Children and Young Persons (Amendment) Act 1986.	The whole Act.
1986 c. 33.	The Disabled Persons (Services, Consultation and Representation) Act 1986.	In section 16, in the definition of "guardian", paragraph (a).
1986 c. 45.	The Insolvency Act 1986.	In section 281(5)(b), the words "in domestic proceedings".
1986 c. 50.	The Social Security Act 1986.	In Schedule 10, paragraph 51.
1986 c. 55.	The Family Law Act 1986.	In section 1(2), in paragraph (a) the words "(a) or" and paragraph (b). Section 3(4) to (6). Section 4. Section 35(1). In section 42(6), in paragraph (b) the words "section 42(6) of the Matrimonial Causes Act 1973 or", in paragraph (c) the words "section 42(7) of that Act or" and in paragraph (d) the words "section 19(6) of the Domestic Proceedings and Magistrates' Courts Act 1978 or".

Chapter	Short title	Extent of repeal
1987 c. 42.	The Family Law Reform Act 1987.	In Schedule 1, paragraphs 10, 11, 13, 16, 17, 20 and 23. Section 3. Sections 4 to 7. Sections 9 to 16. In Schedule 2, paragraphs 11, 14, 51, 67, 68, 94 and 95. In Schedule 3, paragraphs 11 and 12.
1988 c. 34.	The Legal Aid Act 1988.	Section 3(4)(c). Section 27. Section 28. In section 30, subsections (1) and (2). In Part I of Schedule 2, paragraph 2(a) and (e).

Index